THE CULTURE OF NATURE

Hunters on U.S. national forest land, late 1950s.

Alexander Wilson

THE CULTURE OF NATURE

North American Landscape from Disney to the Exxon Valdez

Between The Lines ❡ Toronto

Published in Canada by
Between The Lines
720 Bathurst St., #404
Toronto, Ontario
M5S 2R4

Cover and text design by Greg Van Alstyne, Toronto.
Design assistance by Vilip Mak.
Cover photo by Jeff Wall.
Printed on acid-free, recycled paper by Best Book Manufacturers
Printed in Canada

Portions of this book have appeared in different
versions in *Borderlines, Wildflower, Impulse, Socialist
Review, Massachusetts Review, Fuse,* and *Utne Reader.*

Between The Lines receives financial assistance from
the Canada Council and the Ontario Arts Council.

Third printing February 1998

Canadian Cataloguing in Publication Data
Wilson, Alexander, 1953–
        The culture of nature: North American
        landscape from Disney to the Exxon Valdez

ISBN 0-921284-51-9 (bound)
ISBN 0-921284-52-7 (paperback)

1. Man – Influence on nature – Canada.
2. Man – Influence on nature – United States.
3. Nature – Social aspects – Canada.
4. Nature – Social aspects – United States.
5. Philosophy of nature.
6. Human ecology – Canada.
7. Human ecology – United States.
I. Title

GF75.W55 1991   304.2   C91-095167-5

Contents

7 Acknowledgements

11 Introduction

1   19   The View from the Road: Recreation and Tourism

2   53   Nature Education and Promotion

3   89   Nature at Home: A Social Ecology of Postwar Landscape Design

4   117   Looking at the Non-Human: Nature Movies and TV

5   157   Technological Utopias: World's Fairs and Theme Parks

6   193   City and Country

7   223   From Reserve to Microenvironment: Nature Parks and Zoos

8   257   On The Frontiers of Capital: Nuclear Plants and Other
Environmental Architectures

293 Notes on Sources

326 Picture Credits

329 Index

...Five hundred northern pike, including 15 with radio transmitters will be released. The greater numbers will enable growth rates to be measured and also indicate what impact a pike fishery may have on the yellow perch populations. ...John Garter, representing Hamilton-Wentworth, said there was an "inordinate preoccupation with fish to exclusion of people" in the report. Too much attention was paid to improved water quality and fishery

Acknowledgements

Writing a book is never done alone, as much as it might often seem so. It's a great pleasure to thank all the people who have over the years offered encouragement, advice, friendship, hospitality, and love, among them: Rosemary Donegan, Melony Ward, Peter Fitting, Lisa Bloom, Ioan Davies, Bruce Kidd, Colin Campbell, Gordon Montador, Dinah Forbes, Fredric Jameson, David Galbraith, Caroline Underwood, Marc Glassman, Janice Palmer, Audrey Sillick, Peter Baran, Frank Baumann, Pat Aufderheide, Carol McBride, Ron Ansbach, Victor Barac, Ian Balfour, Jim Winders, Christi Perala, Linda Aberbom, Raynald Desmeules, Bruce Russell, Robbie Schwartzwald, Tom Keenan, Monika Gagnon, Melanie McBride, Elena Orrego, Alejandro Rojas, Julia Mustard, Henry Kock, Chris Creighton-Kelly, David Orsini, Mark Lewis, Annette Hurtig, Jeri Hise and Kim Delaney.

Special thanks to Robert Campbell at the Department of Fisheries and Oceans, Margaret Kelley at the East Bay Regional Parks District, Linda Barnett at the CBC Design Library, Bob Gray and Jim Taylor at Parks Canada, the Public Archives of Canada, the National Film Board of Canada, Monique LaCroix and Dawn Conway at the Canadian Commission for UNESCO, Ann Rowles at the Forest History Society, Bill Andrews at the Faculty of Education, University of Toronto, Jack Vallentyne at the Canada Centre for Inland Waters, Mary Keeling, Architectural Librarian at the Colonial Williamsburg Foundation, Sherry Pettigrew at the Northwest Wildlife Preservation Society, Steven Price at the World Wildlife Fund in Toronto, and the many other people who have generously answered my phone calls and inquiries.

Susan Willis, Roy Merrens, Deborah Esch, Mark Griswold Wilson, Stephen Andrews, Jody Berland, Andrew Ross, and Meaghan Morris read chapters and drafts of the manuscript over many years. Their comments gave me plenty to think about, and helped immeasurably to enrich the text. My editor Robert Clarke has with care and graciousness helped me clarify my arguments.

A book about landscape calls for more than just words. Thanks to Lorraine Johnson for looking after the enormous task of picture research and to Greg Van Alstyne for the book's design.

Ian Rashid, Marg Anne Morrison, and Pat Desjardins at Between the Lines have supported this book from the beginning, and I thank them. Generous grants from the Explorations Programme of the Canada Council and the Ontario Arts Council allowed me intermittently to take weeks and months off work to travel, lecture, and write.

Lastly I'd like to thank my family: my mate Stephen Andrews; my late parents, Gris and Betsy Workman Wilson, who taught me early on to love this Earth; and my brothers Mark, Will, and Andy. To all of them this book will look and sound very familiar.

A.W.
Toronto, Ontario
December 1990

A rigidly managed forest in Ontario. Clearcutting has been the preferred method of harvesting timber since the 1950s.

Introduction

Ecology is permanent economy.
> — slogan of the Chipko tree hugging movement among
> women in Himachal Pradesh, India

Take courage, the earth is all that lasts.
> — Lakota song

This book is framed by two events, two places. It began taking shape in my mind during a 1982 visit to Disney World in Florida, and was finished during the summer of 1990, when a band of Mohawks in the town of Oka outside Montreal took up arms to stop the expansion of a golf course into a century-old pine woods planted by their mothers and fathers. The intervening years emphasize that the distance between Disney World and Oka is not only one of time and place, but of history: of everything we think of as culture and politics, and of very different ideas about the human place in the natural world.

What fascinated me about Disney World was its immense mission. It wants to bring everything into its sunny world — past and future, memory and desire, even nature itself. On the long drive home from Florida, north into winter, I wondered what a history of places like Disney World might reveal. What do theme parks and world's fairs, science museums and golf courses, tell us about the North American continent and its history of human settlement? And what do these constructed environments have to do with what is now everywhere called *the* environment — the non-human world of rocks and water, plants and animals, that seems to both precede and envelop our many cultures? Do they help us understand that world? What do they promote, conceal, or exclude?

The North American landscape, and our presence on it, constantly takes on new meanings. Disney World is a good place to take stock of how the dominant culture of North America — the largely white, male culture we see on TV — makes sense of both historical and ecological change. But as big as it is, Disney World cannot contain all the ways we know and experience this land.

And what a contested land it is! The war at Oka was in part a war over the meaning of the earth. The earth as home or habitat, as resource, as refuge and inspiration, as playground, laboratory, profit centre — in recent years all these ideas have flourished in the place where human and natural economies meet.

That place is called nature, and this book is a cultural history of nature in North America. It does not dwell on destruction or cataclysm, as convincing as those familiar stories might be. Rather it attempts to understand how nature is lived and worked with, copied and talked about in contemporary society — especially in those environments we consider natural.

Nature is a part of culture. When our physical surroundings are sold to us as "natural" (like the travel ad for "Super, Natural, British Columbia") we should pay close attention. Our experience of the natural world — whether touring the Canadian Rockies, watching an animal show on TV, or working in our own gardens — is always mediated. It is always shaped by rhetorical constructs like photography, industry, advertising, and aesthetics, as well as by institutions like religion, tourism, and education.

There are many natures. Raymond Williams calls nature the most complex word in the language. It has also become one of the most common. Today nature is filmed, pictured, written, and talked about everywhere. As the millennium approaches, those images and discussions are increasingly phrased in terms of crisis and catastrophe. But the current crisis is not only out there in the environment; it is also a crisis of culture. It suffuses our households, our conversations, our economies.

To speak uncritically of the natural is to ignore these social questions. Indian ecologist Anil Agarwal distinguishes between a nature "geared to meet

urban and industrial needs, a nature that is essentially cash generating," and a nature "that has traditionally come to support household and community needs." That distinction is buried in the Western term "resource."

Those who wish to speak on behalf of nature must be especially careful. Writing some years ago in *Radical Science,* Ben Crow observed that "the concept of 'nature', a powerful part of many ideologies, needs to be handled at least as carefully as any endangered orchid or panda. Sadly, environmentalists do not do so." In the past few years that has begun to change; the environmental movement has become more self-critical and begun to intervene in the *discourse* of nature, in the convergent environments of economics, science, and promotion.

We should by no means exempt science from social discussions of nature. To say, for example, that radioactive isotopes — radiation, in everyday language — are a natural occurrence is to hide the economic and political decisions taken about nuclear power development. Similarly, the presentations of baboons in zoos or movies as members of "families," or as "aggressive" or "territorial," tell us far more about our own culture than they do about captive or performing animals. All of this is to say that nature too has a history. It is not a timeless essence, as Disney taught us. In fact, the whole idea of nature as something separate from human experience is a lie. Humans and nature construct one another. Ignoring that fact obscures the one way out of the current environmental crisis — a living within and alongside of nature without dominating it.

Confronting the many conflicting ideas of nature at large today will help us to understand the kinds of land development that in the past fifty years have so altered our towns and cities, farms and wildlands. Some of those ideas are new ideas, and they correspond to new ways we live on and transform the earth. The way we produce our material culture — our parks and roads and movies — is derived from and in turn shapes our relationships with the physical environment. I call all of this activity *landscape.*

In the broadest sense of the term, landscape is a way of seeing the world and imagining our relationship to nature. It is something we think, do, and make as a social collective. In this sense, the North American continent is a region where Canadians and Americans play out the conflicts between culture and nature as we understand them. The idea of landscape — that the physical world is something we can know, enjoy, and control — is linked historically to the growth of European science in the sixteenth and seventeenth centuries. The task of that science (initially called "natural") was to establish that a world of fact existed quite apart from human value and intention. During the rise of industrial capitalism in eighteenth- and nineteenth-century Europe, landscape as a cultural practice — particularly in painting — came into its own, only to become devalued and mystified for much of the twentieth century.

This study is an attempt to return landscape to the centre of cultural debate. Thus it is as much a social as a geographical history. It comes back to the land over and again, but it is a land understood as both subject and object, an agent of historical processes as well as the field of human action.

❂

In North Atlantic societies our connection to the land has long been characterized by domination and greed. This is especially true of the years following the Second World War, and it is in that era that I begin. English journalist David Nicholson-Lord has called the thirty-odd years between wartime food rationing and the threat of oil rationing in the mid-1970s "the high summer of industrial society"; a time when "ecological considerations" were "thrust aside in the urge to acquire and consume." Today that summer seems long passed. Yet we live with many of its consequences, good and bad: with the choices perceived, and the decisions and cultural assumptions made.

The social and environmental changes of the postwar years were many and far reaching. The industrialization of agriculture, the development of nuclear fission, the construction of suburbs, recreation areas, and new transportation networks like interstate highways and air travel — all of these wrenched North Americans from their traditional associations with the land. They were accompanied by equally large changes in the economy, changes most crudely symbolized by the rise of giant corporations (not least of them the information/entertainment/image-production industry centred in New York and Los Angeles). In the period 1940 to 1960, self-employment in the United States fell from 26 per cent of the workforce to 11 per cent. Since then, the corporate economy, which is heavily dependent on resource extraction, has expanded to encompass the entire globe.

We shouldn't overestimate these changes, or their effects. Some of them have happened slowly, and many have their roots far earlier, not just in the present century, but many centuries ago. But the Second World War — which U.S. writer John McPhee has called a "technological *piñata*" — had the effect of magnifying the force of these changes in the culture, and their presence on the land. After a period of austerity, many North Americans experienced an explosion of affluence and consumption. Even if cars, camping, and suburbs were around before the war, they were phenomena available largely to the elite. After the war, they were much more popularly available, and it is popular history that I want to engage in this book. Part of that history is one of social conflict and dissent. The new global economy has been built at great expense to land and community, and the many movements mobilized in opposition have developed their own very different ideas about nature.

There have been two booms in land development over the past fifty years: the immediate postwar boom; and the boom of the 1980s that was the result of the completion of the interstate highways in the United States and similar though less extensive road systems in Canada. How much do we know about the extent and patterns of that forty-year project? We all recognize the changes in our own neighbourhoods: the razed buildings and new parking lots, the retirement condos and golf courses, the marinas and industrial parks that encroach upon wetlands. But how do those newly developed places connect across the land? How do river and field, shopping centre, industrial park, and highway interchange cohere? What are their ruptures? Some sense of those changes can be tracked by satellite, with Earth-imaging technologies like Landsat TM and SPOT. But most of the information gathered from remote sensing is unavailable to people outside of the upper ranks of corporations and state planning agencies.

◉

I have made no attempt to present this history in chronological order; instead it is organized according to a set of themes that are broadly illustrative of the changing relations between contemporary North Americans and the natural world we inhabit. The book shifts from small to large landscapes and back again, from TV and domestic space to world's fairs, agricultural lands, nature parks, and, finally, to the industrial, military, and technological grids laid over the entire continent.

These are global phenomena, but I am writing from this place, North America. The places I talk about are *exemplary* places: places that reveal both the cohesions and disruptions of the past fifty years; places redolent of the power of

the land; places overlaid with another, cultural, environment — that of advertising, or tourism, or telecommunications. I have tried to remain sensitive to
local and bioregional histories (and faithful to my own biography and travel
habits), concentrating on the Great Lakes Basin, where I live, Southern
Appalachia, and some disparate sites in western Canada and the United States.
While natural environments know no political boundaries, cultures certainly do.
The border between Canada and the United States — which used to be called
"the longest undefended border in the world" until it became a joke — drops
in and out of view in this discussion. Rarely is there a specific comparison
between Canadian and U.S. places, although I have tried to draw out distinctions where they are revealing.

This discussion necessarily cuts across many disciplines, and because of this
I owe a great debt to people working in geography, cultural and natural history,
popular science, and ecological theory. I comment on writing I have found
indispensable, and that has moved me, at the end of the book. My other sources
are mostly drawn from a wide range of newspaper and magazine accounts; discussions in journals, newsletters, broadsheets, and manifestos; lectures, TV shows,
and radio interviews. Especially useful have been the publicity materials that anticipate, explain, recall, and surround many of the geographies I discuss in this
book. These ephemeral materials remind us that there is now also an environment of promotion and advertising that reaches far into our lives and bodies, as
well as out into the natural world itself.

◔

Readers will sense in these pages an intermittent hopefulness, a desire to explore
the terms of an alternative future. My optimism about current trends in landscape design, park policy, and nature movies is tempered with the knowledge
that none of our relations with the natural world will change until we change
the basic relations of power in the Canadian and U.S. societies. Without broad
social empowerment and true democratic institutions — neither of which I
believe exists in any systematic way in North America today — our connections
to the natural world will continue to be characterized by greed and exploitation, the very values so rampant in our social lives.

With respect to landscape, the task of building a new world (or rediscovering an old one) in harmony with the other species of this earth must begin
with understanding the process of contemporary land development and the
changes it has brought to this continent and our experience of it. I hope this
book contributes to that work by making the places we inhabit and visit resonate
simultaneously with social and natural history.

Moving beyond understanding means continuing to build oppositional cultures and politics. On the most simple level, that involves relearning old skills and lifeways — recalling, for example, that only fifty years ago people separated garbage and weeded their lawns by hand rather than using herbicides. But halting the further domination of the Earth also means withdrawing social consent for the expansion of industrial society. Just how we do that is still very much an open question for me. On the one hand there is a lot of encouraging work being done at the local grassroots level: decentralized and cashless economies, small-scale development, appropriate technology, and so on. Yet are these micropolitical endeavours enough to stop a machine that is truly global in scope?

It will take some time to work through this dilemma. We can make a beginning by untangling the intricacies of two simultaneous tendencies in contemporary society. One tendency is towards globalization: a world economy, free trade, information oligarchies, and all the other stratagems that were laid bare for North Americans by Reaganism. This tendency has been destructive on the economic level, but in other ways holds some promise. There is after all a real need for confederations, for large-scale co-operation — not for competitive reasons, but to bring people together culturally and to solve truly global problems, the most pressing of which are environmental in some sense of the word.

Against this, there is a widespread movement towards localization, autonomy, and self-reliance. It is this tendency that underlies the breakup of large states. It can also be sensed in a yearning for community, for regional and cultural identity, for a sense of place. This is the arena of the small-scale production and social organization that are variously described as tribal, bioregional, or subnational. The danger here is that the local can descend to the level of the parochial: to petty nationalism and patriotism, or to racism and xenophobia.

❂

In an era of ecological crisis, it's no surprise that many of these contradictions are being worked out on the land itself. My own sense is that the immediate work that lies ahead has to do with fixing landscape, repairing its ruptures, reconnecting its parts. Restoring landscape is not about *preserving* lands — "saving what's left," as it's often put. Restoration recognizes that once lands have been "disturbed" — worked, lived on, meddled with, developed — they require human intervention and care. We must build landscapes that heal, connect and empower, that make intelligible our relations with each other and with the natural world: places that welcome and enclose, whose breaks and edges are never without meaning. Nature parks cannot do this work. We urgently need people living on the land, caring for it, working out an idea of nature that includes human culture and human livelihood. All of that calls for a new culture of nature, and it cannot come soon enough.

Icefields Parkway.
Photograph by Douglas Curran.

I. The View from the Road
Recreation and Tourism

Modern tourism was born out of the application of social policies which led to industrial work-ers obtaining annual paid holidays, and at the same time found its expression through the recognition of the basic human right to rest and leisure.
— United Nations declaration on tourism, 1980

In the mid-1980s I took a railway trip from Toronto to Vancouver. The train, called The Canadian, was old and tatty and filled with grumpy American trav-ellers who were in the country by default — Canada was a tourist destination without terrorists. But no tourist experience comes without its own logic, its own way of organizing the landscape and our sense of it. The train carried us to Vancouver, all right, but on the way it stirred us to pay belated though still sincere homage to the Canadian landscape.

The dining car was the most intact remnant of this vestigial nationalism. Called the Queen Alexandra, it was a royal blue ode to prairie songbirds and prairie hospitality, with wonderful etched glass dividers and stars on the ceiling. Here was a colonial nostalgia whose restraint and innocence spoke of the early 1950s, yet it was overlaid with the ruthless corporate reality of our own day: mass-produced meals and packaged travellers who probably wanted to go to Greece but ended up in Saskatchewan.

Out the window, as always, the vast land itself flitted by, so familiar from postcards but silent and untouchable from inside our glass cases. I remember wanting to get off the train at every point and lie in the sweet summer fields. While it's nice to think that my image of those fields came from within, from the memory of authentic, animated, *real* space, I know that it is also part of the repertoire of images of nature that tourist culture produces in great number and variety, and that in some ways are indistinguishable from nature itself.

Tourism organizes our experience of the world and its many aggregate cultures and landscapes. In the past fifty years or so it has become a global

phenomenon involving millions of people. It is also a big and growing industry — and the principal one for the economies of many countries and regions
in the Third World. It may also be the largest industry in North America by the
turn of the twenty-first century. The history of tourism is a confusing one,
because no one knows quite what it is or when it started. What we can say is
that its history parallels that of modern industrial society. While people travelled
for pleasure before that time, and the wealthy classes of imperial Rome or
China had holiday villas in the country, modern mass tourism represents a vastly
different way of moving through the world. It has created a whole range of new
landscapes: motel strips and campgrounds, airports, beach compounds, amusement parks, and convention centres. It has promoted the growth of a managerial class whose job it is to organize human desires and leisure time. It has
extended the commodity form both out into the natural world and back into
our imaginations. The Caribbean holiday, after all, is a mass-marketed product
as well as a place. Like a tin of fruit cocktail, the promise of a holiday experience has been manufactured out of the material and ideological resources available to contemporary culture. The "destination," as they say in the business, is
an integral part of the identity of the Caribbean holiday product at the same time
as it's strangely irrelevant: basically, anything with sun and palm trees will do.
Lastly, modern tourism is a phenomenon that is both urban and rural, and at the
same time it breaks down the distinction between the two. It has vastly reorganized not only the geography of North America but also our perceptions of
nature and our place in it as humans.

Tourism has more than a coincidental relationship with modern industrial society. As the 1980 United Nations declaration on tourism points out, the
phenomenon is one of the byproducts of that society. Certainly one outcome
of the long history of industrial capitalism has been the creation of leisure time.
But leisure isn't time like any other. It's supposed to be a discretionary kind of
time, different from the productive time spent at work. Leisure is a nineteenth-
century idea, introduced by a culture that defined work itself as a separate
sphere of life, an activity that had its own politics and increasingly its own place
in the landscape. In the nineteenth century, work was still a redemptive activity. But work has changed, and so has the politics of labour. Because new technologies have eliminated certain kinds of work and made much of what's left
meaningless, leisure time is increasingly the time, and creates the space, where
we look for meaning in our lives. A lot of social institutions are now organized
around buying, eating, or sightseeing rather than around the social bonds built
through labour. It isn't always this way, of course. People also use leisure time
to engage in other kinds of activities altogether: to build local cultures and
communities — or simply to work in the garden.

An expressway under construction on the outskirts of Toronto in the 1960s. Sightseeing helps us make sense of a landscape continually demolished and rebuilt.

These shifts in the nature of work and leisure are also part of the history of tourism. By the mid-twentieth century, technological change in North American industry had created considerable wealth. The response of most Canadian and U.S. workers, however, was not to gain more control over the labour process — to demand shorter working hours and more time of their own, for example — but to settle for higher wages and easy credit as an entrée into the growing culture of affluence, what was usually talked about as the American way of life. The cycle of ever increasing growth and consumption became a near universal creed. Thus, during the 1950s and 1960s, the modern utopian visions of a beneficent technology ushering in a society of ease and plenitude easily translated into mass desire for leisure commodities. Cars, trailers, motorboats, camping equipment, home appliances, vacation cottages, televisions — in other words, people sought out shopping centres, superstores, and everything inside them. These were the forms that leisure and tourism had taken on this continent by the middle of the present century.

The links between tourism and contemporary society are not only economic. Tourism has all along had a particular role to play in our experience of modernity. By circulating through the material and natural world, we juxtapose the many contradictions of our everyday lives and try to make them whole. When I recall my experience of the train that summer, I begin with images of dead queens and terrorists and grain elevators; then I remember the microwaved Pacific Salmon Almandine in the Rockies, the gleaming bank towers in

Opposite:
Tourism redefines the
land in terms of leisure.
This 1950 ad promotes
Canada as a roomy, handy
place with a "foreign
atmosphere."

Calgary, and a man fishing from a boat in the Precambrian Shield at sunset (the Korean monk in the next seat took a snapshot of him). Sometimes I read while all this was going on, and sometimes I listened to music I'd brought along. That train trip, and its many small pleasures and disruptions, somehow coalesce for me into orderly but still ambivalent images of life in Canada in the late twentieth century.

This ambivalence characterizes much of what's called modern life, and as modernity gets updated we must keep sightseeing just so we can understand our place in it. Our cultures, our landscapes, our social institutions are continually demolished and rebuilt. Each new moment of modernity promises to heal the wounds it continues to inflict, while at the same time encouraging us to imagine an open future. We tour the disparate surfaces of everyday life as a way of involving ourselves in them, as a way of reintegrating a fragmented world. Tourism is thus a thoroughly modern phenomenon. Its institutions — package cruises, museums and amusement parks, self-guided nature trails and visits to a shrine to the Virgin Mary, the grave of Wild Bill Hickok, or the site where a president was assassinated — continually differentiate and reorganize our experience of the world. One way they do this is by naming the modern and separating it off from the premodern — or the merely old-fashioned, which in contemporary culture often amounts to the same thing. Thus the tattered VIA Rail cars that hurtled us across the continent that summer were "outdated," as our U.S. visitors pointed out more than once, while Calgary was somehow "new," or in any case, different from that. The outdated is sometimes demolished (as much of it has been in Calgary) and sometimes preserved as a reference point for us, an "authentic" curiosity that reminds us of the victory of the modern over the ever receding past.

Tourism locates us in space as well as time. It has redefined the land in terms of leisure. It began to do this at a moment when most North Americans were being wrenched from traditional relations with the land. It's no accident that industrial agriculture, the spread of suburbs, and the growth of mass tourism all coincided in the mid-twentieth century.

The Roots of Nature Tourism

Nature has figured large in leisure activities since the mid-nineteenth century and the history of nature tourism provides a good sense of the history of relations between humans and the natural world over the past 150 years. It also reveals how tourism *organizes* those relations.

Nature tourism is simply the temporary migration of people to what they understand to be a different and usually more "pure" environment. It's going out to nature for its own sake, and it's all of the ways we talk about that

A MILLION LAKES TO CHOOSE FROM...WITH TROUT, BASS, MUSKY WAITING FOR A FIGHT.

Canada... *There's* the place to play hooky! Trade your fountain pen for that neglected fly rod, your double-breasted blue for a gaudy wool shirt, and light out for the roomy, relaxing outdoors. You'll sleep, and you'll eat, and you'll forget everything but how good that breakfast bacon smells and how good the sun feels on your back. Collect a party of kindred souls and head North... this year. Write for information or use the coupon.

7 VACATION POINTERS — ALL POINTING TO CANADA IN 1950

1. New, interesting — "foreign" atmosphere. **2.** A million square miles of scenic playground. **3.** Friendly cities, hospitable people. **4.** Friends and relatives waiting to welcome you. **5.** Lots to do — sports, recreation, sightseeing. **6.** Near — easy to get to — no border "red tape". **7.** Your vacation dollar buys more, goes further.

NO PASSPORT NEEDED.

CANADIAN GOVERNMENT TRAVEL BUREAU
Ottawa, Canada   D. Leo Dolan, Director

Please send me your illustrated book, "CANADA, VACATIONS UNLIMITED"

Name ....
Street and No. ....
(PLEASE PRINT)
Town .... State ....

Vacations Unlimited

Deep-sea fishing too, on both East and West coasts, from tuna to Tyee salmon. Knowing guides have a "fix" on the likeliest fishing spots.

Cast off for a vacation cruise! Thread inland waterways or skirt interesting new coasts. Canada is rich in choice, safe cruising grounds.

Or swing into a saddle. On a dude ranch among the blue hills of Canada's West, life quickly slows down to an easy canter.

experience. The modern history of nature tourism is a history of altered land-forms and changed ideas and experiences of the non-human. Broadly speaking, it involves a shift from a pastoral approach to nature to a consumer approach. This in itself is a huge and significant transition.

In the 1850s and 1860s the parks movement got underway in the large cities of the United States and Canada. It grew out of a widespread dissatisfaction with industrial culture and its momentous effects on the landscape. This dissatisfaction was not a new sentiment in its time. The myth of nature as a lost garden permeates both the Greek and Hebraic roots of Western culture. In the nineteenth-century version of that myth, in the age of what would be called the Industrial Revolution, popular nostalgia for nature overlapped in key ways with the culture of Romanticism. Cities grew quickly, becoming crowded and polluted. Many people began to see nature as the tonic for an unhealthy urban life. In the 1850s in the United States, and somewhat later in Canada, amateur horticultural and urban reform organizations built small parks to "improve" urban life. These parks were to have a moral as well as physical function: healthy open spaces, reformers thought, would alleviate the cities' many social and physical ills. The parks movement was followed by the playgrounds movement in the last years of the century, and like the parks movement the playgrounds movement was originally a citizens' initiative, in this case largely organized by women's groups. Typically, a neighbourhood improvement association organized itself to save a vacant lot from development; the undeveloped urban land was versatile and could be devoted to play of all kinds. In the long term the social goal of the playgrounds movement was to convince the public of the beneficial aspects of play and games and see that "supervised" recreation of all types was provided for in schools and neighbourhoods. By the last years of the nineteenth century, parks in both Boston and Montreal had sand gardens for infants, ball fields and instruction in games, folk dancing, first aid, and story-telling. Outdoor organizations like the Camp Fire Girls and the YMCA date from this period.

These movements had two effects that interest us here. One was the new possibility of thinking about recreation as an activity apart from our other everyday tasks. Recreation assumed its own schedule and its own locations in the landscape. It had become a form of leisure. In the contemporary literature of the tourist industry, this is talked about as an increase in demand for outdoor experiences. At first these new activities were organized around the dominant social institutions of their day, like schools and churches, and in fact the collectivization of recreation was closely related to the collectivization of work and the formation of unions.

The other effect of these movements was a general reawakening of interest in the natural world. To be sure, it was at first a natural world shaped by the shears and spades of urban culture, for nature appreciation directly coincided with urbanization and industrialization. By the late nineteenth century, almost half of North Americans lived in cities. It was not until then — the moment that in the United States is called "the closing of the frontier" and in Canada "the opening of the West" — that wilderness itself assumed value in popular culture. In the United States, progress was measured by how far nature — and the aboriginal peoples who were often understood to be part of it — had been pushed back, and the feeling at the close of the nineteenth century, at least in the United States, was that the job was nearly done. It became possible to argue then that the wilderness had to be preserved. In Canada, where nature was not so easily pushed back, the wilderness ethic did not gain currency as quickly as in the United States.

The love of nature flourishes best in cultures with highly developed technologies, for nature is the one place we can both indulge our dreams of mastery over the earth and seek some kind of contact with the origins of life — an experience we don't usually allow urban settings to provide. Since at least the witch burnings of the sixteenth century, people of European origin have regarded nature as separate from human civilization, which makes it possible to argue for its protection. The Native peoples of North America have never shared these attitudes. For them, the natural world is not a refuge — the "other" to an urban industrial civilization — but a place that is sacred in and of itself. In Native cosmologies, human cultures are compatible with natural systems, and it is a human responsibility to keep things that way.

Recreational Resources

By the 1870s and 1880s, wealthy city-dwellers were taking curative holidays at Rocky Mountain spas and seaside resorts. At the same time, the recreational activities available to the growing middle class were also edging out of the city. Hunting and fishing and canoeing had evolved into sports, and the urban dwellers now flocking to the country on holidays encouraged this trend. Church and youth organizations established outdoor education programs as part of their regular activities. It was out of this general social matrix that the Woodcraft Indians, Boy Scouts, national parks, and modern conservation movements emerged.

Transportation technology was also key. Town squares and commons, for example, are old phenomena in North American cities, but public parks *per se* didn't show up until people could get to them on public transit. By the late nineteenth century, railroads allowed the growth of suburbs on the edges of cities and provided access to beaches and lakes well outside city boundaries. After World War I, the car propelled recreation out of the cities for large numbers of

An outboard motor ad from the 1960s. In campaigns targeting the working class, the recreation industry promoted the outdoors as a place to "get away from it all."

the middle class. By the 1950s these trends had all magnified, and country and city now bear a very different physical and philosophical relation to one another.

This general rekindling of interest in nature and the new possibilities of access to it had effects that we still feel today. As more and more people travelled to the natural areas of the continent for a "change of scene," the areas themselves ceased to be thought of solely as sanctuaries from the ills of civilization. Instead, they were now often talked about as "outdoor recreation resources" — a jargon that came out of the popular movements to preserve the parks and forests of North America for the future. The language underscored the new ways rural spaces were appended to urban cultures and to the expanding North American economy. Recreational nature became a place of leisure on weekends and summer holidays; it became attached to the schedules and personal geographies of an urban society.

Several things happened during the years following World War II. In the first place, most North Americans had a lot more money. The war had inflated the economy, and while women were unceremoniously escorted back from factories to the hearths where they were now supposed to marshal the new armies of consumerism, men for the most part were able to move into regular employment. Many people had savings from the war, government grants were available, and if nothing else credit was easy to arrange. (Diners Club and American Express credit cards both appeared in the early 1950s.) After a long period of austerity, the 1950s was a time of exploding affluence. Families were larger and now usually included one car if not two. Leisure time was organized into discrete activities matched to the products of a leisure industry. Outdoor recreation had become a mass phenomenon. For holidays, people often went on automobile trips along new roads that reached far into the natural areas of the continent. There was a new mass market for recreational services and commodities: motels and drive-ins, both of which were around well before World War II, sprang up in large numbers along highway strips and at interchanges. Shops and chain-store catalogues were filled with outdoor equipment of every kind.

There were exceptions to this general trend. For one thing, the idea of nature as an untrammelled refuge is most attractive to cultures situated at some distance from the rural world, and whose values tend to rest on a rigid distinction between the human and the non-human. Utopias, after all, are culturally specific. Thus the non-European peoples of this continent, particularly African-Americans and Amerindians, have traditionally regarded the idea of vast nature reserves with some scepticism and bewilderment. Moreover, both of these peoples have associations with the North American soil — associations as painful as they are deep. Black slaves were imprisoned on the harsh plantations of the South, and freedom historically meant flight to the northern cities. Latinos have had a similar history in the industrial plantations of the modern sunbelt and in Puerto Rico.

Native people, on the other hand, have been explained away as savages almost to the present day. Their ancient kinship with the animals of North America has often been turned into a slur. In the early years of the U.S. national parks, especially in the Southwest, Native families were simply part of the scenery; their production of handicrafts was a popular attraction for the white tourists who were herded through Indian households as if those homes were museums. Non-white people have enjoyed very little of the immense wealth that has saturated Canadian and U.S. societies since the Second World War. For all of these reasons the postwar boom in recreation took place largely without the direct participation of non-whites — a fact usually ignored in the professional literature on the subject.

Regardless of who participated, the rapid development of a recreational infrastructure brought about a new set of relations between humans and everything we call nature. While the places visited might all have existed before, people experienced them in new ways. Nature tourism catalogued the natural world and created its own spaces out there among the trees, lakes, and rocks. It sold us nature-related products, and indeed it began to sell us natural space and experiences too. All of these activities served to fragment the land: here we have a sunbathing beach, over there a nature trail for the blind, further along there's an RV(recreational vehicle) campground or a petting zoo or a "singles' crosscountry weekend." Nature tourism differentiates our experiences of the natural world, with several consequences. The most obvious is that this differentiation makes it easier to package and sell nature as a product. It also means more people can enjoy natural areas. It means that it's now more difficult to experience nature as a whole, as the total environment that for centuries and centuries has been our *home* — which is, after all, a very different kind of space from a "recreation resource."

The Car and the Road

By the 1920s the car had become a popular means of transport, and with the beginnings of a highway infrastructure intercity travel increased dramatically. Between the two world wars, the construction of surfaced roads increased four-fold. Even during the Depression of the 1930s, large-scale road construction continued unabated, often as a part of government relief programs. By the mid-1950s multi-lane parkways and freeways had been built to expedite traffic from city to suburb and city to city; and the car had insinuated itself into the daily habits and desires of millions of North Americans.

While the population of North America has roughly doubled in the past fifty years, highway travel has increased almost tenfold. The private car accounts for more than 80 per cent of all travel — 75 per cent of all tourist travel — in North America. These trends — from highway construction to car acquisition and use — have remained relatively constant for the last five decades. They are a good indication of how the automobile became the keystone of the postwar North American economy. These changes didn't happen by themselves of course; several U.S. corporations, most notably General Motors, practised ruthless marketing strategies that would ultimately ensure the car its central place in North American culture. This meant designing cars with what's now called planned obsolescence and making them the only choice for millions of commuting workers. The control over choice was achieved partly by buying up and eliminating mass-transit companies.

This is a well-known history, with consequences that most people understand. But what does it mean in terms of the landscape and our relation to it? In the first place, the car and the modern highway bring with them a different

ordering of space. Before the car, most roads took care of all manner of traffic. But once the car was in general use, traffic had to be functionally separated: trucks and cars from pedestrians and bicycles, local and feeder traffic from inter-city travel. Expressways, for example, are usually set off on a different grade from surrounding land, and access to them is strictly controlled — changes that imply a rationalization of space. Certain roads come to have certain purposes: some are for whisking travellers and goods past places (whether urban or rural) as quickly as possible. In this case, the landscape you move through is subordinate to your destination. Other roads, such as the nature parkways begun in the 1930s, bar commercial traffic and in the design of their curves and rest areas instruct drivers about how best to appreciate the scenery out the window. In both cases, the car further divides the landscape, and our experience of it, into discrete zones. It promotes some landscapes and discourages others.

In the 1950s new road-building technologies carried more people than ever before out of the cities to play in the country. In 1944 the U.S. Congress passed the Defense Highway Act, which authorized the construction of a massive national network of roads that would supposedly allow for movement of troops and materiel in case of foreign attack. In Canada, the Alaska Highway, authorized in 1948, had similar military beginnings. In 1956, U.S. workers began construction on the Interstate Highway System, aided by revenues from a gasoline tax. The tax, in fact, could only be spent on highway construction for the first sixteen years. The highways encouraged car acquisition and use, the cars in turn consumed more gas, and the tax on the gas ensured the construction of more highways. The interstate highways, completed in the mid-1980s, amounted to a massive government subsidy to the auto industry and its many dependents, including tourism.

Tourism grew by about 10 per cent annually during the 1950s and 1960s, and it was largely a tourism organized around the car and the highway. Pleasure driving had become the most popular form of outdoor recreation and for many people older forms of outdoor activities — camping, for example — became an adjunct of car travel. Car and camping technologies merged. The new highways were thus not only a measure of the culture's technological prowess but they were also fully integrated into the cultural economy. They were talked about as though they had an important democratizing role: the idea was that modern highways allowed more people to appreciate the wonders of nature.

The car also made possible the establishment of a vacation-home industry during the 1950s and 1960s. This changed the physiography of resorts in interesting ways. It used to be — and here we might recall the great nineteenth-century spas — that resorts were typed according to the natural features of the landscape they were part of. So there were mountain resorts like Banff, there were spas, ski resorts, seaside resorts, and so on. Once mass second-home building got under way in the late 1950s, resorts lost many of their ties to locale. The most obvious effect of the car on nature tourism was a large-scale diffusion of recreation across the landscape. Holiday-goers no longer took rest cures at one place, but sought out ever more distant and "unspoiled" recesses in their cars. When A-frame and other pre-fab homes replaced resorts in many people's itineraries, there was a proliferation of tourist sites, and consequently the experience of nature became more private for many people. By the mid-1960s, the resorts themselves had changed in character: either they went out of business or they adapted to the demands of a new and different clientele. Today, travelling families have been replaced by convention-goers and corporate head officers attending marketing seminars. These clients expect familiar surroundings — amenities, they're called — that are not specific to locale.

As the growth of rural tourism proceeded, the geographical focus shifted from natural features of the landscape to artificial ones such as golf courses or African animal-safari parks. The reasons for this are complex, but they had mostly to do with the need for the industry to differentiate its products to serve a rapidly expanding market. Marine parks and Santa's Villages, whether in California or Kansas, were like so many interchangeable brands of cigarettes or pain relievers, each with its target audience. Thus scenic legitimacy came to rest partly on the marketing strategies of the tourist industry as well as the vagaries of land speculation. All of these changes led to new fields of study including tourist motivational assessment and scenery evaluation, which by the 1960s had become the subject of intense scrutiny within the industry.

Where the landscape itself was adaptable to this new industrial situation, so much the better. For example, in the forest-lake complex of much of the north-central area of the North American continent, the aesthetic values already in place coalesced with the demands of a growth industry. The two most desirable features of a woodland cottage-site are the illusion of solitude and the view out over water. In the sinuous lake and river country of the Great Lakes-St.Lawrence watershed, the land is relatively flat and yet densely vegetated. There are no sweeping vistas, so the aesthetics of this landscape in its more or less wild state is built on experiencing nature in its details. The activities that make sense here are intimate, even private, like canoeing or mushrooming. Yet the geography allows for great numbers of people to have this experience of the immanent frontier all at the same time. When you add the automobile and the express highway to this equation you end up with a well-populated region of the continent colonizing large portions of the remaining bush with millions of second homes, each with its private road and intimate view.

The car is not the only vehicle that roamed the new highways of the 1950s. A related technology, the trailer, has had a profound effect on the way we move across and inhabit this continent. Originally — in the early 1930s — trailers were a kind of house on wheels, like a covered wagon for vacationers or itinerant workers. Now they're called mobile homes and they've become the predominant form of prefabricated housing. They are permanent features of the landscape, as the evolution of their town names indicates: from trailer camps to trailer parks to mobile-home estates. In the U.S. Southwest, these communities are simply called parks, and the trailers themselves are called park models. Temporary dwellings — which are an ancient phenomenon — imply a kind of freedom and have thus found a special place in the North American ideological landscape. This phenomenon is usually expressed as freedom from ties to place, to family, and to job; freedom to move across this land as we want and to make new connections with it. For people who work at migratory or temporary jobs — and today this includes work in sales or mid-management as well on farms — moving from one place to another is often a necessity. It's as if physical mobility is standing in for the dream of social mobility that North

American society has been unable to deliver. Camping is one form of this refusal of station; so is desert retirement in a mobile home.

In any case the trailer is now something people use to tour nature (among other places) and dwell there temporarily. In fact, technologies like the trailer, and the cultures that surround them, construct nature as a place of freedom and repose. As our technical mastery over nature has progressed, the idea of nature as freedom has flourished — an idea that would be meaningless in a time or culture other than this one.

Other transportation technologies have been developed since the Second World War, and all of them have helped to transform the landscape and our perceptions of it in some way. Most fall under the name of recreational vehicle (RV), and they include the snowmobile, the off-road vehicle (ORV), the van, the camper, and so on. Many of these technologies have insinuated themselves into everyday North American life, and the social activities of clubs and vacation caravans are now often planned around them. Indeed, a new kind of campground has been designed for people who travel with recreational vehicles.

The trucking industry was also born in the postwar years — often as a result of the car companies' marketing strategies — and it too has had a curious effect on how our culture perceives nature. Before continuous streams of trucks plied highways of every size, trains carried most freight, including foodstuffs. Refrigerated train cars were first put to use in the late 1920s. As John Steinbeck's novel *East of Eden* documents with some bitterness, refrigeration allowed produce from warmer parts of the continent, such as Florida and California, to be shipped to large markets in the cooler regions. Like the car, however, the transport truck is a more versatile, if less efficient, technology than the train. It was able to get right into the fields and collect the avocados and grapefruit soon after they were picked. This development coincided with two others of equal import. Postwar agricultural research bred fruits and vegetables to be part of an industrial process — they could be mechanically picked, were resistant to biocides, and took well to shipping. This led to great increases in farm productivity during the 1950s. At the same time the transportation industry was consolidating itself: trucking firms began to be vertically integrated with food growers, processors, and retailers.

This is a complex tangle of changes, and there were a number of consequences. One was the replacement of local and regional market gardeners by large, often corporate growers in the new agricultural zones of the sunbelt. They in turn introduced vast amounts of biocides, with ecological effects that in many cases remain unknown today. The industrialization of agriculture — which included the development of supermarkets — also led to a homogenization of the seasons as summer produce (or some semblance of it) began to appear in winter as well. This in turn led to a very different relation between the culture and the geography and climate of North America. The land began to look and feel different. As models of domination began to flourish in North American cultures in the 1950s — and the industrialization of agriculture was mirrored by the U.S. military policy of the time — it became possible to think of nature as a servant, or a well-loved pet. It also became possible to think of nature as a victim — a sentiment that underlay much of the thinking of the environmentalist movement in its earliest years.

The Blue Ridge Parkway

The car also had a more instrumental effect on the landscape. Most obviously, it brought massive environmental change in the form of roads, traffic, and deteriorating air quality. These all have had their own secondary and tertiary effects, most of them bad if not catastrophic. But much less discussed are the aesthetic and psychological changes the car has brought to land forms and our perception of them.

Once the roads were full of cars, there had to be a physical infrastructure to service them. Thus we get the creation of the strip: gas stations, roadside motels and drive-ins, coffee shops, muffler franchises. These came with their own logic. Highway businesses had to design their buildings and advertising to attract motorists. Recognition from the road became paramount, and this led to the spread of the franchise business and use of standardized images and eventually logos in advertising, both on and off-site. Consider the repetitive architectures of chains like Howard Johnson's or the Holiday Inn, or indeed of national parks. Tourist services had to be built on a scale compatible with the automobile. Large signs and façades and small cheaply constructed buildings were the lessons learned from Las Vegas. Motorized access and parking lots became necessary adjuncts to every new building, whether souvenir shop or campground office. These in turn were often "naturalized" by planting gardens around them; and work like this became the bread and butter of the newly prosperous profession of landscape architecture. A roadside coffee shop or gas station was transformed into an oasis in the midst of the created deserts of parking lot and highway. Similarly, driveways and garages — and the reappropriated ranch architectures they complemented — contributed to the sprawling character of postwar urban design. More recent architectures like shopping malls turn inward from their parking lots, towards the retreats of indoor gardens. The roadside environments of just thirty years ago are now largely in decay.

The car imposed a horizontal quality on the landscape as well as architecture. The faster we drive, the flatter the earth looks: overpasses and cloverleaf interchanges are almost two-dimensional when seen from the car window.

They are events in automotive time. As highway and tourist space has become more homogenized — like the universal space of modern communications — distance is experienced as an abstraction: suburbs lie "minutes from downtown," and the miles per gallon we achieve getting to them quantify field and stream. Compare this experience of the landscape with that suggested by aerial photography, which wasn't really accessible to people outside the military until the 1960s. Seen from a plane window the landscape flattens out to something like a map: it is a landscape of fact (or to the military, of secrets). With more advanced satellite photography, the landscape has been inscribed with representations of resources — healthy crops, or deposits of subsurface minerals, or Cuban missile bases. The image of the Earth from space, and its Whole Earth counterpart, are extensions of this impulse to picture the planet as a resource. But in the 1950s, travellers weren't yet able to perceive this factual landscape. What we saw out the window of the speeding car — the Futurists were right after all, it is one of the great experiences of modern life — was the future itself. Consider the thrill of entering New York along the Henry Hudson Parkway or Vancouver crossing the Lion's Gate Bridge. The speeding car is a metaphor for progress. It is always moving ahead — although the effect is the opposite, as if the landscape were moving past us, into the inconsequential shadows of history. In this very limited respect, time has replaced space as the predominant way our experience of the world is organized.

These effects are somewhat more attenuated in the design of nature roads. The best examples of these are in the national parks, although parkways, as they are often called, are prominent features of the working landscapes of eastern North America. The Hutchison River, Merritt, and Taconic parkways in Westchester County and the lower Hudson River watershed are good examples of the long-distance and commuter type; the shorter Gatineau, Niagara, and Thousand Islands parkways in Ontario or the Seventeen-Mile Drive in California function more strictly as nature appreciation roads for tourists. These parkways are designed to present nature to the motorist in a way that sanctifies the experience of driving through it. Nature can't really be said to be sacred in this culture, but nature appreciation comes close to being a sacred activity. The entrances to parks are important in establishing the terms of this activity and in defining the relationship between "natural" and "artificial" space.

My favourite nature road is the Blue Ridge Parkway in the southern Appalachians, one of the supreme public landscapes of the New Deal period. It was begun during the Depression as a job-creation project and link between the Shenandoah and Great Smoky Mountains national parks. Managed by the National Park Service, it is 470 miles long and built along the crest of five mountain ranges in Virginia and North Carolina. The road was designed as a rural national parkway restricted to leisure traffic; local residents call it The Scenic, because it bypasses towns and other commercial landscapes.

The Blue Ridge Parkway pioneered many of the techniques of landscape management taken up by the tourist industry in the 1950s and after. One of these techniques is signage: like railroads, the Parkway is periodically marked by mileposts, their purpose being to orient motorists *vis-à-vis* their itineraries and to aid road maintenance and administration. Talked about in the original plans as a way of relieving monotony, the mileposts also introduce the notion of progress to the motorist's experience of the landscape; the miles tick off as nature unfolds magnificently before us. The Parkway has a logo — a circle enclosing a roadway, a mountain peak, and a wind-swept white pine — and like all logos it is repeated. Other road signage, especially at the entrances, is standardized to underline the special quality of this created environment. Gouged wood signs point out road elevations, local history, and the names of distant features of the landscape. Other diversions organize the motor tour: parking overlooks, short hiking trails, local museums, campgrounds, and parks spaced every thirty miles. In this way, the planners designed tourist movement into the land itself. All of these management strategies are today a very common part of the tourist economy.

The Parkway is a prototypical environment of instruction, and this has become as typical of modern tourism as it was of New Deal public works projects. The Parkway's landscape architect, Stan Abbott, had worked on the Westchester parkways. In the southern Appalachians he wanted to create "a museum of managed American countryside." One objective was to reclaim and preserve marginal mountain lands. Another was to create a landscape pleasing to the motorist, which involved using the land in a way that would "make an attractive picture from the Parkway."

To the planners, some land adjoining the Parkway was decidedly not a pretty picture, especially the shacks and worn-out farms of hillbillies — an outsider's term for the impoverished whites of the southern Appalachians. In some cases, these people were moved elsewhere, out of sight, under President Franklin D. Roosevelt's Resettlement Act. Abandoned homesteads were planted over with native succession species and made into parks. In other areas the Parkway administration bought "scenic easement rights" from local landowners or allowed farmers to work Parkway lands.

In both cases, land use was restricted to activities compatible with a Parkway aesthetic. The planners encouraged split-rail fences, grazing cows, or sheep but not abandoned cars or, for that matter, weeds. This policy encouraged soil and watershed conservation; the ecological education of local residents was a high priority with Parkway administrators, who liberally dispensed the

The logo of the Blue Ridge Parkway in Virginia and North Carolina.

fertilizers and agricultural advice of the day. The policy also allowed the road's designers control over the verges — the place the car driver's eye first comes to rest after scanning the pavement. These were planted in a pastoral style — the meadows and groves that have been equated with naturalism ever since the great landscape parks of eighteenth-century England. Today almost the only communities visible from the road are the native plant communities established by Stan Abbott's staff and crews, who were early restorationists: rich and perfumed copses of red maple, rhododendron, flowering dogwood, Carolina hemlock, and white pine flourish as they probably haven't since the arrival of European civilization. That civilization locally, meanwhile, has been removed from view, apparently incompatible with nature.

Control over the verges also allowed the landscape designers to organize the vistas. They screened inappropriate views. They designed curves that restricted speeds to thirty-five or forty miles an hour and placed those curves in a way that organized the long looks. Since the road follows mountain crests for most of its length, distant views tend to be views down over deep valleys and countless ranges receding into the blue distance. Motorists feel like they are at the top of the world, and they share this new universe with the car. The designers have organized this national public landscape around the private car and the private consumption of nature.

The Blue Ridge Parkway is landscape management at its most accomplished. Driving along it is a beautiful and exhilarating experience. I think the pleasure of the experience can be attributed to three strategies that the road's planners adopted. The first strategy was to control virtually everything within the field of vision. The organizing poles of this field are verge and horizon, and the road successfully manages the natural and cultural landscapes that fall within it. Control over the cultural landscape has been a matter of instruction and public relations. The new culture of tourism instructed motorists in how to appreciate nature from the car; farm agents, social workers, doctors, and the Parkway's local newsletter, the *Mileposts,* coaxed destitute Appalachian peoples into modern national life. Once this education took place, mountain cultures could be reinserted into the Parkway motorist's field of vision. In the early 1960s, "Hillbilly Shows" were performed for tourists on the edges of the road. Men in crooked hats and women in long, flowered dresses with holes in them played music and demonstrated whisky stills and other putative trappings of a culture in dissolution. By the 1970s, these people had gone — to Beverly Hills perhaps — and in their place state and federal governments built craft museums.

The second, related strategy of the Parkway was an aesthetic one: separate productive and non-productive landscapes. In this aesthetic, nature is best appreciated "on its own." The road allows no trace of commercial society, save for the occasional nostalgic glimpse of a farm or mill, the shadow of economies that have given way to the single economy of tourism.

The third strategy, and the overriding one, is the production of nature itself. All of the road's design features organize our experience of nature. The result is that nature appears to produce itself with no apparent relation to the cultures that inhabit it, or used to. Magnificent vistas now happily present themselves to us without the clutter of human work and settlement. The seasons begin to be synchronized with the tourist calendar: June is Rhododendron Time, autumn is Fall Foliage Time, winter is a Wonderland.

The Blue Ridge Parkway was built as a landscape of leisure, with both an aesthetic and economic component. The road's pictorial composition of Eastern woodland, lake, and stream would remain the symbolic landscape of U.S. leisure society until well into the 1960s. As federal and local governments built parks in nearly every state, driving and camping became part of the modern tourist economy as well.

❂

The car itself was increasingly laden with technology in the postwar years, and some of these devices accentuated the kinds of changes underway. Air conditioning was the most obvious. It began to be sold as a feature of a few luxury cars in the mid-1950s and soon became a sign of status, especially in climates where it was unnecessary. Of course, as more asphalt was laid down and more engines circulated, roadside temperatures rose, and air conditioning often did become a necessity even in temperate climates. High-speed cars also encouraged the use of air conditioning.

In a car or a building, air conditioning allowed the illusion of human control over environment. This was made possible by the "magic" of what was understood to be a benign technology. Of more interest to us here is the aesthetic effect of air conditioning on the natural world. Nature was now even more something to be appreciated by the eyes alone. Never mind the dust and heat or the snow, nature was now accessible year-round and under any circumstances. There were no longer any contingencies — just the purely visual experience that lay outside the picture window. The other senses were pushed further to the margins of human experience as nature came to play a role in human culture that was at once more restricted and infinitely expanded.

Although car travel is largely an *individual* activity, this is not to say that people usually drive alone, although for commuters and truckers that tends to be the case. It's more that driving is a private exercise, whether done alone or with company. It is a technology that fits well with the North American psyche, and Detroit has done its best to manipulate this. The individual hero on

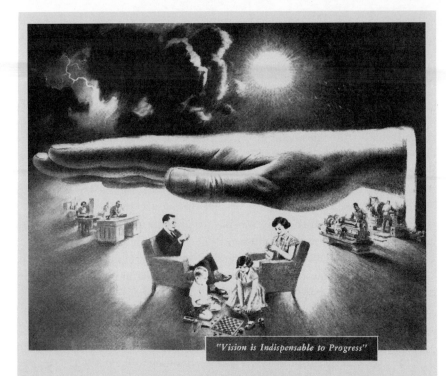

the road, pushing back the frontiers and discovering this land for "himself": this myth has a long and bloody history, particularly in American culture, and the car continues to play a part in it. It's hard to imagine a technology that better discourages communal activity and an egalitarian experience of the non-human world. After all, the private car and the nuclear family have a parallel history. They are both founded on an act of exclusion. Within is radically different

Tourism developed side by side with the resource industry. "Multiple-use" policy has often resulted in poorly-resolved conflicts – such as at Haida Gwaii along the British Columbia coast.

from without. The family and the car — and the family car — are bounded entities that discourage unregulated exchange.

The mobility the car has brought to North American society has contributed greatly to the restructuring of the traditional nuclear family. Its privatizing functions have been splintered by cultural practices like hitchhiking or drive-in movies. The car has also given kids the freedom to get out, put some miles between themselves and the home. It has carried many North Americans, myself included, far away from the consumer culture that engendered it, and into closer contact with the natural world.

Conserve — and Develop

Like tourism and cars, the histories of tourism and conservationism are closely connected. The conservation movement in North America began in the late nineteenth century as a moral crusade to conserve "wilderness" — places supposedly uncontaminated by the physical traces of humanity, meaning people of European origin. As an expanding industrial infrastructure began to extract more and more raw materials from the land, the movement demanded regulation and protection of wild areas for non-industrial uses. In hindsight, those non-industrial uses have by and large turned out to be tourism.

By the early twentieth century, both the Canadian and U.S. governments had adopted conservation strategies as part of what they understood to be the efficient management of natural resources. At first many people saw this project as incompatible with the protection of wild lands for aesthetic reasons. But in time — and the watershed years were the tenure of Gifford Pinchot at the newly created U.S. Forest Service during the Theodore Roosevelt administration — the consensus, at least among the elite sectors of the population, was that tourist development and resource exploitation could be complementary. In Canada, tourist development and mining were part of the mandate of the national parks from the beginning: the government created Banff National Park as an agreed-upon part of the development portfolio of the Canadian Pacific railroad.

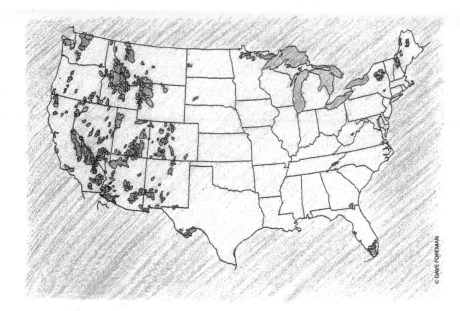

Like all social movements, nature conservationism has had both reactionary and radical moments. In general, the state has adopted conservation measures consistent with its own interests, including the "wise use" of timber, water, grazing, mineral, and, later, recreation resources in the more remote parts of the continent. Conservationism became a matter of resource management — an expedient measure ensuring the greatest return on investment for what is usually called the foreseeable future. There are several other strains of conservationism historically, and all of them have grown up alongside tourism when they haven't actually promoted it. The principal ones include: animal welfare, an anti-cruelty movement that originated in England in the nineteenth century; nature appreciation, an off-shoot of art appreciation with roots in the same era; biological conservationism, which seeks the protection of endangered species of plants and animals from land development of all kinds; and preservationism, which argues for setting aside nature in reserves, protected "for all time" from human manipulation, places that will function as a eulogy for what industrial civilization has destroyed.

Today the outlines of this history are hotly debated within the environmental movement, which inherited conservationism from its various constituencies. The organizers, spokespeople, and gurus of the early movement — Henry David Thoreau, John Muir, Ernest Thompson Seton, Rosalie Edge, James Harkin, Grey Owl, Aldo Leopold, and Rachel Carson, among many others, are also the subjects of considerable debate, alternatively claimed and rejected by the various streams of contemporary ecological thought.

What we can say about these early nature philosophies — aside from the fact that they have been largely ineffective even on their own terms — is that they are reductionist. They invariably understand nature to be good and civilization — or, in the formulation of deep ecology, humans — bad. This is hardly the basis for a politics of social change.

❂

While conservation politics and nature tourism nourished one another, the growth of a tourist industry was contingent upon a substantial contribution by the state. Early recreation advocates had campaigned for government involvement in initiating and promoting outdoor activities, and governments began making this commitment around the time of the First World War. Governments at all levels started to acquire parkland, build recreational facilities, draw up wildlife regulations, and write resource-management policies. They zoned cabin and cottage lands to control development, supervised boating activities, inventoried land, drew up maps, and in general began to divide up the continent according to how humans used it: resource extraction, farming, recreation, wilderness, and so on. In 1924 the U.S. government held its first National Conference on Outdoor Recreation in Washington, D.C. Many Canadians attended.

In the United States, the years of the New Deal saw the development of recreation facilities everywhere. The Civilian Conservation Corps and the Works Progress Administration embarked on a massive program to build a national public landscape. They organized unemployed workers into what was basically a military life. Crews of one hundred men and more constructed parkways, playgrounds, rose gardens, campgrounds, arboretums, parks, and lodges, as well as roads, bridges, and public buildings. The landscape work was sturdy, and much of it remains today. Its rough and earnest design reveals the moral underpinnings of the formative years of the recreation movement: these were environments meant to build character through hard work and wholesome play. Work camps organized by the Canadian government during the same years carried out similar projects, although on a much smaller and less ambitious scale.

The Tourist Industry

There were other exemplary landscapes. In the 1930s the Tennessee Valley Authority (TVA) began to build immense reservoirs in the southern Appalachians. The TVA justified these projects by referring to increases in population and energy consumption and to the need for large-scale public recreation sites. But the reservoirs were also a chance to put the new techniques of flood control, hydro generation, and irrigation into operation.

During the same period, the Civilian Conservation Corps built summer camps for inner city kids — one of them, Camp David in Maryland, is now the weekend retreat of U.S. presidents. The National Park Service promoted these camps to the tourist industry as Recreation Demonstration Areas. In 1936 Congress passed the Park, Parkway and Recreation Area Act, which provided funds for much new construction.

All of these projects involved creating new spaces and new organizations to manage those spaces. As the tourist industry became more sophisticated, designers made sure that travel became a part of the landscape itself. Scenic car routes, photo opportunities, campground layouts — these built spaces have become part of our experience of nature. Thus the booming recreation and tourist organizations of mid-century — which would include older groups like the Boy Scouts, the Girl Guides, and the YMCA as well as professional organizations like the National Recreation Association, the Canadian Association for Health, Physical Education and Recreation, and self-organized clubs for canoeists, trailer owners, gardeners, birdwatchers, and flyfishers — produced new landscapes, and new aesthetics of nature.

It is the mission of any bureaucracy to shape its project according to the internal needs of the organization. Promotional strategies tend to influence our experience of the places and activities they advertise. So do development schemes to maximize public use. Natural beauty, for example, was inevitably quantified as a result of applying bureaucratic and industrial models to the landscape. Industry consultants encouraged landowners considering tourist development to list the "natural attractions" of their sites: was there a marketable topography such as a seashore or trout stream? Were there unusual geological formations, or perhaps Indian ruins? "Scenic value" soon came to be a monetary concept as well as an aesthetic one. All of these developments contributed to the institutionalization of tourism. Sightseeing was no longer an individual activity, at least not in the eyes of those in the business. It was the organized mass consumption of familiar landscapes. Facilities had to be standardized and the "tourist object" — in this case an idea of nature — transformed into recognizable terms. As we'll see, this involved the creation of many new landscapes.

Although much private recreational resource development got started with state assistance — and the state still heavily subsidizes the tourist industry, when you take into account the public funds spent on facilities like convention centres, corporate sports stadiums, and the infrastructures that support them — by the 1950s private tourist development began to outstrip government initiatives. The governments of the day produced publications that outlined how to construct private campgrounds or design summer camps for kids. Other pamphlets suggested hunting policies for industrial landowners, or encouraged farmers and ranchers to add recreational enterprises to their existing operations. Most U.S. agencies made money available for either public or private development of these facilities. These agencies were often concurrently working on improved resource exploitation strategies; as we've seen, tourism and resource management have gone hand in hand for most of this century (although not without many problems). This relationship was made official in the multiple use policy adopted by most government agencies throughout the continent in the late 1950s.

Tourism involves a massive conceptual reorganization of the landscape. Lands once productive in a traditional industrial or agricultural sense were reclassified as recreational zones. Marginal cattle-raising operations, for example, got turned into fishing camps or dude ranches; dairy farms became tourist farms or bed-and-breakfasts; in more recent years, agricultural lands near cities have been turned into sod farms, golf courses, and theme parks. One of the historical functions of tourism, then, is to be a kind of parasite feeding off sectors of the economy that seem to have become superfluous.

Nature tourism grew enormously in the postwar years and, as in other parts of the economy, the industry had to run to keep up with it. For most middle-class North Americans, car holidays had become the norm. By 1960, 75 per cent of U.S. families owned at least one car, and these now brightly coloured vehicles filled the new highways on weekends and during the summer months. A mass market developed for recreational services and commodities; by the late 1950s annual sales in this sector had reached $5 billion in the United States. Shops and chain-store catalogues were suddenly full of outdoor equipment of every kind, much of it making use of the new plastics being pioneered by the petrochemical industry. Among the most significant commodities were the lighter, more easy to use cameras and, later, colour film. The snapshot and colour slides structure the postwar experience of nature. Colour, which by the mid-1950s was common in magazine ads and movies, gave images of nature added authenticity. At the moment of the greatest estrangement between North American culture and the natural world, nature opened up as real space, luring us back with saturated reds and greens.

Governments were quick to lend additional support to the new economy. In 1958 President Eisenhower appointed the Outdoor Recreation Resources Review Commission, chaired by Laurance Rockefeller. Its mandate was to gather data on The Great Outdoors and the people using it and thereby help produce a comprehensive national policy on recreational lands. It released its twenty-seven volumes of recommendations in 1962. A similar study, the

Canadian Outdoor Recreation Demand Study, released reports in 1967, 1969, and 1972. The reports from both commissions suggested that outdoor recreation, far from being a fad, was a component of the national character. The powers that be saw recreational land as critical not only for economic reasons but also because, as the ORRRC put it, "The outdoors is part of what is and was America, and it's being lost." U.S. citizens needed the outdoors more than ever, the report continued, since most people now lived in cities and suburbs rather than on farms. This was much the same as the argument of the recreation and parks movements in the late nineteenth century: people need to escape the everyday urban setting and experience a change in scenery where they would have a different relation to nature. Now these needs were felt to be even more critical. The contradictory recommendations of both Canadian and U.S. commissions were basically this: conserve what was left of natural areas, and develop them for maximum enjoyment by all.

These government commissions hired demographers, geographers, sociologists, and other consultants to come up with ways the tourist industry might adapt to the new situation; and the industry in turn took up many of their recommendations in the expansionary years of the 1960s and early 1970s. The tourist industry began to take a more active role in developing both markets and destinations. In other words, where vacationers once considered a holiday in the countryside, they might now consider many different holiday experiences in many different kinds of places. In a report for the ORRRC in the early 1960s, anthropologist Margaret Mead suggested that the category "family vacation" was quickly becoming outdated. She said that planners ought to be considering what children's holidays might be, and how to entertain adolescents now drifting "aimlessly" around the new suburbs. She wondered if there might not be a vacation market for single women, or "minorities," or "foreigners." And — Americans are always thinking ahead — what might be the recreation possibilities in outer space?

In some ways the culture had already made these distinctions. Men had long since had their own fishing and hunting trips, and the outdoors was still largely identified with what were widely understood to be masculine qualities. The identification of women with nature and the biological would be strictly interpreted until the 1960s: their domain was the physical and social reproduction of the species, and most of that was supposed to happen indoors. For the most part outdoor space for women continued to be confined to the garden and places (like playgrounds) associated with childrearing.

But, in the past thirty years, as families and gender identities have splintered, so too has the social organization of recreational space. Resorts like Club Med or Leisure World cater to specific consumer profiles generated by market research. So does a place like Eco-Village in North Carolina, run by *The Mother Earth News,* a back-to-the-land magazine begun in the 1960s. Most tourist destinations now include a choice of specialized environments: picnic sites, swimming pools, souvenir shops, nature trails, hard surfaces for organized games, places of solitude. The industry has diversified outdoor sports too: ice sailing, windsurfing, jogging, skindiving, hang-gliding, snowmobiling — these have all been developed to meet what the industry talks about as new recreation desires. Not all market research has resulted in the creation of new environments, however. Studies done in the mid-1960s indicated that foreign tourists, especially Europeans, were most interested in the expansive nineteenth-century landscapes celebrated in Western movies. These are the spaces embalmed in the national parks of the West. This desire for the primitive — which has always included aboriginal cultures, however they're constructed in the popular imagination — has become more pronounced in recent years.

The boom in nature tourism of the 1960s brought to a head some of the contradictions inherent in public policies that encouraged both nature conservation and tourist development. Debates around this issue were common in the early years of the modern environmentalist movement. For some, the debate was resolved by the creation of another legal category of land. In the United States, the Wilderness Act of 1964 gave wide statutory protection to designated roadless areas that were over 2,025 hectares in size. The government usually continued to honour prior resource-extraction rights and activities on these lands, which has neutralized the law's effect in many areas of the U.S. West. Both the U.S. and Canadian governments passed similar legislation in the 1960s, naming endangered animal species and setting out national environmental policies.

But a review of the environmental legislation of the past twenty years — which would require a book in itself — doesn't begin to address the deeper cultural changes that were underway during that time. Public attitudes towards nature — or the environment, as it has come to be known — have shifted considerably. Nature tourism is not what it used to be. Consider the encounter of the contemporary tourist with other animals. It used to be that animals were hunted and killed as part of the (male) tourist experience of the outdoors. While sport hunting is still practised today, it has a deservedly bad name. *Photographing* animals has become the preferred trophy-taking activity, especially if the beasts can be "captured" on film in a wild setting. In 1977 a U.S. Forest Service report concluded that by the year 2000, "The primary use of wildlife resources will change from hunting to non-consumptive uses like photography and observation." This is what present-day "ecological safaris" are about. The photograph documents a vanishing species at the same time that it authenticates the nature experience. The animals are temporarily "preserved" on film for the enjoyment of the maximum number of sightseers, including the reluctant friends who end up viewing the vacation slides and movies.

In the 1970s, the expansionary days of the tourist industry began to wane. But by that time the industry had consolidated itself. Alternating cycles of over-expansion and crisis favoured large operators. Almost gone were the mom and pop motels and the family riding-stables that had done so well during the days of the circuit tour by auto. The prestige products were now capital intensive — multifaceted "destinations" like Disney World became the industry model. Tourism was no longer so much about service provision as it was about the mass production and management of sightseeing experiences.

The growth of the tourist industry had produced an enormous infra-structure. Professional planners and bureaucrats, advertising consultants, graphic designers, and cost-benefit analysts were all a seemingly necessary part of the industry, turned out by faculties of leisure studies and courses in hospitality management. The industry had vertically integrated agents, tour operators, car-riers, and destinations. Its publicity and marketing had become highly sophistica-ted, using strategies such as demographics and psychographics invented by Madison Avenue in the 1960s. The mass-marketed package tour sold the tourist experience as a single commodity, concentrating activity in a smaller number of well-produced locales. These "place-product packages," as they're known in the industry, aim for total design of buildings, landscape, services, signage, and spin-off products. In the well-managed business, these tourist sites become in-dustrial plants whose goods are aesthetic experiences and hospitality services. All of these strategies have made good use of the photographic image, now an inte-gral part of most people's experience of the outdoors.

Research in leisure studies has been responsible for many of these changes. In the 1960s, social scientists and management consultants produced volumes of

Graphs like these are supposed to help planners predict people's responses to a "visual recreational environment."

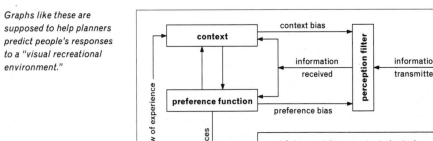

studies related to tourism. Favourite topics of the day were destination perception and scenery evaluation. A good place to look for some of this work is the *Journal of Leisure Research,* published in the United States by the National Recreation and Park Association. The first issue, published in the winter of 1969, featured an article on how to develop a model for testing people's landscape preferences. By quantifying responses to photographs of different landscapes, park and recreation planners could determine which "landscape features" should be purchased, developed, or preserved. The industry could then locate a scenic road or hiking trail, for example, in a way that would maximize visitor pleasure. Subsequent issues of the journal have pursued this research logic: one article draws up a typology of campers according to motivating factors; another talks about measuring eye pupillary response to landscapes — when they see a trout stream, for example, do male eyes dilate more than female eyes?

Other research has aided the administration of natural lands and control over the organisms within them. U.S. government studies have recommended certification of wilderness users, the use of robots for park maintenance, and the captive rearing of endangered species "rather than rely on natural reproduction." Thanks to researchers, we now know the maximum noise levels for optimum human enjoyment of national parks. They've also come up with statistics on the carrying capacities of ecosystems, which presumably help determine the maximum human presence those areas will tolerate. They have studied the further penetration of technology into recreation areas: the possible development of personal hovercraft and helicopters, as well as jet-powered backpacks. Scientists have invented remote sensing devices that monitor animal migrations in some areas and could be used to monitor park use by humans as well.

All this work has implications for the experience of nature, especially when we consider that the mass media, and the vast numbers of images they produce, are part of the modern environment. For example, contemporary tourist research indicates "pre-trip anticipation" is one of the key determinants of a tourist's satisfaction with a holiday destination. The images of the holiday produced by the industry must entice the potential traveller but at the same time they must preclude the cultivation of false expectations. Obviously, not just any picture of Lake Louise will do.

Tourism: From the Recreational to the Social

Today, recreational opportunities, as they're called, are produced almost exclusively by government agencies or transnational corporations — at least at the level of investment. Development decisions are taken in the board rooms of the metropolis and rarely take into account the nature of local communities or working landscapes. Because tourism is largely about the experience of difference — whether it's cultural or geographical — the industry has played an important role in the globalization of Western industrial culture.

This leads to fascinating paradoxes. Industrial logic demands standardization, yet we've come to define natural settings in part by their uniqueness. The result has been an increasing *production* of natural attractions. For a long time now our culture of nature has typed certain topographies and climates — mountains, coastlines, islands, exotic or fragile ecosystems — as special places. But inevitably, even in culturally valorized scenic places, certain elements have to be rearranged to meet tourist expectations. In the game preserves of East Africa, for example, the elephants or lions must be visible and uncontained when the sightseers go by in their tour buses, and preferably the beasts will be eating other animals. But we don't want other buses full of tourists angling for good photos crowding the scene and causing a distraction. Native human communities, moreover, might or might not be an acceptable component of the safari experience. If they are acceptable they're perhaps best presented in traditional, that is, archaic, dress.

Signs for scenic drives on Prince Edward Island, Canada.

Or consider the case of Prince Edward Island. It has a tourist identity as a regional, working landscape. Here, the story goes, the old values predominate: family farms, picturesque villages, benign seascapes. The cosmopolitan tourist requires authentic space: Prince Edward Island should look "distinctive," which in this case means anachronistic. Town buildings should be restored to their original state; rural vistas should conform to the standard image of a bucolic potato-growing backwater. Tacky motels and drive-ins, on the other hand, should be discouraged.

These needs have led to fascinating conflicts with the people who live on Prince Edward Island, for the elite taste of the educated tourist is often insensitive to the vernacular design of the local inhabitant. In the mid-1970s a controversy arose over billboards and abandoned cars along the highways. Tourists found they detracted from the island's identity; islanders considered them part of their culture. Another conflict involved the traditional applications of manure on the fields. Tourist organizations lobbied to have manure use prohibited near highways — its smell was apparently not part of the repertoire of bucolic experience. Because the modern tourist has been constructed as a guest rather than a client, islanders have found it difficult to oppose these changes without breaching the hospitality norms of their culture.

☣

Other recent developments in tourism continue the earlier trends towards diversification of the industry. Sport tourism and earthquake and disaster tourism are obvious examples. Self-catering, another trend, means that tourists provide many of their own services, such as food or accommodation, while they travel. The most common form of self-catering is to travel in a RV, fixing your own meals and making your own bed. Since you carry most of your household with you in a RV, all you require is a parking lot close to the highway with a place to dump your sewage and maybe a play area for the kids. More sophisticated RV sites have club houses and swimming pools, laundry facilities, video games, hot showers, and cable-TV hookups at the campsite: all the conveniences of home.

Private campground chains like KOA have been a familiar part of the landscape for some time now, but franchises of time-sharing campgrounds and cabins are a more recent phenomenon. For an initial investment, often on the order of $6,000, you can buy a 200-year membership in a camping club. In one club this entitles you (and your heirs!) to use the club's private campgrounds for a fee as long as the lease holds, at which time the "vacation license" reverts to the developer.

There are other, quite different, tourist possibilities. Social tourism is the name given to an economy in which public funds are dispersed in a way that distributes the benefits of tourism evenly across society. As it is usually practised, however, it is a kind of subsidized tourism for the "disadvantaged." It includes large institutions like the YMCA, the Boy Scouts, and Outward Bound, as well as many smaller urban groups who offer cheap nature outings for working-class urban dwellers. Trade unions and large industrial enterprises have often participated in these activities by providing vacation villages for workers. So have religious organizations such as the PTL Club. Vacation pay is also a form of social tourism. In Switzerland, state-sponsored holiday-savings plans are available that operate on a sliding scale according to the income of the subscriber.

In 1980 a United Nations conference on World Tourism in Manila affirmed that social tourism is necessary if millions of people are to enjoy "discovery, rest, and the beauty of the world."

Another development is adventure tourism and its recent offshoots ecotourism and biotourism. Standard offerings in this sector of the industry are river rafting, jungle safaris, trekking, and mountain-climbing. For wealthy tourists seeking more, there's skiing in Antarctica, dog-sledding in the Arctic, grizzly bear viewing in Alaska, and kayaking in Greenland or Baja California. An unquenchable appetite for the exotic and "uncharted" distinguishes much adventure travel. This description of one outfit's 1990 trip to Irian Jaya illustrates the point:

These jungles are the home of still uncontacted upper Asmat tribes living along the rivers and on the swamps in great treehouses, and we must travel with caution.... As the terrain, river conditions and tribal situations have many unknowns, we have allotted a good

A whale-watching
expedition in the northern
Pacific. By the mid-1980s,
"eco-tourism" was big
business.

chunk of time for this exploration. This is the leading edge of adventure and we must emphasize that you must be in extremely good physical condition and ready to accept unknown hardships en route.

The World Wildlife Fund defines ecotourism as travel to "protected natural areas, as a means of economic gain through natural resource preservation." The economic gain spoken of accrues to the host country. Governments in Costa Rica and Kenya, for example, have recognized that tourism to natural areas brings in more money than mining, forestry, or ranching would on those same lands. Some tour companies offer working vacations: harvesting crops in Third World nations, or assisting wildlife conservation work. These tour operators make a point of educating their clients about the effects of development on natural systems. Some also donate a portion of their fees to environmental groups in host countries.

Ecotourism raises questions about how a *socially* useful tourism would work. Surely it would be designed to meet local needs. At a minimum it would mean building a sustainable local economy and providing rewarding and well-paid jobs. It might also mean working the landscape in a way that invites care and participation; unpolluted swimming places for people to go to after work, for example. Lastly, it must strengthen cultural and political bonds within and between communities. Cultural exchanges and group vacations are ways of bringing people together.

An admittedly remote example of an alternative tourism is that promoted by the Annapurna Conservation Area Project (ACAP) in west-central Nepal. The Annapurna region is home to forty thousand subsistence farmers — and the annual host to twenty-five thousand foreign tourists who come to hike in the Himalayas. The area is in ecological crisis, part of a downward spiral of malnutrition, deforestation, erosion, fuel scarcity, overgrazing, and species extinction. ACAP has set itself the task of reconciling ecological restoration with sustainable community development and low-impact tourism. Based and directed in the villages, its programs include alternative energy generation, tree planting, literacy campaigns, trail repair, health centres, cultural festivals, and wildlife inventories. ACAP charges tourists a fee to enter the area and gives them a sophisticated brochure that discusses the connections between land and life in the region. Hot showers, diet, meal times, plastics, electrification, drinking water, price haggling, shitting, and begging: the brochure traces the connections between these tourist issues and both the Annapurna ecosystem and its cultures.

French social theorist Guy Debord has called tourism "a by-product of the circulation of commodities." The mass circulation of the middle classes around the globe is a phenomenon of vast proportions — now over 400 million people a year — overseen by an industry that has extended its management techniques out into the land itself. That world is a changed one, fragmented by development, diversified by marketing strategies, and overlaid with technologies like the car and the camera. As we'll see in the pages to come, the Annapurna project is just one example of another kind of circulation of people through the world, of a tourism directed in a way that encourages connections between community and region.

*Photograph by Lynne
Cohen.*

2. Nature Education and Promotion

Today, as in the past, ideas about things natural must be examined and criticized not only for ways they help us understand the material world, but for the quality of their social and political counsel. Nature will justify anything. Its text contains opportunities for myriad interpretations.

— Langdon Winner, *The Whale and the Reactor*

While our sense of the natural world has always been encumbered by our sense of human culture and history, there was a time, not long ago, when you could get out of your car at a curve on a scenic road and admire the view on something resembling its own terms. There were no signs directing your gaze, no coin-operated binoculars, and no brochures answering your unasked questions about local flora, geology, or the history of land use.

Today many people would regard such an unadorned curve in the road as a missed opportunity. Environmental educators, government agencies, and corporate public-relations departments all make claims on our understanding of nature and its place in our everyday lives. By the mid-twentieth century, it seemed, nature had to be explained to its human inhabitants; it was not enough to just try to experience it.

As a result, conflicting information about the natural world blankets our visual and aural environments. Much of this information is promotional — that is to say, often misleading, mystifying, or simply irrelevant. On the other hand, we often find it difficult to gain access to vital data — for example, success rates of reforestation programs, or locations of toxic waste dumps, interpretations of remote sensing data, or the results of studies in health, geology, or freshwater ecology. In fact, as U.S. historian Samuel Hays has documented, the control of information has been the most powerful weapon used by anti-environmentalists.

For all of these reasons, public discussion and democratic decision-making about environment are difficult to come by. Despite this, one of the most innovative and politically competent social movements in decades has mobilized

An exhibit on Appalachian forest ecology, Sugarlands Visitor Center, Great Smoky Mountains National Park, Tennessee.

itself in opposition to environmental degradation — and it is a movement driven largely by the grassroots efforts of people working in their own communities. In the formative years of the 1960s, environmentalism was a reaction to contamination of air, water, and food. Since that time the movement has become far more sophisticated in both tactics and management of the media. It has also changed (and splintered) as emerging issues like deep ecology, feminism, animal rights, and social justice have added to its analysis and altered its direction.

All of these social changes have been paralleled by changes in the scientific disciplines whose subject is the natural world. Sciences such as natural history, biology, and ecology have opened out into new interdisciplinary fields, among them environmental studies, urban and landscape design, neurophysiology, and environmental psychology.

These changes indicate the possibility of a new understanding of landscape as cultural activity. Debates about our relations with animals, about the perceptual mechanisms of the brain or the place of aesthetics in urban design — these are all attempts to discover how the land means what it does. Such debates raise questions of value and aesthetics that have too long been absent from both popular and scientific discussions of environment. These debates are part of what I broadly define as nature education, which is today a vast and disparate endeavour, a complex and changeable subject with many currents, both official and unofficial.

Nature Interpretation

As more and more people have taken to sightseeing over the past forty years, recreation managers have begun to offer their "interpretations" of the world out there in the wilds. This nature interpretation, as it has come to be called by the people who do this kind of work, is a kind of popular education for people visiting parks, museums, roadside historical sites, and other places of leisure. First used in the context of natural history education, interpretation is now a term

common in other contexts, such as museum design. It is a profession that is practised for the most part in public and non-profit institutions.

The primary purpose of interpretation is to teach visitors about what
they're seeing first hand, using signs and pathways, guides and actors, games,
plaques on buildings, stories told round a campfire, video monitors, slide shows,
photographs, and other visual displays. A 1969 Parks Canada annual report
described the objective of interpretation as "not only to increase the visitor's
awareness, understanding and appreciation of the park's environment, but to
help him assess his own natural surroundings and his place in them." The sexism of this explanation aside, interpretation also accomplishes various management objectives, such as resource protection, public safety, law enforcement, and
public relations. All of these activities have had an effect on the land and the way
we experience it.

A U.S. journalist, Freeman Tilden, elaborated an interpretive method in
a 1957 book called *Interpreting Our Heritage*. Tilden argued that the purpose of
interpretation was to "reveal": to reveal the perhaps hidden processes that
underlie forest succession, for example, or the everyday life of a seventeenth-
century fishmonger in Cape Breton. This is done "through the use of original
objects, by firsthand experience, and by illustrative media, rather than simply
to communicate factual information." But Tilden's goal was not what you'd call
an education in popular science. Interpretation had a moral purpose:

*The appeal for a renaissance of the appreciation of Beauty — in the abstract and in its
particular aspects — must not be allowed to falter. It is vital to our moral growth. It is a
program of education. Perhaps it is truer to say that it is a program of re-education, for
we have always known, in our innermost recesses, our dependence upon Beauty for the
courage to face the problems of life. We have let ourselves forget. It is the duty of the interpreter to jog our memories.*

It's hard to know what to make of this appeal, which came in the middle of
the 1950s. It calls to mind some of the moral wholesomeness of the New Deal,
but the deference to "Beauty" must have seemed strangely out of place in a
consumer culture devoted to the pursuit of happiness and the good life. It was
certainly out of step with an increasingly dominant scientific progressivism. By
the 1950s few among even the traditional sectors of the conservation movement
would have used such an anachronistic language. In any case, Tilden's book,
and his work as a park activist, inspired many professionals who worked in parks
and other natural areas. They quickly sloughed off references to Beauty and
moulded the new discipline to the requirements of the tourist industry.
Interpretation joined the ranks of the popular social sciences — sociology,

statistics, psychology, and demographics, among others — whose methodologies were by the 1960s a familiar part of the public culture of television, mass-market magazines, and advertising.

Professional nature guides and naturalists date from the late nineteenth century, the same period as the early recreation and conservation movements and the formation of Boy Scouts, Girl Guides, and Campfire Girls. Popular nature study was an important part of a broad outdoor-education movement with roots in Germany and Switzerland. Typical activities included field trips to natural areas, sketching classes, bird watching, and evening lectures and travelogues sponsored by local naturalist organizations. These activities persist to this day, but are very different from more recent phenomena, such as Native survival schools or "restored" natural landscapes.

It is no wonder that naturalist activity proliferated in the late nineteenth century, for the preceding century had been a time of tremendous scientific investigation of nature. North American flora and fauna had been the object of intense professional scrutiny since the mid-eighteenth century. Most of the field work in European natural sciences was done among the rocks and flowers and beasts of North America. The fruits, so to speak, of this work were widely displayed in natural-history museums and at world's fairs in both the "old" and "new" worlds. At about the time the natural and physical sciences began to split, their practitioners formed professional organizations such as the Audubon Society, the National Geographic Society, the Society of American Foresters, and the various academies of science. Many of those organizations were important advocates of the establishment of national, provincial, and state parks, and continue today to be important in nature education.

As the parks opened and began to attract tourists, their administrators began to hire naturalists and educators. By the 1920s, parks at all levels of jurisdiction had initiated education programs. In 1959 Parks Canada established its Education and Interpretation Section. In the same year park rangers at Banff National Park in Alberta built a nature trail, the first of thousands all over the continent — although some reports indicate a nature trail in the park as early as 1915. The rangers erected intermittent signs to identify tree species, point out wildlife habitats, and explain geological features.

The rise of interpretation closely followed the increased recreational and leisure activity of the mid-twentieth century. In a perhaps more innocent time, someone going camping or slogging round the edge of a marsh had no choice but to encounter the natural world "on its own." Now, with nature education moving out onto the land itself, the ruptures of contemporary culture began to intervene in more obvious ways. Nature interpretation coincided with a growing realization in the culture that modern land-use practices had a massive and detrimental effect on natural ecosystems. Rachel Carson's *Silent Spring,* a denunciation of pesticides published in 1962, was widely read and quoted and helped launch the environmental movement.

In the postwar years interpretation was quickly institutionalized. Major parks and museums created positions for interpreters, colleges offered courses, institutions developed policies in nature education, and scholars developed a professional literature. Park administrations began to build visitor centres and theatres, publish pamphlets, and offer guided walks, slide shows, movies, and amphitheatre performances. They hired personnel to demonstrate, lecture, and explicate, and they built gift shops to sell nature art, guide books, and local crafts. In the words of a Parks Canada memo, the parks would now be "explained and interpreted as living museums of nature, where people can observe and appreciate the beauty that surrounds them."

Living or not, museums require good visual access, and interpreters have also worked to enhance the "visibility" of nature by building roads and trails, observation towers, underwater viewing booths, boardwalks, blinds, and telescope platforms. Some parks use boats and aircraft to give visitors increased access to natural experiences.

The Construction of the Visitor

In the past thirty or forty years the early focus of interpretation on natural history has given way to a concern with attracting a broader audience and keeping people entertained. In this regard, the history of nature interpretation parallels that of modern marketing and communications, much as tourism has. In 1967 the Canadian Outdoor Recreation Demand Study called for "an in-depth examination of the characteristics of the park visitor," and much demographic work has since followed. Typically, researchers create "visitor types" in their studies and then discover them among the people who show up at a park or museum. They construct profiles of a visitor's age, sex, nationality, family composition, ethnicity, consumption habits, and recreational preferences. Some visitors belong to clubs — trailer and RV clubs, Scouts, garden clubs, Rotary, and so on. Some are disabled. Some come by bus, others by private car. Some are outdoor types, some just happened to be driving by looking for a good restaurant or a place to swim.

Park administrators use these visitor profiles to help design educational programs and modify the physical landscape of nature reserves. The data are in turn transformed and recirculated in visitor surveys that both gather background information and monitor the "performance" of the park — looking at how well it has produced a meaningful experience of nature. At Wye Marsh, a private non-profit nature centre along the southern shore of Georgian Bay in Ontario,

Kids in an interpretive program at Wye Marsh, Ontario.

visitors use microcomputers to evaluate their experience of the marsh and to indicate how well it lived up to their expectations. In times of scarce public funds, visitor surveys also become part of making up budgets, very much like Full Time Equivalent formulas are used in schools. Park managers establish ratios of caretakers to visitors by season, which almost always results in layoffs and less full-time work for employees.

Interpreters often divide parks into "interpretation management units." Each area is assigned a theme and a target audience that will then "discover" the area and its theme. The interpretive activities that take place in a given unit will develop the theme in different ways. For example, a theme in a campground area might be "the forest ecosystem." The signs and exhibits at the washrooms and water pumps might explain forest diversity, seasonal cycles, and wildlife communities, while trails might lead through examples of different forest types.

Another unit might aim for a different audience. At the scenic turnout at the Bow Summit in Banff park, the strategy is to keep people from immediately jumping back into their cars after they step out to admire the view. A short booklet enlarges on the sights with capsule discussions of glaciation, wind erosion, and soil formation. It concludes with a few paragraphs about the devastating effects of tourism on alpine ecosystems.

Interpretation and Environmentalism

Just as visitors are divided into "types," so is the land rationalized: splintered into discrete yet overlapping management jurisdictions, use zones, narratives, sights, and experiences. This process of differentiation — which the advertising industry refers to as product diversification — simultaneously diminishes and expands

An organized wolf howl at Algonquin Provincial Park, Ontario. Imitating wolf howls has long been used by wildlife managers to track populations, and is now a tourist activity.

our experience of the natural world. Because parks are by definition a limited resource, managers must predict and control their use by humans. At the same time governments over the past thirty years have actively promoted park use. In Canada the Glassco Commission mandated the development of visitor facilities in the national parks in 1963. Administrators have been able to deal with this contradiction by rationalizing the very landscapes of natural areas. They differentiate parks one from the other and divide them into zones that situate our experience of nature within management objectives. They match each of these rationalized spaces to an appropriate educational program or advertising campaign. This process is similar to the creation of audiences for the electronic media: the market is first limited to specific groups of potential consumers — commuters, youth, housewives, yuppies — and each group is then expanded into an audience that can be sold to an advertiser.

At its most scientistic, interpretive ideology has collided with the more philosophical currents of the environmental movement. Is the forest there for its own sake, or is it there to offer visitors an experience set apart from their lives in the city, or perhaps to remind them of the last example of a particular plant community in the region? Where it has been successful, interpretation has inevitably encouraged heavy public use of natural areas; this in turn has often had detrimental effects on the very "aesthetic resources" that are the object of all the instruction. Tourism and conservationism, though complementary, have had contradictory results throughout the present century.

While interpretation has encouraged the further management of the world and its inhabitants, it has also brought to the public the insights of relatively new disciplines, such as social history and ecology. Since the 1970s, in fact, many interpreters have been anxious to engage people in environmental politics. Today displays frequently talk about acid rain, the warming of the planet, urbanization, or demonstrate how to build a compost in the backyard.

But the biosphere — the thin surface of the Earth that supports life and is both our home and a vastly complex web of interrelationships — is not easy to explain to people on holidays in a way that will immediately speak to their hearts. I remember a long and pleasant chat with an interpreter at the information centre at Cape Hatteras National Seashore in North Carolina one brisk grey day in February in the mid-1980s. I was curious about a few things, like the diet of pelicans and the presence of subtropical plant species in the freshwater marshes behind the dunes. It's always a treat to talk to someone who really knows those kinds of things first hand, and the woman I talked to was such a person. But best of all, her knowledge was not confined to the natural history of the locale. She told me a wonderful story about the creation of an adjacent park, Cape Lookout National Seashore. When the U.S. National Park Service proposed a second park for the Outer Banks in the 1970s, they included the Shackleford Banks in its boundaries. The Shackleford Banks are a series of sand-spits that have been used for centuries by local fishers who have built shacks on the dunes to store equipment. At the time, U.S. national park ideology didn't allow for shacks on dunes; the park was to be a pristine nature reserve. In the early 1980s the park administration bulldozed the shacks and built a small interpretive centre. The local people were outraged and some of them promptly torched the park building. The interpreter was clearly aware of the ironies of this unconventional environmental history, and I came away with, as they might say in the profession, a better understanding of the place I was visiting.

◐

But not all nature education is about parks or even takes place in them. Many new museums work hard at combining cultural and natural history. The Oakland Museum in California is an ambitious attempt to talk about the natural history, popular culture, and fine art of a region all at once. Discussions of beach ecosystems, for example, spill over into presentations of surfing culture. The building itself constantly shifts its position from just above ground to just below ground. Outside, in grids that move from roof to terrace to sunken courtyard, landscape architect Dan Kiley has worked back through Modernism using a northern Californian idiom.

Another example of the breadth of contemporary nature education is the Frank Slide Interpretive Centre in the Crowsnest Pass of Southern Alberta. The narrow Rocky Mountain valley is rich in examples of the interdependence of natural and cultural history. It is the site of a major railway crossing of the

Continental Divide, several abandoned coal mining towns, and one of the world's largest rock slides. The centre has been built at the edge of the slide rubble. Its construction directs the visitor's gaze out over the valley as exhibits tell the stories of railroad construction, coal and oil extraction, and the collapse of the mining economy just before the First World War. Outside, paths radiate out to platforms where exhibits tell about railroad alignments and the arrangement of the town sites — all within the context of the valley's physiography and geology. Beyond the centre, visitors are encouraged to explore the old mining communities, which are physically intact because of the quick collapse of the local economy.

Unlike the old natural history museums, these new museums are about interconnections: the links and parallel histories of our social and natural environments. Such places are one of the legacies of the diffusion of ecological ideas in the culture.

Nature in Schools

Until the 1960s, the study of nature in schools had remained relatively unchanged since the early part of the century. Most of it went on within the "hard" sciences like biology or physics — or, in rural areas, vocational agriculture, which concentrated on animal husbandry or crop production. Ideas of "environment," let alone "biosphere" or "habitat," were foreign to this scientific discourse, which since the sixteenth century had viewed the natural world as, in environmental historian Carolyn Merchant's words, "a machine built and repaired by men."

The official curriculum guidelines left teachers who wanted to introduce a sense of the relationship between humankind and the natural world with little room to manoeuvre. The exception was vocational agriculture, although these guidelines (rightly) required that the courses be tied to local economies. But because modern agricultural economies are skewed towards industrial production and resource exploitation, it has been difficult to teach subjects such as organic gardening or integrated pest management. There was a minor tradition of "nature studies" programs and "outdoor schools," basically biology field trips in which teachers took kids outside to explore frog ponds or forests. Geography classes sometimes raised issues related to technology and the land. These optional courses were often taught by people afraid of the biases of science and were never well integrated into the curriculum. They were further marginalized by science teachers, often with good reason, for they typically fostered little understanding of what might be considered the basics of ecological science: the interactions of food webs, photosynthesis, soil fertility, plant genetics, speciation, hydrology, reproduction, and succession. It's not unreasonable to expect formal education to be strong on conceptual principles. Outdoor education in parks and at rural conservation centres, after all, is constrained by its recreational context; kids go there by and large to play and swim, to snow-shoe, to learn about bees or maple syrup — not the axioms of science.

There have also been professional reasons for the institutional antagonism to nature education. "Easy" environmental science courses have often attracted students away from the supposedly more serious or focused courses such as biology, which have retained the upper hand in attracting dwindling school funds. Guidance counsellors have helped police these disciplinary boundaries by steering brighter students towards the traditional sciences where higher degrees and careers have often awaited them. "Low achievers" are shunted off to voca-tional programs. Lastly, many of the ethical questions raised in environmental science courses have challenged the traditional "neutrality" of scientific study and insisted that the natural sciences themselves have a social history as well. These are legitimate fears, for, properly taught, environmental science has a broader scope than science, and transcends it. Ecology addresses nature at a higher level of organization — that of communities and systems.

That said, ecology has not been altogether ignored in school curricula, for some of its lessons have long since penetrated even the most parochial sci-ences. Ecology is also not intrinsically sympathetic to moral philosophies that value natural systems on their own terms. It is as rife as any science with in-strumental thinking about the Earth. It has remained to the environmentalist movement to invest ecology with an ethics.

By the 1970s, in any case, many governments had begun to introduce environmental science to school curricula. Slowly over the past twenty years — very slowly in fact — ecological ideas have permeated most levels of formal education, although often unsystematically. Environmental science courses are seldom integrated into the full range of courses and almost never allowed sci-ence credits. Courses rarely explore connections between ecology and disciplines such as economics, history, literature, or sociology — or even, for that matter, horticulture or agriculture.

These changes have happened unevenly, and from the top down. Universities were the first institutions to offer environmental science courses. By the late 1980s, such courses were offered in some secondary and elementary schools; other schools, however, still balk at offering both science and envi-ronmental science courses. In cost-cutting and "Back to Basics" campaigns, environmental science — like many of the "permissive" 1960s-era outdoor pro-grams — has been the first to go. Even where it is offered, schoolyards are often covered in asphalt — an unlikely place for anyone to become familiar and at home with nature.

What ends up being taught goes under many names. Course units have titles like "Organisms and Their Environment," "Science in Society," "Food and Energy," and "The Social Implications of Technology." What exactly is being talked about: farming? biology? ecology? These semantic and professional rivalries are in part due to the broad and synthetic nature of ecological science. They also indicate deeper rifts in thinking that permeate both the natural sciences and the environmental movement — rifts about the social applications of ecology. For instance, UNESCO documents state:

The goal of environmental education is to develop a population that is aware of, and concerned about, the environment and its associated problems, and which has the knowledge, skills, attitudes, motivations and commitment to work individually and collectively toward solutions of current problems and the prevention of new ones.

There is little in this definition suggesting that "the environment and its problems" have anything to do with the social. Solving environmental problems will involve far more than the technological fixes implied here, for they do no more than reinforce the boundaries between a natural world understood to be pure and irrational and an urban-industrial civilization bent on domination. A radical environmental education would explore ways of re-establishing a culture that is more or less in harmony with the land. Some environmental studies programs at the university level recognize this by including issues related to development, health, housing, advertising, urbanism, and the quality of working life in their courses.

Not surprisingly, the same contradictions that have flourished in scientific thinking about the Earth for several centuries can be seen in the divergent teaching materials and activities of environmental education. Project WILD, for example, is a popular school program developed in the United States in the late 1970s by the Western Regional Environmental Education Council. It was launched in Canada in 1984. In both countries the program receives considerable funding from government education and resource agencies. Project WILD was designed for teachers who know nothing about wildlife but want to impart an animal-conservation ethic to their students. They do this through a heavily structured series of games and activities integrated into other subjects. The program can be used with students all the way from kindergarten to high school and illustrates principles of population dynamics, migration, and habitat to promote the "wise use" of resources.

Both animal-welfare and animal-rights organizations have criticized Project WILD. They charge that the program is infected with the languages of commerce and sport. The program's administrators argue that it is "neutral" on contentious issues such as hunting, trapping, and sealing. Yet when referring to animals, words like "game," "sustained yield," "resources," and "harvest" are laden with the imperatives of corporate capitalism. On the other hand, all languages spoken at the intersection of human and natural economies — whether they are referring to plants, domestic or wild animals, or for that matter gardens — are full of ambivalence. That ambivalence is difficult to explore within the confines of a conservationist discourse.

Habitat 2000, a recent program sponsored by the Canadian Wildlife Federation and Environment Canada, supports school projects to restore wildlife habitat. These include building nests and planting hedgerows and windbreaks in both urban and rural settings. Students can also adopt a species by studying its habitat requirements and ensuring that they are met in a given locale. Many teachers have integrated this kind of hands-on environmental work into their courses in a promising way. Students at a Seattle high school, for example, hike into the Cascade mountains several times a year to collect the seed of rare and endangered plants. They propagate these in school greenhouses for use in restoration work in wilderness areas. In other high-school programs in the Western United States, students adopt streams, build erosion control structures, and conduct watershed education workshops in community centres. Portland Community College in Oregon runs an educational program at a wetland on its campus. Urban students spend up to a week a year working in the wetland and learning about plant communities, weather monitoring, fish habitat, and water quality testing.

The New Alchemy Institute, a non-profit farm and research centre on Cape Cod, Massachusetts, has developed an activity-based science curriculum for New England schools. The Green Classroom curriculum includes the development of a school garden, thus fostering a respect for the earth while providing the experience for its care. Students learn about seed germination, plant growth, and soil formation, as well as the origins of agriculture, food production in New England, and how food travels from farm to table. The institute keeps educators abreast of its research through its publications and on-site and off-site education. Current research includes resource-efficient housing, small-scale waste-water treatment, greenhouse horticulture, organic market gardening, and integrated pest management. The New Alchemy project is similar to urban farm initiatives that have recently become popular in England.

Because they were developed in an era of a declining public sector, many of these school programs rely on volunteer labour and funds solicited from conservation organizations, corporate foundations, government grants, and private donations. In the salad days of the welfare state, public agencies co-ordinated and funded most conservation work. Today public funds support pri-

A community-initiated project to stabilize and revegetate a streambank. Projects like these educate local communities about water quality, erosion control, and wildlife habitat.

vate industry while school kids, community organizations, and local natural history societies — all of which lie outside the official economy — carry out the rehabilitation of many disturbed natural areas. A typical example is the "America the Beautiful" program launched by the Bush administration in 1990. Its stated objective was to neutralize carbon dioxide emissions from cars and coal generating stations by planting billions of trees across the country. Corporations such as Texaco and the International Paper Company contributed $1 million each and committed their employees to volunteer their labour after hours. The effect has been a shift of funds away from state-run (and salaried) reforestation programs and into a volunteer organization overseen by the private sector.

The voluntary sector has also taken over interpretation work in some parks. Central Park is a good case in point. In the mid-1970s the city of New York didn't have the money (or, apparently, the interest) to restore Frederick Law Olmsted's paths, bridges, and plantings, so several communities surrounding the park — as well as the larger community of conservationists — raised money and organized work brigades. This new economy is another legacy of the environmental movement.

❖

Not surprisingly, there are many conflicting ideologies of nature at large in environmental education. School curriculum guidelines and texts are often infected with the market imperatives of the resource managers who operate in

Conservation campaigns have long relied on photogenic animals or scenic beauty to raise funds, as with these Canadian Wildlife Federation holiday stamps.

both industry and state agencies. Do we protect deer or duck or fish habitat, for example, out of kinship and a general respect for life, or to provide ample populations for sport hunting? Traditional conservation and sporting organizations like Trout Unlimited or the National Wildlife Federation play an ambiguous role in this respect. They can be counted on to mobilize their large constituencies to help save wildlife habitat (even the National Rifle Association has at times been distracted from gun rights long enough to lend its support). Yet broader issues like nuclear power, consumerism, or aboriginal rights lie well outside their concerns.

The terms of the debate about nature and its relation to society have shifted enormously since the advent of the modern environmental movement some thirty years ago. That movement has produced a vast amount of educational material, ranging from pamphlets and books to games and movies. Most of this is generated by local groups engaged in very specific issues — such as wetland preservation, waste disposal, acid rain, or energy. Non-profit clearinghouses distribute many of these materials to schools and media, as well as organize "environmental festivals" for children. The movement has also nurtured a vast number of small businesses and publications over the past thirty years.

Many teachers of environmental science came of age during the first flush of the movement in the 1960s and have brought its social, political, and ethical imperatives to their work. The teaching of biology offers an example of how an environmentalist ethic has found its way into the schools. In the last ten years many biology teachers have stopped using animal dissection as a classroom exercise. Dissection was introduced in the 1960s as part of an new emphasis on demonstrating scientific process in the study of natural systems. By 1981, however, a changed social climate prompted the U.S. National Science Teachers Association and the National Association of Biology Teachers to adopt a code (later weakened) forbidding investigations that caused animals pain or endangered their health. The subsequent abandonment of dissection was hastened by declining school budgets and concerns about the toxicity of formaldehyde. Many teachers have instead introduced live captive animals into the classroom. It is a momentous shift from severing the vertebrae of a live frog with a pin to watching its daily cycles in the approximated habitat of a terrarium.

Countertraditions

As environmental education has made its way into schools over the past twenty years, primarily under the reluctant aegis of science, a number of alternatives to formal nature study have emerged. Like interpretation, these countertraditions draw on postwar social sciences as well as the energy and political commitment of contemporary social movements.

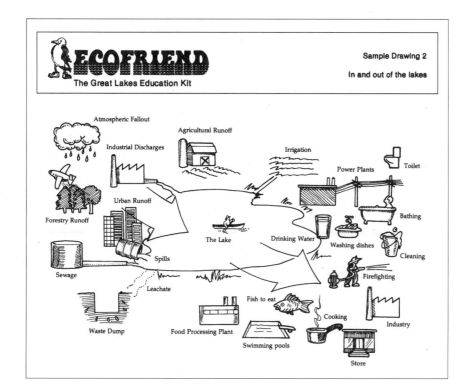

ECOFRIEND
The Great Lakes Education Kit

Sample Drawing 2

In and out of the lakes

Atmospheric Fallout

Industrial Discharges

Agricultural Runoff

Irrigation

Power Plants

Toilet

Urban Runoff

Forestry Runoff

The Lake

Drinking Water

Bathing

Washing dishes

Cleaning

Spills

Sewage

Firefighting

Leachate

Waste Dump

Food Processing Plant

Fish to eat

Cooking

Industry

Swimming pools

Store

A diagramatic explanation of a lake ecosystem, produced by the Ontario Ministry of Natural Resources, for use in primary schools.

One of these alternatives is the Institute for Earth Education (IEE), an organization based in Illinois that has developed extensive outdoor programming for children's camps and nature centres not just in Canada and the United States, but in Australia, England, and France. In recent years the IEE has begun training programs for environmental education teachers as well. The organization is typical of a certain kind of pedagogy often found in the environmental field. It was begun by Steve Van Matre, a student of environmental perception who became involved in nature education through the Boy Scouts and as director of various summer camps in the U.S. Midwest.

In *Acclimatization* and *Acclimatizing,* two books written in the early 1970s and published by the American Camping Association, Van Matre outlined his methods. The immediate goal was to teach about the "Web of Life," which he defined this way:

Light, air, water, and soil are the elements of life,
Life is divided into producers, consumers, and decomposers,
Everything is becoming something else;
Everything has a home,
Homes in a defined area form a community;
Inhabitants of these communities live together in competition, cooperation or neutrality;
Man is the chief predator.

Van Matre wanted to marry the science of ecology with the experiential methods of education that had gained ground in the 1960s. He was bluntly critical of
traditional nature education, with its various strategies of observation, identification, collection, and laboratory experimentation. For Van Matre the pedagogi-
cal strategies of acclimatization, as he has called his approach, are similar to those
of language immersion. They stress the sensorial over the taxonomical: wading
in marshes, climbing trees, crawling through a forest at night on hands and
knees. The aim of these activities is to foster a "personal awareness" of nature.
His approach arranges acclimatization programs according to ecological concepts
such as habitat, community, soil formation, food chains, and plant succession, as
well as the more dubious concepts of "territory," "competition," "producers," and
"consumers." In teaching lessons the instructors draw on group-process techniques such as role-playing, consciousness raising, sensory awareness training,
Gestalt, and even "grokking." The goal is for students to become familiar with
the Earth and eventually feel themselves part of the biosphere.

One of the theoretical bases of this pedagogy is the work of the Swiss child
psychologist Jean Piaget, who argued that children acquire knowledge of their
environment by actively exploring it. Van Matre's terms "producer," "consumer," and "decomposer" derive from a very different tradition, a widely dif-
fused model of energy transfer first proposed by U.S. freshwater ecologist
Raymond Lindemann in the 1940s. Using a flow chart, Lindemann explained
how energy enters a lake as light, passes through a number of organisms, and
exits as heat. Lindemann's explanation of community energetics — which gave
scientific legitimacy to the ideas of interrelatedness and dynamism in natural systems — has become one of the central metaphors of ecology.

Acclimatization activities have trademarked names like Sunship Earth,
Earth Caretakers, Earthkeepers, Earth Encounters, and Earthwalks. Laden with
gimmicks and props and hands-on activities, they rely on anthropomorphic
narratives whose objective is to make the earth, including mud and spiders,
familiar. Kids "scratch and sniff" leaves and branches, explore the "underworld"
of fungi and crickets, visit "nature's basement" (the soil), and stage a "performance" of dancing seeds and leaves.

All of this activity usually takes place outside the city. IEE argues that
urban environments hide natural processes from the incurious and distort
perceptions. For the IEE, nature education in the city is too centred on an understanding of the Earth as human environment rather than as a "system of energy
and materials." This argument, common to deep ecology, reproduces the ideology of "humanity vs. nature." After all, the Earth is human environment: the
question is not whether we should touch it, but how we belong to it. To name
"man" as the chief predator of natural communities is an outlandish reduction

of human history that ignores the many examples of societies that have lived in equilibrium with the Earth.

Acclimatization is typical of a certain kind of pedagogy emphasizing discovery and "magic." Its objectives are to change perceptions of the natural world and develop attitudes more conducive to the long-term survival of the Earth and its inhabitants. Yet its ideas about how culture mediates our sense of the natural world are naive. Restoring this planet will involve more than just "feeling" it. Indeed, an emphasis on perception and attitudes has an unfortunate depoliticizing effect. Programs of this kind rarely consider questions of social power and historical change, much less the entanglements of social, natural, and electronic environments. Nor do the educational activities themselves intervene in the material world by actually doing something collectively to restore the earth — like plant a stream bank or start a waste-reduction project.

Acclimatization is justly critical of most nature education, whose roots often go no further than the most traditional science and the market imperatives of the leisure industry. A rhetorical rejection of science, however, with no attention paid to oppositional currents within the discipline, amounts to little more than anti-intellectualism.

Here and there — for the most part outside institutions — there are other educational currents that draw from local, regional, and historical wisdom about the Earth. These are the kinds of teachings you encounter when talking to gardeners who know the parent soils beneath their gardens and the location of sacred groves, or aboriginal healers who can surmount the boundary between the human and non-human worlds and reaffirm our connections to the planet as well as to human society.

Indeed, the aboriginal cultures of North America have much to teach us about how to survive the current crisis of the land. Despite centuries of oppression and dislocation, Native cultures have survived. The resilience of those cultures comes, I believe, from a collective experience of the Earth as home, as a place that is animated and sacred. Respect for the Earth is something that must be taught, however, and for Natives living away from traditional lands, survival schools have been a critical way of adapting traditions to new social circumstances. One of the hopeful progeny of survival schools is a movement to establish Rediscovery Camps for youth. The first camp was begun in Haida Gwaii (the Queen Charlotte Islands) in 1978, and there are now about fifteen in Canada and the United States. The camps are usually initiated by a local tribal council and set up at ancient campsites or villages in the bush. Participants are Native and non-Native, youth and elders, men and women. Each camp is autonomous and develops programming according to local culture and geography and the needs of the community. They teach social and outdoor skills as well as traditional Native lifeways. They also provide an alternative for youth who are at risk or in crisis. Programs like this politicize the land.

Another community-based project is the Adopt-a-Stream Foundation in Seattle, which has set up stream enhancement programs in schools, neighbourhoods, and community groups. The Foundation's handbook — easily adaptable to other regions — provides a thorough introduction to stream ecology and the relationship between land-use patterns and watershed quality. It details how local groups can become stewards of degraded watersheds: everything from how to conduct wildlife surveys and fish incubation, to planting stream banks, monitoring storm-drain outfalls, and talking to the media.

The East Bay Regional Parks District in the San Francisco Bay Area runs an educational program that ought to be a model for parks departments everywhere. All its activities are on-site and involve active participation in the specific ecosystem of each of its fifty parks (which comprise about twenty-five thousand hectares of urban, urban fringe, and undeveloped areas). In Sunol Park in the headwaters of Alameda Creek, for example, hikes and workshops focus on food webs, stream studies, and larger watershed issues. At an Ohlone village site in Coyote Hills Regional Park, kids learn how to make baskets and construct shell-mounds. In Contra Loma Park, a hike climbs to a ridge to view the California Delta, then descends to a proposed landfill site to discuss the impacts the site would have on the area.

A sophisticated teacher's guide divides the parks into types of habitat. It discusses both the natural and cultural history of the East Bay, moving from geology to climate and on to agriculture, ranching, Native American history, mining, the effects of importing eucalyptus from Australia, and the ecology of salt marshes, oak woodlands, chaparral, and grasslands.

Staff naturalists in the East Bay parks are adamant that nature education involve restoration. A walkathon proposed by a business group to raise money for the parks was turned by staff into a "rockathon," in which kids solicited donations for each bucket of rocks they carried to an eroded stream bank. The Junior Rangers is an after-school and weekend group for nine to twelve-year-olds. For a $100 annual fee, they go on two backpacking trips in the parks as well as log hundreds of conservation hours. They are taught various skills: camp craft, map reading, shelter making, survival techniques, afforestation, and exotic plant removal.

The East Bay Parks have an enormous amount of public support. Adult volunteers meet weekly to work at clearing debris and replanting, and the parks recently won a $225 million bond issue from local communities for programming and land acquisition — an extraordinary accomplishment in an era of a declining public sector.

There are many other promising educational projects under way in Canada and the United States. Many of the best are small efforts that address local biological and social situations. Save the Rouge Valley System, an organization dedicated to preserving a river valley on the eastern edge of Toronto, has found that its links to local schools have broadened and strengthened its constituency. Denver public schools, the parks department, and two foundations have sponsored the Greenway Experience, which trains "educationally-at-risk" high-school students to lead elementary-school kids on tours of the Platte River Greenway, which traverses downtown Denver. The students build self-esteem while teaching others about the history of the river and its relation to the city. The Land Institute in Salina, Kansas, offers courses in permaculture and perennial prairie cultivation — bucking a century of industrial agriculture. Conferences are important places for smaller environmental groups and isolated bureaucrats to exchange information and compare strategies. Most large environmental organizations have also found that education is an essential part of their work as well. The Audubon Society, the World Wildlife Fund, and Ducks Unlimited all sponsor school programs.

Promoting the "Safe" Environment

Governments produce an enormous amount of material about the natural world — for schools, non-government organizations, tourists, rural property owners, and the mass media. The materials include curriculum guidelines, maps, technical studies on pollutants or recycling, fishing quotas, development guidelines, tourist brochures, synopses of research on sewage treatment, pamphlets on vegetable gardening and crop rotation, prospectuses for investors in the recreation industry, videos on water quality, resource assessments, species profiles, instruction kits for schools, contracts with industrial developers, pesticide and mining regulations, and environmental assessment documents.

In part, all that paper is a byproduct of an immense research apparatus whose chief task is to manage the natural world according to the priorities of those in power and the common sense of the day. But the reports and pamphlets and magazine ads are also publicity, for in any modern organization, public or private, public relations is a central activity. This publicity is also a key component of nature education.

In most Western economies today, one of the primary roles of the state is to ensure maximum freedom and profitability for the private sector. An important part of this task is the building of consensus about what constitutes a sound and just economy. How is wealth created and distributed? What are the relations between growth, progress, consumption, and the quality of life? Which activities are included in official accounts of the economy, like Gross National

Smokey the Bear, the mascot of the U.S. Forest Service and symbol of its fire suppression campaigns since the mid-1940s. Smokey had another life as the cartoon character Yogi Bear of Jellystone Park, but today his official career is in some jeopardy as ecologists come to understand the beneficial effects of fire on many ecosystems.

PLEASE...ONLY YOU CAN PREVENT FOREST FIRES!

Product? How are we to account for the declining states of our air, water, and soils? How much of the "lifespan" of a commodity or development — from production and marketing to distribution, consumption, and disposal — is entered into the "environmental impact" ledger?

The assumptions of Western economies are rarely debated in public forums, yet they have a direct and enormous impact on landscape, on the way we think about and live in the natural world. The task of building consensus about the economy, however, is complex, and differs from one era and culture to another. Debates about forest management, for example, resonate differently in the United States than they might in India or Germany; similarly, a dam that was built without opposition in the 1950s might not win public acceptance today.

Increasingly, therefore, the state has found that management of public opinion about what has come to be called environment is at least as important as management of natural systems themselves. Over the past thirty years there has been a growing sense in North America (as elsewhere) that the assimilative capacity of the biosphere — a capacity long used as an unacknowledged economic resource — is reaching its limits. Examples of degraded ecosystems have become more frequent and familiar, more talked about. We understand them to be more serious than ever before. We have entered an era of continual and systemic environmental crisis.

As the crisis has deepened, it has spread outward to encompass the entire planet and inward into our very bodies, further blurring the distinction between human and environment. Consider these "natural" disasters of the past thirty years: regular oil spills in all the world's oceans since the 1960s, the use and test-ing of atomic weapons, the corporeal deformations of thalidomide, blanket aerial spraying of herbicides in Vietnam, DDT in Arctic mammals, smog, can-cers, AIDS and other widespread immunological disorders, eutrophication of the Great Lakes, flooding and starvation in Bangladesh, deadly industrial chemi-cals at Love Canal, dying whales and dolphins and caribou, PCBs in gasoline and rainfall, overlogging, desertification and famine in the Sahel and in Haiti, acid rain right across the northern hemisphere, "accidents" at nuclear power stations, ozone depletion, global warming, destruction of agricultural lands and tropical rain forests.

The Earth is dying. The scientific evidence, if we need it, is staggering. In 1989 the "Vancouver Declaration on Survival in the 21st Century" summed it all up:

An accelerating increase in population growth over the past 150 years from one billion to over five billion with a current doubling time of 30-40 years;

a comparable increase in the use of fossil fuels leading to global pollution, climate and sea-level change;

an accelerating destruction of the habitat of life, initiating a massive and irre-versible episode of mass extinction in the biosphere — the basis of the Earth's ecosystem;

an unimaginable expenditure of resources and human ingenuity on war and prepa-ration for war.

And all licensed by a belief in inexhaustible resources of the planet encouraged by political and economic systems that emphasize short term profit as a benefit, and disre-gard the real cost of production.

Catastrophism, however, is an approach that neither government nor industry can afford. As the crisis has grown, state resource agencies have become locked into crisis management. As early as the 1950s, when controversy began to rage in the United States about damning river canyons in the Southwest region, state and federal officials organized sophisticated media campaigns in sup-port of development. Ironically, while some government agencies continue to promote increases in the consumption practices of the North American mid-dle class, other agencies fight a rear-guard action to preserve what's left of nat-ural systems. The apparent contradiction is conscious government industrial strategy: provide industry with security of supply, manage public opinion, and create and maintain markets through trade regulations and foreign policy.

For instance, in the administration of fish and wildlife, resource agen-cies manage animal populations and habitats by monitoring migration and feeding patterns, regulating hunting and fishing, and encouraging "compatible"

Extinct	Blue-eyed Mary
Endangered	Cucumber Tree, Furbish' Lousewort, Gattinger's Agalinis, Heart-leaved Plantain, Hoary-Mountain Mint, Large Whorled Pogonia, Mountain Avens (Eastern Population), Pink Coreopsis, Pink Milkwort, Prickly Pear Cactus (Eastern Population), Skinner's Agalinis, Slender Bush Clover, Small White Lady's Slipper, Small Whorled Pogonia, Southern Maidenhair Fern, Spotted Wintergreen, Water-pennywort
Threatened	American Chestnut, American Waterwillow, Anti-costi Aster, Athabasca Thrift, Bird's Foot Violet, Blue Ash, Bluehearts, Colicroot, Giant Helliborine, Ginseng, Golden Crest, Kentucky Coffee Tree, Mosquito Fern, Nodding Pogonia, Pitcher's Thistle, Plymouth Gentian, Purple Twayblade, Red Mulberry, Sweet Pepperbush, Tyrrell's Willow, Western Blue Flag
Vulnerable	Broad Beachfern, Dense Blazing Star, Dwarf Hackberry, False Rue-anemone, Few-flowered Club-rush, Green Dragon, Gulf of St. Lawrence Aster, Hill's Pondweed, Hop Tree, Indian Plantain, Lilaeopsis, Marcoun's Meadow-foam, Prairie Rose, Prairie White-fringed Orchid, Shumard Oak, Soapweed, Swamp Rose Mallow, Victorin's Gentian, Victorin's Water Hemlock, Western Silver-leafed Aster, Wild Hyacinth

industrial and recreational development. Government and business try to manage public debate, such as it is, by producing educational materials for rural communities, hunters and anglers, and school kids. These include information signs posted on highways and in parks, as well as innocuous fact-sheets distributed at shopping malls and county fairs. Most of this material — like profiles of wood ducks, coyotes, or cod — has changed little in the past forty years. Other pamphlets, however, have had to explain the complex relations between resource development, regional employment, and global trade. Still others have had to introduce entirely new vocabularies. They use new terms, for instance, to describe the slow retreat of plants and animals from the landscape. They now classify vanishing species as rare, vulnerable, threatened, endangered, extirpated, or extinct.

While the resource ministries still talk about harmony and wise use — their mandate, after all, is to promote the exploitation of natural resources — the newer government environment agencies have the far more difficult task of explaining the radically changed relations between humans and environment; so their educational materials tend to be more sophisticated.

Consider, for instance, the task of promoting, or even describing, the quality of water in North America. In many parts of the continent we can scarcely swim in lakes, bays, and rivers that for centuries have nourished us. Subsurface aquifers are often either contaminated or drying up.

Popular descriptions of water quality range from pure to potable to safe to polluted. The meanings of all these terms have subtly shifted over the past thirty years. For water quality specialists the criteria for purity number in the hundreds. These break down broadly into chemical, microbiological, physical, and radioactive categories. The factors involved in measuring toxic substances include lethality, sublethality (promoting cancer or infertility), mutagenicity, persistence, and bioaccumulation. In one process, biomagnification, many substances become more concentrated as they move up through the food chain. For this reason, for example, the presence of toxins in the Great Lakes can be detected in gull eggs long before they show up in air, water, or human tissue.

Environmental health issues have become a tangled problem, not only because they pose grave liability problems for governments (witness industrial conflicts such as Johns Mansville with asbestos, Union Carbide with pesticides, Kerr McGee with radioactive materials), but also because so little is known, or knowable, in the little time we seem to have. The effects of long-term exposure to most of the hundred thousand chemicals now in commercial use are not known.

Since the 1960s the task of monitoring and testing the environment has grown into an immense enterprise that employs millions of North Americans and takes up the bulk of most environment ministry budgets. Technicians study the contribution of farm runoff to nutrient overloads in streams and lakes, pesticide residue on foodstuffs, the concentration of heavy metals in sewage sludge, the effects of acid deposition on forests, and the effects of introduced parasites on pest populations. Treatment facilities tend to lag behind detection technologies. Chlorine-based water-treatment plants, for example, introduce a highly toxic group of chemicals known as trihalomethanes into drinking water. Detection technologies in turn lag behind the introduction of new chemicals, many of them untested, or tested under dubious conditions.

Testing for toxins presents distinct technical and epistemological problems. Some chemicals can't be measured because they're present in concentrations too low to be determined with existing technology (which is currently able to detect parts per quadrillion, or the equivalent of one second in thirty million years). The existence of other chemicals is not yet proved. Once chemicals are isolated and studied, their health risk can be extremely difficult to ascertain — not the least because science refuses to acknowledge its cultural and social biases. Risk assessment, which has grown into a vast activity, often focuses solely on the human organism — despite ecological evidence that the biosphere is a whole system in which it is impossible to single out one organism for study. "Maximum Acceptable Concentrations" of toxins are determined by a complex formula that is extrapolated from such social factors as size and character of the population

Consumption guidelines for fish caught by anglers

Consumption Frequency	🐟	🐟	🐟	🐟	🐟
Long-term consumption	No restrictions	0.2 kg/wk. (0.5 lb./wk.)	0.1 kg/wk. (0.3 lb./wk.)	1 or 2 meals per month 0.5 kg/mo. (1 lb./mo.)	None
One-week vacation	No restrictions	10 meals 2.3 kg (5 lb.)	7 meals 1.5 kg (3 lb.)	1 or 2 meals 0.5 kg (1 lb.)	None
Two-week vacation	No restrictions	5 meals per wk. 1.3 kg/wk. (2.8 lb./wk.)	4 meals per wk. 0.8 kg/wk. (1.9 lb./wk.)	1 or 2 meals/wk. 0.5 kg/wk. (1 lb./wk.)	None
Three-week vacation	No restrictions	4 meals per wk. 1 kg/wk. (2.1 lb./wk.)	3 meals per wk. 0.6 kg/wk. (1.4 lb./wk.)	1 or 2 meals/wk. 0.5 kg/wk. (1 lb./wk.)	None

Children under 15 and women of childbearing age should eat only fish in 🐟 category.

Some government agencies publish consumption guidelines for fish contaminated with industrial toxins like mercury, mirex, DDT, and PCBs. The relationship between toxins and human health is rarely one of cause and effect, leading to endless technical debates about safety. In this chart from the 1990 Guide to Eating Ontario Sport Fish, *fish in the first column are the only species recommended for "women of childbearing age."*

at risk, average body weight, life expectancy, typical daily intake of air and water, reliability of toxicology studies, and relative danger compared to other social risks. These maximum figures are typically adjusted (usually upwards) to conform to existing detection and treatment technologies.

Often, government publicity announces that levels of a given contaminant are "safe" — or the now more common term, "acceptable" either because they are present in minute quantities or because they exist in the "background," that is, in some other, imperceptible environment. Scientists often use risk/benefit analysis — yet another interpretation of toxicological data — in defence of industrial chemicals or nuclear-power generation on the basis that their social benefits "outweigh" their potential risks. They often count growth and profit generation among the benefits, while leaving social and environmental costs outside the calculus altogether.

It makes for an odd world. On the shores of Lake Ontario, government signs guide fishers through the complexities of what kind of species to eat how often and at what time of year, how to remove cancerous tumours, and how to avoid ingesting the fatty parts where toxins are most concentrated. Official pronouncements deem the same waters safe to drink.

Toxic chemicals and their intimate relation to cancers and immunological disorders have reintroduced an immanent sense of the biological to everyday life. Note, for example, the rich social and cultural history substances such as lead and mercury have assumed over the past few decades. These metals have escaped the worn path from soil to industry, entered households, foodstuffs, blood-streams, and genes, and finally ended up as the subjects of television documentaries and art. The other formerly "invisible" materials of air and water now have a tangibility they didn't have before. Many other substances, however — most of them new to the biosphere since the 1950s — are imperceptible. We find it difficult to see and feel evidence of PCBs, radiation, ozone, and pesticides in the environment, a fact that has encouraged the development of disciplines with names like "risk perception management."

The cultural and political consequences of these physical transformations are complex. Canadian geneticist and broadcaster David Suzuki argues that the imperceptible and incremental nature of some forms of environmental degradation — the slow rate of global warming, for instance, compared with something like a new expressway — encourages cultural adaptation rather than opposition. U.S. historian Stanley Aronowitz, on the other hand, points out that these developments also indicate a new awareness of nature as a constraint — a boundary condition for human endeavour — as well as an historical and moral agent.

As evidence of Aronowitz's argument, there are sensitive programs emerging from government environmental agencies at every level. Where backed with funding and political commitment, some of these programs can have a far-reaching effect. The U.S. Environmental Protection Agency — an agency still on its feet despite the attempts of the Reagan administration to sabotage it — has declared water quality its top priority for the 1990s. Following this lead, the U.S. Fish and Wildlife Service is encouraging people to have their backyards or neighbourhoods declared wildlife refuges. The agency will help with plans and contribute plants. A similar program in the city of Eugene, Oregon, offers tax breaks for property owners who create wetlands or other wildlife habitat on their land.

Corporate Environmentalism Comes of Age

Advertising and promotion about nature are not restricted to government agencies. The history of corporate advertising also has much to tell us about the contradictory ideas of nature that have flourished in contemporary culture over the past forty years. Until well into the 1970s, the private sector flaunted its capacity to extract materials from the earth. By the end of that decade, however, corporate publicity had shifted towards a more conservationist, resource-management model. Environmental advocacy advertising became common, particularly among oil and petrochemical companies. Today many of these campaigns are part of "image enhancement" and "damage control" initiatives launched by newly expanded public relations departments.

In the mid-1980s, for example, the Agricultural Chemicals Association changed its name to the Crop Protection Institute, thus shifting attention away from its work and towards a hackneyed construction of nature as adversary. Most readers will be familiar with the rapid growth of corporate environmentalism that has followed industrial phenomena such as toxic chemical discharges

Streambank protected by willow plantings.

Trees that are not windfirm can blow down in a timbered leave strip.

A promotional pamphlet from the logging transnational MacMillan Bloedel, explaining why their clearcuts often extend right down to the water. The willow plantings on the left are usually not done. In the rejected scenario on the right, fallen logs catch sediment, and help create the pools many fish need. Neither option proposes an alternative to clearcutting.

in Bhopal, India, oil spills in Alaska and the Gulf of Mexico, and radiation discharges in the United States, Canada, and the Soviet Union.

These publicity campaigns are aimed at recapturing political initiative from the social movements. They are also part of the business opposition to a decade and more of environmental regulation — a system that has not only raised costs within industry but also rendered capital much less flexible. By the mid-1980s, corporations had made decisive moves to contain and co-opt the environmental movement. Within the energy and resource sectors, a recent tactic has been to organize community support among citizens', church, and labour groups. The Center for the Defense of Free Enterprise, a U.S. business lobby, has organized small anti-environmental groups all over North America. Typical names are Share the Forest, Northeastern Nova Scotia Truth in Forestry, and Oregonians for Food and Shelter. The Centre for Conflict Studies, a military think-tank in Fredericton, New Brunswick, runs seminars to instruct corporate image managers in counterintelligence tactics. A less benign corporate strategy is legal harassment. Tactics include bringing charges against environmental groups and demanding "deposits" from plaintiffs in class-action pollution cases.

Environmental law has become an industry in itself. In early 1990 the U.S. government filed criminal charges against Exxon for dumping oil in Prince William Sound, Alaska, in 1989, an occurrence Exxon long claimed to be "an accident."

Since the mid-1980s, corporate ethics has been a "growth industry," as an Ontario Hydro official remarked at a conference. Many corporations, especially those in the chemical and energy business — the most polluting sectors of the

An old-growth sitka spruce talks to his grandson about the uncertain future of old-growth forests in a TV spot called "The Talking Rainforest" from British Columbia. Environmental groups now spar with corporations for access to the media.

industrial economy — have formed internal "social issues committees" to consider corporate responsibility, corporate "citizenship," and the ethics of technology. As the Canadian and U.S. economies become more privatized, corporations can no longer depend on governments to mediate between corporate industrial decisions and what is usually called the public interest. Corporations have also begun to claim for themselves the civil liberties that in liberal democracies have usually been reserved for individuals. Other questions typically debated in corporate forums are social equity, "right-to-know" legislation, non-human rights, risk allocation, risk management, and risk perception management.

Certainly, nuclear power lies at the centre of many of these controversies. From the perspective of the nuclear industry, opposition concerns have shifted from health and safety issues towards morality. A number of Christian churches have participated in these discussions, through panels such as the Interfaith Program for the Public Awareness of Nuclear Issues and the Task Force on the Churches and Corporate Responsibility. The following questions, from an issue of the industry periodical *Ethics and Energy,* give a good sense of how the issues are framed. What is our obligation to future generations? What is acceptable risk? What are the rights of local communities relative to the rights of the majority? Does nuclear energy violate the trust given by the Creator? Is it appropriate technology? Are the risks worth the benefits? If not, what would be appropriate compensation "for unmitigable impact and for assuming the burden of risks?"

The other major corporate initiative has been investment in the "ecosector" of the economy. At the most superficial level, this has meant capitalizing

"Green" commodities at Loblaws, a Canadian supermarket chain. A broadening environmental consciousness has provided many corporations with new marketing opportunities.

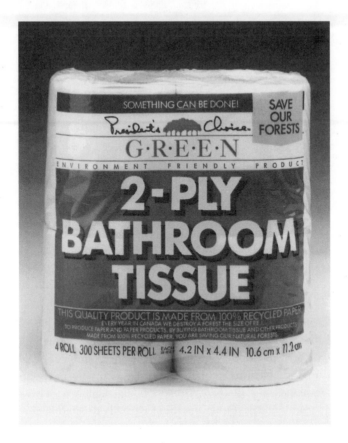

An "affinity card" from the Canadian Wildlife Federation and the Bank of Montreal.

on the eagerness most people have for making some contribution to "saving the planet," as it's usually put. Colgate-Palmolive has developed "ecopaks" (thin-walled plastic containers) for household toxins such as Mr Clean. Supermarket chains promote "green" disposable diapers, made in part with unbleached cotton imported from Sweden. "Biodegradable" plastic bags made a brief appearance in the marketplace in the late 1980s, until environmental groups objected that they merely break down into plastic dust and do nothing to alter consumption patterns. EcoLogo, sponsored by Environment Canada, is a government attempt to regulate this new marketing strategy. Companies stamp its logo — three green doves in a maple leaf configuration — on commodities determined to be "environmentally friendly" after research into the production, consumption, and disposal of the products.

The Canadian government's EcoLogo, a symbol of "environmental friendliness."

There seems to be no end to the inventiveness of the commodity process. A U.S. firm called The Nature Company markets wildlife calenders and T-shirts, suntan lotion, microscopes, and maps of the universe. Banks offer "affinity" credit cards, so that consumer purchases can help finance the conservation of wildlife habitat. Gas stations sell tumbler collections that commemorate endangered species. "Ecologically responsible" companies and investment services have also set up shop. The big industrial profits, however, are concentrated in two areas: new technologies, particularly in packaging and waste management; and recycling. The lure of recycling profits and "biodegradable" packaging has in many cases discouraged efforts to reduce and reuse materials.

Ecology and Ideology

Industrial environmental advocacy and the attendant shifts in consumption patterns have had a measurable social effect, mostly by broadening and popularizing environmental politics in North America. In the larger picture, however, the grave imbalances in our relations with the natural world run far deeper. The domination of nature is linked to domination in social relations, and a serious environmental advocacy must address global economic disparities. It must understand the relations between the financial and corporate institutions of the industrial West and the subservient economies of Third World nations, which are locked into a spiral of export production, overgrazing, fuel shortage, famine, drought, pollution, chronic disease, and infant mortality.

Interest in the environmental effects of development began at the top in the mid-1960s, at a time of widespread ecological illiteracy at every level of the bureaucracy and throughout most of the media. Federal governments in both Canada and the United States created agencies whose mandate — to "protect the environment" in the U.S. formulation — was expected to complement that of the old natural resources ministries, which themselves had been responses to the conservation movement of the early century. Thirty years later, however, it is clear that the mandates of these new environmental agencies have simply not been broad enough to address the social, economic, or cultural aspects of the problems they have attempted to remedy. (Stopping pollution coming out of pipes, for instance, is easy; but once that's done the remaining problems become more diffuse and more cultural.) Cabinet-level decisions regarding taxation or investment, or for that matter, international relations, rarely take ecological questions into account. Co-ordination between government agencies is notoriously poor.

Consequently, environmental agencies have come to rely on react-and-cure measures to problems, when what is needed is an approach that anticipates and prevents deterioration of the biosphere. A preliminary report issued by the World Commission on Environment and Development (the Brundtland Commission) in 1985 put the problem succinctly:

Questions of conservation versus development that were once thought to be rather straight-forward, subject to "rational" benefit-cost assessment and confined to one or two political jurisdictions, are now seen to be highly complex, involving linkages and feedbacks among agriculture, energy and forestry development and transportation and trade policy, and raising questions of economic gain in the short term versus unsustainable development and massive economic loss and social dislocation in the medium and longer terms.

In the 1980s, to address these more long-term questions non-governmental organizations launched several initiatives, including the World Conservation Strategy as well as the World Commission on Environment and Development.

The World Conservation Strategy was prepared by the International Union for the Conservation of Nature and Natural Resources in 1980, with the support of the United Nations Environment Program, the World Wildlife Fund, the Food and Agriculture Organization, and UNESCO. The document was an early proposal to arrest environmental degradation and integrate conservation with development. It lays out an international framework for the development of conservation policies, to which it invited all countries voluntarily to accede. Its three principle objectives are: "Maintenance of essential ecological processes and life-support systems; preservation of genetic diversity; and sustainable utilization of species and ecosystems." The document also notes a number of high-priority global conservation issues, including the reduction in quality and quantity of agricultural land, overexploitation of fisheries, degradation of river systems, and desertification. More administrative objectives include a broader approach to conservation, enforcement of legislation, and better trained personnel.

Distribution of Old Growth Coniferous Forests in the Mattole River Watershed

1947

1988

Maps showing forest decline between 1947 and 1988, prepared by the Mattole Restoration Council in Humboldt County, California. This kind of information is critical for local environmental education but hard to obtain from corporations and public agencies.

Similar discussions have surrounded other international conventions concerning the "global commons," such as the International Law of the Sea and the Antarctica Treaty. The stakes are high in Antarctica. At least seven nations claim authority in the territory, and many more fish and undertake scientific research there. The continent is known to have large deposits of oil, copper, iron, uranium, lead, coal, zinc, gold, and silver, although most of these are not recoverable given low oil prices and current technology. In 1959 twelve nations signed the Antarctica Treaty to establish a legal framework for exploration and research and in 1988 treaty countries adopted the Convention on the Regulation of Antarctic Mineral Resource Activities, known as the Wellington convention, which adopted legal standards for resource exploitation on the continent. The U.S. State Department argued at the time that the convention gave the continent "legal protection," but in the late 1980s Australia, France, Belgium, and Italy backed out, arguing that resource exploitation in Antarctica should be banned.

These recent studies and documents suggest that there are natural limits to the biosphere and thus to the human capacity to use the external world for continued development. Yet they don't state this directly. Nor do international treaties provide any social critique — a recognition, for example, that the environmental crisis has in the past fifteen years been displaced to the Third World, or that the consumptive patterns of the affluent nations must be changed.

In its 1987 report the Brundtland Commission addressed some of the shortcomings of the World Conservation Strategy (which has since been updated). The Commission was emphatic in linking environmental and social crises, arguing that the burden for restoring the Earth must be borne by the North — the wealthy 20 per cent of the world's population which at present consumes 80 per cent of its resources. It argued that global equity must be part of any discussion of the ecological state of the Earth. What was not clear, however, was whether the Commission supported increased industrialization to bring the rest of the world up to the profligate standards of the North American middle class — something that would require an increase of five to ten times the current increase in industrial activity. Or are industrialization and consumerism themselves the problem?

The Commission offered a long-overdue critique of government economic-environmental policy:

Environmental policy needs to become a comprehensive, horizontal policy field and an integral component of economic and social policy, whose mission is, at least, to anticipate damage and reduce the negative external effects of human activity and, at best, to propose and promote economic and social policies that expand the basis for sustainable development. In doing so, it should allow for the diversity and uniqueness of specific regional and local situations.

The Brundtland Commission has its share of critics within the social movements. While it succeeded in putting the environmental crisis on government agendas and front pages, the Commission's report did not stray far from the "bottom line" of the global market. In the event, its catch-phrase "sustainable development" has ended up endorsing the status quo. It has become an empty phrase escaping the mouths of administrators and executives, who use it to justify expansion of the nuclear industry, "sustained yield" in forest management, and limitless growth in productive capacity — all to further accumulate capital. At the end of the day, the Commission was not able to relinquish the development model, whose "trickle-down" effects will allegedly have social benefits: "It is essential that economic growth be revitalized. In practical terms, this means more rapid economic growth in both industrial and developing countries, freer market access for the products of developing countries, lower interest rates, greater technology transfer, and significantly larger capital flows."

There have been other critics of the Brundtland Commission. A UNESCO symposium held in Vancouver in September 1989 — "Science and Culture for the 21st Century: Agenda for Survival" — dismissed the idea of sustainable development as an excuse to continue destroying the Earth, because the "social and political will" to disengage with development is lacking. The meeting declaration argued that a mechanical notion of the universe — once a cornerstone of science but now repudiated by it — has over the past two hundred years led to a life-threatening fragmentation of body, mind, spirit, and environment. Science and culture are beginning to reconverge, and survival into the next century will hinge on "the perception of an organic macrocosm that recaptures the rhythms of life" and allows us to reintegrate ourselves with nature. "Science and technology are indispensable for the attainment of these goals," the declaration continues, "but they can succeed only through an integration of science and culture."

If we fail to redirect science and technology toward fundamental needs, the advances in informatics (hoarding of knowledge), biotechnology (patenting of life forms) and genetic engineering (mapping of the human genome) will lead to irreversible consequences detrimental to the future of human life.

❦

Discussions of the future of the Earth are by no means confined to international agencies or the academy. Once science confirmed the notion (long held by primal peoples) that humans are merely one part of the biosphere, dependent upon the stability of the whole, an immense and fascinating debate opened within the environmental movement on the social implications of ecology. In part, the aim of this debate has been to elaborate a social-ecological theory that will move beyond the dualism inherent in conservationism and resource management, and suggest ways of living in and with the world. From this debate new philosophies (and ideologies) have emerged, including environmental ethics, social ecology, ecofeminism, deep ecology, animal rights, and animal liberation.

This debate is also part of an attempt to build a broad and oppositional social movement that will work at transforming modern society along ecological lines. The environmental movement has come a long way since the 1960s. Its initial constituents — and in many ways still its strength — were local groups who focused on local environmental and conservation issues: air and water pollution and pesticides. Since then the movement has grown into a folk culture impelled by a new sense of global limits. Its focus has broadened from contamination to human survival. The impact of the environmental movement has been felt even within the sciences; its ideas have moved back into ecology itself, investing that science with an ethics and a metaphysics. The political strategies of the movement are as sophisticated and imaginative as any of the twentieth century. Anarchism, feminism, and the politics of European Greens have been particularly influential among radical environmentalists: note, for example, the direct-action tactics of women's peace and anti-nuclear organizations at places like Greenham Common in England or Seneca Air Force Base in New York State.

The debates within the movement have had variable results, as could be expected with any vibrant social movement. After all, the intellectual roots of modern environmentalism are spread wide: American transcendentalism, individualism and survivalism, libertarianism, the Frankfurt School, bioregionalism, existentialism, phenomenology, Marxism, and an eclectic mix of spiritual traditions from Buddhism and Taoism to witchcraft, shamanism, animism, and goddess worship. Movement publications resound with arguments over hunting and trapping, the value of wilderness, spiritual relations to plants and animals, immigration and population policy, vegetarianism, and the nature of forestry and agriculture.

Many of these are questions that could never have been raised as recently as ten years ago and are symptomatic of fundamental changes in the way nature is talked about in contemporary culture. As these waves of activity have moved over the terrain of the "biosocial" over the past decade, however, one thing has become clear: ecological thinking cannot form the sole basis for social theory or political action. Restoring this land must also mean making a place for ourselves within it.

Alongside the environment of the biosphere, though, there is now also an environment of promotion and advertising and speech about nature — its management, its protection, its fragility, its sacredness, its marketability. It is an environment that encompasses the print and electronic media and suffuses the language of both corporations and social movements. It is also an environment in which we must intervene. As George Bradford has argued:

Every scar on the Earth's body, every broken thread in its tapestry, diminishes us, undermines our own evolutionary destiny. To save ourselves we must save the Earth. To save the Earth, we must find a way to create a humane, egalitarian and ecologically sustainable society. If we cannot, we will continue around this vortex created by urban-industrial capitalism down to extinction and poison this planet beyond recognition. It may even be already too late, but there is still life in us, so we keep on.

As Bradford points out, debates about the social meaning of ecology are taking place at a time when the web of life is unravelling before us. Yet the way forward will not be found within nature (wherever we think that might be), for nature is not "on our side." Clearly, a sense of urgency about the degraded biosphere is not in itself an adequate politics. If we are once again to feel our-selves part of the Earth, rather than its masters, we must learn from the long history of opposition to domination — whether social or planetary. Our oppo-sition to the destruction of the Earth must entail a refusal — and an obstruc-tion — of the institutions and practices that support it. The environmental movement has begun to undermine the social consensus for growth, develop-ment, and the promotion of commodified relations with the land. It must now directly engage social debate, for the culture of nature — the ways we think, teach, talk about, and construct the natural world — is as important a terrain for struggle as the land itself.

Suburban landscape design in Los Angeles, 1980s. Photograph by Peter Menzel.

3. Nature at Home
A Social Ecology of Postwar Landscape Design

We don't just talk and dream about our relations with the non-human world. We also actively explore them in the real places of our streets, gardens, and working landscapes. By crossing to the sunny side of the road on a winter's day, or by arranging some flowers in a vase, we both respond to and address the animals and plants, rocks and water and climate that surround us. Those working landscapes — the ordinary places of human production and settlement — are enormously complex places. Their history is in part a history of engineering — of how we build bridges, contain water, prune trees, and lay sidewalks. But it is also an aesthetic history. It is about shaping, defining, and making the world beautiful in a way that makes sense to us in the time and place that we live.

Throughout the twentieth century, landscape design ("landscaping," as opposed to landscape) has expanded into new spheres. Regional planning agencies have built new towns and reorganized entire watersheds, all of which require landscaping. In addition to traditional sites such as public parks and private estates, landscaping is now done alongside freeways and in industrial parks. We see landscaping at airports and outside restaurants and shopping centres, as well as inside buildings. Some of these sites either didn't exist before or weren't typically planted and tended by humans.

There have also been changes in the way people have come to make their domestic spaces fit their ideas of — or felt needs for — nature. In the twentieth century, millions of North Americans left rural communities and settled in cities and suburbs, disrupting their traditional physical relationship with the non-human world. Yet in the construction of suburban yards, victory gardens, and, later, shopping malls, community parks, and "wild gardens," people have addressed and replicated nature in other ways, developing new aesthetics in the process.

Changes in North American settlement patterns have been slow and uneven, and they have had complex social and geographical repercussions. City and country can no longer be thought of as the two poles of human settlement on the land. As agriculture was industrialized and the economy shifted its centre to the city over the course of the last century, many people abandoned rural areas, leaving whole regions of the continent both socially and economically impoverished. By the 1960s, when this trend peaked, more than two-thirds of North Americans lived within the rough boundaries of urban agglomerations. But those boundaries have gradually become indistinct. In the postwar years, regional planners directed most population growth to the new geography of the suburb, which took over rural lands on the margins of cities. By 1970 almost 40 per cent of U.S. citizens lived in the suburbs, which became, ideologically at least, the dominant land form on the continent.

Yet the next twenty years brought further changes. Many people moved back to rural areas, or to more intact examples of the small towns that were engulfed by the rapidly expanding cities of the postwar years. In the 1960s the back-to-the-land movement (only one among many in North American history) was merely one symptom of a much more systematic development that brought about an increasing interaction of urban and rural economies. Rural areas became very different places than they were two decades earlier. Agriculture, for its part, became closely (and perhaps fatally) linked with urban money markets. In legitimated scenic areas, the leisure industry — a sector that epitomizes many of these changes — propelled itself into existence through the mass marketing of raw land, recreational communities, resort condominiums, and second homes.

As the nature of the capitalist economy shifted towards information and commodity production, production was decentralized. Now, many industrial activities no longer rely on concentrated workforces or physical proximity to resources or markets. Data processing centres and small more specialized industries have parachuted themselves into forests and fields well away from metropolitan areas, giving rise to new kinds of exurban settlements that some commentators have called "technoburbs." All of these developments have intensified the reinhabitation of rural space.

These complex displacements and resettlements — and North American society in particular thinks of itself as mobile — have contributed to a jumble of landscape design styles. Predominant among those styles, however, are two aesthetic traditions, which I broadly call pastoralism and modernism. Since the 1970s those traditions have collided with pronounced regional and ecological tensions that leave the future of landscaping (and landscape) wide open.

In recent years a great many critical and alternative landscaping practices have emerged. Some of these try to combine modernist forms with an environmentalist ethic — by using conservation and wildlife plantings, for example. Some, like urban agriculture projects, insist on integrating horticulture with local economies. "Natural landscaping" and wild gardens attempt to reintroduce indigenous land forms to horticulture and to reanimate the city. Current trends in horticulture suggest a movement away from concentrating on individual species and towards the creation of whole communities of plants, of habitat.

All of this work challenges the orthodoxies of postwar landscaping, the culture of golf courses and petrochemicals and swimming pools that many of us grew up aspiring to. In the best of this work — and there is more and more of it — we can see the re-emergence of a pre-modern relationship with nature, a relationship that is not about domination and containment. We can begin again to imagine nature as an agent of historical forces and human culture.

The Planting of the Suburb

The postwar suburb has had an enormous influence on modern landscaping practice and its aesthetic continues to influence human geographies the world over. Some of its forms — from mobile-home architecture to street layout to the choice of trees planted — have since followed urban emigrants "back" out to rural areas.

Mobility is the key to understanding contemporary landscape design, because in the last forty years planners and builders have organized most land development around the automobile. This has had enormous effects on how most of us see the landscape. It has also changed the look and feel of the land itself. The car has encouraged — indeed, insisted on — large-scale development: houses on quarter-acre lots, giant boulevards and expressways that don't welcome bicycles or pedestrians, huge stores or plazas surrounded by massive parking lots.

The mass building techniques practised in North America both require and promote uniformity. To build on land, property owners first have to clear and level it. Everything must go. Once they put up the structures they replant the land. Biological life is allowed to reassert itself, but it is always a life that corresponds to prevailing ideas about nature. Obviously, building contractors cannot restore the land to its former appearance — an impossible task, because they've had the topsoil removed and heavy machinery has compacted the remnant subsoils. But it is also ideologically impossible. A suburban housing development cannot pretend to look like the farm, or marsh, or forest it has replaced (and often been named after), for that would not correspond to popular ideas of progress and modernity, ideas based more on erasing a sense of locale than on working with it. By and large, contemporary design and materials strive towards universality. Regional character, as Michael Hough points out in his book *Out of Place: Restoring Identity to the Regional Landscape,* is now a matter of choice rather than necessity. When buildings were made of local stone, wood, and clay, they had an organic relationship to the soils and plants of the region.

We can get a direct sense of these changes by considering what has been planted in the suburban landscape. First, the plantings have had to be species able to survive the harsh conditions of most North American suburbs: aridity, soil compaction, salt spray from roads, and increasingly toxic air and water. Where I live, the plants that "naturally" grow in such places are pioneer species like dandelion, sumach, tree of heaven, and brambles of various kinds — plants that, ironically, are usually considered weeds. Yet instead of recognizing the beneficial functions of these opportunistic species, university horticulture departments spent much of the 1950s and 1960s breeding properly decorous plant varieties and hybrids able to tolerate the new urban conditions. The plants had to be fast growing, adaptable to propagation in containers, and, perhaps above all, showy. By definition these requirements preclude most native North American species — for the showy very often means the exotic. Unfortunately, with so much effort put into breeding the top of the plant for appearances' sake, the resultant hybrid invariably has a shallow, weak root system, a bare base, and needs frequent pruning, fertilizing, and doses of pesticides during its short life.

Evergreens became another common feature of the suburban aesthetic. The junipers, spruces, yews, and broadleaf evergreens planted throughout the temperate regions of the continent constantly say "green" and thus evoke nature over and again. The implication is that nature is absent in the leafless winter months (or perhaps all too present), because by some oversight she does not produce green at that time of year. So evergreens are massed around the house as a corrective.

But what are the economic strategies of the culture in remaking the domestic landscape? Certainly some already existing ideas were carried over to the postwar suburbs. Many people planted fruit trees and vegetable gardens when they moved to the suburbs, and indeed, some even brought their pigs and chickens — at least until municipalities passed anti-husbandry legislation in the name of sanitation. Yet the backyard could not serve as a displaced farmyard. Too much had intervened. The suburb quickly became locked into a consumer economy in which agriculture, energy, transportation, and information were one consolidated industry. Sanitation and packaging technologies further mediated relations with the environment. So while suburban hedges and fences could recall the now ancient enclosures of farm and range, for example, they also promoted reinvigorated ideologies of private property and the nuclear family.

Lawns, the most prominent feature of home landscapes in North America, depend on massive doses of pesticides, synthetic fertilizers, and water.

Most of the North American suburb was built quickly in the years following the Second World War. One result of such an immense undertaking was a standardization of landscape styles. Several extant styles were drawn upon to create an aesthetic that everywhere is synonymous with modernity and that until very recently dominated landscaping practice. In its caricatured form, the most prominent feature of the modern suburban aesthetic is the lawn, in which three or four species of exotic grasses are grown together as a monoculture. Native grasses and broadleaf plants are eradicated from the lawn with herbicides, and the whole is kept neatly cropped to further discourage "invasion" by other species, a natural component of plant succession. Massive doses of pesticides, synthetic fertilizers, and water are necessary to keep the turf green.

In a perverse example of this trend, the lawn industry removed dutch clover from grass-seed mixes because the clover was incompatible with 2,4-D, a common broadleaf herbicide. Besides being drought-tolerant, clover can retrieve nitrogen from the air, making supplementary fertilizers unnecessary. The aesthetic value of the lawn is thus directly proportional to the simplicity of its ecosystem, and the magnitude of inputs. The "byproducts" of this regime are now familiar: given the intensive inputs of water and fossil fuels, there's a related output of toxins that leach into the water table.

Typically, the suburban lawn is sparsely planted with shade trees and occasionally a small ornamental tree bred to perform for its spectators: it either flowers or is variegated or somehow contorted or stunted. These species are planted to lend interest to an otherwise static composition. The house is rung with what are called foundation plantings, very often evergreen shrubs planted symmetrically or alternated with variegated or broadleafed shrubs. These are usually clipped into rounded or rectangular shapes. The driveway and garage otherwise dominate the front of the lot. A hard-surfaced area for outdoor cooking and eating is off to the rear or side of the house and a bed for vegetables or flowers is usually at the far side of the backyard. The house's positioning on the lot has little to do with the movement of the sun or any other features of the place. The determinants of the design are more often the quantifiable ones: number of cars per family (the industry standard is 2.5 cars, plus recreational vehicles and lawnmowers), allowable lot coverage, and maximum return on investment. Such is the suburban garden as it has been planted in countless thousands of communities up, down, and across the continent.

The Persistence of Pastoralism

The lawns and trees that are so important to the postwar suburban landscape derive from the English landscape park of the eighteenth century. Lancelot ("Capability") Brown and others designed country estates in a pastoral style that was revived in the United States in the nineteenth century through the "rural cemetery" movement and later popularized by Andrew Jackson Downing, Frederick Law Olmsted, and others. Following this style, workers thinned forests and planted meadows with scattered groups of trees to create a landscape of woodland edges and openings. Sheep kept the meadows shorn, and the enclosures that had been built of hedging and walls were replaced by ha-has, sunken fences that allowed garden to recede unbroken into countryside. Some landscape gardeners even had vistas culminating in ruins — usually manufactured — of medieval abbeys or Greek temples, in this way placing a human presence in the middle ground, just as the landscape approached the wildness of the forest. These landscapes were above all idealized versions of the pastoral, and their own antecedents stretch back to the classicist painting prominent in the salons of the European continent.

But what interests me here, looking back from the very different situation of the North American postwar suburb, is how this pastoral tradition continues to have meaning today. Versions of the English park persist right through the Romantic, Victorian, and Modernist landscape work of the nineteenth and twentieth centuries, and an impoverished version of it — lawn-and-tress — is still the mainstay of contemporary municipal park work.

Pastoralism has a long history in Western culture. It promotes a view of nature as a kindly mother, a refuge from the demands of urban life. The Earth, in this view, is a garden of Eden, generous and fertile. Mother Earth provides us with food, rest, diversion, and solace. Nature in this tradition — and it is an ancient tradition, predating both science and Christianity — is an analogue of the female body. The pastoral tradition is the obverse of another Western tradition — equally primal — which understands nature as chaos and death.

Pastoralist ideas flourished during the European conquest and settlement of North America. Colonial explorers and promoters lavishly described the

Atlantic seaboard — and later, the upper St. Lawrence and the Transappalachia — as bountiful gardens, as virgin lands to be tamed and cultivated. The historical record is ambiguous on this point, however. The accounts of many Europeans suggest that North America, a continent so unlike their own, troubled and lured them in ways their dominant spiritual traditions hadn't prepared them for. Judeo-Christian civilization emerged in the inhospitable semi-arid zones of West Asia. But when that civilization encountered the Americas, whose indigenous peoples lived mutually with nature, the rush to destroy this land and its inhabitants was by no means universal. As the 1990 movie *Dances with Wolves* documented, some white people — more than our historians teach us — resisted the impending genocide. Some of them even "went native" — an inconceivable act that was interpreted by the priests and administrators of the day as a kidnapping and punished with incarceration or death.

By and large, the Western pastoral tradition has been compatible with the idea of nature as a resource to be manipulated by human enterprise. Very often in this tradition, the image of nature presented is that of a passive mother and

The Reservoir in Frederick Law Olmsted's Central Park, New York City, in the 1960s. The pastoral landscape style promotes a view of nature as a refuge from the demands of urban life.

bride to an active male spectator. The image of the Earth as a benevolent female is an ancient anthropomorphic gesture, and one that in pre-modern societies had a normative function. Before the rise of a mechanistic world-view, for example, proscriptions against rape could be used to argue against mining. Yet as Mary Daly, Marilyn French, and other feminist historians have documented all too well, the identification of women with nature and men with culture was used to justify the emergent power of men and their machines over the land and its history. It was far easier to turn pastoralism on its head than to incorporate more marginal traditions that understood nature as a unity of male and female principles.

In any event, it is easy enough to see why pastoral traditions in landscape design have persisted in an urban industrial society. While Romantic landscaping practice tried to reintegrate the human and non-human worlds, the dynamo of modernity required a passive image of nature for the dual purposes of escape and exploitation. In our own day, this trajectory has perhaps run its course. American art critic Lucy Lippard argues that the identification of the Earth with a woman's body need not only reinforce the inferior and submissive role relegated to women in male-dominated societies like our own. It can also be an abiding source of female strength. Moreover, there is a growing feeling in North Atlantic culture that the Earth will no longer yield to human (or male) domination; that unless we reinvent pre-modern conceptions of nature, the present "environmental crisis" may be the last.

But the persistence of pastoral traditions in landscape design can't be explained only in terms of domination. The English landscape park and its North American reinterpretation are landscapes of woodland edges, a place where several plant and animal communities overlap. In temperate climates, the woodland edge — where forest and meadow meet — is the most complex and textured ecosystem of all. There the number of species is greatest, the degree of co-operation and symbiosis the most advanced. The edge is the richest feeding ground for all animals, including humans who rely on hunting and gathering. It is one of our oldest and most sacred abodes. The persistence of the English park has to do, I think, with the impulse to create and inhabit edges, the diverse and dynamic places that connect, that bind the planet together. The woodland edge is the principal model in the design of most parkway landscaping in the eastern part of this continent, for example.

In the mass-produced bungalow and ranch houses of the 1950s and 1960s, much of this impulse was brought under control or stylized beyond recognition. There, edges are not so much about diversity and interrelationship as they are about separateness. In the suburban landscape the edge is typically the property line, an assertion of conformity to the ideology of the home as private domain.

Men and Women in the Suburban Garden

In postwar North America, patterns of management and domination suffused popular culture. The pastoral lawn, for example, not only predominates in suburban frontyards, but also stretches across golf courses, corporate headquarters, farmyards, school grounds, university campuses, sod farms, and highway verges. For such enormous expanses of this continent to be brought under the exacting regime of turf management, an entire technological infrastructure had to be in place. There had to be abundant sources of petroleum and electricity to provide for an increasingly mechanized horticulture. Power mowers, clippers and edgers, weed whips, leaf blowers, sod cutters, fertilizer spreaders, and sprayers brought nature under control. Hedges and shrubbery were closely clipped. Each housing lot needed its own driveway (a large one, to accommodate the 2.5 cars). In colder climates this often necessitated the purchase of a snow plough or blower. In the 1950s, the new petrochemical industry introduced chlorinated hydrocarbon pesticides as virtual miracle products that would liquidate unwanted weeds, insects, or fungi. Popular horticultural literature reduced the soil — the very source of the ancient metaphor of the life-giving mother — to a lifeless, neutral medium that did little more than convey water-soluble fertilizers and help plants stand up. As a site of mediation between humankind and nature, the postwar garden had become technologized.

While contemporary garden chores may still be a source of pleasure, the chores themselves have changed. Many people talk fondly today about climbing onto a tractor mower and cutting an immense lawn — not unlike the way a combine harvests a field of grain. This is an activity that ends up integrating the human body into a mechanistic view of nature. The idea of the body as machine has been around since the Enlightenment and the beginnings of industrial capitalism; gardening had also begun to be mechanized by the early nineteenth century. But in postwar North American culture, a great many people became gardeners for the first time, for street trees and parks were no longer the only horticultural presence in the city. The space that surrounded the suburban tract home was of a new kind, however. It was neither the kitchen garden and barnyard familiar to women nor the rural field or urban street that was most often the domain of men.

As gardening became both less exacting and more technologized — in other words, as it came to be synonymous with turf management — it was increasingly an enterprise carried out by men. Previously, for men technics had always been confined to the workplace. The home, and the symbolic clearing in which it stood, had been thought of as a refuge from the world of alienated labour. But changes in the economy brought changes in the relationship between work and home. In some ways the workplace has been demasculinized as industry has shifted away from primary production towards what are

In the micro-geography of the idealized middle-class suburb, men presided over the barbeque, while women looked after the "flowers."

B.F. Goodrich

This ad for men only

MEN should buy the garden hose—but keep the women very much in mind. If you do it right you can sell them the idea of doing more outdoor work *and liking it.*

If your wife never uses the hose maybe you don't need Koroseal. It costs a little more—but only $9.80 for 50 feet and makes up for it by being so easy to handle. It is *guaranteed to last ten years.*

"Garden Club", also made by B. F. Goodrich, also guaranteed 10 years, is lighter than most rubber hose, a wonderful value.

But Koroseal is a third lighter still (weighs only half as much as some hose). It's *clean:* the surface has a high polish, doesn't hold dirt. No need to drain it or lug it in

either. Leave it out all year round if you want to. Its brilliant colors (fire engine red and bright green) may fade a little, but neither sun nor air will weaken it.

Look for the label. Every length is plainly marked. Be sure you see the name to be sure you're getting the real thing. *The B. F. Goodrich Company, Industrial & General Products Division, Akron, Ohio.*

Koroseal—Trade Mark—Reg. U. S. Pat. Off.

Koroseal

GARDEN HOSE BY

B.F. Goodrich

It's Fun to Spray the Hudson Way

A pesticide ad from the early 1950s. For many, gardening became a military operation: new "miracle" pesticides promised to liquidate unwanted plants and animals.

called "services." As consumption, rather than production, came to dominate Western economies in the second half of the twentieth century, men often took up more exacting "hobbies" to compensate for the loss of physical labour. Care of the garden was one such hobby.

That's not to say that women stopped gardening, any more than they stopped cooking when men began to preside over the backyard barbecue. But women's presence in the garden tended to become associated even more with everything that could be generalized as "flowers": perennial borders, herb gardens, arbours and trellises, window boxes, bedding plants, and greenhouses. The landscape profession often dismisses this horticultural work (and horticulture is not a strong tradition in North America) as being too fussy or labour-intensive, when it is perhaps better thought of as evidence of a keen awareness of and interest in the other communities of the biophysical world. For women, the domestic spheres of food and sanitation had also gradually become mechanized; flower beds remained one of the few household locations not mediated by technology. Men wielded a lawnmower over the grass; women dug into the soil with a trowel.

The suburb was a new form of human settlement on the land, a new way of living. Often far from friends and kin, and "independent" of neighbours (as the suburb was supposed to be independent of city and country), the nuclear family of the 1950s clung to newly revived ideologies of togetherness. Yet the suburban form itself accentuated the feeling of absence at the centre of middle-class family life. The new houses replaced fireplace and kerosene stove with central heating, thus dissipating social experience throughout the home. A fridge full of "raidables" and supper-hour TV programs broke down the pattern of meal-times. Separate bedrooms for all or most of the children and the evolution of men's spaces like the workshop and the "yard" further encouraged rigid gender distinctions. At the same time, communal experiences within the family often became more a matter of choice than necessity. The growing independence that children felt from their parents and siblings opened up the possibility for an affective life outside the confines of the nuclear family for both men and women. These changes were as subtle as they were contradictory; many of their social implications are still not entirely clear.

The suburb stands at the centre of everything we recognize as "fifties culture." Beneath its placid aesthetic appearance, its austere modernism, we can now glimpse the tensions of a life that for many had no precedent. Until these tensions were brought to the surface in the 1960s, the suburb was a frontier. There were no models for a family newly disrupted by commodity culture, any more than there were for garden design in a place that had never existed before. It was as if nature and our experience of it were in suspension. Things were unfamiliar in the suburb, and it's no surprise that people who could afford it fled whenever they could. Weekends and summer holidays were often spent not in the ersatz idylls of Don Mills, Levittown, or Walnut Creek, but in what was imagined to be nature itself: newly created parks and lakes and recreation areas. Here, at last, out the car window or just beyond the campsite or cottage, was an experience of nature that was somehow familiar. In fact it seems that this holiday place — and not the suburb — was nature.

But the idea of nature that was invented by postwar suburban landscaping was not a unitary one. The distinction I've made between "lawn" and "flowers" — and the parallels with gender roles — were and continue to be refuted by many people's gardening habits. Organic gardening, for example, is a very old practice that allowed many people to resist the technological incursions of the 1950s. And technology was resisted in more obvious ways, too. The mass movement against the bomb was perhaps the earliest expression on this continent of modern environmentalism.

Outside of the suburbs, in the older settled areas of the cities themselves, other forms of resistance gathered strength. The social movements whose beginnings we casually ascribe to the "sixties" — civil and human rights, feminism, peace, free speech, sexual liberation, as well as environmentalism — were in part struggles over the nature and use of urban land. Urban activism developed its own very different ideas about landscape design — ideas that are now more influential than ever.

Modernism

Another important influence in postwar landscape design was modernism. It was introduced to North America from the top, at the Graduate School of Design at Harvard in the 1930s, a time when there were fewer than two thousand landscape architects in the United States. At the time the dominant landscape tradition was "Beaux-Arts," an eclectic and ornamental school that combined axial European forms with the more Romantic and informal ideas popular in England at the turn of the century. Onto this scene Harvard graduated a number of influential graduates who took a new approach: among them Daniel Urban Kiley, James Rose, and Garrett Eckbo. As the landscape profession grew during the development boom of the postwar years, the influence of modernism grew as well, first in larger scale, public work.

A gravel garden in Albany, California, early 1980s. A severe vernacular interpretation of modernism.

Modernist design principles were derived from the art and architecture of early twentieth-century Europe, from a movement whose preoccupations were as much social and functional as aesthetic. In landscape design, this meant that the site and the client became an important part of the process: existing land forms were used to relate human beings to environment. In domestic work, the garden became an extension of the living space.

The most elite modernist tradition — which remained independent of English landscape design — brought a spare formalism to aesthetic strategies. Modern landscape work relentlessly enclosed, encoded, patterned, and abstracted nature. Thomas Church, an influential San Francisco landscape architect who championed modernism very early on, composed asymmetrical geometric patterns using walls, fences, pavings, trellises, and pools, in the process connecting garden to house. Church and other designers used plants as foils, both accentuating and blurring the lines. They massed vegetation, limited the palette, and de-emphasized bloom. Since the 1970s, U.S. modernist design has travelled back across the Atlantic. The work of John Brookes, for example, has combined modernism with an English respect for plants to produce a new garden aesthetic of great interest.

There are other crosscurrents. In the first half of the twentieth century the early beginnings of ecology in Europe influenced a number of young German, Scandinavian, and Dutch modernists. Their work, much of it public, juxtaposed organic and inorganic forms, marrying a sometimes rigid formal aesthetic with ecological principles. Many of these principles were drawn from phytosociology, the study of plant communities. In recent years this work has come to light among landscape designers in North America, who see in it a prototype of landscape work that is at once social and ecological.

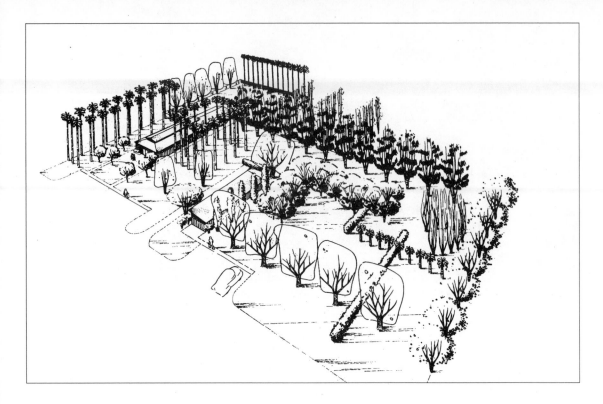

Garrett Eckbo's design for
a common area in a
migrant workers' camp in
central California, late
1930s. Eckbo managed to
infuse modernist
aesthetics with both a
social agenda and a sense
of region.

A San Francisco roof
garden designed by
Thomas Church, 1950s.
Japanese design
strategies contributed to
the hybrid California style
of the postwar years.

North American modernism has other roots as well. It borrowed from Japanese and Moslem gardens, as well as from Latin America. Roberto Burle Marx, a Brazilian, introduced flowing biomorphic patterns into his landscape projects, which rely on complex pavings of many different materials and a sculptural use of native plants. Luis Barragán used the basic, almost primal forms of water, earth, walls, and trees in his work in and around Mexico City.

The most obvious characteristic of all this work — and I have been very selective — is its emphasis on form. But it is form as it is derived from local cultures and topographies, a sensitivity to region that often carries over to the use of native plants. The tension between modernism and regionalism, in fact, is a recurrent theme in twentieth-century landscape design. Modernist aesthetics generally have ransacked and colonized non-European cultures in a search for authentic expression. Sadly, the formulation of this "international style" — with its parallel in the standardization of building techniques and industrial processes — means that many of our built landscapes today are indistinguishable from one another.

Some designers, however, have attempted to combine modernist ideals with a sense of region. In much the same way that early European modernists tried to infuse the movement with a social and ecological mission, there is a North American landscape tradition that is honest about the specific cultural, ecological, and historical circumstances of locale. In this design work, which saw a revival in the 1980s, naturalist and nativist idioms predominate. In regions with a strong self-identity, like New England, the U.S. Southwest, and the Northwest coast, it was often only a matter of learning from existing landscapes, both natural and cultural. A. E. Bye and Cornelia Hahn Oberlander have done this kind of work along, respectively, the eastern and western coasts of North America. These are exercises in abstracting nature — and here it is worth recalling that the modernist painter Wassily Kandinsky argued that the purpose of abstraction is to liberate the essential patterns and forms of nature from its chance aspects. In what is now often called a "naturalized" landscape style, designers retain mature trees and fit the house into a slope or opening using local materials. They plant meadows or fields right up to the windows and leave streams unimpounded. Their work understates, even effaces, human intervention in the natural world.

Frank Lloyd Wright based his career on the rejection of European styles in favour of an indigenous American design. Wright did much of his work in the U.S. Midwest, a region with a poorly developed sense of itself (and one that is still almost ignored in studies of the North American landscape). Wright was part of an aesthetic movement that developed a distinct prairie vocabulary for buildings and landscapes — houses, for example, that sit low on the land, accentuating the subtle topography rather than dominating it. The prairie revival began in the early years of this century. Its principal exponent in landscape at that time was Jens Jensen, a Danish immigrant who worked for many years as a superintendent in the Chicago parks. Jensen pioneered efforts to introduce native prairie plant communities to parks and gardens.

Garrett Eckbo was another regional modernist. His first work was with the Farm Security Administration, designing and planting camps for migrant workers in the San Joaquin valley of California. Eckbo moved to Los Angeles in the late 1940s, where he specialized in suburban residential work. In *Landscape for Living* (1950), Eckbo helped introduce ecology to landscape architecture. He understood his work — which manages to be stylish while still sensitive to elements such as microclimates — to be about "reuniting people and nature."

But these regional and nativist impulses in landscape design have been carried out some distance from the mainstream of the landscape and architectural professions — which in turn have not had a direct influence on most of the land development that has changed this continent in the last forty years. Yet recently, those impulses have resurfaced, mostly outside of the profession, in gestures that go under names as various as natural gardening, wild gardening, habitat creation, and ecological restoration.

California and the Standardization of Horticulture

One regional garden tradition has had an influence far surpassing any other. The various styles that make up what is usually called "California" have contributed to the recent North American landscape as much as the many traditions of the English garden. The California style has co-evolved with popular architectural forms such as the shopping centre and drive-in, the freeway and roadside motel — many of them introduced in California. Pool and palm tree have become indivisible in the cultural imagination, just as California itself has come to signify everything modern and desirable.

The style has also drawn on the proximity of Californian and East Asian cultures. Japanese people have long tended the gardens of the wealthy up and down the west coast of North America, and Japanese styles as well as plants themselves have fused with both native Californian and colonial Spanish flora. The spare use of stone, the presence of water, the textural possibilities of wood and gravel: these are Japanese design strategies that have had a far-reaching (and sometimes disastrously inappropriate) influence on North American gardens. There is a similar history in plant use. Juniper and yew and false cypress, euonymus, azalea, weigela, spirea, honeysuckle, and scores of other plants in common use today all originated in the temperate forests of Japan and China. Many of them were brought to the West by the British, who first propagated them in their own botanical gardens in the eighteenth and nineteenth centuries. But many more temperate Asian plants — especially dwarf plants — were cloned and hybridized in California nurseries in the postwar years. Junipers in particular proved to be adaptable to virtually every North American climate and along with a small number of indigenous California species have become the most common garden plants. Most importantly, these California species have been able to survive the droughty conditions of the modern city and suburb.

The diffusion of the California style was not only a matter of plant adaptability. Hollywood also did much to popularize the suburban ranch house and its exotic surroundings. Casual outdoor living, an urban geography that stressed the ease and pleasure of movement through the landscape, a countryside of immense and exhilarating vistas — these popular West Coast images continue to attract many North Americans. The images still resonate with the frontier myths that have always overlapped with the Western landscape. The presence of Californian culture in the contemporary imagination must also have much to do with its specifically coastal geography. The seacoast is an edge of another kind. The ocean is the source of all terrestrial life, and the places where it meets the continents always speak to us not only of worlds far beyond but also of our own beginnings as a species.

To understand how landscape forms became so rapidly standardized throughout the continent, we also have to consider how the landscape industry was reorganized in the postwar economy. Until the 1960s, most nurseries and seed houses were small family-owned businesses. Horticulturists propagated plant species native to their own area and grew exotic species on site, so the plants were well adapted to the local soils and climate. Open-pollinated, non-hybrid seeds were still common, and catalogues offered vegetable and flower varieties that had been in cultivation for decades, even centuries. All of this knowledge was passed on from one generation of breeders and growers to another.

Along with the postwar industrialization of agriculture and the introduction of larger machines to carry out more complicated tasks, the work of hybridization also accelerated. Agricultural petrochemicals were developed. Much of this work was done at agricultural colleges and land-grant universities in the United States and Canada, where it was well funded by corporations and governments.

At the same time North American capital was reorganizing itself. Whole new sectors of the economy were consolidated and brought into national and international markets. As small companies were bought out by large firms, locally produced goods were standardized and made into national products. Many of these changes penetrated the horticultural industry quite late. Local production of beer and plants, for instance, was able to be revived in the late 1980s precisely because it was never fully abandoned and integrated into national markets. Nonetheless, standardization of plant propagation and distribution, as well as design work, did begin to get under way in the 1950s. By the 1970s, through aggressive marketing techniques directed at the new housing industry and the usual practices of underselling small competitors, large regional growers had driven many local nurseries out of business.

Some nurseries eliminated their propagation fields and greenhouses altogether and became "garden centres." The garden centre had an expanded retail section to accommodate the immense influx of non-horticultural, mass-produced commodities aimed at the exterior of the home: lawn and patio furniture, swimming pool accessories, bird baths, concrete or plastic animal ornaments, miniature golf sets, wheelbarrows, lawnmowers and snowblowers, barbecues. The stores had entire aisles of new pesticides. The plants sold were bought from the mechanized farms of a small number of regional growers and wholesalers and trucked into urban areas via new cross-country four-lane highways on a strictly seasonal basis. Year by year there were fewer varieties to be found. Today, garden centres — which have the largest share of the horticultural market — tend to sell a standard list of versatile plants propagated by large industrial growers in central climates. Native species have all but disappeared from the lists of these growers; they've been replaced by hybrid junipers and hollies and euonymus, and clones of a few of the less interesting European maples — including the hybrids developed to grow in the new and arid microclimates of the suburb. Where thirty years ago an average-size nursery would have offered sixty species of trees, many of them native, today a garden centre might offer ten, most of them exotic. In the seed industry, many native and traditional varieties have likewise been eliminated from catalogues, and probably lost forever.

Similar changes have been brought about by new micropropagation techniques. A minute piece of cell tissue from one plant can now be used to propagate millions of plants. But tissue culture propagation — a type of biotechnology — has had mixed results. Plants with too little "natural intelligence" — genetic and ecological information drawn from their communities — often mutate unpredictably and are vulnerable to pests. Yet industrial plant research continues, aiming to create a whole new generation of patented, privately owned and marketed plant species resistant to pesticides.

The standardization of the horticultural industry coincided with an increase in planting all over the continent, which accompanied the development booms of the last forty years. The result has been virtual plantations of single species in the parks, neighbourhoods, and shopping centres of many cities. This simplification of the ecosystem has led to both increased susceptibility to pathogens and a consequent dependence on pesticides. It is a development that is structurally integrated with modern agriculture, an industrial process that depends on abundant and temporarily cheap petroleum and triggers a downward spiral of genetic simplification, pesticide resistance, poor nutrition and health, habitat destruction, and species extinction. To a whole new profession of landscape contractors and maintenance companies, meanwhile, horticulture has become an adjunct of housecleaning; and landscape design an endlessly repeated exercise that bears little relationship to its own bioregion.

In the last ten years or so, a number of small "post-sixties" businesses have bucked many of these trends. In every region of North America, specialized growers have begun to propagate native plants once again and to organize conferences to promote these plants to landscape architects, government agencies, and amateur gardeners. Botanical gardens have long recognized the need for local seed sources to maintain a gene pool large enough for plants to adapt to disease, insects, and climate change. Now amateur naturalists and small nurseries have also begun to collect and propagate seed from diverse communities of native plants. Clearinghouses for heritage and open-pollinated (non-hybrid) vegetable seeds have been started in Iowa and Ontario, and similar organizations are conserving old varieties of fruit and nut trees. In the Southwest United States, drought-tolerant crops such as blue corn are once again being grown in place of varieties dependent on irrigation and petrochemicals. These last developments are related to changes in Canadian and U.S. diets and, some people argue, to "hippy ethnobotany" — the introduction of plants, medicines, and foods like yoghurt, bulgur, falafel, amaranth, miso, and seaweed to North American culture. Larger businesses have also responded to these cultural changes. For example, *Sunset* magazine, which once promoted regular use of pesticides, now emphasizes integrated pest management and organic gardening.

❧

One legacy of an industrialized horticulture has been a discontinuous and contradictory landscape. In the case of domestic gardens, people have developed a great variety of vernacular and idiosyncratic ideas about nature over the past forty years. Some public work has been innovative as well. Given its severe environmental limitations, for example, freeway landscaping has often successfully integrated urban form and natural surroundings. There are also magnificent woodland and meadow plantings along parkways in Ontario, New York, New Jersey, Connecticut, Texas, and Wisconsin. In most public or publicly visible landscape, however — at shopping centres, airports, parks, and apartment complexes — the results are less encouraging. Planners have spent little effort on integrating these projects into their urban, suburban, or rural surroundings.

In their designs for the enclosed shopping mall, designers have altogether abandoned the exterior of the complex. Inside, however, something else is going on. In the chic upmarket malls of wealthy areas, plantings are lavish: trees ten to twenty metres tall, formal hedges, fountains, beds of massed tropicals, often in a late nineteenth-century ornamental style that had been banished by modernism. Many malls, in fact, consciously imitate glass-roofed Victorian botanical gardens. Even in the shabbiest of contemporary malls there are constant references to gardens and to nature.

That nature is so lavishly replicated within these new spaces and yet so repudiated without is telling. As new transportation and communications technologies penetrated the natural world in the 1950s, people began to experience nature as something manipulated, altered, composed by humans. As primitive landscapes have vanished from the planet, we've surrounded ourselves with our own replications of them. Plants now proliferate in places they haven't been seen in decades, if ever: bars, offices, bank-tower lobbies, and restaurants. These interior landscapes have been produced since the late 1960s, once the most intensive period of exterior suburban planting had been completed. Plant maintenance and plant leasing services now flourish in indoor horticulture.

But the cultivation of these new gardens is not only the result of an industry expanding its market but also part of the culture (and, increasingly, the economy) of environmentalism. Indeed, it is safe to say that much of the innovative work in recent landscape design has come from the grassroots — amateur gardeners, community activists, and a great many people working in the unofficial "voluntary" sector of the economy. These people have strongly influenced the way our world looks and feels. Verdant shopping malls and fern bars are only one manifestation of this change. Neighbourhood economic development, squat cities, people's parks, the urban muralist movement, neighbourhood greenhouses, food co-ops, cluster housing, "open space" and "green city" campaigns: these projects represent a radical critique of modernity and its relationship with nature.

Two phenomena deserve special attention because they have been responses to changing urban forms over the past century. Rural "intentional" communities have been around since the rise of the industrial city in the nineteenth century. These communities, sometimes called communes, which numbered about two thousand in the United States by the early 1980s, are diverse: some are farms or crofts, others ashrams, others nurseries, schools, retreats, publishing enterprises, or study centres. All represent a desire to revive community by forming a new relationship to the land. Those that work the land have repopularized long-term and sustainable land-management techniques (sometimes called permaculture); those that do not have helped reintegrate rural development.

Community gardens — also called allotment, victory, and leisure gardens — have even earlier beginnings. In late eighteenth-century England, they were

A school garden in Vancouver supplements kids' lunches and brings some life to the science curriculum. Community gardens have reintroduced agriculture to urban landscape design.

a response of local governments and philanthropists to rural starvation brought about by the slow move to "enclose" common lands and introduce modern agricultural techniques.

Where they have been permitted by municipal authorities, urban food gardens have traditionally not only fed people who might otherwise be undernourished but also performed an important ecological function by absorbing organic wastes, dissipating heat, and improving drainage and air quality. Urban agriculture is also enormously efficient, as proved by the wartime victory gardens popular in Canada and the United States. (Intensive food gardening is over a hundred times as efficient as industrial agriculture.) During the First World War, the U.S. campaign was organized by industrial conservation interests such as the American Forestry Association. By the Second World War the gardens were associated with patriotism. "Every Garden A Munitions Plant!" was the slogan on one poster.

Since the 1960s the politics of community gardens — like the politics of ecology — has shifted markedly to the left. The watershed events took place in 1969: the fight for People's Park in Berkeley and the establishment of Tent City on a parking lot in Boston. Urban geopolitics have changed. The relevant indices are industrial flight, altered demographics, a militant civil rights movement, land abandonment, demolition (which at one time went under the name of urban renewal), highway clearances, and changed residential densities. As public institutions decline, local community organizations have had to step in to initiate community gardens. Projects like these are an informal land use that lies outside of the profit-generating economy. They remind us that except during periods of intensive urban land speculation (the longest being roughly 1750-1930) cities have *always* had gardens. They also remind us that cities, too, are habitat.

The Ecological Imperative

The suburban landscaping of the immediate postwar years is still the spatially predominant model, but it has come to mean something different today. As modernity itself is being questioned right across the culture, we experience its expressions with much more ambivalence. Consider these examples: the "no-maintenance" garden of coloured gravel that was once popular in Florida and the U.S. Southwest is on the wane. Its matrix was the Japanese-Californian work of the early 1960s, and when well done it was striking. But it turned out that no-maintenance meant that you got rid of weeds with regular doses of 2,4-D or a blast with a blow torch or flame thrower. It's unlikely that in a culture that has been through Vietnam and the Love Canal such a regime can have quite the cachet it once did. Likewise with "growth inhibitors" that you spray on hedges so they don't need to be clipped. These are landscaping strategies that deny change and the presence of life.

In recent years, ecological science has begun to change the way North Americans think about and work their gardens. Ideas of ecosystem and habitat have become new models for landscape work. There is new interest in native plants and wildflower gardens, in biological pest control and organic foods, as well as in planting for wildlife. These are all symptoms of a new understanding of urban land as animated, dynamic, and diverse.

These issues are now often forced into the open. Many North American cities mandate water conservation, for example. The city of Santa Barbara, California, forbids people to water their lawns with municipal water. Marin County, California, pays residents to remove their lawns and replace them with drought-tolerant plants. In many parts of the western United States, new land development is contingent on no net increase in water use, forcing communities to investigate composting toilets, the reuse of grey water (non-sewage waste water), and what is now called "xeriscaping," water-conserving planting schemes. Sometimes these schemes mean drawing strictly from the region: cactus and rock landscapes in Arizona, for example. But they can also mean working with composites of native plants and plants from similar bioregions elsewhere. In southern California this means rejecting the tropical and subtropical plant species that have been so long associated with Los Angeles and drawing instead from the chaparral and dry woodland plant communities of the Mediterranean regions of the world: southern France, central Chile, South Africa, Australia, and of course southern California itself. All of this work gives the places we live a sense of regional integrity.

Painting dead grass in Santa Barbara, California, 1990. In arid regions of the continent, water shortages have forced people to choose between eliminating their lawns and painting them green.

A backyard in Kitchener, Ontario. Prairie eco-systems are particularly well adapted to the sunny, arid conditions of North American suburbs.

The role of ecology in landscape aesthetics is not new. In the 1920s and 1930s the new discipline of regional planning dedicated itself to the design of *whole* landscapes. Its mission is best exemplified by the work of Lewis Mumford and, later, some of the public agencies of the New Deal years. Ian McHarg, a Scottish immigrant to the United States, made the most celebrated professional intervention in 1969, with the publication of *Design With Nature*. This ambitious book, which is everywhere cited but seldom taken seriously within the land-design professions, attempted to introduce natural science to the planning process.

McHarg taught in the landscape architecture program at the University of Pennsylvania in the 1970s and 1980s. His lectures ranged across ethics and aesthetics, lurching from the advent of agriculture to Christianity, science, and space technology — all with an aim to understanding better the relations between

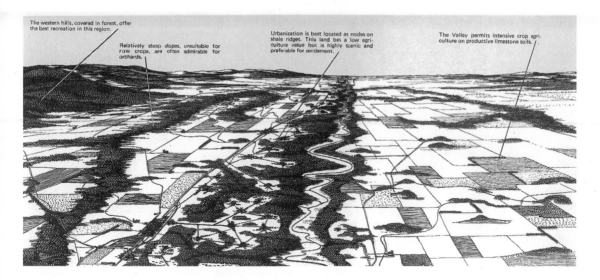

The western hills, covered in forest, offer the best recreation in this region.

Relatively steep slopes, unsuitable for row crops, are often admirable for orchards.

Urbanization is best located as nodes on shale ridges. This land has a low agriculture value but is highly scenic and preferable for settlement.

The Valley permits intensive crop agriculture on productive limestone soils.

Regional planning maps from Ian McHarg's Design with Nature, *1969. Drawing on the land forms of the Atlantic seaboard, McHarg helped reintroduce natural science to the land design professions.*

human settlement patterns and natural systems. The discussions anticipated many of the philosophical debates in ecology today.

McHarg's work, which has given rise to a small but influential school of ecological designers and consultants, is both descriptive and prescriptive. While the philosophical discussion in *Design With Nature* is broad and at times sloppy, the examples are instructive. For McHarg, those examples were close to home: the landforms of the Atlantic seaboard, and particularly the city of Philadelphia and its environs. McHarg provides detailed discussions of local geology, plant communities, hydrology, dune formation, soils, and topography. He places maps of these systems over one another to indicate the importance of detailed site analysis well before development.

From there his discussion moves out into the interior river valleys of east-central North America. McHarg argues for changes in settlement patterns, for design work that begins with nature — indeed, he advocates a kind of ecological determinism. Steep slopes, he notes, are unsuitable for row crops but good for secondary agriculture such as orchards, or for recreation. Cities should be kept well away from the aquifer and are best encouraged on the nodes of ridges, which have low agricultural value but high scenic value. Agriculture is best directed towards alluvial valleys, where the soils permit extensive row cropping. Using these principles McHarg fashions an aesthetic that promotes development compatible with the bioregion. This is not an anti-urban polemic. Rather it is about bringing nature into the city.

McHarg's lessons have been all but ignored within the land-design professions. A great deal of development has taken place in North America since

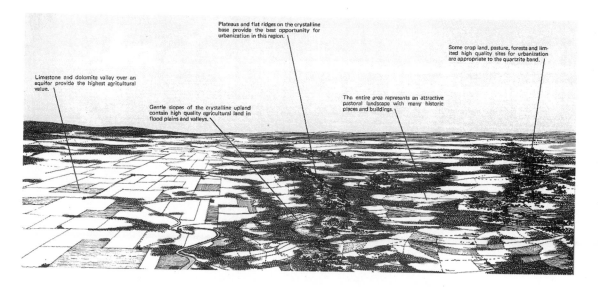

Limestone and dolomite valley over an aquifer provide the highest agricultural value.

Plateaus and flat ridges on the crystalline base provide the best opportunity for urbanization in this region.

Some crop land, pasture, forests and limited high quality sites for urbanization are appropriate to the quartzite band.

Gentle slopes of the crystalline upland contain high quality agricultural land in flood plains and valleys.

The entire area represents an attractive pastoral landscape with many historic places and buildings.

1969, and little of it shows an understanding of ecological principles. For its part, landscape architecture is in disrepute, having for the most part degenerated into a service industry that provides "amenities" and adornment for real estate development projects. Many land designs are undertaken by people who have never been to the site.

If the landscaping professions are in disarray, it is because they are awash in the flood of environmentalism. For better or worse, an entire generation of people now understands landscape design as applied ecology. As the idea of bioregion gains currency as an organizing strategy, Ian McHarg's work is once again relevant, this time to people working in the social movements. It offers a methodology of place, a way communities or watersheds can map their identities according to climate and landforms. "Place," McHarg writes, "is a sum of natural processes and … these processes constitute social values."

Questions of place and values resonate differently across generations, classes, and political cultures. But some landscape work is able to galvanize both communities and professions. A promising example is ecological restoration, an emerging discipline — and movement — dedicated to restoring the Earth to health. Restoration is the literal reconstruction of natural and historic landscapes. It can mean fixing degraded river banks, replanting urban forests, creating bogs and marshes, or taking streams out of culverts. Since the early 1980s, this work — a great deal of it carried out by people working for free in their spare time — has been going on in forest, savannah, wetland, and prairie ecosystems all over North America. The Society for Ecological Restoration was founded in 1987 to co-ordinate the endeavours of its disparate practitioners: farmers, engineers, gardeners, public land managers, landscape architects, and wildlife biologists, among many others.

Restoration ecology is multidisciplinary work, drawing on technical and scientific knowledge for a generalist pursuit. It is more than tree planting or

A prescribed burn of an oak savannah in a suburban Cleveland, Ohio, park. Landscape design and management now often include the restoration of specific ecosystems.

ecosystem preservation: it is an attempt to reproduce, or at least mimic, natural systems. It is also a way of learning about those systems, a model for a sound relationship between humans and the rest of nature. Restoration projects actively investigate the history of human intervention in the world. Thus they are at once agriculture, medicine, and art. William R. Jordan of the University of Wisconsin Arboretum writes:

Watching a group of volunteers collecting seed on Curtis Prairie one fall day, I realized that they were repeating the experience of hunter-gatherers who inhabited this area centuries ago, and who actually, through their hunting, gathering and burning, had helped create the prairie communities we tended to think of as "native," "original," or "natural." At this point I realized that restoration represents a reenactment — not only of the forces that created the communities being restored in the first place, but of the entire passage of cultural evolution, from hunting and gathering through agriculture, to the analysis and synthesis of modern science. I now see restoration as providing the framework for a system of rituals by which a person in any phase of cultural evolution can achieve a harmonious relationship with a particular landscape.

These are not new ideas, but they are ideas newly current in the culture. Frederick Law Olmsted, Jens Jensen, Stan Abbott, Aldo Leopold, and others have all been part of efforts to replant and restore this continent. The recirculation of these ideas has led to some fascinating philosophical and political debates. What is an authentic landscape? What is native, or original, or natural? These are cultural questions, and it's refreshing to see them raised within a technical — even scientific — profession.

Restoration actively seeks out places to repair the biosphere, to recreate habitat, to breach the ruptures and disconnections that agriculture and urbanization have brought to the landscape. But unlike preservationism, it is not an elegiac exercise. Rather than eulogize what industrial civilization has destroyed, restoration proposes a new environmental ethic. Its projects demonstrate that humans must intervene in nature, must garden it, participate in it. Restoration thus nurtures a new appreciation of working landscape, those places that actively figure a harmonious dwelling-in-the-world.

What we see in the landscaping work of the late twentieth century is residues of many traditions: romantic, modernist, environmentalist, pastoral, countercultural, regionalist, agrarian, and, now, restorationist. The suburban aesthetic was able to accommodate some of those traditions, but today suburbia is clearly a landscape that can no longer negotiate the tensions between city and country — much less those posed by the many people and movements already busy making new relationships with the non-human world.

Changing environmental and cultural circumstances have brought changing aesthetics. If these changes have left the landscape profession (and the landscape) in disarray, they have also allowed large numbers of people to become involved in shaping the physical world as never before. As landscaping ideas have been reinterpreted and reversed, the boundaries of the garden have become less distinct. Much recent work attempts to reintegrate country and city, suggesting that what was once nature at home may soon become nature as home.

An unidentified beast at Green Animals, a topiary garden in Portsmouth, Rhode Island.

4. Looking at the Non-Human
Nature Movies and TV

To anyone not hopelessly prejudiced by the metaphysical apartheid of Christianity and Western thought generally, human beings closely resemble in anatomy, physiology and behaviour other forms of life. The variety of organic forms themselves are closely related, and the organic world, in turn, is continuous with the whole of nature. Virtually all things might be supposed, without the least strain upon credence, like ourselves, to be "alive," that is, conscious, aware, or possessed of spirit.
— J. Baird Callicott, *In Defense of the Land Ethic*

What goes on in the brain of this amazingly human-like creature?
— Voiceover from a National Geographic movie about gorillas

In *Nature's Half Acre,* an Academy Award-winning movie made by the Disney studios in 1951, the opening shot is of a painting. It's the kind of landscape painting familiar from the calendars that insurance agents or gas stations used to give out in the days before colour photography. The painting shows the edge of a meadow in spring, with some aspens to one side and the standard snow-covered Rocky Mountain peaks in the background. On screen the painting slowly dissolves and becomes a movie explaining the everyday life of plants and animals in the wilderness.

Like most nature movies of its time, *Nature's Half Acre* worked a number of themes: friendships, animal instinct, predation and violence, natural disasters, and the idea of territory. But as the title of the movie suggested, nature was itself a theme; and nature's backyard, like our own, was accessible, enthralling, understandable. We were invited into a world so familiar we could hang it on our wall like a calendar illustration.

Today that movie could not be made. Its intimacy with its subject now seems naive, its science bogus, its ethics dubious. The world it tried to depict, and a whole tangle of ideas about that world, have changed too much. Hundreds of nature and wildlife movies have been made in the forty years since *Nature's Half Acre.* Their discontinuous history includes such genres and approaches as animal stories, science journalism, conservationism, ecological advocacy, social anthropology, adventure stories, and tips on hunting and fishing. Often a single TV program will be a hybrid of different documentary forms and will express deeply contradictory ideas about nature and its relation to human culture.

If we look more closely at the history of these popular movies and television programs, we can see the emergence of an untold version of life in North America since the Second World War. In disentangling this history, we will see how changing ideas about nature correspond to changes in geography, economy, science, and politics.

Geography and Progress

The Disney studios popularized the genre of the wildlife movie in the early 1950s, and the influence of their work was felt in nature education for the following two decades. Their first effort was *Seal Island,* which Walt Disney himself booked into a Pasadena, California, cinema in 1948. By the mid-1950s the studios were producing about one wildlife movie a year in their "True Life Adventure" series, including *The Vanishing Prairie* (1954), *The African Lion* (1955), *Perri* (1956), and *White Wilderness* (1958). All of them turned a good profit, and many won Academy Awards.

The Disney movies always told stories, and the stories always began at the beginning — the spring, the dawn, the birth of a bear cub or otter. They ended at the beginning too, with words like new life, rebirth, hope. These were old "eternal" stories about the land, not very different formally from the woodland lore traditionally taught at summer camp or the stories of paradise that have drifted down to us from the Bible and garden history. What does distinguish nature movies from learning how to tie knots or build a snow cave or send semaphore signals is that they often precede all those experiences.

Our ways of thinking about and altering our landscapes these last forty years or so have been shaped and framed by the narrative and dramatic conventions of movies and, especially, television. For example, the time-lapse film sequences of blooming cactus in the 1953 Disney feature *The Living Desert* (another Academy Award winner) did something far more than reveal "nature's mysteries": they spoke to us of a living and intelligible world beyond the fence of civilization, a world we could enter at will and experience in something like human time. The stories and memories of the non-human world were meant to stand in for the stories and memories of our human world, and vice versa.

Yet for all they opened up and "revealed" of life, the early Disney movies also came with their own constricting logic. The animal stories they trafficked in were among other things transparent allegories of progress, paeans to the official cult of exploration, industrial development, and an ever rising standard of living. Those blooming flowers in "living colour" — a signature of Disney's film work — legitimized our metaphors about economic growth. The flowers were typically shown only to the point of "perfection." Rarely did we see them fading, decaying, consumed by microorganisms that returned them to the earth — part of some other economy, a larger collective cycle of life and death of which we humans are also a part. Like nineteenth-century accounts of the "winning" of the American West, these postwar nature stories were told over and again. They were fictions of victory for the new Century of Progress.

Walt Disney's insistence on natural rhythms in the organization of his wildlife movies tells us much about the social and geographical disruptions of the postwar years. Amid the race-related violence and catastrophic urban "redevelopment" of the U.S. city I grew up in, for example (not to mention the disintegration of my family), Disney's stories of a nature "in balance" and somehow outside of history functioned as a kind of utopian fantasy for me. They were myths that I lived.

The narrative summary at the close of *One Day in Teton Marsh* (1966) is especially revealing. It's the end of the day, a thunderstorm has just broken up, and as the clouds move off a rainbow appears over the Teton Range in Wyoming:

Even as the day had begun in calm, so it ended in calm.
As twilight fell, a sense of peace returned to this valley,
A peace heralded by nature's oldest sign and symbol.
The golden orb of the western sun touched the scene with its last probing arrows of light,
And mirror-smooth waters caught the jewelled rays and held them back
          in joyous brightness.
As night fell a sense of peace returned to the valley.
All was again as it once had been.
Life was once more triumphant and undefeated.
For the beavers, the otters, and all the denizens of Teton Marsh,
It had been a good day to be alive.
A day to live through and remember.

Disney's nature movies shared another organizing strategy. At their very beginning, just after the credits, they usually showed an animated tableau. A paint brush might appear on the screen and create a verdant Earth. Oceans were sloshed on, mountains dabbed in, deserts and clouds added. Quickly it became clear that we were looking at a cartoon of North America, and we'd look to find where we lived ourselves. Canada, predictably, was white with snow and ice, the West mountainous, the Southwest dry and strewn with John Ford cowboy-movie props, the East green and steamy — or already civilized. Off the coast of New England, where human history always began in these stories, European ships were painted in. Sometimes there would be wagon trains on the plains, or lumberjacks felling trees in the Rockies. It was all about the conquest of an unpeopled land, a totalizing view of a continent as seen from a helicopter or space ship, a map of the empire. The camera would zoom in, usually on the mountains of the West, and dissolve to a helicopter shot of an alpine valley in spring.

In the 1950s, the West (and its annex, Alaska) could still be the backdrop for frontier myths about an American civilization destined to grow and expand. In the TV show *Space Invaders,* Buzz Corey rid the skies of communists in order to free outer space for U.S. settlement. In the movie *Beaver Valley* (1950), beaver offspring followed their fathers' trails to their ends and beyond, driven on into the unexplored wilderness of the New World. As succeeding generations of beavers settled ever more remote and beautiful valleys, undesirables like coyotes moved in too, taking up some of the elbow-room. And so the West was won.

The movies were not only stories of victory and settlement — natural versions of Daniel Boone legends. Sure, the wildlife movies were the fantasy preserves of an older order, tales of hidden places supposedly untouched by the dislocations of modern society. But they also functioned as lived myths of freedom and space, helping to give shape to the cultural and environmental politics of the coming decades. As such they were part of a long and distinguished tradition of North American nature stories. The people who swelled the ranks of environmental organizations in the 1960s and 1970s grew up on Disney's utopian tales of cuddly fawns and lost but clever dogs — a fact not ignored by the organizers of the campaign to ban hunting of baby seals in the Gulf of St. Lawrence two decades later.

The site of most of the early Disney stories, the American West, was soon enough thrown into crisis, however. By the 1960s the West was closely identified with radical politics, of both left and right. But it was the physical changes of the Western interior that made it a landscape too laden with contradictions for any more *Beaver Valleys.* A voracious resource industry had by the 1960s begun to extract hydrocarbons, uranium, timber, and water power from the earth in quantities never before imaginable. Moreover, the military cordoned off many of the more remote areas of North America over the forty-year course of the Cold War. Enormous tracts of desert and tundra (regions Disney called "incredibly ugly, yet fantastically beautiful") were taken over by the U.S. armed forces in western and northern regions of both the United States and Canada — for bomb tests, practice battlefields, and chemical weapons research.

In those same years, however, a broad-based resistance arose to militarism and the degradation of the planet. For instance, Native people, whose presence in the Disney wildlife movies had been in every way impossible, began to speak their own stories about the Earth — or rather white culture began to listen to them. As the environmental movement mobilized itself and ecological ideas spread through the culture, nature movies shifted their focus from animals to science.

Itinerant nature photographers and filmmakers who didn't take up environmentalism abandoned North America for "undiscovered" lands that could still support narratives of exploration and domination. Africa — the continent, but also the film location that has conflated so many cultures and biogeographies — was an obvious destination, as were other amorphous and historical places, like the South Seas. In more recent years, the Arctic and Antarctic have served a similar purpose.

For their part, the Disney studios began to abandon the puppy-dog movies (the last of the type was 1968's *Charlie the Lonesome Cougar*). The "True-Life Adventure" series itself was canned in 1960, perhaps because the most dramatic outdoor footage had already been used up and maintaining a field crew had become too expensive. Future Disney wildlife movies were filmed on the Burbank lots using trained animals, and they came to resemble popular TV shows like *Lassie, Flipper, Daktari,* and *Sea Hunt.*

Moving the Laboratory Into the Orchard

Following the Disney example, wildlife movies proliferated in the 1950s and 1960s, a trend closely linked to the increased consumption of visual images in all modern industrial societies. The new photographic and video technologies marketed in the years before and after World War II were key to this media wave. Among many other things, these technologies encouraged us to translate our experience of nature into forms accessible to the camera. As a result, our culture today is saturated with the photographic image. The metaphors we use to talk about the act of photography are strangely revealing: we take pictures, we capture or even shoot something on film. These are metaphors of the hunt, an activity that in modern urban culture retains few of the meanings it has in traditional societies. In the sealing and trapping controversies of recent years, for example, the hunt — the activity at the centre of the debate — is represented in completely different ways by the opposing sides.

Most popular representations of nature are organized around the eye, an organ that is itself surrounded by ideologies encouraging a separation of the human individual from the natural world. This tendency is accentuated by the imperatives of science, an activity that ascended in Western culture at about the same time as perspectival painting, in the sixteenth century. The roots of Western science lie in Greek natural philosophy and Pauline Christianity, which conceived of nature, in the broadest sense, as the corrupter of a transcendent human soul. Canadian environmental philosopher Neil Evernden argues that the problem is still older than that, that the eye is the predominant human sense.

*It provides access to the world in a particular way, and while it gives us much, it also con-
ceals. Vision permits us the luxurious delusion of being neutral observers with the ability to manipulate a distant environment. The gain is objectivity, but the loss is any
notion of interrelation between the elements of the visual field. We see only what is, not
how it came to be.*

But it is not so much the predominance of the visual that is important here as
it is the *separation* of the visual from the rest of the senses. The camera, with its
insistence on perspective and the narrow field, exaggerates the eye's tendency
to fragment, objectify, and estrange. Staring through a viewfinder, we experience the physical world as landscape, background — the Earth as if seen from
space, or as map. At the same time, the snapshot transforms the resistant aspect
of nature into something familiar and intimate, something we can hold in our
hands and memories. In this way, the camera allows us some control over the
visual environments of our culture.

Wildlife movies — like realist wildlife genre paintings — promise us that
photographic intimacy with nature. Over and over again we're led to remote
valleys "where time is still measured by the passing seasons," where there are hidden places "inaccessible to man," where the entire photographic field is in focus
and the animals return our anxious glances. Very often nature movies can't
deliver because this restricted medium alone — and its appeal to the eye and, less
so, to the ear — can't bridge the cultural and philosophical abyss between us and
what in recent years we have come to call environment. Most North Americans
see wildlife on TV or at the movies before they see it "live" at the farm or the
zoo, animal park, or campground. In films nature is easily constructed as a
resource or a commodity to be consumed as scenery, or it is shown in some
abstract form as matter capable of producing energy. Usually in these movies
we're supposed to be able to sit back and "view" nature without becoming
involved in it. This detachment is an illusion that nature movies at least partly
promote. Many of them don't reveal the deep involvement with nature necessary to their making: large crews, helicopters, camera blinds, sets, telescopic
lenses, remote sound, and trained animals flown in from another part of the continent. In other words, nature films traffic in images that are ordinarily invisible. Our ability to produce these films of "life in the wild" is an index not only
of our power over nature but also of our distance from it. For the closer the
members of a film crew get with their cameras and paraphernalia, the further
nature recedes from their experience, and ours.

On the other hand, we are aware of the technical apparatus that makes
this "visual experience" possible, because we are surrounded by it every day. In
this technologized culture not many of us can watch a wildlife movie without

*Canadian nature film
maker Bill Mason. Nature
movies traffic in images
that are ordinarily
invisible. Our ability to
produce them is an index
of our power over nature,
as well as our distance
from it.*

asking ourselves how it was made. At the beginning of the Disney nature movies it used to be explained that we were about to be told a "True-Life Adventure Story" — a narrative form with an especially rich history in North America. With a movie, however, special problems come up about how to represent the natural world as truth. Before the invention of photography, it wouldn't have made sense to say that the story you're about to tell is "true to life." But Disney went out of his way to assure us that the scenes were "completely authentic, unstaged and unrehearsed."

None of that is true of course. There is ample documentation of animal training — and animal abuse — in nature movie productions by the Disney studios. As well, film footage for many of the early Disney productions was acquired from independent filmmakers. The studios themselves explained that "filming nature" is more complicated than it seems. *Filming Nature's Mysteries,* a 1956 Disney production for the education market, examined how the nature movies of the day were made. It showed how, in the "True-Life Adventure" department of the Disney studios, engineers designed camera fittings and lighting systems for a variety of field conditions. It showed experts building blinds in marshes, igloos in the High Arctic, and watertight boxes for underwater filming. Technicians brought animals out of the wild and into the lab for equipment tests. They used time-lapse photography to film "the miracle of plant growth — a process so slow it can only be disclosed by special camera techniques that compress time." Eventually, the film says, by "moving the laboratory into the orchard," time-lapse photography is able to reveal "the lifeforce surging within the core of the apple."

In another example, scientists cut away an ant hill and insert a window pane and shade for observation. The next day, we're told, "The ant colony is performing in a normal manner, and photography can proceed. The cameras can now probe the secrets of life." Yet those cameras were set up according to the conventions of TV drama: multiple cameras for action and reaction shots, close-ups, slow motion. There's a lot of editing involved. In many wildlife movies, animal performance in front of a camera is presented as animal behaviour. These approaches continue to the present day in work that is popularly understood to be scientific. In a recent program funded by the fur industry and the governments of Alberta and Canada, captured animals were herded into immense fenced-off pens in the bush so that video cameras could record the effects of various alternatives to the leg-hold trap. Regardless of what we think of trapping fur-bearing animals, there is something odd about assuming that the behaviour of animals in a pen will tell us something about the right way to go about living with them, and killing them.

In that sense, Disney's early wildlife movies were an outlandish enterprise. They mobilized the latest technology, pointed it at the earth and tried to imagine a vital world with no humans in it. The contradiction that Disney's work flaunted — this is nature as she really is even though we've staged it all — only works if the culture draws a sharp distinction between the human and the non-human. Nature is in part a human construction after all. Like a set of maps laid over the earth, our culture's ideas about nature are already out there on the land itself as we move around it.

◌

The history of animal movies is closely linked to the development of both the movie camera and field biology. Eadweard Muybridge began his research into moving pictures by studying animal locomotion in Sacramento, California. In the 1870s he used twenty-four still cameras to take serial photos of a racehorse galloping along a track. A few years later he staged a tiger attacking a buffalo at the Philadelphia Zoo, setting a precedent for the sacrifice of animals that became a standard in TV entertainment. Muybridge's interest in animal locomotion still finds an echo in the wide use of slow-motion in wildlife movies. Etienne-Jules Marey, a zoologist at the Collège de France, used movies as data in his studies of animal behaviour. His shots of a flock of birds, taken in 1878, provided the first moving picture of animals in the wild. From the time of Muybridge and Marey the camera — still and moving — has played a key role in the development of biology. Many early movies were made by scientists at a time when field research was still a marginal activity within most disciplines.

The spread of photographic technologies in the early twentieth century promoted what the National Geographic Society called, in its 1989 video *Cameramen Who Dared,* "the golden age of photographic exploration." Much of this exploration was of the non-human world, and shots of animals became common in travelogues and Hollywood adventure movies. Carl Akeley, a U.S. taxidermist, used a movie camera to document animal poses. John Williamson, a cartoonist for a Virginia newspaper, took the first underwater pictures from a "photosphere" that he built below the surface. In 1914 Williamson filmed *20,000 Leagues Under the Sea*.

The most celebrated wildlife filmmakers of the early century were Martin and Osa Johnson, a husband-and-wife team from the U.S. Midwest. Martin had learned photography using an early Kodak camera while travelling around the world as a cook for Jack London. Between 1917 and 1937 the Johnsons made about thirty immensely popular adventure movies. Most of them were shot in Kenya or New Guinea, with titles like *Among the Cannibal Isles of the South Pacific, Jungle Adventures, Trailing African Wild Animals, Congorilla,* and *Baboona*. The best known work, done in Kenya, had the backing of the American Museum of Natural History and Kodak founder George Eastman. The Johnsons set up a lavish mountain camp alongside a Kenyan lake used as a film set for most of the animal action. Martin Johnson, mechanically adept, developed all his film in the camp and devised a field movie camera that became an industry standard. The Johnsons believed they were filming "the world as it once was." Today their movies seem an embarrassing amalgam of bad anthropology, natural history, and adventure — a formula that has meant "box office" right up to *Raiders of the Lost Ark*.

❂

Our ideas about nature are drawn not only from movies and television, but also from our experience of the land. For many North Americans living in the postwar years, the natural world was the site of great ambivalence. Rural cultures were massively displaced during and after the Second World War. Modernization brought suburbs, expressways, and industrial agriculture to the landscape. In everyday material life, nature was a laboratory full of "things" to be observed and increasingly managed in the name of social mobility and economic progress. Yet at the same time people persisted in inventing a kinship with a natural world understood to be in some way authentic, primeval, and immanent — as if trying to make sense where there was none.

Disney's *Filming Nature's Mysteries* opens by talking about the long history of animal photography — something the film says has been going on "since the invention of the camera...and that will continue for as long as man is fascinated by nature." The pictorial landscape is far older than the camera, of course. But by the 1950s Disney was able to invest the depiction of landscape with a new urgency: it was now necessary to "get wildlife on film before civilization could wipe them out." That not only takes technical expertise. It also requires an understanding of what the project is about in the first place. For Disney, nature movies (like most of his work) were made both to educate and to entertain. It was as if, in living our modern urban lives, we had few other ways to experience nature, to "understand her mysteries." Disney wildlife movies would explain, map out, *show* nature for all to enjoy. Nature was worth learning about, worth saving from the encroachment of civilization — whatever that might be taken to mean.

Science and tourism had drawn maps of nature long before Walt Disney. Movies, television, and amateur photography introduced a new populist imperative for nature: it had to entertain. How do you film the environment of a fish? If you're Disney, you look for what's both unusual and familiar. You film some fish chasing each other and have the voiceover comment: "Here, drama is everywhere. These waters have their full share of life's problems and conflicts." Nature in these movies is both impossibly close and impossibly distant, and perhaps that is our fascination with it.

From Cry of the Wild, *a 1971 film by the National Film Board of Canada. Popular culture has invested the wolf with the most savage and barbaric characteristics.*

Looking at Animals

"The cameras probe the secrets of life..."

"For the first time on the screen, the mysteries of ants are revealed..."

"Our search also leads to the beauties of nature's garden..."

What is this search about? What are they trying to get on film? The object of all this scrutiny of nature is first of all the land itself. Western (that is, North Atlantic) cultural history is full of examples of a desire to live in a world of nature uncontaminated by human presence. Yet this quest for paradise — which in the history of colonialism has placed aboriginal peoples in an impossible position — is not just a negation of modern civilization. It is also a positive reaching out to embrace the other animals that inhabit this Earth. But what is it that we see when we look across the abyss of ignorance and suspicion and yearning that separates human from wolf or elephant or cow? What do animals mean in human culture?

English writer John Berger points out that, historically, animals interceded between humans and our biological origins. They worked and played alongside us on the land. Mortal and immortal, like us and unlike us, animals have until very recently been at the centre of our world. Human language is saturated with their presence, and in traditional cultures animal fables continue to be a central form of expression. Animals led lives parallel to and yet distinct from ours. This dual relationship made for a companionship like no other.

In the last hundred years, however, animals have been slowly excised from the everyday lives of most Westerners, an excision recorded in the subsequent proliferation of zoos and animal toys and animal movies. No longer our companions or workmates — except non-autonomously as pets — animals seem to have no more secrets to tell us about ourselves. They've been reduced to machines devoid of spirit, to everything that is strictly biological in the world. Indeed, industrial animal husbandry and scientific research construct animals as *less* than machines. They're merely components of production. We cannot be fond of the animals we eat from the supermarket, for example, any more than most of us today can eat the animals we are fond of. This is a history that parallels that of science and capitalism. Over the past two hundred years the natural world has been inscribed with the logic of production and consumption, and, conversely, human social distinctions are now understood to mirror the diversity of species found in the non-human world.

If we ponder the recent history of the wildlife movie industry — everything from Walt Disney's early work through *Mutual of Omaha's Wild Kingdom* and Lorne Greene's not-so-*New Wilderness,* to the more science-oriented traditions of National Geographic and CBC-TV's *The Nature of Things* — we see a record of the slow recession of animals into history. There they begin to merge with all that we call primitive in the world: primal landscapes, indigenous peoples, and a displaced human biology. The archaic becomes synonymous with everything we understand to be lower on the evolutionary ladder. The wolf is a good example of this. As a figure of the primitive, the wolf has been invested with the most savage and barbarian characteristics. It stands in opposition to everything that is meant by civilization. Unlike modern *homo sapiens, canis lupus* fills an appropriate niche in its environment, rather than seizing a thousand.

The wolf has been shunted to the margin physically as well as culturally. For decades, many Canadian provinces and U.S. states had official wolf eradication programs. Other predator species, like the coyote and bear, are under similar pressure in the western United States. With the encouragement of trophy hunters and developers, wolf eradication programs were government policy in British Columbia until late 1988, and unofficial wolf kills appear to be on the increase. These programs are carried out through a bounty system, aerial gunning safaris, and bait laced with strychnine, cyanide, and "1080" (sodium monofluoroacetate, a nerve toxin). The poison bait ends up killing many other species as well. The provincial government of British Columbia has even argued that wolf control programs preserve forests; its logic is that the government cannot justify "the retention of unlogged caribou habitat if, because of wolf predation, caribou cannot use, or underutilize the habitat currently being reserved from logging."

I bring up the wolf not so that I can argue for the preservation of yet another wildlife species, although in the short term we'll have to rely on such

*charasmatic
mega-fauna
!*

rearguard tactics. Instead I want to signal that the wolf lives at one extreme of human contact with the natural world; pets live at the other. In the territory between dwell the remaining thousands of animal species, each grafted with a different human value, from the exotic to the useful, from the pestiferous to the ignored. Most wildlife movies focus on the larger, "higher" mammals and pay little attention to invertebrates or plants. Moreover, the dramatic conventions of TV insist on individual protagonists to carry the story along, usually ignoring serious discussion of animals-in-community, or habitat.

❂

In part, wildlife films are a record of lost species, a memento of times and places we once have felt close to in the natural world. But why are these things important to us? Perhaps it is because we feel ourselves to be also out there in the world, beyond our skins if not beyond our culture. For all the clumsiness and naiveté of the probing cameras, these movies reveal a deep desire simply to be in the world. That "lifeforce" in the core of the apple that Disney tried so hard to film must finally be the life in our own human bodies, which are inextricably connected to the rest of the biophysical world.

When Disney moved the laboratory into the orchard, the orchard was a changed one. It was changed first of all by the techniques of industrial agriculture in the postwar years. It was also changed by the eye itself, for as the eye casts itself out over the earth, it constructs the landscape as it goes. But the landscape we make images of changes from one moment to another. In other words, human culture, as well as human biology, intervenes in our experience of nature. Part of our cultural heritage in the West is a deep belief that humans are the source of all value and meaning in the world, that we are the Earth's only subjects. Since the advent of science, the "exterior" world of reality has been disenchanted, purged of its spirit.

But as much as that is the dominant tradition in modern industrial societies, there remain everywhere vibrant cultural traditions that still imagine (and experience) the world as place to live rather than space to colonize. We articulate those traditions above all in popular cultural forms. In our snapshots and movies and music, and in the way we tell fishing stories or plant our gardens (to say nothing of our rituals), we try to speak of a reciprocal experience of an Earth understood to be animated, even sacred.

One of the ways human societies have always done this is to transfer human behaviours and motivations onto the natural world: the act of anthropomorphism. Anthropomorphism can be a radical strategy in a culture like our own, where the frontier between the human and non-human is well policed, where nature is usually talked about as a field of objects to be observed and managed for the "public good." Yet domination of our natural neighbours has perhaps had its price in alienation and loneliness as a species. It is also becoming clear that the Earth resists all our attempts to control it.

Humans have always invented ways to form an interactive relationship with the Earth, often by endowing that Earth with the qualities of the only subjects we know — ourselves. Nature and wildlife movies (and particularly the early work of Walt Disney) are thus one expression of a long human tradition of investing the natural world with meaning. Those meanings are as often as not laden with sexism, colonialism, and species hierarchy — witness the number of cars, tractors, and military machines named after animals. Still, the anthropomorphic gesture is a means of making the world beyond the garden wall intelligible to us, and of breaking down the ideology of "humanity vs. nature."

Bear Country and *Beaver Valley* are good examples of Disney's early work in the genre. Made in the early 1950s, they are stories of human families living like bears and beavers in a North American Arcadia. Here, we're told, "Nature is the dramatist." Mother bear looks after the youngsters while papa bear hunts for food. The cubs are taught to be obedient — to stay out of trouble or they'll get sent to the den to bed. Meanwhile, when he's out fishing papa bear greets lordly moose, timid deer, and Mrs. Wren opening her family's summer cottage. Over in Beaver Valley life is much the same, only in that society beavers seem to be mired in wage labour while otters practise primitive communism. Beavers are solid (Canadian) citizens who build solid houses. And not only houses, but dams, canals, bridges, and other engineering works. They're helped in this by crayfish bulldozers. Well-mannered and unassuming, the beavers disapprove of the carefree otters — vagabonds who sleep anywhere and have no respect for honest work. All of the animals in the valley are heterosexual, of course, and observe marriage — with celebrations and proper honeymoon protocol.

The stories are punctuated with a Disney trademark that persists from his cartoons: orchestrated vignettes of organic rhythms. Mud gurgles, frogs croak, blooms bloom. Grebes stage pageants, pelicans perform classical ballets. It's enthralling; the world hums and cooks to a human choreography and middlebrow orchestral music. Just like in the cartoons — the most pointedly anthropomorphic of Disney's work — these humanized animals are able to break all kinds of sexual and bodily taboos. They are always farting or falling on their asses.

The barnyard was the scene of Walt Disney's first cartoons, whose subjects were mice, cows, ducks, and dogs. The domestication of animals is an ancient anthropomorphic act. It is the transformation of the non-human into human surrogates. Disney's move from the U.S. Midwest to Los Angeles was part of a rural migration that took place throughout North America in the first half of the twentieth century. His animal cartoons and nature movies must be understood in the context of the reorientation of the North American economy away from farming and its culture.

In the 1960s and 1970s, scientific (and pseudoscientific) understandings of animal behaviour began to supplant the anthropomorphism that for so long had characterized popular representations of nature. Pop anthropologists such as Desmond Morris and Robert Ardrey used animal studies to excuse contemporary social organization. This new tradition dismissed Disney's beaver families and cricket orchestras as being "subjective." Instead the new science taught us that animal "guards" aggressively patrol well-marked territories; that the dominant male fights with other males to control the clan and its women; that the animal kingdom is divided into predator and prey.

For the moment, it will be enough to refute these last pronouncements in passing. Feminist anthropologists and others have pointed out that terms like aggression, dominance, and instinct have been used by scientists in so many different contexts that they have lost all meaning. More recently still, many biologists have argued that it might be more useful to look for paradigms of co-operation and symbiosis in nature; and sure enough, they are there to be found. If we think of boundaries in experiential rather than visual terms — or even rather than in the legal terms of property — territoriality comes to mean something quite different too. Current biological theory suggests that animals sense themselves to be truly part of the larger world; their selves extend beyond their skins to encompass an invisible region that includes the whole integrated web of relationships they're part of.

Looked at again in this light, Disney's wildlife movies take on new interest. At least in Beaver Valley the world looks habitable. Compare that to the sterile and militaristic baboon societies portrayed in the science documentaries of later years. In *One Day in Teton Marsh,* made by the Disney Studios in 1966, we learn that animals aren't just a bundle of DNA — they're social beings that need to hang around with friends. In Disney's work the otter is often chosen as the prime social vertebrate. When the otter protagonist of this story loses his friends in a landslide, he becomes lonely, "and loneliness can destroy the will to live." Without others of his kind he is out of his world. Eventually, being the hippy that he is, the otter wanders around, hooks up with a new network of friends, and is able to resume his hunting and gathering.

Humans were never visually present in the natural settings of Disney's early movies. But then, with such familiar, utopian stories, we don't need to be. Despite the otters' respect for private property and the sexual division of labour, the world of Teton Marsh is at least a world full of life, a dwelling-place. To the extent that films like this sum up our relations with nature, they are about us. But more than that, Disney's early work anticipated some of the debates in the natural sciences today. Among biologists there is a countertradition to the usual arguments about territory and boundaries. Scientists now argue that the central tenet of ecology — that everything in the world is interrelated — is to be taken seriously, not casually. It seems that for science itself, there is no longer any certainty about where to draw the lines between one organism and another, about whether the living and non-living worlds are truly distinct, about whether we can study humans outside of the context of the natural world we live in. Organism-and-environment are now thought of as a unity. Despite their juvenile anthropomorphism — or maybe because of it — Disney's early movies lie within this tradition.

From Pastoralism to Scientism

The dominant trend in nature movies in both Canada and the United States has always been conservationism — the idea that the natural world should be used wisely or it won't last. Walt Disney's work of the 1950s was in many ways a departure from this trend. By foregrounding the anthropomorphic character of our relations with the natural world, his movies emphasized the *experience* of the non-human (as problematic as that might be) over the use of it.

Disney's early work had coincided with a momentous change in human demography. In the postwar years, rural cultures were in rapid decline as large sectors of the population resettled in urban areas. Nature was newly out of reach for most North Americans. Disney's wildlife movies were one way the culture reintroduced the idea of nature into everyday life, in what were obviously very changed social circumstances. Like Disneyland, or even the long tradition of the suburb with its extensive lawns, the movies functioned as a bucolic idyll for a popular culture saturated with images of technology and the domination of nature.

It was not only society that was changing. The land itself was being extensively developed — "harnessed" was the word most often used in government and corporate publicity — not the least by new technologies of transportation and communication. The conservationist movement, which seemed to be in decline in the North America of the 1950s, had re-emerged by the 1960s, ironically reinvigorated by two decades of technological expansion. In the public imagination, it had once again become necessary to protect and save the Earth and its resources.

The difference between *showing* the animals and *saving* them is a telling one. A charming fable produced by the National Film Board of Canada (NFB) in 1960 gives a sense of this transition. *Beaver Dam* tells the story of two farm

boys who discover a new beaver dam downstream from a hayfield ready for harvest. These beavers are cut from Disney cloth; they sing a "work song" as they
go about their earnest industry:

Work will keep you merry
Work will keep you well
So don't be in a tizzy
Just keep busy, you'll feel swell

When Dad notices the flooded field, he tells the boys he's afraid the beavers will
have to be killed. While their old man hides on the bank with his rifle, the boys
alert the beavers and break open the dam. The field dries out and the hay is
saved. After the harvest, the beavers rebuild the dam and at the end of the
movie the boys go swimming in the restored pond.

The presence of humans in this story signals the change. Conflict has
"inevitably" developed over the presence of a rudimentary technology — the
plough — and its effects on nature. Two children step into the breach and heal
the wound. The world is restored to a garden where humans and animals can
live in harmony. What is important here is that it is humans who take the initiative. By saving the beavers the boys help us all re-establish what we understand
to be the proper constitution of the natural world. We also, in this parable at
least, invent an ultimately non-intrusive role for technology.

As the effects of the immense physical development of the postwar years
began to be felt at large in popular culture, it seems that Disney's vision became
too limited. The human role in the natural world (for good or bad) could no
longer be ignored. The Disney studios also took part in this change, most obviously in *Hang Your Hat on the Wind,* a 1969 fable in which a kindly Franciscan
missionary who runs an animal shelter helps a Navajo shepherd boy find a lost
white colt. The padre and his charge spot the napping Chicano rustlers from a
pesticide plane and get some tourists to help chase the bad guys in dune buggies. In the end the colt is returned to its owner (a blond California woman who
drives a convertible) and peace is restored to what is imagined — to put it in more
contemporary terms — to be the ecological society of the Navajo.

◦

The seminal body of work in the conservationist tradition is probably *Mutual
of Omaha's Wild Kingdom.* Begun in 1963, the show was still being produced in
1990 and has been syndicated in forty countries. It was originally hosted by
zoologist Marlin Perkins, the director of the St. Louis Zoo and host of an early-
1950s TV show, *Zoo Parade,* about animal behaviour. At the beginning of each

A swift fox reintroduction program on the Canadian prairies. "Drug-and-tag" TV shows like Wild Kingdom *justify their action-packed plots by promoting biological research.*

program Perkins sat in a leather armchair in his library and talked about saving animals. Thanks to his zoological colleagues and the valiant efforts of professional photographers, Perkins would report, scores of species had been rescued from the brink of extinction.

On *Wild Kingdom* animals had to be captured before they could be saved. The show's strict formula (known in the industry as a "drug-and-tag movie") involved chasing animals around a savannah in a Land Rover long enough to get some action shots. Tranquillized and caged, the beasts were hauled off to be studied in the laboratory, where if all went well they would reproduce. The argument that Perkins, Jim Fowler, and other TV biologists made is that because of the incursions of human civilization, the natural environment could no longer support wild animals in an efficient way. Human expertise — which turned out to be a tangle of medical technology — would be necessary for the survival of wildlife.

The *Mutual of Omaha* commercials that punctuate the show emphasize this point. One tells how the insurance company has not only saved a disabled man from certain death but also made his life worth living again by buying him a remote-controlled TV and a wheelchair van. (It was in a car accident that the man was crippled in the first place.)

You might say that good intentions are the only thing that separates *Wild Kingdom* from Buffalo Bill Cody's Wild West Show. As a scout and sharpshooter in the second half of the nineteenth century, Cody had helped open the U.S. shortgrass prairie to settlement by whites. White agrarian civilization was thought to be a more efficient use of the land than the "wasteful" nomadic traditions of the various aboriginal civilizations of the plains. In his later years Cody staged a travelling Wild West Show celebrating the victory of farmer and cowboy over bison and Indian. In the circus tents that toured Europe the tamed American wilderness lived on, just as today the same tawdry and ambivalent story of civilization is retold in TV wildlife shows.

Perkins always insisted he was telling "the animals' side of the story" on *Wild Kingdom*. In an interview with the Canadian Broadcasting Corporation (CBC) program *The 5th Estate* in 1982, he explained the methods of TV conservationism:

The philosophy is educational, you see. But if you don't have a little entertainment and action, you don't get the opportunity to tell your story. We have excellent wildlife photographers. Sometimes it takes weeks to get something on film....We never predetermine the exact script. Our footage is taken in the wild kingdom itself.

What Perkins wouldn't talk to the CBC about was the wildlife photography industry. In the salad days of the 1960s and 1970s, several U.S. and Canadian TV production companies worked full time on the many wildlife shows that followed Wild Kingdom. Most outdoor footage was shot in Florida with trained animals and the assistance of the Florida Freshwater Game Commission (which rightly saw no contradiction of their mandate). Like doctors, lawyers, or horticulturists, wildlife photographers belong to professional societies and go to conventions where film footage is bought and sold along with animals for use in movies, zoos, game farms, and private collections. The films made with this footage often differ little in their formal conventions from the Disney work. Shots and sequences are worked out beforehand on story-boards similar to those used in filming television dramas. Whatever research the biologists might be doing off camera, what ends up in the programs teaches us little about animals.

Since *Wild Kingdom* began, other conservation shows have developed new techniques and themes. Sound production has become more sophisticated, and a show with a decent budget might use up to twenty-four tracks to record wildlife, narration, music, and sound effects. *Wild Wild World of Animals,* produced by Time-Life from 1973 to 1976, is a good example of more recent work that is still trapped in the contradictory logic of wildlife conservation. Its mission is to document the rescue of animals from human recklessness. (It's as if we set out to destroy other species in order to save them.)

An episode on the Okefenokee Swamp in the southern United States attempts to lay out the basics of ecological science. The swamp, we learn, "can take care of itself." Forest fires, once the bane of conservation efforts, now "serve a definite purpose." Humans are unwelcome here. Even our presence in the production of the show is denied by the narrator's syntax: "These are pitcher plants. One *has been slit open* to reveal the downward-pointing hairs which trap the insect." Too destructive of natural systems, the narrator banishes us from the swamp: "Like spanish moss, which supports itself and exists apart from its surroundings…Okefenokee Swamp is a wilderness in a capsule, existing by, and of, itself."

These are not the lessons of ecology. No life exists apart from its surroundings. The myth of the self-supporting organism is an appendage of the ideologies of the frontier and the free market, in which it's every "man" for himself.

Typically there are two roles for humans in the conservation TV shows. Either we are destroyers of nature — developers, poachers, careless campers — or we are saviours of nature — scientists intervening to save an endangered species or citizens organizing to create a park. Sometimes, most of the time in fact, we're both. Likewise, there have been two dominant models for land use since World War II: total development or total preservation.

The immediate vicinity of most national parks is a good illustration of this. Many park borders are lined with everything high-brow culture considers the most hideous manifestations of humankind: motel strips and gas stations, hydroelectric projects, mining and timber operations, fast food outlets. Many parks and wild areas were created as part of a trade-off between conservation organizations and industry. A dam here for a grove there. This is institutionalized in many urban situations where developers who want to build a skyscraper are required to build its "opposite" on an adjacent lot — a park (or, increasingly, the mere gesture of a few trees). Conversely, when wilderness areas are built, existing human settlements must be bulldozed, not because they're too indecorous, but because the boundary between the "human" and the "natural" must be well marked.

Over the past thirty years, TV conservationism has continued to document nature, enumerating the decline of this or that species, presenting schemes for crisis management, and assuring us that aggression and the notion of private property have a natural origin. Yet increasingly these programs have also begun to critique the doctrine of economic growth. Perhaps they've been forced into this new position by the collision of the conservation ethic with rural lands increasingly burdened with shopping malls and leisure developments. On an episode of *New Wilderness* from the mid-1980s, host Lorne Greene inveighed against hydroelectric projects in Tasmania that are threatening the habitat of the Tasmanian devil. Yet on the same program Greene presented a brief report — a "tip of the hat," he says — on the saving of the California condor. The young birds of prey are now being bred in the lab, "well away from the rigours of the outdoors." We watch scientists feed them with eye-droppers. Another success!

The suggestion in the Tasmanian case seems to be that human civilization should not encroach on the territory of the natural world; nor should the natural world move too far into human territory, like the Tasmanian devils who "steal" from farmers. But, as in California, the laboratory seems to be a special place, a kind of demilitarized zone where the rules are in suspension, or at least in the human favour. Perhaps the lab is the new wilderness itself. If so, it is a wilderness in which the natural and the human are inextricably bound up with technology. In the U.S. films of the past thirty years — think not only of *Wild Kingdom,* but of the National Geographic series, *Wild America,* and *Nature* — the focus of the camera has shifted from the *face* of the racoon or shark or what have you to the hypodermic needle or submarine or helicopter — in other words, onto the technics that intervene in rescuing nature on our behalf. This work is able to sound an alarm about the developing crisis at the same time that it recuperates conservationism within the most traditional kind of scientific practice.

❧

Humans have always "intervened" in nature, but by the early 1960s our relations with the natural world were broadly understood to be in crisis. From the mid-nineteenth century on, a great many popular social movements had mobilized in response to an accelerating rate of species extinction and displacement. The urban parks movement, wilderness preservationism, communitarian socialism, Romanticism, agrarian populism: as much as these anti-modern movements developed different approaches to the cult of progress and the domination of nature in North America, they were all responses to the industrialization of the land.

Conservationism had its beginnings in the same period. Land was recognized as a limited resource that must be used efficiently. The movement's initial objects of concern were buildings and natural areas; protection of animals, trails, and rural land came later. As it became articulated by Gifford Pinchot and other U.S. agronomists and industrialists of the early twentieth century, conservation was not at all opposed to the production economy. Nature and its products were commodities, subject to supply and demand, scarcity and abundance, and constantly in need of management. As an industrial strategy, conservationism is deeply intertwined with the modern Western world-view.

Today we're surrounded by the shortcomings of conservationism as a political strategy. Despite a century or more of hard work by lots of well-meaning people, the Ark is sinking. The complex and diverse organism of the Earth that has taken millennia to develop is in steady decline. As species after species disappears from the planet forever, complex relationships are simplified and life of all kinds becomes more vulnerable. Even on its own limited terms, the conservation movement has been a dismal failure.

By the 1960s this failure was obvious to many critics and conservationism began to be reshaped. The modern environmentalist movement that mobilized itself over the following twenty years rearticulated conservationism in a way that drew from both ethical and scientific traditions while often compromising its opposition to industrialism.

The environmental movement arose at a moment when North American economies were trying to find ways to convert an immense military apparatus into "peaceful" enterprises — industries, government agencies, and universities that produced not only commodities for the "good life," but also ideas about the relation of science and consumer society to the natural world. Not many years after the bombing of Nagasaki and Hiroshima, for example, the U.S. government began talking about "atoms for peace." In the late 1950s it proposed Project Plowshares, a scheme to use nuclear explosions to redirect rivers, drill for natural gas, move mountains, and dig harbours.

Sea Stories

Since the mid-1970s especially, the place of science and technology in coming to terms with the natural world has preoccupied most nature and wildlife movies. Two influential nature programs document the shift from animals to technics.

One of those programs had its beginnings in France. Jacques-Yves Cousteau launched his career as a broadcaster by making movies about aqualungs, an underwater exploration device he invented in the 1930s. By 1951 he had outfitted his first ship, the *Calypso,* with funds from the Direction générale du cinéma français, the French navy, and the ministry of education. Not long after, he began a financial association with the National Geographic Society of the United States.

The diverse funding for Cousteau's expeditions gives us some clues about the hybrid nature of the documentaries. Cousteau talks about his work as "diving for science." For each voyage, he assembles a technical research team under the auspices of his Office français de recherches sous-marines. The scientific purpose of the voyages is never all that clear. The crew do basic field work, such as collecting specimens and observing animals, but Cousteau spends a large part of the edited programs on what can loosely be called sightseeing: boating, diving, and underwater photography. This arrangement — travelogue cum scientific documentary — became the model taken up by National Geographic and other filmmakers in the 1960s and after.

Cries from the Deep, a 1981 movie about the North Atlantic fishery co-produced with the National Film Board of Canada, is a good example. Like most Cousteau movies, things begin in a relaxed way, with the *Calypso* and its crew roaming around the Gulf of St. Lawrence, periodically stopping to lower camera equipment into the sea or to disembark and talk to people in the outport

The dominant tradition in nature movies is conservationism, a political movement with few victories in its one hundred-year history.

Act Now, While Supplies Last.

The eight varieties of the modern tiger are going fast. Four are extinct or near extinction. And the habitat of the others is dwindling.

Between 1920 and 1960, the over-all tiger population dropped from an estimated 100,000 to less than 1,000. Today, thanks to "Project Tiger" and World Wildlife Fund, they've clawed their way back to 6,000. It's an encouraging comeback but their existence is still threatened.

That's why AGF started the "Eye of the Tiger" Program.

AGF is one of Canada's largest and most successful investment management companies. In our family of mutual funds, we manage 1.8 billion dollars for over 200,000 clients.

But we also know how important it is to manage our environment. And that's what makes our "Eye of the Tiger" Program with World Wildlife Fund so special.

Every donation you make will be matched by AGF.

And if you make a donation of $250 or more, we'll send you a

beautiful, hard cover coffee table book that intimately details the life of this intriguing predator.

So send your tax creditable contributions to: Eye of the Tiger" Program, World Wildlife Fund, Suite 201, 60 St. Clair Avenue East, Toronto, Ontario, M4T 1N5. Or to find out more about how you can help, contact Anna Roman in our Toronto office at (416) 367-1900.

Please hurry. This offer could expire at any time.

AGF

Industrial fishing practices have decimated marine communities in most of the world's oceans.

IF YOU KNEW HOW MANY DOLPHINS DIED TO MAKE THIS TUNA SANDWICH, YOU'D LOSE YOUR LUNCH.

Over 6 million dolphins were killed by tuna fleets in the eastern tropical Pacific over the last 30 years.

These dolphins weren't killed for food or for use in any product. They were killed purely to increase net profits.

It was just these dolphins' bad luck that schools of large, profitable yellowfin tuna often swim below dolphin herds. And in the late '50s, fishermen realized that if they could snare the dolphins, they could net tons and tons of

the tuna below.

First, the dolphins are chased and herded with speedboats, helicopters, and underwater explosives. Then, an enormous net is set around the herd and drawn closed at the bottom.

Exhausted and entangled in the nets, many dolphins suffocate. Some are literally crushed to death.

The Marine Mammal Protection Act of 1972 has helped. But it hasn't helped enough. Over 100,000 dolphins continue to die each year at the

hands of the tuna industry.

Please donate your time or money to Greenpeace so we can continue our efforts to save the dolphins. If you must eat canned tuna, buy only Albacore or chunk white tuna which isn't caught "on dolphins."

Better yet, don't buy any tuna at all. It will only leave a bad taste in your mouth.

GREENPEACE
1436 U Street, Washington, DC 20069

communities. The discussion lurches from nineteenth-century whaling economies to cod habitat to the relation between icebergs and the geography of the sea floor.

By and by the diving crew notices that they are seeing very few fish, even among the shipwrecks that typically function as both marine feeding areas and stage sets for underwater photography. Almost reluctantly Cousteau raises the question of overfishing. He does this by showing different methods of catching fish: line fishing, jigging, the "squid pump," drift nets, and trawling.

We learn that by far the method most destructive of marine habitat is trawling, a massive enterprise conducted in the Grand Banks area, off the coast of Newfoundland, by ships from both Atlantic and Pacific nations. The film shows us the truly industrial operation of the trawlers — including the conveyer belts and assembly lines that help haul fish out of the sea in vast nets (some of them 150 kilometres long), and the on-board equipment that processes and freezes the fish for trans-shipment. Fully 50 per cent of the catch is of species that are unmarketable; they are discarded, dead, a "prodigious waste," Cousteau tells us. While the film doesn't discuss the global economy that encourages industrial fishing, it does succeed in conveying, on a visceral level, its character.

Most discussions of fish methods and quotas mask the problem of over-fishing in talk of interspecies conflict: between whale and caplin, whale and human, lobster and seal. The offshore fishery has been seriously (and perhaps irrecoverably) depleted by trawlers in recent years. The industry has driven large sea mammals close to shore where they compete with inshore fishers for dwindling numbers of fish. Grey seals "raid" lobster habitat, and whales get caught in driftnets, often destroying them. At the time *Cries from the Deep* was made, the Canadian government, in a particularly obtuse response to the crisis, was hiring crews to shoot seals thought to be endangering fish quotas. The cull has since been discontinued, and the government is now researching biological control of the seal population.

The issue is not surprisingly more complicated than it appears at first. For centuries, seal populations off the Newfoundland coast have been controlled by a spring hunt. Local hunters clubbed the pups of these harp and hooded seals, called whitecoats and bluebacks respectively, on ice floes not far from shore. The seal carcasses were used for clothing, tools, and food. As the hunt was capitalized, an international luxury fur industry grew up based on rifle hunting from large ships. Greenpeace successfully targeted this hunt for "baby" seals in the early 1980s and the market in seal furs subsequently collapsed. Yet after opposition from aboriginal groups who argued that the hunt is part of their traditional economy, Greenpeace retreated, even admitting that its campaign had been a mistake. The hunt has since resumed its place in the local subsistence economy, although the Canadian government no longer permits the use of large vessels or the hunting of pups.

The resulting increase in seal populations has had an effect on the fishery well beyond the ability of seals to eat up commercial fish. At least one species of seal is an intermediate host for a worm that attacks cod. Yet there is one other factor to consider when puzzling through this vortex of changes, and that is the effect of pollution from the Great Lakes–St. Lawrence watershed. As *Cries in the Deep* tells us, the small beluga whales of the St. Lawrence River, to name only one species, are now "technically extinct." The remaining 350 belugas are sterile, due to upstream pollution (mainly aluminium smelting in the Saguenay and Akwesasne regions), although the movie does not name the source of the problem.

As with other Cousteau films, the filmmakers organize the narrative in *Cries from the Deep* using shots of divers entering and leaving the water, followed by a brief chat about their findings with Captain Cousteau as they peel off wetsuits and warm up on board the ship. The other device is a recurrent helicopter shot (the *Calypso* has a landing pad) that situates the ship for us in its changing seascape. Like Disney's work, Cousteau's movies are marked by an impulse to beautify the natural world. *Cries from the Deep* offers several long and rhapsodic shots of jellyfish. At one point the narrator speaks of the beauty of this "theatre of the deep" — not far off the mark, considering the pivotal role in these movies of music and lighting, and the often flamboyant *mise-en-scène*.

Cousteau's nature movies emerged from a very particular cultural milieu. Cousteau is perhaps above all a sailor. He likes ships and old yarns as much as the technical knowledge his expeditions are supposed to collect. Cousteau's persona as a *bon vivant* helps carry the narrative of these movies. It is the collective life on board the ship, in fact — the meals, the discussions of which wine to bring up from the cellar, the endless stories and jokes told round the dining table — that endears us to the life below the surface of the ocean. This sociability among humans, which on this side of the Atlantic seems somehow "foreign," is rarely sensed in North American nature movies, which go out of their way to present themselves as scientific and objective. Nonetheless, we can say without exaggeration that Cousteau opened up a frontier, and a landscape. His work presented some of the first undersea photography to appear on television, and his style became an industry norm.

National Geographic

The National Geographic Society released its first wildlife film, *Miss Jane Goodall and the Wild Chimpanzees*, in 1965. The movie focused on Goodall and her research on speech and tool use among chimpanzees in Africa. In this early

who are the "actors" @ PLC?

what are their roles?

movie the Disney tradition was still strong: all the animals had names, and the movie was edited to ensure plenty of drama and comedy. By 1967 those traditions had apparently been repudiated. In *Grizzly!,* a drug-and-tag classic, the focus shifted almost entirely away from animals and onto their human saviours. The plot was driven by the work of wildlife biologists. For perhaps the first time in a wildlife documentary, the filmmakers decided to foreground photographic technology. We see them shooting the movie. This technique not only gave an air of objectivity to both movie and field work but also connected the film to the public image of the National Geographic Society. Ever since its founding in 1888, the organization has funded the research of numerous scientists (among them Jane Goodall and Dian Fossey); but it is best known for its photographic documentation of global exploration and "exotic" cultures, particularly in *National Geographic* magazine. The style of *Grizzly!* made it clear that this was as much a photographic expedition as a scientific study.

The Society's first TV special, aired in 1963, was about the ascent of Everest by U.S. climbers. The program's mission, in the words of its narrator, was "to record the first moving pictures ever taken from the summit of Everest." The Society returned to Everest a few years later to send *live* pictures of the summit into North American homes by satellite. Since then, National Geographic film crews have roamed the world in an incessant drive to "uncover the secrets of the past and present." The subjects of their work range from insects to alligators, whales, circuses, railroads, ocean liners, computers, circuses, and gold rushes — as well as the ever-popular search for the lost *Titanic.* Yet despite their broad interests and often cool, scientific airs, the Society's filmmakers created adventure movies that fit squarely in the photosafari tradition of Osa and Martin Johnson. Nature in these films becomes an object of a much larger investigation of the world that goes under many names, among them science, colonialism, and tourism.

A look at some of the animal movies of the past twenty years offers a sense of how this works. The voiceover of the video *White Wolf* (1989) goes out of its way to demystify wolves, denouncing their popular image as "vicious predators." The filmmakers interview wildlife biologists and show them taking their own film of wolves — cameras in front of cameras. On camera the biologists speculate about wolf language and child rearing, play, security, and feeding, all in a way that helps connect wolf society to the taiga, which forms the scenic backdrop of most of the shots. Yet the structure of the movie undercuts the script. The tension of the show is a *dramatic* tension, organized around an edited hunting episode rather than the ideas set out by the biologists. Its structure reproduces the clichés and "typical" behaviours rampant in the wildlife genre right through the twentieth century.

In photosafari movies, nature becomes an object of a much larger investigation of the world that goes under many names, among them science, colonialism, and tourism.

The Grizzlies (1987) is an ambitious film that attempts to address both the cultural and ecological aspects of one of the largest surviving mammals in North America. Narrated by actor Peter Coyote, the program is set principally in Alaska, a state long associated in the American imagination with the idea of wilderness. It opens with a discussion of the place of bears in human, especially aboriginal, history, about how the grizzly is "our elder brother," "our spirit helper" who taught us what to eat and how to survive. The film explains some of the work of wildlife managers — habitat studies, population control — that has been necessitated by conflicts with human activities. Like most National Geographic projects, the movie quietly backs away from political issues. For example, it refers to economic development of the grizzly habitat ominously, without focusing on specifics. It fails to mention the petroleum industry — the paramount disruptive force in the Alaskan ecosystem. The one conflict that does get considerable attention is the clash between recreation and bear habitat. But the film sums up that situation by documenting "a daring experiment": an attempt by tour organizers to cram sport fishers and adventure photographers onto the same narrow river delta where grizzlies are feeding on migrating salmon. The filmmakers wonder aloud how close these outdoor enthusiasts can get before being attacked. The narrator asks somewhat facilely, "Can Man and bear coexist?" If we are expected to understand the conflict in this way, the answer is clearly no.

But in the program's coda the narrator reformulates the question. "In the old stories," he says, "the bear taught humans how to survive. In this changing world, it seems the secret of how the grizzly will survive is known only to humans." That "secret" might well be known, but the National Geographic Society has cloaked it in its own old stories about the irreconcilable conflict between humankind and the natural world. While this film gestures towards other cultural possibilities, its cynical and accommodationist politics carries the message that the industrialization of wild lands is inevitable; it's only a matter of managing the bears so they'll be able to survive it. Whether or not *we* will survive continued industrialization is a question never considered.

Many of the National Geographic films give science a bad name. They leap over the species barrier just long enough to conclude that nature too is ruled by despots and that only the fittest creatures will survive. Here is the voiceover from a lurid trailer advertising *Africa's Stolen River* (1989):

Beneath this stark façade, the Savuti region of Southern Africa is a land of violent extremes. Savage storms erupt without warning and set the night ablaze. Huge dust clouds loom like an inescapable shroud. This is a world ruled by the sun, the cruel relentless force that binds predator to prey together in a desperate search for water.

*But now the river is disappearing. Nature has cut the Savuti's only lifeline. Now death becomes nature's constant companion, and the quest for survival the all-consuming fact of life. Join National Geographic in search of...*Africa's Stolen River.

Or consider this trailer for a documentary on archaeological work in Africa. As the film cuts between shots of the Olduvai Gorge and a science lab, the narrator invites us to see a video whose subject, curiously, remains unspoken:

It is the greatest detective story known to man. It springs from a curiosity shared by people everywhere. To understand where we came from and how we got here. Scientists the world over search for the pieces of the puzzle, and then the newest technology is focused on this most ancient of mysteries. We even study our own simian cousins for clues to our own primitive past.

Science Journalism

There is another television tradition that discusses science, and its history, with more honesty and intelligence. By the mid-1960s, basic scientific knowledge about the natural world began to work its way into the scripts of some nature programs. Here at last were the things we never learned from Disney: the diet of a mouse, for example, or the habitat requirements of caribou or sycamore, the sexual preferences of a stickleback, or the place of mosquitos in the food web. The increasingly rich diversity of subject-matter ranged far beyond the anthropomorphic or drug-and-tag stylings that had dominated the genre. In essence this represented a shift from nature to science programming, with all the emphasis those words imply.

But only a few programs have been able to present that kind of research in any larger context, speculating about the social implications of science, perhaps, or acknowledging other ways of knowing the world. The most prominent of these programs are *Nova* (produced by WGBH in Boston) and *The Nature of Things* (CBC), both of them weekly series that examine a broad range of technical and social issues.

The diversity of the nature films that have been produced since the late 1960s reflects the diverse origins of ecology, as well as changes in the way natural science has been carried out over the course of the twentieth century. I can give only the barest outline of those changes here. Over the past century, science has slowly undergone a cultural revolution of sorts. This is especially so in biology, where the retreat from rationalism was most marked and the mechanistic and materialistic biases of science became widely questioned from within. The biocentric (or ecological) world-view that emerged from within science has had an impact far beyond it. One reason the mass media have been able to take up environmental issues over the past thirty years is because those issues were understood to be "scientific" — quantifiable, reasonable, and perhaps above all articulated by scientists working in official institutions. At the same time non-scientific gestures — such as Romanticism, spiritualism, or anthropomorphism — have been de-emphasized or actively attacked. Ecological ideas were now backed by a legitimate science, ecology, so to understand humans as animals it was no longer necessary (and no longer desirable, its proponents would have argued) to develop an ethic.

Anthropomorphism has been a specific target of science journalism, especially on TV. The attack initially arose from the groundbreaking work in animal behaviour that was carried on during the late 1950s and early 1960s. Field

"The Kingdom of the Ice Bear," a mid-1980s mini-series about the Arctic, on Nature. *By the late 1960s, basic scientific knowledge about the non-human world had begun to work its way into the scripts of some nature shows.*

observations of primates and other mammals — in part an attempt to get the biological sciences out of the laboratory — sought another way of understanding our long history of relations with animals. The seminal work in this tradition was Konrad Lorenz's 1966 book, *On Aggression*. The recognition of the animal roots of human society led Lorenz, an Austrian biologist, to conclude that aggression could only be controlled by cultural means. His book was intended as a call for non-violence and an end to war. Ironically, as it was presented in countless TV programs and newspaper articles of the time, Lorenz's work was misinterpreted as a justification of violence and aggression. For some programming, this was an acceptable theory of behaviour. In others, it was condemned, and Lorenz himself was denounced as a Nazi.

Necessary or not, however, ecology has an ethics. It is derived in part from the close association the science has had with the social movement I call environmentalism. But what is now generally called environmental ethics has earlier beginnings. The science of ecology emerged from two distinct traditions: holistic (or contextual) biology, with roots in Germany and England; and energy economics, a sub-discipline with some currency in the United States. The biological tradition developed the idea of the ecosystem, and in a sentiment new to science, came to regard human action with regret. Energy economists drew similar conclusions from the Second Law of Thermodynamics, which states that energy dissipates. If biological equilibrium is to be maintained, energy economists argued, drastic changes to internal energy flows must be avoided.

By the 1970s, these two strains of ecology combined into a unique science that, in historian Anna Bramwell's words, fused "an intensely conservative moral and cultural critique with the full apparatus of quantitative argument." Ecology is thus uniquely both a descriptive and a normative science. It can not only tell us how to do something in the world but also tell us what to do and whether. As conservationism has increasingly come to be seen in North Atlantic societies as an inadequate way of perceiving and organizing the natural world, ecology has emerged as the dominant natural philosophy. It has also become, Bramwell argues, a new political category, with its own history and ideology, and right and left wings.

❂

The shift from nature to science programs on TV also has to do with the economics of the entertainment industry. The drug-and-tag movies that flourished in the 1970s were in decline a decade later. Their rise had been due in part to a loophole in U.S. broadcasting regulations that allowed nature shows to be exempted from the requirement that one hour of prime time be given over to non-network programming. Once the rule was dropped, the costly nature shows were simply unable to compete for ratings. Science series, on the other hand, have done well. They're cheaper to make, especially since they're popular in Europe (particularly in Germany and England) and can be co-produced with state television agencies there. European co-production has also introduced a different aesthetic to U.S. nature shows, moving them away from quick cutting and melodrama.

There are limits to science journalism. While it is relatively easy for a program like *Nova* to describe bear mating or criticize the whaling industry (now a negligible business compared to whale tourism), the subject of nuclear power has proved impossible for the program to discuss with any integrity. An episode entitled *Back to Chernobyl* (1988) bills itself as "a behind-the-scenes look at the accident and its aftermath." The program is lavish in its descriptions of the 1986 nuclear meltdown in the Ukraine. It shows how entire contaminated forests were cut down and buried in concrete. The robots shipped to the plant to help with the cleanup were unable to be used because their transistors were sensitive to radiation. Some fifty thousand humans, working ninety-second shifts, filled in. Nearly twenty countries received a full spectrum of radioactive fallout, and radioactive material travelled half-way around the world. Estimates of cancer related to the disaster range from two thousand to a half-million cases.

The program mocks Soviet experts who maintain that a meltdown could only happen once every ten thousand years and then tells us with a straight face that "it couldn't happen here." It makes no mention of the several plants identical to Chernobyl that the U.S. military operates for weapons production. When it comes time to evaluate what happened at Chernobyl, the program shrouds itself in objectivity. While acknowledging a widespread opposition to nuclear power, even among many governments, it incessantly invokes the authority of the nuclear priesthood. These aging men — a vestige of the dominance of physics in traditional twentieth-century science — see room for hope. They argue, "We've survived the worst nuclear accident, with modest but not catastrophic results; that's a good start for doing better, for improving safety."

Environmental Advocacy

In recent years many nature films and TV shows have adopted an overtly political stance. The model is the humane investigative science journalism of *The Nature of Things,* produced by the Canadian Broadcasting Corporation. The Canadian nature-TV work occupies a kind of middle ground between the pastoral and scientistic poles of the U.S. tradition. The Canadian films are produced by public agencies — usually the National Film Board or the CBC. The social strategies they develop thus assume the existence of national and public debate on these issues in Canadian society at the same time as they try to articulate regional cultures. *The Nature of Things* has been around since 1960. Hosted by dissident geneticist and journalist David Suzuki since 1975, the show deftly combines science, natural history, and political culture. Its programs are consistently critical of the way science and popular aesthetics talk about nature. Its productions contain no majestic and unpeopled landscapes, no uncharted regions full of bounty. Instead the programs talk about nature in the full social, moral, and spiritual context of human history.

A late-1980s episode, *The Great Lakes: Troubled Waters,* engages politics rather than beauty or paeans to industrialism. The program summarizes current environmental issues in the Great Lakes basin: industrial toxins, agricultural runoff, erosion, and loss of habitat. It quickly dismisses a technical fix: "Science won't give us answers for seventy-five years. By that time we'll all be statistics." Its discussion engages cultural issues, talking about how the Great Lakes region offers its inhabitants "a sense of place." It says that "having lost our spiritual link with nature, unlike the Natives who once lived here," we have to reinvent that important sense of place. Another program, *Manitoba Wetlands,* argues that it's pointless to talk about an ecosystem without reference to humans. It directly relates the loss of wetland habitat and the consequences for human societies to current agricultural practices.

In 1985 David Suzuki and the CBC produced an ambitious eight-part mini-series called *A Planet for the Taking.* Co-written by Suzuki, William Whitehead, and John Livingston, the program is an eclectic and intelligent historical overview of Western science and technology. Surprisingly philosophical while still being accessible, the show emphatically rejects the domination of nature that has been the mission of North Atlantic societies for the past five hundred years. It argues that humans are part of the natural world, rather than outside of or above it.

The National Film Board has produced a "Perspectives in Science" series for school kids that tries to situate science within a social context. Program topics include biotechnology, acid rain, ecofeminism, multinational corporations and the environment, water quality, and agriculture. Studio D, a women's production office at the NFB, has made a number of films examining nature and gender.

In recent years TV specials have been produced by some of the large U.S. environmental organizations, among them the National Wildlife Federation and the Audubon Society. A 1989 Audubon program, *Arctic Refuge: Vanishing Wilderness?,* narrated by Meryl Streep, cogently examined the debate about further resource development along the North Slope of Alaska. Unlike National Geographic projects, this program did not back away from political issues and in fact thoroughly examined the relationship between Arctic ecology and North American consumption levels.

Social Anthropology Movies

While nature and wildlife films produced over the past ten years have slowly taken up social questions, another film genre has come to nature from the other end, that of human history. These films, which I very loosely call social anthro-pology movies, demonstrate how difficult it has become to represent nature as uninhabited or "wild." Like biologists, anthropologists have taken movie cam-eras to the field with them for a long time. Some of their movies — the earliest probably being Robert Flaherty's *Nanook of the North* (1922) — have reached a broad audience. In the years that followed the Canadian centennial, the National Film Board made a series of short movies that documented the cultures of the Inuit and Cree. Movies such as *Group Hunting on the Spring Ice* or *Tuktu and His*

Animal Friends (both made in 1967, around the time of Disney's *Hang Your Hat on the Wind*), and *Cree Hunters of Mistassini* (1974) were sensitive attempts to combine human and natural history for the classroom and TV. They provide no voiceover, no explanation, no translation of Native languages. What we see is simply a putatively primitive people going about their everyday lives. The strength of the NFB movies was that they encouraged an encounter with "the other," in much the same way that the Disney movies attempted to show us the "unknowable" aspects of nature. Again like the Disney work, the NFB movies were marred by a naive attempt at realism that erased the presence of the field-worker or observer. As powerful as they were, the movies were also deeply conservative — and mistaken — in their understanding of aboriginal cultures as static and unchanging and thus doomed in a modern industrial world.

The Tuktu movies were part of a series that attempted to tell "a story of the old days, when people were different from us." A man at the edge of a fire would tell stories of the world as it used to be, when Tuktu's friends were as likely animals as humans. Just as in many TV nature programs it is a young boy who is our entrée to this world of the primitive, of harmony with the world and kinship with animals and other life. The films' introductory remark — that "a minimum of reconstruction is required to film the traditional life of these people" who have had "little contact with white men" — links them to the conservation films. And like the animals and ecosystems that were their subjects, by the time the Tuktu movies were made, Inuit culture had already gone through generations of changes as a result of contact with Europeans — changes unacknowledged by the film.

Things changed further between 1967 and 1974. *Cree Hunters of Mistassini,* made by the NFB for the aptly-named Department of Indian Affairs and Northern Development, was more of a political intervention. Its subject was a modern hunting society in the James Bay area of northern Quebec, a region about to be transformed by a massive hydroelectric development. The film argues that the planned roads and dams and river diversions (and reversals) would destroy Cree society.

The narrator explains that Sam Blacksmith has allowed film crews on his land "to record the quality and dignity of native life." The movie methodically discusses what it means to be part of a subsistence economy in the northern woods. In winter families fly north for six months to hunt and build winter lodges, set traps, skin beavers and rabbits, make clothing, canoe paddles, and toboggans, and navigate the lakes and rivers. We learn that family hunting territories were a cultural adaptation to Western society, but that old land-management strategies, like monitoring game yields and sharing trap lines while the land restores itself, remain.

The movie provides a sense of the complicated web of kinship, land tenure, and wildlife management. At a communal bear feast, part of the food is given to the fire, and care is taken that children and elders get plenty. The Crees bring out drums and sing hunting songs, and three families — sixteen people — pose for the camera. They keep bear bones for the dogs and rub bear grease into hair and guns. At the end of the film a family leaves on foot for its land. "The women will be walking with us, and we will be taking our time."

❂

Throughout the 1980s a number of feature-length movies and TV mini-series explored the natural world in a way that foregrounded human culture and history. *Clan of the Cave Bear* (1986), *Quest for Fire* (1981), and *Koyaanisqatsi* (1983) are examples of this genre. One of the most ambitious films was *Millennium: Tribal Wisdom and the Modern World,* a ten-part Canadian TV series produced by Richard Meech and Michael Grant and shot in Latin America, Australia, Asia, Africa, and North America. The program was sold to Global TV, the BBC, the Australian Broadcasting Corporation, and PBS, to be aired in early 1992. It is hosted by David Maybury-Lewis, a Harvard anthropologist who also heads Cultural Survival, a Massachusetts foundation (and journal) promoting the survival of indigenous peoples throughout the world. In North America its coverage includes the Mohawk, Ojibway-Cree, and Navaho, all of whom are in the middle of bitter political campaigns against military occupation and resource extraction on their lands.

The script is a synthesis of current issues in anthropology, ecology, and cultural theory. While it is driven by a discussion of contemporary tribal societies, it consistently refers back to the historical and contemporary concerns of the West. Through wide-ranging discussions of ecology, art, power, religion, economy, science and magic, and ideas of self and community, the program carefully critiques modern thinking and modern life. One of its themes is that, far from being victims of modern life, tribal cultures have much to teach us in the West. Cultural survival, the movie argues, is now bound up with ecological survival; both depend on the reintegration of nature, culture, and technology.

All of these movies raise questions about what, exactly, a "nature movie" is. Behind that question lie others, namely, what is nature and what has it to do with us? These have become pressing questions in the last years of the twentieth century, and they are not easy to answer — although contemporary popular culture is full of attempts to deal with the issues. Too often, many of those attempts simply collapse the terms, equating the natural with the tribal, the biological and the "primitive." Examples would include *The Gods Must Be*

A scene from Millennium, a ten-part TV series that examines the relations betweeen tribal and industrial societies. Movies like this make us ask what a "nature movie" is – or can be. Here, a Makuna man and his son fish in the Amazon basin. The Makuna do not farm near the river banks, which they believe belong to the fish. Ecological knowledge is often fully integrated with traditional cultures.

Crazy (1980), *Greystoke: The Legend of Tarzan, Lord of the Apes* (1984), *Iceman* (1984), *The Emerald Forest* (1985), *Where the River Runs Black* (1986), *Mountains of the Moon* (1989), as well as such Werner Herzog work as *Aguirre: Wrath of God* (1972), *Fitzcarraldo* (1982), and *Where the Green Ants Dream* (1984). At the end of the day, their well-meaning attempts to critique modern civilization differ little from the neocolonialist laments for "a vanishing culture" familiar from the full-colour pages of *National Geographic*.

☉

Among the many types of recent nature movies there are two noteworthy tendencies. The first is a willingness to do something more deeply political than merely argue for conservation. For instance, the fairly traditional movie *Never Cry Wolf* (1983), based on the book by Farley Mowat and coproduced by a private Canadian company and the Disney studios, tries to imagine a world in which humans and animals can once again be proximate, a world in which all life is interrelated and yet autonomous. For the film's main character, a white government biologist, this happens through an encounter with Native culture, which here — unlike in many of the movies noted above — speaks in its own voice without being fashioned as "primitive." To come back to the idea of the eye and its organization of the landscape: one thing that happens in *Never Cry*

Wolf is that the look is reversed. The movie often shows the biologist from the wolf point of view.

Usually animals are the observed. The fact that they can observe us as well has lost all significance in everyday life. At the zoo, animals don't return our intense stares; they're too set apart from the world. But on video and film we can make them return our look (something Disney is famous for) as if they could speak to us. Thus in some contemporary explorations of nature, it is not so much yet another frontier that is charted and explored as it is the memory of an archaic habitat — a time and a place where we could communicate with animals. In films like these, our looking at nature became a looking *back* (or out) to a world in which human cultures have a precise knowledge of their habitats.

The other recent tendency in nature movies — and it is very much related to the first — is the reintroduction of the social into depictions of the natural world. Two recent French films with wide North American distribution, *The Claw and The Tooth* and *The Bear* (1989), seem to once again raise questions about the historical function of anthropomorphism in North American cultures. *The Claw and the Tooth* is an eye-opening documentary about the large East African mammals long familiar from TV and movies. This time, however, we see all of their bodily functions. The movie is full of sex and death, eating and shitting — in short, everything Disney didn't show us. But while the theme of this movie encourages a biological sympathy with lions and antelopes, its aesthetic strategies at once distance us from them. The movie was shot mostly at night, with bright lights like those used in the viewing areas at a safari resort. The filmmakers say the animals get used to the lights with time — a comment that confuses the animals' awareness of filming with a comprehension of it.† In any event, this technique wrenches them from the familiar brown and green context of the African savannah. Bathed in white light against a black background, the animals take on a life that is outside the conventions of realism.

The Bear was made in 1988 by Jean-Jacques Annaud, the director of *Quest for Fire*. It's about the adventures of an orphaned bear cub after his mum was killed in a rock slide. Here again, the acts of eating, farting, fucking, and sleeping are prominent. The bear cub dreams and even has an acid trip after eating some psilocybe mushrooms. Both of these sequences are filmed in wonderfully chintzy animation. There are other ruptures. Despite its Disney theme, the movie explicitly locates itself in human history. Its opening shot of the Canadian Rockies is identified as being British Columbia in 1885. After some scenes that

---

† This is not very different from the "laboratory in the orchard" films where animal performance is presented as animal behaviour.

*A moose relocation
underway at Mew Lake,
Ontario.*

establish the bear cub's story, the movie shifts to the arrival in the area of a small group of hunter-trappers, perhaps scouts for a European settlement party. As the plot develops, the point of view shifts back and forth between human and bear protagonists. While the human plot uses the conventions of the adventure movie, the bear plot is not self-consciously organized around the seasons or other allegories of pristine nature. In Disney's work, the cycle of the seasons — "always enthralling, never changing" — sits in for real historical change. Nature rarely changes in Disney: there is little depiction of succession, fires, or disturbance. In this way, the Disney movies function as an analogue for conventional ideas about the "unchanging nature" of human society. In *The Bear,* on the other hand, there is at least an attempt to locate the movie's "nature" within human culture, to relate natural history to the conventions of time.

As we might expect, the plots converge and bear and human "inevitably" meet. But here again there are surprises. One of the men wants to kill the bear, the other suggests capturing it for a zoo. The movie's titles had included the motto "The greatest thrill is not to kill but to let live," along with an endorsement by the American Humane Society and the World Wildlife Fund. While the imputation of a conservation ethic to one of the hunters may seem anachronistic, the turn in the plot allows the movie to flirt briefly with the conventions of the drug-and-tag movies. The cub is captured and tied to a tree under the guard of a vicious dog. The presence of the dog — and the threat of incarceration in a zoo — allows us to ponder the role of pets as an intermediate species, as intervenors and protectors of humans. In the end, the bear escapes, not to a life of "freedom" in the wilderness but to bear society.

Both of these movies return to anthropomorphism as a cultural strategy for addressing relations between humans and the natural world. John Livingston, a Canadian naturalist, argues that anthropomorphism is a way of seeing wildlife in a human light: that is, in terms of dominance and submission. Many of the movies we have looked at here use human criteria to impose interspecies rank and order on the rest of the world, a notion very likely inconceivable — and certainly incomprehensible — to non-human species. Livingston criticizes the "inferred despotism" of animal study and argues that human observation of animal society often mistakes compliance for submission.

Yet I wonder if an historical appreciation of anthropomorphism doesn't reveal other things at work. At the very least, Disney's anthropomorphism allows animals to be addressed as *social* beings, and nature as a *social* realm. This suggests a breach in the species-barrier between human and animal. The conservation and preservation documentaries insist on that barrier and reject the possibility of interspecies intimacy — a possibility suggested in *Never Cry Wolf.* Anthropomorphism is thus not a program, but an historical and strategic intervention, a step on the way to understanding that the wall between humans and the natural world is not an absolute. It is permeable, movable, shifting, able occasionally to be leaped over — as it always has been by hags and shamans.

Wildlife movies are documents of a culture trying to come to terms with what Bill McKibben calls "the end of nature." Their short history is one of intricately overlain traditions: animal fables, technological fetishism, dissident science, sea and adventure stories, and conservationism. Nature is alternately (and sometimes simultaneously) understood as refuge, community, and commodity.

The history of these movies is thus a figure for the many histories this book wants to tell: cultural, biogeographical, environmentalist, and technological. They have moved from the North American West, to Africa and the North, and back again to North America as the land and its meanings have changed. The movies have both anticipated and responded to the ideas of the environmental movement, and their televised images have helped to organize the way we experience the natural world. Here and there they demonstrate the possibility of entering into social relations with that world.

The surviving icon of the 1964 New York World's Fair, Flushing Meadows, Queens. Photograph by Rose Kallal.

5. Technological Utopias
World's Fairs and Theme Parks

[Modernity is] the guiding principle of a system of social control which justifies its dynamism and its notion of progress by repeating ad nauseam *the litany of constant improvement and technological happiness through unlimited consumption.*
— Michèle Mattelart, *Women, Media and Crisis: Femininity and Disorder*

Built and torn down within a few years' time, world's fairs are telescoped models of industrial hyperdevelopment.

— Edward Ball, *Village Voice*

More than anything else, the monumental splendour of scores of trade fairs, expositions, and amusement and theme parks from the mid-nineteenth century to the present has revealed our shifting and contradictory responses to the land. Inscribed in their very grounds is a popular history of the organization of the landscape — urban, rural, suburban, utopian, collective, public and private — and of the tensions between real and ideal space in the North American imagination. The history of these expositions is closely linked to the history of advertising as well as to the time and place each was built. Chicago 1893, New York 1939, Montreal 1967, Vancouver 1986 (as well as all the many theme-park developments of the intervening years): all of these fairs mark shifts in cultural expression, geopolitics, and the spatial organization of the North American continent.

It used to be that world's fairs engaged landscape in a specific way. At one time they were full of model cities and suburbs, and demonstrations of new agricultural processes. In recent years the fairs have all but obscured the land itself through their focus on technology. This shift from geography to technology can be seen in the move towards outer space in fair themes. The subject is no longer where we live. The "new frontier" is somewhere else, an abstract alibi: the atmosphere, the impenetrable depths of the ocean, or "communications." While technology still organizes ideas about the land, explicit references to the land as habitat are now usually left to theme parks to develop.

The New York World's Fair
In Flushing Meadows in the first days of the Second World War, U.S. industry unveiled its vision of a capitalist utopia. The 1939 New York World's Fair, with

its theme "The World of Tomorrow," introduced television, domestic air conditioning, and any number of other objects that would eventually fill the homes and lives of North Americans during the postwar years. But the fair did more than promote commodities. It anticipated many of the conflicts that are in part the subject of this book: conflicts over the meaning of the North American earth and over the range of utopian ideas the culture is able to invest in that earth.

. The New York World's Fair consciously drew upon American utopian thought. Its vision of industrial society was that of a world whose citizens were now free from the necessity of arduous labour for the sake of subsistence. By the year 1960, the fair promised, there would be boundless leisure time for all U.S. citizens, and indeed for all humanity. The car, the highway, the fluorescent light, and the household appliance were to be the mass-distributed expressions of equality. "It is important to remember," the narration at one exhibit intoned, "that the people of 1960 will have more time, more energy and more tools to have fun." The new technology would democratize society from top to bottom. The automobile was perhaps the most critical component of these hopes; and as we've seen the intervening years have made clear the immense role — both liberating and destructive — it has played in the transformation of the North American landscape.

The landscape was in fact the subject of many of the fair's exhibits, as it had been the subject of much of the work of U.S. intellectuals from the late nineteenth century through to the New Deal. Urban reform and planning, the parks movement, model towns, the various regional movements — all of these were responses, whether traditional or progressive, to the dissolution of an agrarian order in the United States and its replacement in the early years of the century by an urban-industrial complex.

The New York fair introduced these polemics to the general public. The most visited exhibit was General Motors' Futurama, a large-scale model of a future city influenced by two projects of the Swiss-born Modernist architect Le Corbusier: the Contemporary City of 1922 and the Ville Radieuse of 1935. In both plans, the city centre is the intersection of two superhighways surrounded by symmetrically placed skyscrapers.

Housed within the Perisphere — which with the Trilon was the symbol of the fair — was Democracity, another model landscape. Its site plan was drawn from Ebenezer Howard's radial-plan Garden City designs and Frank Lloyd Wright's models for Broadacre City, which were built by his students in Arizona in the early 1930s. Here again, the automobile, which for Wright was the supreme expression of American individualism and freedom, was paramount. Democracity was traversed by expressways that whisked drivers from the classicist city centre (a concession to the City Beautiful movement that Wright would have abhorred) past the surrounding greenbelt, suburbs, and industrial ring and into natural preserves.

This road-link to the natural world, which made more ideological than practical sense, was to "contribute to the definition of a native American culture." Thus the very plan of Democracity attempted to resolve the myth of the American frontier with the demands of a high-technology industrial society. Precarious at best, it was a resolution not to be attempted again so assiduously until the 1956 opening of Disneyland in California.

In the popular imagination, the inventor and hobbyist assumed a crucial role in this resolution. Neither political theorists nor dreamers, the applied scientists working in the laboratories and basements of the nation would privately produce the products and tools necessary to usher in a future of leisure. This popular vision of the future turned its attention, then, to a rising commodity culture rather than to the idea of radically different social and ecological relations. "Quality for all" had been Wright's dictum. For him, it was a promise informed by the Arts and Crafts movement and the history of American "inventiveness." Yet in an increasingly massified U.S. society, that promise could no longer be realized, as it had once been, in the self-sufficient utopian communities of the rural United States.

The promise of quality for all was now the promise of two peculiar and contradictory spaces in the U.S. landscape. On the one hand was the utensil-laden home, bursting with new petrochemical products that promised miracles. On the other was the pristine wilderness areas of the national parks — all that remained of the frontier by 1939. Strangely, neither of these spaces made sense without the other. The utopian impulse of the fair was to reconcile this paradox, to forge an indigenous, bountiful, and egalitarian society consonant with a persistent though by that time largely baseless nostalgia for the land. Those hopes would not emerge intact after the Second World War.

The Canadian pavilion at the 1939 fair put the land right up front, as usual. Its interior displays were overseen, aptly enough, by W.D. Euler, the minister of trade and commerce. The main feature was a huge copper map of the country presenting the main points of interest to its U.S. neighbours: hydro projects, forests, mineral deposits, agricultural areas, tourist destinations, shipping routes, and RCMP detachments. Nowhere on the map was there mention of social or cultural institutions, or even of the people who lived among the bountiful resources of Canada. A two-sided mural, "Canada at Work" and "Canada at Play," continued the invitation to foreign investment that was to be the legacy of the Mackenzie King Liberal government. "Canada at Work" depicted a giant power plant generating electricity for industry. In "Canada at Play" the railway hotels

Main Steet U.S.A., Disney World. In this replica of the original Disneyland, the American small town stands at the centre of the park, reconciling "America" with the world.

and Rocky mountain lakes familiar from calendars beckoned sightseers northward to a vacant land ripe for the picking.

The 1939 fair's theme of "Building the World of Tomorrow" was a dictum that Robert Moses, who worked on the fair and was just rising to power in New York at the time, would take literally and spend a lifetime putting into practice. The vast American suburb Moses and his many disciples so doggedly promoted has long since swallowed up the splendid indigenous buildings designed by Wright and others — and with them their distorted visions of a new U.S. society.

Disneyland

It would be difficult to overemphasize the importance of Disneyland in the American imagination. Opened in 1956 in Anaheim, a then-distant suburb of Los Angeles, Disneyland was the Californian fair, a celebration (much belated because of World War II) of Los Angeles as a non-urban city.

Disneyland is organized around Main Street U.S.A., a facsimile of an early-century small town. Situated at the entrance to the park and extending to a circular plaza where paths to other amusements converge, Main Street U.S.A. is the spatial mediator between "America" and all the other cultures and landscapes of the park. Thus the American small town, and the American popular culture it represents, is capable of reconciling Amazonia with the terrain of the

A new freeway, Los Angeles Basin, 1956. Disneyland was built on citrus groves, and popularized the new geographies of cloverleaf and shopping centre.

moon; the Wild West with medieval fantasy; and an imaginary pre-bourgeois agrarian society with the L.A. freeway.

Like the fairs before it, Disneyland is history in the service of the market. But that history in turn, as French theorist Louis Marin has argued, is an imaginary one: Disneyland is the geographical representation not of American history itself but of an imaginary relationship that the dominant groups of U.S. society have with their history. "I don't want the public to see the world they live in while they're in the park," wrote Disney, who himself lived in an apartment above Main Street U.S.A. "I want them to feel they're in another world." The Pirates of the Caribbean, Cinderella's Castle, the Jungle Cruise, Frontierland — these are all familiar fantasies organized (or "illusioneered" as they say at Disney) to become with all the other "attractions" part of a larger narrative, the history of U.S. capital. The Jungle Cruise is a good example. For Disney publicists, it's "a favorite attraction among armchair travelers."

It compacts into ten minutes the highlights, mystique, fun and excitement of an adventure that could only be duplicated through weeks on safari. Best of all, it has none of the mosquitoes, monsoons, and other misadventures of the "not always so great" outdoors.

This brand of "spruced up reality" is integral to the Disney Theme Show. As a key designer said, "The environments we create are more utopian, more romanticized, more like the guest imagined they would be. For the most part, negative elements are discreetly eliminated, while positive aspects are in some cases embellished to tell the story more clearly.

On the Jungle Cruise, the gaze of American pop culture penetrates the dense canopy of the tropical landscape and finds, not fruit plantations or tin mines or the vestiges of ancient ecological societies, but "crocodiles, fearsome natives and ancient Asian temples": simulacra of local pasts now increasingly transnationalized. In the collapsed time and space of the adjoining gift shop, imported commodities become the displaced souvenirs of a trip through history never taken.

In Tomorrowland, the Disney imagineers turned their attention to the future. At the replicated Tomorrowland at Disney World in Florida, much of the discourse of the future current in the postwar period — and later popularized by the Jetsons and Robert Moses's 1964 New York World's Fair — has been preserved intact: superhighways, space ships to the moon, orange-and-aqua-coloured monorails. There are more recent futures too: pitches for nuclear power from concealed speakers and a natural foods snack bar sponsored by Tenneco, a food, oil, and agriculture transnational corporation. Yet by the mid-1970s, Tomorrowland could no longer adequately represent the penetration of technology, particularly the new telematics, into everyday life in North American society. That representation — celebratory, mythologizing, both genuinely enjoyable and suffocating — would only come alive at EPCOT Center.

Expo 67 and the Culture of Expertise

Not to be outdone, Canada has staged two important world's fairs since the Second World War: Expo 67 in Montreal and Expo 86 in Vancouver. But these fairs are notably different from the U.S. extravaganzas, mostly because the Canadian relation to land and technology is deeply ambivalent.

Canadians inhabit the physical and electronic margins of the U.S. empire, and the modernity (and post-modernity) of the United States saturate Canadian culture. Living in a specific time and space — an urban society thinly strung out along the U.S. border, with a vast and sparsely populated hinterland — Canadians experience a natural world as mediated by an accumulation of agricultural, industrial, resource, and transport technologies. The political cohesion of the country has always depended on the control that technology has been able to assert over a vast land and its many nations and cultures.

At the same time, Canadian and especially aboriginal and Québécois cultures have always struggled to remain outside of and positioned to some extent against the U.S. project — to emancipate modernity from within, or to preserve

Both Canadian fairs examined some of these tensions between technology, geography, and nationality. Expo 67, produced to mark the centennial of
Canadian confederation, was part of a year of celebrations and public-works projects that included train, truck, and canoe caravans that crossed the country
with exhibits of the history of Canada. Yet if 1967 was a time of celebration for
some Canadians, it was also a time of crisis. In Quebec, the host province of
Expo 67, a movement for self-determination had broad and growing support
among the francophone community. In that same year the Laurendeau-Dunton
Commission on Bilingualism and Biculturalism had issued a report calling for

*The Canada Pavilion at
Expo 67, Montreal.
The fair's memorable
architecture imposed
social order on a fractious
society in the throes of
industrial development.*

"equal partnership" in the collective institutions of Canada. Fearing the deepening crisis, the Liberal government passed national legislation establishing both French and English as official languages. For the federalists soon to come to power around Pierre Trudeau in Ottawa, the future of Canada lay along the continentalist path of growth, industrial expansion, and progress. Expo 67 was their invitation to Quebec to join the technological society of North America and leave behind what they openly regarded as its infantile ethnicity.

The demands for self-determination in Quebec were the most obvious threat to the federalist vision of the Canadian nation. There were other dissenters too. At the official "Centennial Birthday Party" in Vancouver on July 1, 1967, Chief Dan George read his "Lament for Confederation":

How long have I known you, Oh Canada? A hundred years? Yes, a hundred years. And many many seelanum more. And today, when you celebrate your hundred years, oh Canada, I am sad for all the Indian people throughout the land. For I have known you when your forests were mine; when they gave me my meat and my clothing. I have known you in your streams and rivers where your fish flashed and danced in the sun where the waters said come, come and eat of my abundance. I have known you in the freedom of your winds. And my spirit, like the winds, once roamed your good lands. But in the long hundred years since the white men came, I have seen my freedom disappear like the salmon going mysteriously out to sea. The white man's strange customs which I could not understand, pressed down upon me until I could no longer breathe.

When I fought to protect my land and my home, I was called a savage. When I neither understood nor welcomed this way of life, I was called lazy. When I tried to rule my people, I was stripped of my authority.

My nation was ignored in your history books — they were little more important in the history of Canada than the buffalo that ranged the plains. I was ridiculed in your plays and motion pictures, and when I drank your fire-water, I got drunk — very, very drunk. And I forgot.

Oh Canada, how can I celebrate with you this Centenary, this hundred years? Shall I thank you for the reserves that are left to me of my beautiful forests? For the canned fish of my rivers? For the loss of my pride and authority, even among my own people? For the lack of my will to fight back? No! I must forget what's past and gone.

Oh, God in Heaven! Give me back the courage of the olden Chiefs. Let me wrestle with my surroundings. Let me again, as in the days of old, dominate my environment. Let me humbly accept this new culture and through it rise up and go on.

This was hardly the first time a Native elder had denounced European domination of the North American soil and its first peoples. Yet Dan George's message was scarcely heard, for at the time it was obliterated by the cacophony of the technological dynamo. In Canada, as elsewhere in the Western world, the 1960s brought great physical as well as cultural change. Based on the U.S. boom of the postwar years, government strategy was to encourage exploitation of natural resources and expand the branch-plant manufacturing infrastructure in Ontario and Quebec. New development was everywhere: in cities, in manufacturing and resource extraction, in space exploration, and in research in medicine, petrochemicals, electronics, and agriculture.

Many of these developments involved the introduction of new technologies to the land. This was most visible in the part of Canada least colonized at that time: the North. By the mid-1960s government and industry were committed to greatly increased development of mineral, hydrocarbon, and timber resources throughout the northern edges of the provinces as well as in both territories. It was during these years, too, that Canada signed a number of military agreements with the United States — including the Distant Early Warning system and NORAD. This massive technological transformation would have a tremendous effect on the northern landscape and the way we perceive it.

Expo 67 was a first-category exhibition (the first in the Americas), meaning that it was to be "universal" in both theme and participation. The theme of the fair, which is now often referred to as the best ever, was "Terre des Hommes/Man and his World," from the title of a book by Antoine de Saint-Exupéry. The fair attempted to examine the full range of relationships between humankind and environment. These were explored in a series of theme pavilions: Man the Explorer, Man the Producer, Man the Creator, Man in the Community, Man and his Health, Man the Provider, Labyrinth, and Habitat 67. This was the discourse of the United Nations, and it presaged the idea of a multicultural Canada in a multinational world that would be promoted by the Trudeau government in the early 1970s.

Expo 67 had a strong architectural presence, as if to impose a model of social order and corporate vision on a fractious society in the throes of massive development. Today it is the individual buildings that visitors recall most vividly. Many of the pavilions introduced new architectural forms to popular culture, such as Arthur Erikson's pyramid at the Man in the Community pavilion, Buckminster Fuller's geodesic dome at the U.S. pavilion, and the parabolic plastic tent of the West German pavilion. Man in the Home was a "model house for modern living" sponsored by *Chatelaine* magazine. According to the *Expo 67 Official Guide,* features included a "gardening center, sewing center, swimming pool and forever-green man-made lawn that you vacuum, never cut or water."

A more serious project was Moshe Safdie's Habitat 67, a prefabricated concrete housing complex at Cité du Havre along the north shore of the St. Lawrence. Safdie explained that the building was modelled on the ancient idea

of a village by a river. As more people settled there, the village grew organical-
ly: people added stories to the buildings and expanded the settlement out along
winding paths and past small squares. It was an intriguing experiment, and
although Habitat is one of the few fair buildings still standing and is a popular
place to live, its ideas have never been replicated.

The Man the Explorer complex was divided into exhibits on space, the
oceans, and the polar regions. The Man the Producer pavilion raised questions
about resources, progress, and control. The emphasis throughout the fair's
pavilions was on the progress of science and its broad social benefits. Designers
made lavish use of kinetic displays, photographic collage, and multi-screen film
in highlighting postwar advances in production technologies. But the exhibitors
made the same old promises, only this time in the "universal" language of a non-
U.S. fair: with automation, computers, and modern medicine, with all the new
tools at our disposal, the guidebook promised, "Man is moving towards an era
where working hours will be less and leisure hours will be substantially more
than at this moment of time." In both form and content, Expo 67 was a model
of the technological humanism then being popularized by Marshall McLuhan.

"How long can Man go on meeting ever-increasing needs for energy
and raw material to serve the world's soaring population?" This was a question
frequently asked in the theme pavilions. The answers were, not surprisingly,
optimistic: with proper management, there was plenty for all.

Private-sector industries echoed this call for expertise. International
Nickel, Polymer, Kodak, Air Canada, Canadian National, Alcan, and Canadian
Pacific-Cominco built buildings and public spaces where they hawked their own
versions of the future. So did consortiums of steel producers, breweries, and
manufacturers of pulp and paper, asbestos products, and telecommunications
equipment.

Expo 67 was built in a park-like setting on two artificial islands in the St.
Lawrence River, just opposite the city centre. Fair promoters like Montreal
mayor Jean Drapeau heralded the creation of the grounds out of "water and a
few rocks" as an example of the magic technology could accomplish. The parks
themselves functioned as a passive, non-programmed space for relaxation. There
were places to picnic, and naturalized areas were set aside for wildlife to reinhabit. But while our shared history with the natural world was actively explored
in the hightoned theme pavilions of Man and His World, it was ignored in the
manufactured pastoral landscapes of the park itself.

Expo planners separated off rides, nightclubs, and other amusements at
La Ronde, at the far end of Ile Sainte-Hélène. Recreation areas at La Ronde
included an aquarium, Pioneerland-Fort Edmonton, an "old-time" French-
Canadian village, and a "safari-jungle." This jumble of amusements underscored

the difficulty of exploring the tension between technology and geography. The harmonious human settlements touted in the pavilions were repudiated in the real space of the fairgrounds.

Looking back now, nearly twenty-five years later, the naive optimism of Expo 67 seems curious. Outside of the work of Walt Disney, which has its own peculiar logic, it would be difficult to mount such an exhibition today. It's not only the "man-made lawn"; the shallow soul-searching of the fair now rings hollow because too much has happened in the interim. Communications technologies have done nothing to strengthen democratic institutions. Increased productive capacity has brought unemployment, despondence, and habitat destruction instead of an end to scarcity. Unlike Habitat 67, our urban housing hasn't "answered the suburban dream of gardens" and has not led to community solidarity. For its part, McLuhan's global village has turned out to be a model for "free trade" and militarization rather than for cultural exchange.

The technological utopianism promoted at Expo 67 was based on the old assumptions of the productive economy and the culture of expertise that supported it. The official response to crisis — whether social, industrial, economic, or, later, ecological — was management. Hunger, poverty, and pollution, to use the terms of the day, were understood to be technical problems that could be solved with "objective" research, planning, and administration.

In retrospect, the questions so baldly posed in the Expo pavilions were the wrong ones. By 1967 the environmental movement was gaining broad-based public support — support based on a different set of values from those of the conservation movement, whose mission was the scientific and efficient use of physical resources. The consumer society that developed in the decades following the Second World War no longer only thought of air, water, and land as resources; people now understood them to be part of the quality of their everyday lives, part of the human environment.

The struggle over the meaning of the land in contemporary culture can be illustrated by a single, widely circulated image from Expo 67: the image of the Earth as seen from space. For the first time, our visual environment allowed us to imagine the planet as a single organism. Environmentalists quickly picked up the image and used it on bumper stickers, decals, logos, flags, and magazine covers. The image was commemorated on Earth Day in 1970, and it eventually penetrated advertising. It became significant in ecological theory with the publication of James Lovelock's *Gaia* in 1979.

The image of the Earth from space also signalled the wide use of "remote sensing" — a satellite photography employed by resource industries and the military. In fact, such photographs were only possible as a result of military technology. Since 1967 those industries have continued to exploit the Earth —

Africa as seen from the Apollo 17 spacecraft. Expo 67 popularized the image of the earth from space, prompting us to imagine the planet as a single organism.

as well as the Earth's entire neighbourhood — using every technical and promotional means at their disposal. The promises they made at Expo 67 — promises of wise use, of conservation, of harmony between people and environment — can no longer be believed. For resource managers, the Whole Earth image is the image of the Earth as data.

Expo 86: Megaprojects and Real Estate Development
Nearly twenty years later, at Expo 86 in Vancouver, the theme was transportation and communications, and like the world's fairs before it this one showcased

every new and exciting machine available. But fairs don't only display cars, trains, or satellites: they place those new technics in a certain context and thereby help to build a consensus about their social uses. With the optimism of Expo 67 and the McLuhan years long gone, this task has proved more difficult in recent years. It's no longer a simple matter to galvanize popular culture by touting the wonders of industrial society. The Disney organization has had to construct a virtual universe in Florida to try to convince us that technological progress will lead to human freedom and well-being.

Fairs also play a more obvious political role: like Expo 67, Expo 86 promoted the provincial government and the local economy as well as the idea of progress. In British Columbia the idea of progress turns very much on land and its development, with an economy founded on simple resource extraction. By the 1980s, a once diversified manufacturing sector had gone into decline as raw logs, natural gas, and electricity were being directly exported to Asia and the United States. The recession of the early 1980s had hit British Columbia hard. The response of the province's Social Credit government to those problems offers a glimpse of the true agenda of the hucksters of the technological revolution.

The government's first strategy was a program of deregulation and privatization of the economy, coupled with a broad curtailment of social services and human-rights safeguards. The second strategy was massive spending on megaprojects, including a large indoor-stadium complex in Vancouver, new highways, and "high-tech" coal and uranium extraction facilities in the interior. All of these failed to produce the recovery, even in official terms, that was promised. Expo 86, which cost $1.5 billion (and lost $311 million), was yet another — and the last — of these megaprojects. Its sponsors hoped the fair would provide at least a symbolic boost for public morale and private investment.

The site chosen for the exposition was saturated with these conflicts. The north shore of False Creek had become a derelict industrial area adjacent to the new financial core of Vancouver. In the nineteenth century the federal government had given the land, once the home of the Musqueam Indians, to the Canadian Pacific Railway, and until the 1960s the CPR used it for rail yards and leased out vacant portions to industries that would bring it business. After the exposition closed in late 1986, the 220-acre site on False Creek was sold, amid much controversy and scandal, to a large Hong Kong real estate developer. Later plans for the site called for the kinds of buildings going up everywhere else: corporate towers dedicated to the tertiary sector of the economy, namely, financial services and data processing.

The fair thus transformed its very site from a primary materials manufactory to a capital-intensive real estate development. World's fairs (and Olympic Games) have always been used by government and industry as land development projects — though for perhaps the first time, this strategy was met by well-organized resistance in Vancouver, from the environmental, women's, and Native movements, to the various movements that seek to empower those at the margins of urban life. By the mid-1980s the land itself had become so contested that the fair's exhibits could address it only in abstract terms. In addition, where Native culture or an unmediated nature emerged at Expo, they proved troublesome, for they foregrounded history and tradition, the *time* of the land, rather than its space, which is so easily dominated.

"World in Motion, World in Touch" was the slogan Expo producers adopted to smooth over these ruptures. The exhibits focused on communications technology, drawing on a long utopian tradition that pins social well-being on electricity and electronics rather than machines and primary industry. The fair displaced most questions about the direction of society, its future, onto the technics themselves: if a machine or process is obsolete, you replace it. This is an approach that infects most discussion of science and technology in the popular media, especially in the advertising sector. The idea is that technology is a neutral instrument that can be used for either good or ill. Who finances technological research and development, and for what reasons? These questions are nowhere raised. There were doubts — we were occasionally exhorted to "master the new tools, tame the new demons" — but on the whole the message was, "Look how far the human race has come, and where technology is taking us."

The planners of Expo 86, many of whom trained at Disney Productions, evaded social questions at every turn, opting for an abstract and optimistic celebration of technology that is all too often the impulse of science journalism. Some of the exhibits they rejected give an idea of how conservative the planners were: a giant car crusher that produced uniform metal cubes to be used to build some kind of structure; an iceberg towed from the North Pole to Vancouver harbour; a boxcar that would be lifted several hundred metres by helicopter each day at noon and dropped into False Creek. The only adventurous installation to survive was the SITE design group's *Highway 86,* a freeway overpass with two hundred monochrome vehicles embedded in the concrete.

As benign as the rejected ideas are, they might have indicated the historical dimensions of technological change. Information technologies of all kinds, for example, have been developed in a culture of militarism. The low-intensity regional wars now favoured by modern states depend upon a system of command, control, communications, and intelligence that is probably the most complex organization ever constructed. This system's hardware and software penetrate every corner of the globe. Civilian surveillance systems are equally complex in a wired society like our own. For example, police and security

forces "harvest" and analyse two kinds of information. The first is "transactional information," the routine traces our bodies leave in the electronic environment: FAX and phone calls, credit-card purchases, TV and radio reception, electricity consumption, pass-key and employee-card use. More active gathering techniques include video and audio surveillance and interactive analysis of data bases from police, tax, and credit agencies, health organizations, and so on. The advertising, marketing, and public-relations industries use these techniques of social management as well. What we find, then, is that contemporary technology is saturated with models of domination, which in turn infect our relations with the natural world. As the rationales for resource management have become more sophisticated, so too have the technologies that harvest the "data" and manage the "capital" of the Earth itself.

Expo 86, Vancouver. The fair transformed False Creek from a primary materials manufactory to a capital-intensive real estate development.

similar models
@ PLC?

❂

Early on in the fair, the Expo site was dubbed Sarnia-by-the-Sea, and with good reason. Unlike Expo 67, the Vancouver fair was intensely urban. There was no parkland on the fair site, and rides and amusements were dispersed throughout the grounds. The buildings were drenched with industrial and

A satellite released from the space shuttle Columbia by the "Canadarm." Modern warfare depends on satellites like these, but at contemporary world's fairs, discussions of technology usually ignore geopolitics.

post-industrial iconography. The choice of design vocabulary was in part inspired by the profit-making 1984 Los Angeles Olympics, which had flaunted cranes and scaffolding in a celebration of the transitory quality of the games. Expo's cartoonish struts and beams also worked to make a fetish of science, in the belief that science is the principal way to know the world and live in it. By turning science into spectacle, the fair masked the social policy of the very government that sponsored it: the restoration of free enterprise, the attack on democracy, and the cult of technocratic authority.

The other dominant design principle at Expo was something known as Media Image Anticipation, another form of social management. The object was to ensure that every vista available to a magazine photographer or TV crew be properly composed and convey the right message. This is not unlike the strategy of photo opportunities that has been widely used by heads of state since the Nixon administration.

For a sense of the place culture might have in the technological revolution, visitors were directed to Folklife, a quiet and verdant ghetto stuck in the farthest corner of the grounds. Here there was music and theatre, Native and local crafts, dancing and food. So on the one hand, throughout the fair we had "technology," which was understood to be neutral, modern, international, and fun; and then completely severed from that we had a display of something called "culture," which was coded as parochial and value-laden. Technology was understood to be the future; "Folklife" the past.

There were, however, some exceptions to the "let's party" chorus of the technological discourse. What intruded over and again at Expo was the place of nature in a technological society. And this in turn raised the issue of aboriginal cultures. There had been plans to build a Native pavilion at Expo 86, but they were cancelled as being too delicate politically. Most aboriginal people in British Columbia have never signed treaties with any Canadian government and in recent years they have contested every expansion of white culture and development in the province. As the fair was being built in Vancouver, the Nuu-Chah-Nulth were defending Meares Island from logging, the Haida had mounted a national campaign to reclaim the South Moresby area of the Queen Charlotte Islands, the Gitksan Wet'suwet'en were preparing a land-claim case in the B.C. Supreme Court, and other bands were contesting timber leases and defoliant use and track widening proposals by the railroads. In many of these conflicts, Native people formed coalitions with non-Native environmental groups.

All of these issues lurked behind the high-tech stage sets at Expo 86. Even in the extremely scientistic U.S. pavilion, for example, which was wholly dedicated to outer space, nature was present only by the fact of its utter denial. The central display was a model of a space station, which the narration blithely informed us would bring "untold benefits to mankind." In the simulated shuttle voyage to the station — which got there without blowing up — the planet Earth receded from sight until we could see only blackness outside. In the ensuing narration, that blackness got reconstructed as something foreign and threatening. Nature was no longer our home but the negative space that lay outside the fabricated and patriotic environment of the off-world space station. It was the familiar story of the frontier, only in this new chapter the planet Earth was left behind, discarded like the old winter coat of someone who retires to Florida.

Elsewhere this negation of the natural world was not so total. In the British Columbia pavilion, a Douglas fir was cut away to reveal its age. Nearby some totem poles were plunked down under a monorail. What were they doing at a fair about technology?

For one thing, the B.C. government was clearly paying lip service to Native people in a moment of deep crisis over rights to aboriginal land. But the fair's frequent, almost inadvertent references to the natural world reminded us that nature just won't go away, even when you want it to. Nature is literally the ground of all human endeavour, including the snowmobiles and radars, amphibious tundra buggies, logging helicopters, and mining ships marketed at Expo. In fact, despite all the accolades thrown at technology by Expo, nature was continually evoked and quoted there — sometimes to subdue it, other times to contain it within the anthems of tourism or national identity. Two popular pavilions at Expo explored this issue, and not co-incidentally they did so by talking about contemporary Native Canadian culture. In the Northwest Territories and General Motors pavilions, nature was constructed as something adjacent to, if not part of, our lives.

The N.W.T. pavilion was announced by an inukshuk, a traditional cairn for the Inuit people who live above the tree-line in the north. The title of the pavilion was "The Emerging North/In Search of Balance." The exhibits within were able to engage questions of technology and aboriginal culture simultaneously. The pavilion was no museum of Indian culture but a self-conscious and uncompromising examination of what it means for an ancient people to make a home in the deeply technologized North.

The General Motors pavilion also raised these issues, although in a more philosophical than political way. The GM "Spirit Lodge" consisted mostly of a nine-minute holographic show that was one of the most popular items at the fair. The show was based on the Kwakwaka'wakw culture of the central British Columbia coast and was written by the curator of their cultural centre in Alert Bay. The director and producer of the show both trained at Disney. The audience was herded into a darkened room and the show began with an elder, a story-teller, standing round a smoking fire speaking aloud. He stood on the stage in his great log house at the edge of a wood. It was raining outside, as it often is in that part of the world. The story-teller spoke, and the spirits and memories of his people shaped themselves holographically in the smoke of the fire. He said:

Welcome travellers. Welcome to The Spirit Lodge. Welcome to this pavilion. And welcome to this World's Fair on Transportation.

When I first walked through this World's Fair, I was amazed by all the machines: machines that do great things; machines that try to think like people. At first they all seemed wonderful. Then suddenly I began to feel afraid and the Fair began to look dark and my vision was no longer certain.

For I wondered, where was the heart in all this steel and glass? In these cold, thinking machines, where was the human spirit? Are our machines making us more like humans? Or more like machines? And here I paused to think.

And my thoughts carried me back to another time, long, long ago, when the old ways were strong and magic was real.

Long ago life moved just as quickly as today. Even then, life and the freedom to move were as one. To stop moving is to die. All living creatures know this.

The killer whale who migrates up and down the coast, dances to a slow, ancient rhythm that bids him first north, then south, then north again.

The wild geese also hear the call. They come and they go with the season ...

Our People knew this too.

Our people followed the food. Followed life. Whole villages moved with the seasons. All our belongings — even the planks of our houses — would be packed up and moved by canoe.

The story-teller recalled the great feasts of old, and the masks that the dancers wore. As he talked, the masks of Crooked Beak, Raven, and Thunderbird appeared in the smoke. The old man remembered a magic canoe his grandmother had told him about, and how much easier it would have made life for his people.

Towards the end he addressed Raven, the trickster and bringer of change:

Maybe all the modern changes of the last century are your trickery. Then again, perhaps change itself is an illusion, thin as smoke.

For what has really changed? Our machines have changed, but our dreams remain the same.

I took another look at this World's Fair and saw that the new science of transportation seeks nothing new. It reaches for the same old dream that my Grandmother knew was good.

It reaches for the magic canoe.

Each small improvement brings us closer to that day ...when we will only have to step inside, wish where we want to go, take one stroke ...and we'll be there.

The dream is as real and as old as life. For life and the freedom to move are as one.

The old man vanished in a bolt of lightning, taking with him Raven and Thunderbird and the rest of his world. The rest of us were ushered into a GM showroom.

This archival representation of native culture didn't begin to tackle the difficult issues presented by the Northwest Territories pavilion. I'm also sure most people noticed right away that there was a connection between the "freedom to move" and the Pontiacs we caressed on the way out of the pavilion. ("It's fun to be free!" is the slogan at the GM pavilion at EPCOT in Disney World.)

But a couple of questions nag. In trying to be the soul of Expo 86, wasn't GM at least raising the issue of technology and its introduction as an open question, as something to be debated? More to the point, how is it that it makes sense in contemporary popular culture for General Motors to act as if Native elders had something to teach us?

The Hidden Works of Disney World

Of all Disney's installations, Disney World in Orlando, Florida, calls for special attention. There the tensions and oppositions that organized earlier fairs were recast in a way that anticipated advertising and design strategies at work throughout the North American landscape. The city, the country, the public, the private, the natural — by the time Disney began its projects in Florida, and later Japan and France, those spaces had been wrenched from their historical and topographical referents and given new meanings.

The very scale of Disney World suggests its potential for a total reorganization of the landscape. In 1965, for $5.5 million, Walt Disney Productions of California secretly purchased over eleven thousand hectares of land southwest of Orlando — "enough land to hold all the ideas and plans we can possibly imagine," Uncle Walt gushed at the ground-breaking ceremony. And just as the endlessly prolix Disney publicists remind us, those ideas and plans just keep coming. At present, Disney World consists of a number of resort complexes, recreation and shopping areas, and three large theme parks: the Magic Kingdom (the resituated Disneyland of California), EPCOT (the Experimental Prototype Community of Tomorrow), which opened in late 1982; and Disney-MGM Studios Theme Park, opened in 1989. There are also housing developments, water parks, a monorail system, a conservation area, artificial lakes and streams, hotels, resorts, freeways, parking lots, something called a "Wilderness Area," ancient cities, and modern shopping centres.

Almost all of the workings of Disney World are hidden from the spectator, much as productive forces are hidden in the image of the commodity. Miles of underground corridors — "utilidors" in Disney parlance — allow workers, supplies, utilities, and telecommunications to move out to the various parts of the "total Vacation Kingdom." Storage facilities, staff cafeterias, laundries and dry cleaners, and costume and dressing rooms are all located underground throughout the site. Pneumatic tubes "whisk refuse away like magic" to compactors (where it goes from there the publicity does not mention). Service roads are concealed behind berms. On-site jet generators and solar collectors power the entire park. Nurseries and greenhouses propagate 250,000 species of flora.

Through special legal arrangements made with the State of Florida in 1967, Disney manages the Reedy Creek Improvement Area, a virtual county of Florida that is exempt from filing environmental impact statements and operates outside of the jurisdiction of municipal and regional laws regarding zoning, building codes, traffic, development, power, waste, and flood control. The Disney fiefdom is designed to withstand challenges to its global vision of the future.

Or at least that was the plan. Land speculation, graft, and scandal began within forty-eight hours of Disney's purchase of the property. As the quality of

Making a Western movie at Adventureland, in the Magic Kingdom at Disney World.

life in central Florida declined, opposition to the corporation and its special status broadened. In 1988 neighbouring Orange County had to beg $13 million from Disney to enlarge the roads leading to the park. In exchange the county agreed not to challenge the extralegal status of the park for seven years. A few months after the deal was signed in early 1990, Disney announced plans to develop another five thousand hectares with twenty-nine new "attractions" and seven hotels, almost doubling its workforce. This development would require $1 billion in public funds for roads, drainage, and sewage.

Sewage has been a particular problem for Disney. The park itself is built on a recharge area for the Floridan Aquifer, and the regional development it has encouraged has done irreparable damage to the fragile ecosystem of most of the central and southern part of the state. The wetlands now slated for development are home to many rare and endangered species, among them the indigo snake, the wood stork, and the bald eagle. The Environmental Protection Agency has fined Disney for contaminating these wetlands with toxic waste. The park's sewage effluent exceeds state guidelines, and has been found as far away as the Everglades. Disney has found it cheaper to pay fines than redesign its "state of the art" engineering systems, much of them funded with public money. The company also recently contributed $95,000 to local conservation organizations after the state laid charges of animal cruelty.

A photo opportunity at World Showcase, EPCOT Center. The view across the lake takes in the major trading partners and tourist destinations of the United States.

The Nature of Entertainment — and Commerce

Disney World employs thirty thousand people. Unless they are hired at the professional or managerial level, all staff must begin at the bottom — sweeping streets or taking tickets at minimum wage — and advance rung by rung to their desired station. Staff are trained in "efficiency, cleanliness and friendliness" — the hallmark of the organization — at the on-site Disney University. They live in the sprawling and hideous towns and cities that surround Disney World and must get to work in cars. An announcement of the PA system tells them when they can take a break. The workers the public comes into contact with — that is to say, all lower-level workers — wear uniforms. Garbage collectors wear white French legionnaire outfits and caps; monorail attendants wear chartreuse poly jumpsuits with navy plastic helmets; for gardeners it's green dungarees with white poly polo shirts and matching parkas for the rain. Waiters and ride attendants are turned out in the colours and fashions of the thematic areas they work in.

Many observers of Disney's parks have commented on their elaborate infrastructures and the rigorous control they impose on visitors. Yet Disney World marks a signal departure from Disneyland. Its intention is to represent not merely the Edenic circular space of a 1950s amusement park, but some new post-industrial, post-urban space. Like the airport or the mall, Disney World is indeed an appropriate spatial representation of transnational capital. It is at once every place and no place; it is on the land, but not of it.

What is this new space? It is first of all an anti-urban one. The dominant form at Disney World is not the city but the amorphous continuum of the exurb. The various areas of the park are linked by monorail and freeway, as if they could be distinguished as city, suburbs, country, and wilderness. Yet each of those spaces is structurally identical to the others. Emptied of their historical functions, they can only be told apart by the themes assigned to them.

The city is never explicitly represented at Disney World, except when coded as an archaic or primeval form. In an area of EPCOT called World Showcase, eight "foreign countries" have been constructed around an artificial lagoon. Most of these places are represented by boutiques and rides tarted up with clichéd architectures — an Eiffel Tower here, a Chateau Frontenac or Japanese Garden there. The human scale of these "Olde World" townscapes make for a visual comprehensibility usually absent from the modern metropolis, yet they are understood — perhaps correctly — as nostalgic constructions, as a kind of human settlement no longer possible. In Future World — a series of pavilions, also at EPCOT, that ostensibly address the future — the city is likewise absent. There are references to a Le Corbusier-style metropolis of grids, but it's only a few blinking lights seen from the car at the end of innumerable rides, silent and timeless. These are not called cities in the publicity, but "Cityscapes" — would-be cities.

The North American suburb is figured here too, but in a similarly oblique way. Disneyland had popularized the topographies of cloverleaf and shopping centre in a culture just getting used to the atomized space of what Frank Lloyd Wright had hopefully called the "country-wide, countryside city." In the 1950s, there was enough kick left in modernism for this idealized geography to mean something to people. Disney World still tries to draw on the pastoral energy of the suburb and repeatedly evokes the harmonious image of the model towns and planned communities of the early century. Yet perhaps by the 1980s those visions had been milked dry. Los Angeles, which is the spatial paradigm for a lot of Disney's work, makes considerable historical sense as a polemic against the traditional metropolis. Yet in our own day I wonder if its genuinely democratizing moment has not been overshadowed by its central place in the dystopian imagination. The sets in the movie *Blade Runner,* for example, fascinate us precisely as a critique of a social landscape Disney still takes seriously.

If the vague and shimmering models at the EPCOT pavilions are simulacra of city and suburb, the natural landscape of the park itself is likewise a "countryscape" rather than the country. The artificial lakes at Disney World are made to look like the Caribbean, the woods like a tropical rainforest or a boreal swamp. This is the exoticized locus of the package tour, rather than the matrix of agricultural production and rural culture. Disney's elaborate invasion of the future has indeed cancelled rural space. At EPCOT, experts grow food in laboratories and space stations. Agriculture is thus not only part of a corporate economy, but it also becomes a sphere of human activity that no longer has a place on the land.

A kind of frontier regional planning is at work at Disney World. Development is dispersed in space. The monorails and expressways traverse great expanses of countryside and bring crowds of people to the various centres scattered round the park. Only just as the Disney countryside is a facsimile of the pastoral, so are the various centres, once you get to them, not centres at all, but immense and isolated homages to unsuccessful modernist megaprojects like Brasilia, Chandigarh, or Duvalierville.

In vernacular architecture, it is the shopping mall that is the physical negation of both urban and rural spaces as they have been defined since the nineteenth century. This form is only possible once the agriculture, energy, and information industries are consolidated; it also epitomizes a complex of radical social changes that reach far into our everyday lives — from transportation to diet to sexuality and cultural practice. Most buildings at Disney World look, and function, like shopping malls. Disney World organizes public space according to the market; it understands private space as an architectural adjunct of individual consumption. All other forms of street life have been banished — or at least replaced by signifiers of street life. In the historicized versions of "Italy" and "Mexico" and "Britain," for example, street musicians and theatre troupes give a series of ambulatory performances that both open immense possibilities for a transformation of urban space and simultaneously reinscribe the event within a tourist framework of "days gone by."

Once the city is abandoned, so too are the rich possibilities of a diverse and eclectic human settlement. A monument to a homogeneous and massified society, Disney World has been built on the ruins of the forum. There democracy is a function of the public-opinion poll. Social and cultural diversity are absent from the visitors to the park and resolutely denied by the orthodoxies of the exhibits. The productive labour of Disney World — a figure for the multifarious economy of the city — is concealed underground. Exchange, interdependence, the struggle for power — all the everyday functions of the city have been hidden, or banished.

There is another way in which the city is negated at Disney World, and that is in its playful, spontaneous, and communal dimensions. Nowhere is this more amply demonstrated than in Spaceship Earth, the pavilion that is the symbol of EPCOT. Spaceship Earth is a giant white sphere sponsored by Bell Systems. Its central position and unmistakable allusion to Buckminster Fuller's geodesic dome suggest many of the communal spaces that U.S. utopian history is full of: a phalanstery, a 1960s pleasure pad, or at least an Oneida sitting room. But this building effectively has no interior. It's a ride, with one entrance and one exit. The promise of pleasure within was a false one; the structure denies the utopian locus of many oppositional cultures.

Nature is relentlessly evoked at Disney World, yet it is always a nature that has been worked and transformed; subsumed by the doctrine of progress. The

Conservation Area, for example, is not so much a biotic habitat as it is a release valve for the gigantic transformations of the park. The riparian Florida terrain never stands on its own; it is replicated as a golf course or parkway median. "Wilderness" is the name of an RV campground.

The land, then, is massively developed and then "renaturalized" — just like the suburbs. This process is often highlighted, even ridiculed. Designers have constructed an intersection of a canal and a highway, for example, so that the canal — which carries tourist boats — crosses over the road on a bridge. They have had hedges clipped into topiary of Disney cartoon characters. The Disney publicists call this work "whimsification," and it is the Disney way of annexing nature, of transforming nature into entertainment and inserting it into the overall modern project of development.

In the North American imagination (or at least that of its colonizing peoples), the wilderness has always been the place of the "other" in the landscape. This peculiar vision of an unpeopled natural environment only makes sense when defined against historical notions of the city. The national parks were established a century ago as preserves of an animated nature, in all its virgin immanence. Such a space was understood to be incompatible with the sordid and artificial city. As those last vestiges of primeval space came to be developed in the Reagan era, so conversely their representations were resurrected in distorted form in American culture. For example, in the Cold War TV series *Airwolf* of the early 1980s, Monument Valley and the great calendar settings of the U.S. Rockies were the theme-park headquarters of a top-secret counterinsurgency hit team. Accessible only by helicopter gunship — and the imagination — the mountains continued to dispense a mythical national identity to the defenders of U.S. soil.

At Disney World, the names of national parks are used to identify conference rooms at a hotel called the Contemporary. (All the hotels at Disney World have names like furniture: Polynesian, Sport, Venetian, Grand Floridian.) The theme at the Contemporary is Southwest American Indian. The building is shaped like an Aztec pyramid, a form repeated in the hedges that surround the parking lot. The lobby is called the Grand Canyon Concourse and has a large mural of bucolic Navajo life: kids playing with burros, families eating, bighorn sheep grazing. Turquoise and orange are the predominant colours in the decor. Bars are named after tribes, and have smart hieroglyphic wallpaper of squiggly snakes and dancing shamans. The Indian theme is an ambiguous one. After all, references to Native American culture were absent in Disney's work until the release of *Peter Pan* in the mid-1950s, and they've been sporadic since. Can those cultures now be the theme of a hotel because they're thought to be extinct? Or have we reached an historical juncture at which their voices can be heard — as if they now have something to teach us about the land?

The hotel decor is one of the few oblique references made at Disney World to the oppositional cultures that flourish outside the park. Usually they are recuperated within corporate slogans. In the film *Symbiosis* at the Kraft pavilion at EPCOT, a deep and resonant TV voice instructs us to "take charge of our technology" so we will avoid "pollution and other mistakes of the past."

The organizing principle of the Disney universe is control. It's as if every gaze of a spectator must be directed — just like in the movies. The visual perspectives, aural and olfactory terrains, the kinds of movement permitted — all reinforce and reinterpret the various strategies of transnational capital as they are represented in the themed exhibits and the organization of the site. The map of Disney World — replete with freeways and rest areas — promises a choice of tours; yet the structure of the park attempts to reduce the many possibilities to a single prescribed experience — a kind of spatial corollary of a monopoly capitalism that incessantly produces rhetoric about free enterprise. This is accomplished by a sensory blanketing that renders the environment itself seamless. Signs, sewer covers, trash cans, plantings, uniforms, colour schemes, architectures — all are coordinated, like a series of logos. They shift as you move from one area to another.

From the moment you drive into the park and a voice comes over your car radio welcoming you to Disney World, you are rarely out of earshot of an announcement, a chatty narration, a monition, or music. "Exit on your left." "Visit the unique shops in Walt Disney Village, just a monorail ride away." "Behind us lies the splendour of a lost civilization." All of these interventions shape the environment of the park, much as Muzak, fluorescent lighting, and air conditioning shape the space of a supermarket or shopping mall. By masking inappropriate ambient sound (like machinery and other people's conversations) and directing our attention to the proper object, they attempt to rid our immediate environment of the traces of work and the social aspect of life.

This sort of thematic and directed space is a common one in our society, though seldom is it so systematically applied. When we go to a corporate megashow at an art gallery, for instance, we get a tour mapped by the lighting and the linear arrangement of objects, and scripted by the headphones we rent at the entrance. But as an organizing principle, the "theme" has dominated exhibitions only recently. In the nineteenth century, displays aimed at providing encyclopedic knowledge. By the 1930s, the fair-going public met with exhibits that were organized around the dramatization of a few central ideas. Entertainment, sensation, spectacle — these had become the preferred techniques, and many of them were borrowed from the strategies of persuasion employed by advertisers of the interwar years. Consumers were flattered, encouraged, scolded, cajoled — in short, increasingly managed — by ads and department store displays as commodities began to insinuate themselves ever more intimately into everyday life. The model rooms of the large department stores — whose spatial strategies were very similar to those of the fairs and museums of today — invented an "architecture of merchandising" that eliminated physical and intellectual clutter and concentrated the client's attention on the commodity.

So what we see in Disney World is the recent history of capital relations inscribed on the land. Disney World names and replicates all the landscape types specific to this continent; but replicates them in a way that strips them down to what's intended to be their bare terms, their simplest function, namely, commerce. Disney World is the fullest representation of commodified space we have in North America. This is a relatively new landscape, historically speaking; one in which not only production and settlement are managed but also memory and desire themselves.

EPCOT Center: The Future According to Disney

The vision that was to become EPCOT — the Experimental Prototype Community of Tomorrow — obsessed Disney from the opening of Disneyland in 1956 until his death in 1966. Like Brasilia and countless other modernist projects, EPCOT was to be a community built "from scratch." Technologically efficient in the best Buckminster Fuller manner, it was also to be centrally planned. In a film made shortly before his death, Disney outlined his eccentric and worrisome vision of the future:

EPCOT *will be an experimental city that would incorporate the best ideas of industry, government and academia worldwide, a city that caters to the people as a service function. It will be a planned, controlled community, a showcase for American industry and research, schools, cultural and educational opportunities. In* EPCOT *there will be no slum areas because we won't let them develop. There will be no landowners and therefore no voting control. People will rent houses instead of buying them, and at modest rentals. There will be no retirees; everyone must be employed. One of the requirements is that people who live in* EPCOT *must help keep it alive.*

EPCOT was to be a capitalist utopia, not unlike Henry Ford's plans for Muscle Shoals, Alabama. In Ford's scheme, outlined in his 1926 book *Today and Tomorrow,* the town would be organized around resource extraction and the production of chemical fertilizers and automobiles. Each worker would own an acre of land, which his family would work while he laboured in one of the factories spread throughout the region. Ford thus meant to extend industrial authority over landscape and family relations alike. His thesis influenced the work of Frank Lloyd Wright as well as Disney.

In October 1982, sixteen years after Walt Disney's death, EPCOT Center opened at Disney World. As a taped announcement proclaims when you climb out of the monorail on arrival, "EPCOT is technical know-how combined with Disney showmanship — 550 acres exploring the innovations of tomorrow and the wonders of enterprise." Disney had imagined a community where people live and work. As it turned out, EPCOT is an amusement park whose residents, officials hasten to explain, are the millions of tourists who stay in the hotels.

EPCOT specifically addresses the future in a way Disney's other parks do not. Its publicity says it is dedicated to the imagination, to our fantasies and our "dreams for better tomorrows." Disney publicity makes it seem as though a brighter future were just a matter of "creative thinking" and "futuristic technologies." At EPCOT we're told what the future is going to be and that it is a hopeful one. Here technology figures large as an agent of history. Progress, development, expansion, growth — these will ensure (some day) leisure and well-being for all.

At EPCOT, two developments face each other across an artificial lagoon. On one side is Future World, a series of pavilions set in a vaguely Beaux-Arts arrangement, with Spaceship Earth at its centre. The pavilions are sponsored by such corporations as Kraft, General Motors, Kodak, Bell, Unisys, Exxon, General Electric, American Express, and Coca-Cola. Within are rides and exhibits that try to acclimatize us to their visions of the future.

World Showcase sits at the opposite end of the lagoon. The symmetry of its plan hinges, as it typically does in national exhibitions, on the pavilion of the host country, here the United States. Flanking the U.S. empire, in order of importance, are its major trading partners: Germany, Japan, Italy, France, China, Great Britain, Canada, and Mexico. Each national pavilion is sponsored by a "local" transnational — or, as they say at Disney, "universal" — corporation. More exhibits — for Israel, Morocco, and Equatorial Africa — would follow.

At EPCOT the geographical juxtaposition of past and present — a configuration that with Disney always *progresses* through the landscape, towards the spectator of the present day — is explicit in its intentions. It reconciles, as Louis Marin has argued about Disneyland, an ideal past with a real present.

The most popular pavilion at EPCOT, called The Land, is sponsored by Kraft. Outside the massive complex, which looks like nothing so much as a shopping mall, berms are planted to resemble contour farming. Inside the main attraction is a boat ride called "Listen to the Land." It is billed as "a journey to a place most of us have forgotten about: the place where food is grown." But before we get there, we float by translucent plastic sculptures of plants that highlight cellular and photosynthetic development, a sort of Tunnel of Love with *Fantastic Voyage* sets. Then we sail past simulated examples of biotic communi-

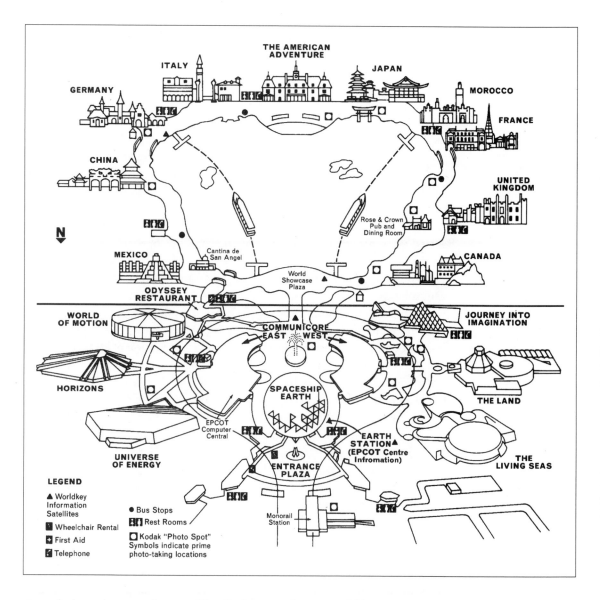

The following locations are labeled on the map:

THE AMERICAN ADVENTURE

ITALY

GERMANY

JAPAN

MOROCCO

FRANCE

CHINA

UNITED KINGDOM

N

Rose & Crown Pub and Dining Room

Cantina de San Angel

MEXICO

World Showcase Plaza

CANADA

ODYSSEY RESTAURANT

WORLD OF MOTION

COMMUNICORE EAST · WEST

JOURNEY INTO IMAGINATION

HORIZONS

SPACESHIP EARTH

THE LAND

EPCOT Computer Central

EARTH STATION (EPCOT Centre Infromation)

UNIVERSE OF ENERGY

ENTRANCE PLAZA

THE LIVING SEAS

LEGEND
▲ Worldkey Information Satellites
🔲 Wheelchair Rental
➕ First Aid
📞 Telephone

● Bus Stops
🚻 Rest Rooms
▢ Kodak "Photo Spot" Symbols indicate prime photo-taking locations

Monorail Station

A plan of EPCOT Center, Disney World. The "foreign countries" at World Showcase surround the lake, while Future World beckons with pavilions sponsored by large American transnationals.

ties, whole underground rooms like display cases in a natural history museum, only here when you cross the desert region a hot wind blows in your face, and the jungle smells of water and decaying plants. Around another bend in the river we reach the Family Farm, which in turn smells faintly of hay and cowshit. As an idealized representation of agrarian life, all is in place: bucolic setting, fence and field, barn and domestic animals, the yeoman farmer and his tightly knit family. The music is what in the business is called "soothing." Yet it can't mask the rupture that follows.

"Each year," the narration intones, "the family farm is being replaced by business as farming becomes a science. With better seeds, better pesticides and better techniques, we're moving into a new era." We round another bend in the river and suddenly we're in a greenhouse, the blue Florida sky high above our mythical boat ride through U.S. history. The farm has been erased from memory; this is a laboratory, and it must be the place they told us about, where food is grown. "This is what's called Controlled Environment Agriculture, CEA for short." We again move through several biomes, only thanks to science they're all blooming this time. "Nature by itself is not always productive." There are buffalo gourds, triticale, and gopher plants growing in eighteen inches of hot sandy soil. The gopher plants are a euphorbia species being propagated as a synthetic fuel. There are demonstrations of trickle irrigation technology, nutriculture, and growing food in outer space: to simulate gravity, they spin lettuce in a mesh cylinder placed around a broad-spectrum fluorescent tube.

In truth, the family farm was far more than the site of food production in North American society. Thus its destruction entailed not only the rationalization of the agricultural landscape but also the decimation of local communities and rural cultures. Yet there is scarcely time for such thoughts, for by now we're passing giant tanks of bass, eels, paddlefish, and catfish. This is something called aquaculture, we're told. The fish are taking part of their nutrition from the red lights above the tanks. We hear children's voices singing a tune lifted from Woody Guthrie; it goes "Let's listen to the land we all love…"

Despite the exhortations, the message is clearly, "Leave farming to the scientists." As the high priests of industrial civilization, scientists are a signal part of the agribusiness complex. For over a century the U.S. government has funded a system of agricultural colleges, experimental stations, and extension services at large state universities. Their imperative has been to substitute a technical revolution in the fields for a social one. The research going on at EPCOT, under the aegis of the University of Arizona, is typical of the kind of work these institutions sponsor. Its beneficiaries are not farm labourers, rural communities, or even the food itself. Even on its own terms, industrial agriculture doesn't work. U.S. energy consultant Amory Lovins estimates that industrial agriculture consumes three times as many calories as it provides in food value — ten times if you factor in the energy used in food processing and distribution. Crop losses to insects are today 13 per cent — double what they were before the introduction of synthetic pesticides. Soil erosion and aquifer mining are producing desert conditions in many parts of North America (two-thirds of all groundwater drawn in the United States is used on crops; one-quarter of that total is overdraft, that is, water drawn at a greater rate than it is replenished). The entire agricultural economy is yoked to oil, which even industrialists admit will last only another twenty or thirty years.

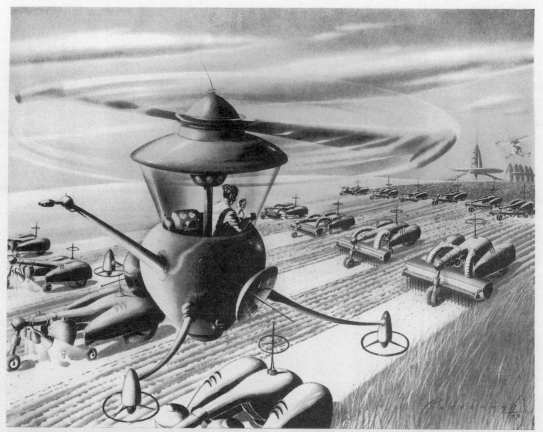

When "push-button" farm machines are a reality...

National Oil Seals will protect their performance

Some day soon, in the air-conditioned comfort of his helicopter "control tower," the farmer will flip a switch and send teams of ingenious machines out to till his fields. In a single integrated operation, the robot gangs will pulverize, condition and furrow the soil, drill seed and fertilize, perhaps implant soluble water capsules and transmit a pest-killing electronic "bath."

Such machines will represent a superb achievement in engineering. Yet, like today's equipment, performance will still depend on oil seals and O-Rings. Oil seals

are steel-and-synthetic rubber or steel-and-leather parts that keep lubricant in and dirt and water out of assemblies. O-Rings are synthetic rubber diameters—pressure seals used in hydraulic and pneumatic assemblies.

National pioneered oil seals and O-Rings, and today is a leader in this field. Perhaps precision National Oil Seals and O-Rings can improve your product's performance, lengthen its life, or make it easier to assemble or service? Our long experience is at your disposal.

NATIONAL MOTOR BEARING CO., INC.

General Offices: Redwood City, California. Sales Offices: Chicago, Cleveland, Dallas, Detroit, Downey (Los Angeles County), Milwaukee, Newark, Van Wert, Wichita. Plants: Redwood City, Downey and Long Beach, California; Van Wert, Ohio. Products: Oil, Fluid and Grease Seals, O-Rings, Airtron*Ducts, Silicone parts, Shims.   *T. M. Reg.

Original equipment on cars, trucks, buses, tractors, agricultural and earth-moving equipment, railway rolling stock, machinery and appliances.

A Controlled Ecological
Life Support System
(CELSS) at NASA's
Kennedy Space Center in
Florida. Experiments on
growing food in space
promote agriculture as an
activity that no longer has
a place on Earth.

It's the end of the ride and we climb out of the boats. A shop is selling plastic fruits and bright ceramic vegetable ashtrays. Then there's a video on "revolutionary" techniques such as interplanting (in fact an ancient farming practice) and photos of a research complex the Arizona labs have built in Abu Dhabi.

From here it's all downhill. The central atrium of the pavilion is taken up by a Farmers' Market, an amalgam of pizza parlour decor, chain-store marketing, and corporate advertising. Here we can buy processed cheese sandwiches from Kraft and ITT, peach nectar from Nestlé, soup from Campbell's, meat alloys from Greyhound, and snack foods from Pepsico. Chairs and tables are of one-piece extruded plastic in colours like salmon and avocado, and the floor is a brown "cobblestone" indoor/outdoor creation. This is pretty well the menu all over Disney World. The monotonous and denatured form of the food is masked — or perhaps enhanced — by the various "atmospheres" in which we can choose to consume it. Just as agriculture has become an industry more than a way of life, so too preparing and eating food are now more a matter of commodity consumption than social activity. On the other hand, in many North American cities, fast-food malls like this have been recuperated as public space; they are hangouts for marginal youth, much as neighbourhood soda fountains were in the past. May we wish the same for the Farmers' Market!

In an adjacent auditorium, a shimmering Kraft curtain rises on "your hostess Bonnie Appetit," an animatronic reincarnation of a 1950s housewife. She and her Kitchen Krackpots — Miss Yoghurt, a Mae West swiss cheese, and the Cereal Sisters ("I'm the toast of the town") — do a cabaret act. The show is not unlike the revue mounted by the fruits and vegetables in the fridge on *Peewee's Playhouse,* only at the Kraft pavilion it carries a dreary message about square meals.

"Kraft's involvement in EPCOT was a natural for them," a Disney publicist explained to me. "They're a family-oriented organization, like us, and their idea was that probably 80 per cent of the American people have never seen a hydroponic garden or a wing bean. We think there's a message of hope in The Land. We're saying that we can utilize our resources and do some wonderful things." The truly wonderful thing Kraft does accomplish at EPCOT is a skilful management of the longing North Americans have for the salad days when agriculture was the matrix of the social and economic life of the nation. The Green Revolution has changed all of that. Today agriculture is a destructive industry.† The land — the complex web of soil micro-organism, fungus, insect, plant, and mammal — is no longer a home for all the life on the planet. Within

† U.S. agronomist Wes Jackson points out that its high yields have been purchased at great cost to fuel, soil, water, genetic diversity, and economic equity.

official culture, the land is talked about as an inert resource to be managed by paramilitary technology.

If there is a message of hope in The Land, I couldn't find it. Surely it lies well outside of Disney World — and outside of industrial capitalism. It is in the sustainable agricultural projects and urban restoration work under way throughout the North American continent that the ecological lifeways systematically denied at EPCOT continue to be asserted. This is a politics that refuses the management of our dreams and works towards a truly emancipatory future.

There is a momentous historical failure at Disney World, and indeed at all world's fairs. It is a failure of imagination. The modernist vision of EPCOT and its antecedents discards the history of genuinely utopian initiatives of the U.S. and Canadian people in favour of an ideology of growth and development. "We would hope the world of tomorrow would be like EPCOT Center," a publicist told me, and that is the project Disney's corporate sponsors are already at work on. For all the scientific exactitude of these futurist plans, they are frighteningly incapable of moving beyond a rigid technological determinism. Increased productive capacity, so the story goes, along with a free flow of inventions and careful management of the Earth's resources, will raise standards of living; this will in turn foster international co-operation and peace. Buckminster Fuller's marvellous illustration of this potential was of seven-hundred-passenger airplanes the size of twenty-three-storey buildings. These would be mass produced and air delivered, "installable anywhere around the world in a day by upending the fuselages. It also means the removal of skyscrapers and their redelivery to any other points on Earth in one day." As Fuller argued, "Whole cities could be flown to any location. This is the consequence of the chain-reaction rate now attained in the man-and-environment interregenerative evolution."

For Fuller, "The new highway leading directly to success for all is now ready for use." At EPCOT, the lucky holiday-goer can travel that lush parkway through a future North American landscape. Yet the scenery looks strangely familiar. Indeed, this is a future that differs from the present only in its details; it is a future of hierarchy, continued industrialization, enforced scarcity, and a ravished planet.

A future of emancipation, on the other hand, can only be reclaimed by a society willing to debate its own survival. Contemporary world's fairs stand squarely in the way of that debate and condemn us to a recurrent and eternal present.

A housing development in central Florida. Photograph by Vid Ingelevics.

6. City and Country

The deepest problems we have now to understand and resolve are in [the] real relations of nature and livelihood.... The central change we have to make is in the received and dominant concept of the earth and its life forms as raw material for generalized production. That change means, necessarily, ending large-scale capitalist farming, with its linked processes of high land costs, high interest-bearing capitalization, high-input cash crop production. But in the equally necessary perspective of...an apparently unmediated nature — the living world of rivers and mountains, of trees and flowers and animals and birds — it is important to avoid a crude contrast between 'nature' and 'production', and to seek the practical terms of the idea which should supersede both: the idea of 'livelihood', within, and yet active within, a better understood physical world and all truly necessary physical processes.
— Raymond Williams, "Between Country and City"

The narratives of the Kraft pavilion at EPCOT Center are familiar to us from countless natural-history museums and TV commercials. They are also familiar because they talk about the real changes in the land itself that North Americans have experienced over the past forty years. Paths we might once have walked along to get out of the city now lead to suburbs. Streams and rivers we used to swim in are often polluted; or perhaps they are gone altogether, piped underground in an attempt to control flooding. Our settlements feel different today because they are different; they have a different physical relationship to the earth. We grow and market food in different ways than we used to; we've adopted new ways of generating power and managing soil and water.

Agriculture appears to give form to, to make comprehensible, these changing relations between what we usually call city and country. Agriculture is, after all, something humans have done on and with the land for a very long time, and more recently something we've done against the land. But the centrality of agriculture as a metaphor makes it both easier and more difficult to understand the connections between recent historical and geographical change in North America. Easier because food production is such a basic human activity. Nearly everyone has had the experience of growing plants, whether an exotic tree coddled indoors or a tomato vine in the backyard. More difficult because this familiarity with growing food — and all the resonances it has in the culture (nurturing, family, hearth) — obscures the reorganization of the agrarian economy that has taken place over the past century.

A mid-1950s ad promoting the benefits of petrochemicals for agriculture. Our familiarity with food and its cultivation obscures the reorganization of the agrarian economy that has taken place over the last century.

Modern agriculture as practised since the Second World War is the result of applying industrial methods to traditional farming practices. The characteristics of industrial agriculture are high-input cropping dependent on fossil fuels, intensive animal husbandry, mechanization, and the reduction of human work. The efficiency of this farming is measured only in monetary terms — the return on investment — leaving the unwanted results of the process (pollution, habitat destruction, unemployment) to be described as "byproducts." Food conglomerates like Kraft have also introduced new transportation and processing techniques and contributed to the consolidation of agribusiness. For example, nine companies — Ciba-Geigy, Sandoz, Bayer, BASF, ICI, Rhone Poulenc, Cyanamid, Monsanto, and Du Pont — now produce (and own patents on) most of the world's agricultural seeds and chemicals. (There is also a semiotic history to be told in the names of some of those chemicals, among them Avenge, Marksman, Fusilade, Attack!, Roundup, and Erase.) Production and distribution have been integrated into a single system, continuously in motion and tracked by computer from land to supermarket to landfill. Industrial agriculture has also encouraged a genetic and cultural uniformity in farm practices that has carried over to an aesthetic uniformity in its food products.

All of these practices have distanced human communities from food production. It is a thorough distancing, at once biogeographical, technological, and political. It is also a cognitive distancing. Many, perhaps most, North Americans are frighteningly ignorant of modern agricultural practices. Yet in the public imagination, links to food production are still significant. McCain Foods, Campbell's, Kraft, Stouffer's, Stokely Van Camp, Libby's, Mrs. Paul's, Aunt Jemima, and a host of other agribusinesses retain their family names (many of them women's) as a marker of home and hearth, the place where food used to be grown and processed in North America, and where it still is in much of the world. There is a significant disjunction, then, between the actual relation of city to country and how we think about and reproduce that relation in our working landscapes.

cow

bovine milk production mechanism

As Raymond Williams pointed out, the contemporary distinction between country and city has been produced by the modern economy, which nonetheless has integrated the two more closely than ever. As money markets have penetrated industrial agriculture in recent years, those links have been strengthened. Yet our ideas about country and city continue to simplify. Popular culture continues to produce what Williams described as a "continuing flood of sentimental and selectively nostalgic versions of country life." It is no accident that this development has coincided with a precipitous decline of the city all over the West, a decline that has a social and cultural dimension as well as an economic one.

Our understanding of these changes has not been helped by most of the land development that has taken place in North America in the past forty years. Suburbs, theme parks, shopping centres, executive estates, industrial parks — not to mention industrial farms or tourist developments — continue to reproduce misleading ideas about city and country. Their forms fragment geographies into those devoted to work and leisure, production and recreation — oppositions that obscure far more than they reveal. The interurban highway projects initiated in the 1950s have since dispersed those landscape forms right across the continent, with little regard for local geographies and cultures. Rather than linking together and reintegrating the working landscape, superhighways have done

Many pesticides are applied from planes, and drift beyond target areas. This air bombardment of the spruce budworm uses Dipel, a bacterium that is non-toxic to humans but kills many species that are not pests. Sevin is a petrochemical that temporarily interferes with nerve transmissions in all animals, including birds, honeybees, aquatic organisms, and humans.

little more than produce a jumble of compromises: bedroom communities, high-tech "parks," green belts, and retirement complexes.

The Shopping Centre

A small number of private corporations constructed most of our built landscape today, with the exception of the older sections of cities. This land development industry was in turn largely the creation of government economic policy, which promoted mass housing and a land-intensive industrial plant serviced by automobiles and trucks. This scheme replaced the older and less energy-intensive model of urban factories serviced by rail and waterways. In Canada, the postwar government subsidized the founding of large construction companies such as Cadillac Fairview, Olympia and York, Daon, and Campeau to create employment and build much needed housing.

Shopping centres are a familiar example of the kind of development that characterized the immediate postwar years. They were first built in the 1920s and 1930s as a row of stores set back from a suburban arterial road to allow for parking. Soon gas stations and supermarkets were added to the developer-owners' formula of providing all retail services for a community in one place. At the end of the Second World War there were only about ten shopping centres on the entire continent. Once large-scale suburban construction began in the postwar years, however, shopping centres proliferated along highways and became retailing outlets for entire regions. Gradually, access to the stores was restricted to pedestrian walkways. In Southdale, a shopping centre opened near Minneapolis in 1956, the pedestrian areas were roofed over, creating a prototype for the contemporary mall.

Today there are some twenty-six thousand shopping centres in the United States, and three thousand in Canada, and they handle about 40 per cent of retail trade. Often fully integrated into the multinational economy, they have had a devastating effect on the small independent business sector and the regional economies that small businesses once supported. Shopping centres have also redefined the social sphere in terms of consumption. Privately owned and managed, they have in many towns entirely supplanted public spaces. Subway entrances and overhead and underground passageways have further contributed to a decline in the quality of street life.

The West Edmonton Mall provides an idiosyncratic example of this kind of development. When it opened in the early 1980s as a forty-five-hectare development in the western suburbs of Edmonton, Alberta, the mall could announce itself as the world's largest indoor shopping centre, with fifty-seven entrances and over 850 stores along its two-and-a-half-kilometres-long concourse. Some fifteen thousand people work there, and the parking lot holds thirty thousand cars. There are cinemas, hotels, video arcades, department stores, car showrooms, restaurants, and every chain store you've ever heard of. At one of the mall's hubs sits an official-size ice rink where the Edmonton Oilers practise hockey. At another there's a one-hectare lake with dolphins and a full-scale model of Columbus's *Santa Maria*. There are rides in one of four full-size submarines (twice as many as in the Canadian navy, scoffed the *Washington Post* in its story on the mall); the ships are equipped with sonar and video surveillance equipment, and they dive through waters full of live and mechanical sharks and octopuses. There is an eighteen-hole Pebble Beach golf course, replicas of Bourbon Street and the Rue Faubourg de Saint Honoré. An amusement park, Canada Fantasyland, has an antique carousel and a thirteen-storey roller coaster.

The statistics boggle. And they're meant to, for the mall is itself a tourist attraction. Everything in the mall is "the world's largest indoor" something. A $5 million annual promotion budget brings in hundreds of thousands of people from western North America on the weekends. World Water Park contains a 2.87-hectare lake — the size of five football fields — and is covered by a glass dome. Palm trees line the edge of the lake, which has six-foot surfing waves. A "tanning sun" shines and the temperature is maintained at thirty degrees celsius year round. There are twenty-two waterslides. To one side of the waterpark is the Fantasyland Hotel. A third of its rooms are theme rooms: Arabian, Polynesian, Truck Stop, Victorian Coach, Hollywood Nightclub, and Classical Roman. In most of the rooms the theme turns around converting things into beds: a volcano, a pickup truck, a catamaran, a carriage, a disco dance floor.

The mall seems endless in both size and enthusiasm. Hyperbole abounds, from the "exquisite statues" to the marble, chrome, and brass lavished on every

World Water Park at the West Edmonton Mall, Alberta. The 45-hectare project attempts to bring all of nature – including six-foot ocean waves – into its climatized, commodified space.

surface. Like Disneyland, nothing here is ever exactly what it seems: fountains breathe fire, and Gourmet World turns out to be a collection of chains like Mr Submarine and McDonald's. Given that nature has become an increasingly important component of artificial landscapes, it's no surprise that in the West Edmonton Mall, according to its promoters, control over nature is part of the attraction: "Heretofore, only the rich could flee winter, travel, follow the sun, play, dine and shop in a sort of endless summer. Now, with the West Edmonton Mall, average families can do likewise." And all under one roof.

The relentless mission of the West Edmonton Mall is to bring everything into its climatized, commodified space, especially objects and species from the natural world. There are hundreds of animals — "hand-picked specimens," the brochures say — in aquariums and cages. The species chosen are displayed in the ways that we've come to know them. First come the most glamorous and evil beasts, familiar from James Bond movies: piranhas, octopuses, alligators, and sharks. Then there are the performers: seals and penguins, peacocks, flamingoes, and dolphins. Then there are the cute animals: spider monkeys, emus, and angel fish. And the "wild" ones we know from TV: black bears, mountain lions, jaguars, iguanas, ostriches. Some of the animals are available for photos. A sign at one stall says:

Have your photo taken with a live cougar cub, $5.99. Extra persons in photo, $2.00 each. Small cub $5.99. Large cub $7.99. Special cuddly cougar prints, regular $30.00 value, now only $5.00 while they last. Lovable lynx prints only $5.00.

There is little effort wasted on contextualization at the Mall. Why bother recreating the pre-industrial farm or a simulated jungle, conceits insisted on in Disney environments? Here the animals are just another commodity form, alongside Yves St. Laurent and Shoppers Drug Mart. As if to emphasize the point, the mall maintains a "retreat" for the animals at an undisclosed suburban site in Edmonton. There the animals can rest from their work at the mall, a fact that hasn't discouraged the local gossip that these non-human employees have a very short lifespan. See them while they last!

Urban Villages and Rural Suburbs

Shopping centres were a new kind of land use that corresponded to shifts in the economy. In the past three decades, there have been other shifts in North American economies, this time away from manufacturing and towards sectors that have to do with information and services. Many manufacturing jobs have been moved offshore where labour is cheap and now some 50 to 75 per cent of all North American jobs are in the new sectors, which include work in computer-related fields, retail sales, information, the professions, fast food, finance, and management of all kinds. The physical needs of these new capital-intensive and data-intensive businesses are very different from those of manufacturing based on raw materials. By the 1980s, telecommunications networks were sophisticated enough that these industries could be located just about anywhere, so long as they were accessible to the cars that now carry the overwhelming portion of commuter traffic.

These changes in the economy have promoted two new forms of land development: the urban village and the rural suburb. I propose these terms tentatively, for as Disney World demonstrates, it is growing more difficult to distinguish the various kinds of urban, exurban, and rural settlement. Urban villages are the mini-downtowns that now surround the old cores of larger cities. They are partly the reason that it has become commonplace for statisticians to speak of Greater Metropolitan Areas rather than cities. As it has developed in the past ten years, the urban village is a type of infill development in an already existing suburb. Typically, corporations will move their back-office operations to office towers widely dispersed among parking lots and semi-public landscaped areas on the edges of cities. The offices are followed by chain restaurants, business hotels, and auxiliary services and industries. The aptly named Perimeter Center north of Atlanta is a good example of an urban village. Its buildings are

In this fanciful mid-1950s idea of meal time in the suburban home of the future, food production and consumption have become one unified system from land to landfill. Yet the view of the "country" out the window obscures those changes.

NEW   DEPARTURES   OF   TOMORROW

Super Chef —1965?

TOMORROW: Pick your favorite foods! Then this **imaginary SUPER CHEF** assembles your choice from a vast freezer storage, cooks it to perfection by infra-red ray and serves it by conveyor in a matter of seconds!

Set the table . . . then set the dial! Future meals could be as easy as that with this miracle meal-getter. And, maybe tomorrow it will be a reality.

When it is, New Departure will play an important part, just as it does in so many of today's work-savers. For example, you'll find New Departure ball bearings in almost every major appliance . . . and for good reason. They keep moving parts functioning smoothly, while requiring virtually no maintenance. They support loads from any direction . . . keep parts always in perfect alignment.

If you're dreaming up tomorrow's time-saver, or improving your present product, call on New Departure for the most dependable ball bearings in the world.

NEW DEPARTURE • DIVISION OF GENERAL MOTORS • BRISTOL, CONNECTICUT

TODAY: The operation of many of today's conveniences relies on New Departures. Specially designed, low-cost New Departure ball bearings in the hinges of this heavy refrigerator door make it swing open at the lightest touch.

NEW DEPARTURE
BALL BEARINGS

NOTHING ROLLS LIKE A BALL

not connected by sidewalks and there is minimal public transportation. The grounds are planted to conform to the suburban landscape aesthetic established in the 1950s.

The rural suburb is virtually the same kind of development, only it's usually located well into the country, near the intersections of continental highways or airports and often within easy commuting distance of wealthy executive communities. Research Triangle Park in North Carolina was a prototype of what is now called a business park. In 1952 the University of North Carolina began to assemble a two-hundred-hectare campus for the newly established North Carolina Center for Research in Institutions and Administrative Organization. Its mission was to carry out research in agriculture, industrial development, ecology, and urban and regional planning. By 1958 a university-industrial consortium had hacked Research Triangle Park out of the second-growth pine forests of the North Carolina Piedmont. In planning terms, the new business park was to be an example of industry in harmony with its environment.

Today the Triangle has grown beyond its original boundaries to overlap the small cities of Cary, Raleigh, Chapel Hill, and Durham. It is an amorphous collection of industrial installations, shopping malls, and four-lane highways spread over nearly one thousand-square-kilometres of rolling and forested uplands. The corporations that have built in the Triangle include large U.S. transnationals in pharmaceuticals, computers, and military research. Their mysterious buildings, awash in parking lots, give no clues about what goes on within. Some seven hundred thousand people live in the region (including the cities), many of them in residential "communities" nestled in pine groves. Inside the security gates of these developments, houses and condos surround lawns, health clubs, golf courses, and shopping centres. The entire development is designed as a package, an advertising strategy that positions a commodity in the marketplace. Their market-researched styles are often of pointedly European origin — Georgian, French, Italian Villa, Tudor — as if it were impossible to address local architectural traditions. You might drive through several kilometres of forest before coming across another development, this time a postmodern "condiminiplex" overlooking an artificial lake. Many retirement communities in North America, particularly in the sunbelt of the United States, are built on the same model. A typical advertisement promises "a quality lifestyle in a self-sufficient, secure setting with superb landscaping."

Promoters in the Triangle talk about these rural developments as "multinodal small town villages." Publicity emphasizes their "exclusive" character. The exclusions are many, for this new landscape overwhelms both the land and its history. In North Carolina, the new communities and the high-tech industries their residents work at have supplanted an economy once organized around

Suburban Mission,
British Columbia, a
distant suburb of
Vancouver, in 1967 and,
opposite, in 1979. Suburbs
often rupture the physical
links between city and
country, place and region.

tobacco and market farming. Most food is now imported from Florida, and traffic, water pollution, and unaffordable housing have become acute problems. The people displaced by the new economy — farmers and the many low-paid service workers of the Triangle — have been dispersed to public housing or trailers on abandoned farm land far out in the country. Whatever we might think about these changes in the economy, it is important to recognize that fenced-off settlements and jobs that have no relation to locale break links between home, community, and land.

Reconciliation

As land-use patterns have changed over the past forty years, the relations between city and country have been thrown into crisis. Land nearly everywhere today is subject to rapid changes brought about by alternating cycles of capital speculation, development, and abandonment. These changes have ruptured both the integrity of urban and rural communities and the physical links between city and country, place and region. The suburb promised to mediate some of those tensions. Its pastoral landscape was meant to negotiate the cultural boundaries between the rustic and the urbane. But its mission was a compromise, and an unsuccessful one at that. Today North American suburbs are surrounded by dead zones — degraded river corridors, abandoned farm land, deforested industrial areas, and the uninhabitable "public" spaces of shopping malls and superhighways. Exclusive bedroom communities deep in the woods are merely another broken promise, for they do not reconcile productive with ornamental landscapes, work with pleasure.

The development of rural areas has met with a great deal of opposition in recent years. Yet the resistance to airport expansion, estate housing on agricul-

tural land, or time-sharing resorts often describes these projects as "urbanization" or "sprawl." This is an incomplete analysis. The dispersal of what we think of as urban society — non-agricultural production, money markets, and state institutions — into rural areas is in part a reintroduction of a stable economy to the country. It is only since the Industrial Revolution, with its unbalanced concentration of production, power, and wealth in the cities, that it has been possible to think of the country as primarily the site of agriculture, and secondarily a place of retreat. Traditional rural society — even in the West — has always included crafts and tradespeople. That is now happening again, as urban dominance of the economy is waning and the social and ecological crisis of the city intensifies.

All of these changes indicate that the distinction between city and country is slowly dissolving. There is considerable debate about what this dissolution means. In many respects, the contemporary ideology of city and country as discrete and exclusive land forms has been destructive. It prevents links between the nodes of local ecosystems, what U.S. writer Barry Lopez calls the synapses of food webs and energy cycles. From the standpoint of social ecology, it would be far better to disperse human settlement across the land in a way that integrates natural and social economies. This is also related to Raymond Williams's idea of livelihood — a reconciliation of work and nature.

What does this mean practically? Firstly, in the city, the key work to be done is the reintroduction of healthy natural ecosystems: urban forests and wetlands, meadows and prairies. Secondly, food production must be brought back to the city, especially the raising of fruit and vegetables, poultry and fish. These old skills need to be recovered and propagated.

In the country, reconciliation will mean preserving and restoring what cultural geographers call "working landscapes," the ordinary places of production and settlement. Rural lands were traditionally places of economic and cultural diversity, of "partnership" with nature. Agriculture was one activity among many. To restore working landscapes we must work the edges of the land, the places it connects, the ways it gathers itself together and draws in human communities: these are the hedgerows, the streambanks and abandoned fields, the road edges, bridges, and swimming places, and above all the boundaries of cultivated fields, towns, and cities. We must also restore a sustainable agriculture that uses little land and few inputs, rather than extensive land and massive inputs.

This new landscape will not come about only by planting and restoring city and country. We must also build a culture that will nurture new relations with the natural world, relations built on harmony and livelihood rather than domination and profit. It is an immense challenge, for it means altering the way we grow food and manufacture goods, the way we log and mine and build our houses. Yet these changes are already under way right across the continent — as the urban agriculture projects that have reclaimed (and resocialized) abandoned land in cities as different as Boston, Vancouver, and San Francisco show. Other rural initiatives have grown out of opposition to industrial forestry and fishing practices. These are for the most part grassroots efforts. But regional planners too are beginning to think about economic, social and environmental problems simultaneously. U.S. writer Tony Hiss has found small but broad coalitions of bureaucrats, professionals, environmentalists, and private landowners working towards extending, and compounding, those areas that still demonstrate the interconnectedness of city and country and offer us a sense of place. Old and new settlements can be reinfused with what Hiss identifies as three forms of connectedness: "the sense of kinship with all life; the sense of partnership with working landscapes; and the sense of community and companionability which is traditionally fostered by villages and urban neighbourhoods."

Some of these projects are well advanced in the United Kingdom and Europe. Many English cities, for example, have working urban farms and forests. New Towns such as Milton Keynes and Warrington have been designed as a complex web of housing, industry, natural habitat, education, and land stewardship.

Nostalgic Landscapes

As the collapse of industrial society draws nearer, the possibilities for a reconciliation of city and country become more distinct. A restructured industrial economy, finite resources, agricultural overproduction, and urban decay — to say nothing of ecological collapse — will make our choices clearer in the last years of this century. Yet the very uncertainty of survival into the next century has elicited contrary responses as well. The last forty years have been a time of dislocation, of ruptured communities and irreversibly altered landscapes. One popular response to these changes, which have been in many cases cataclysmic, has been to retreat to an imagined place and time outside of economy and history. Some people propose the unlikely possibility of the nuclear family as a refuge from violence and other social malaise. Similarly, in the pages of outdoor magazines an "untrammelled" wilderness beckons to us with entire panoramas of amnesia.

These nostalgic gestures of "the good old days" are often organized around ideas of village and countryside. Not surprisingly, rural nostalgia has become an industry, with its own product lines and tourist destinations. There are few regions of the continent that do not have some kind of pioneer village or Old McDonald's Farm. These villages have their origins in nineteenth-century world's fairs, whose organizers combed the globe for objects that could be made to justify industrial progress. But while world's fairs have become infrequent in recent years, theme parks, their progeny, have blossomed. There are hundreds of them in North America, and they function in different ways. Most, like the Wonderland or Six Flags chains, are part of the tradition of midways and county fairs. Others have been inspired by garden history or local historical artifacts. Many combine these traditions. My interest here is in theme parks that are about history and the traces we leave on the land. This is a narrow and very local reading, but one that I think illuminates significant changes in the way contemporary popular culture organizes itself in both time and space.

World's fairs are optimistic enterprises that idealize a "kinder, gentler" future of abundance, thanks to technological innovation. Historical theme parks are decidedly more pessimistic affairs. They construct the idealized past of an organic community in harmony with nature, in the belief that this harmony is something we cannot look forward to again. There was no technology then — or so the story goes — just tools we held in our hands and tasks we kept in our memories. Like world's fairs, historical theme parks draw on social anxiety about the future of human settlement on the Earth.

As environments, theme parks have much in common. Like toys, they are models of social and physical ecologies. They replicate in miniature our cities and towns and gardens, our industrial and agricultural landscapes. They tell us about past and future human settlement and speculate about the meaning of natural areas. As commerce, theme parks have learned much from Disney. They conceal their services, shove the gift shops up front, and lard the whole with lots of authenticity: period architectures and costumes, and plenty of old-time fun.

Knott's Berry Farm is an early example of the historical theme park. Built before Disneyland on the same arid plains of the southern part of the Los Angeles

River basin, Knott's Berry Farm was originally just that: a working farm of soft and stone fruits with a small retail stand along the road out front. Its orchards were irrigated with water that had been expropriated from the Owens Valley far to the north, a scandal that is the main narrative of the movie *Chinatown*.

As time went by and the Los Angeles aerospace economy boomed during the war, the orchards themselves were slowly displaced by tourist facilities. The owners of Knott's Berry Farm bought the abandoned silver mining town of Calico, California, shipped it from the desert to some adjacent land, and "preserved" it as an Old West amusement park. From there, the rest, as they say, is history, and today Knott's Berry Farm resembles nothing so much as every other amusement park on the continent.

The historical juncture this book examines is all there at Knott's Berry Farm: the industrialization of agriculture, the dispersion of the automobile and its culture, the rise of tourism, and the loss of a sense of region.

Four Appalachian Villages

Southern Appalachia provides a sterling example of a geography in crisis, for its old mountains and river valleys have in the past sixty years witnessed the collision of a distinct and isolated regional culture with the relentless project of modern development.

Scattered along the roads of Tennessee, Kentucky, and the western part of North Carolina are restored villages that recall and reconstruct ideas about the way things once were in those mountains. Some are within nature parks, some are part of theme parks, some are simply an assemblage of buildings that evolved out of someone's backyard, some promote religion, others consumerism. All of them are built on the land, and at some point all of them come round to talking about place and the transformation of human production (that is, work). If you drive east from Oak Ridge, Tennessee, and across the divide to Charlotte, North Carolina, you'll find four of these villages: at the Museum of Appalachia, Dollywood, Cades Cove, and Heritage USA.

The Museum of Appalachia, in Norris, Tennessee, calls itself "The Most Authentic and Complete Replica of Pioneer Life in the World." It is a collection of old buildings and artifacts arranged across a clearing in some oak woods, less than ten acres in size. Its founder, John Rice Irwin, set about collecting things in the 1950s. Worried that "the true breed of mountain folk" was diminishing, Irwin wanted to preserve a trace of their material lives. These were a gentle, stalwart, and imaginative people, he wrote, the sons and daughters of pioneers.

The museum is a welcoming and homely place, itself a remnant of another era when roadside attractions were small family operations. There are no back-lighted signs here, the parking lot is unpaved, and the colour schemes are old and funky. You walk around on your own, without the costumed guide of the national parks or a cassette narration, looking over the brochure and wandering in and out of the houses, barns, and schools, past corn cribs, churches, orchards, and vegetable gardens. Irwin strove for authenticity. He rescued buildings from rising reservoirs or interstate highways or bought them from derelict farms, then restored or rebuilt them. The Arnwine cabin came from the Clinch River, the log church was built about 1840 as a mountain meeting house in Madison County, North Carolina, the ice house was built by Ed and Elmer Sherwood "on the same pattern as the one their father had."

Inside, the buildings look lived in. The rooms are dressed with period furniture and clothing. In fact the entire site is crammed with remnants — 250,000 relics, they say in the brochure — of early nineteenth-century material culture: yokes and saw blades and blacksmith's tools, hundreds of old bottles and jars, spinning wheels, ploughs, millstones — and on and on, as if the more accumulated the more authentic the assemblage. Walking around you do get a sense of what people held in their hands and stuck into the earth. You can picture people working.

Like the park, the brochure is folksy, full of stories:

At the age of 86 my old friend General Bunch fell from the top of an apple tree, catching his foot between the forks of a limb. He hung upside down for four hours before he was discovered, and he died a few days later. This was 78 years after he, as a boy of eight, helped to build this house which now bears his name. The last time he visited me he talked of the old homeplace.

The stories are meant to take visitors back to an earlier day: the years of victory over wilderness and savages. I look but can't find documentation of the subsequent years of loss: loss of land to erosion, to inundation by reservoirs, to poverty and all the displacements of modern life. There are no traces here of what happened to these places, to their disappearance in the mid-twentieth century. Nor is there any sense of a culture that predated the white one. So we're left wondering how our own present connects to these tools and buildings.

I have to get back in my car to find some of these things out. Across another ridge or two the rest of the story tells itself in the landscape. To the east, on Interstate 75, lies Norris itself. The town, built by the Tennessee Valley Authority in 1934, is often called a model of American state socialism, with its modest salt-box houses sitting on one-acre and two-acre lots well dispersed across wooded ridges. At the town centre there's a common haphazardly surrounded by a few civic buildings copied from New England. Not far beneath the surface of this landscape is a prototype of the postwar suburb. TVA literature tells us, "The town plan includes a protective green belt, a town forest to protect the city's water supply, and houses set in a park-like atmosphere." To go anywhere — the store, the church, to visit a neighbour — you need a car. Originally inhabited by TVA administrators, Norris is now a satellite of Knoxville and Oak Ridge.

In the Norris town offices hangs a collection of Lewis Hine photographs, donated by the TVA, showing nearby communities before the dams were built: dirt-poor farmers, eroded land, and broken-down tenant houses. In one photo a TVA official interviews a prospective employee in a general store familiar from its reproductions along the roads. These photographs were commissioned by the same agency that built the dams that flooded their subject.

Heading north, the Norris Freeway — a parkway, really, but one of the first roads in the United States to be called a freeway — winds back down into the Clinch Valley to the Norris Dam and the surrounding recreation areas. These are the only sites in Norris where we can see work or its representations.

And then looping back south again, past the entrance to the Museum of Appalachia and innumerable car and boat lots, I come to Oak Ridge, another town built by the government, less than ten years after Norris. It too began with modest, quickly built houses scattered across a dry ridge. What was a pointless (even blasphemous) town-common in Norris is here a more honest U-shaped shopping centre. The Chamber of Commerce sign boasts: "Oak Ridge, City of the Past…City of the Future." The past it refers to is not the past recalled by the rusty farm implements on the road into town, but the past of the Second World War, when Oak Ridge was built as the principal centre for manufacturing atomic weaponry.

Because of the way the land is formed in the Tennessee Valley — long parallel ridges alternating with steep hollows, and broad but winding flood plains along the rivers — you never really grasp it all at once: the dams, the motorboats, the bomb factories, the shopping centres, the model campgrounds, the fertilizer factories and nuke plants and aluminum manufacturing complexes. With so many pasts and futures making claims on us, it's hard to know which way to turn.

Dollywood

I turn towards the mountains, towards Dollywood, which promised much. This place too is a homage to Southern Appalachian culture. It invites us to "experience the only place in America where the tradition and pride of the Smokies are brought to life through old-time crafts, breathtaking scenery, food, fun and friendly folks, and Dolly's kind of upbeat music!" Dollywood was built by one of the mountain South's most famous daughters and spokespeople,

Dollywood, Pigeon Forge, Tennessee, Dolly Parton's homage to the mountain culture of the southern Appalachians, "where the streams and rivers are stocked every Thursday, so there's always plenty for the weekend."

country singer, songwriter, and actor Dolly Parton, a woman much admired by Southerners, especially women, for her chutzpah and pride of place.

The conceit of the park is very much the same as at the Museum of Appalachia: the Tennessee mountain home, back when things were simple. It is built across the floor of a hollow and along an adjacent ridge in Pigeon Forge, Tennessee, near Gatlinburg, a town on the western edge of Great Smoky Mountains National Park, the most popular park in the United States. For decades, Gatlinburg has been a service and amusement centre for people vacationing in their cars. It seems that every U.S. chain restaurant and boutique has a franchise in Gatlinburg. And every idea to attract tourists is here too: trout pond, wax museum, haunted house, waterbed showroom, Biblical garden, taffy factory, medieval castle, sightseeing gondola, miniature golf — "you name it, we've got it in Gatlinburg."

A ridge or so away at Dollywood, there's a vast parking lot. Beyond, frame buildings rise from asphalt paths in haphazard summary of building types once common in these hills: mills, barns, a church, shacks, latrines. A steam train circles the site, which also has rides and craft studios.

On the rainy day in September that I show up, Dollywood is decked out in Fall Festival themes. Bound corn stalks and pumpkins adorn verandahs. Planters are filled with orange marigolds and red geraniums — anything, really, so long as it is bright and colourful and always in bloom.

Dollywood too abounds with *things*. At every turn there are material remnants, and reproductions, of mountain culture: old looms and ploughs, churns, rakes, wood stoves, dulcimers and banjos, corn-cob pipes, skillets, washboards, irons, yokes, stills, and Bibles. Most of these are in turn commemorated on T-shirts, mugs, hats, sweatshirts, posters, and needlepoint. Everywhere too are butterflies, "Dolly's favourite animal," and the memorabilia of Dolly's successful career.

Dolly's story is told on signs and video, and in the songs themselves that emanate, as usual, from everywhere — shrubberies, eaves, and headrests. She was born in a shack right here in the Smokies, in a settlement just like this, one of twelve children born to poor rural folk just trying to get by. Despite its humble situation, Dolly's family was honest and proud. Dolly herself had loved to "pick and sing" ever since she was a little girl. On the rags-to-riches video in the Dolly Parton Museum we see her reminiscing about the early days, before her diet when the wigs were so big they were jokes. She gets to meet Jane Fonda and Burt Reynolds, perform with Emmy Lou Harris, and play for the Queen. At a British press conference, which she handled magnificently, Dolly announces, "I like being a woman. If I'd a been a man, I'd a been a drag queen."

There's something charming about the lack of pretensions at Dollywood. Like Dolly herself, nothing is quite what it seems. Authenticity — what's that? We're all just having a good time here. There isn't a creek running by the mill? Make one! Or take the Olde Lemonade Stand: a rough-sawn wood cart watched over by a woman in a frilly bonnet and long gingham dress. You ask for a lemonade and she digs a can of Kuntry Tyme Lemonade out of the fridge. And so with the buildings scattered willy-nilly in the hollow: once you're past the rustic shingles, pitched roofs, and stovepipes and get inside, it's a gift shop, selling the same T-shirts and coffee mugs as the last one.

Back in my motel in Gatlinburg, rain still coming down, I turn on the TV and catch a promotional video for the Roaring Fork Motor Nature Trail in Great Smoky Mountains National Park. A white couple drive through three seasons of nature in a Porsche convertible. After some ads about the "world-class shopping and dining" in Gatlinburg, there is a fishing report. An "old timer" shows us how to clean and cook a trout. "The streams and rivers are stocked every Thursday, so there's always plenty for the weekend." Then there is an ad telling us, "Welcome Home to Tennessee," and a ranger report, also from the national park, explaining the difference between a spruce and a fir.

Dollywood is built on the idea of home. People lived like this once; it was simple out here in the bush, but it was wholesome. The fact that Dolly doesn't live this way any more seems irrelevant. It is the very artificiality of the enterprise that fascinates. You can buy postcards of the private quarters Dolly stays in when she's at Dollywood. There are lots of butterflies, but otherwise her rooms bear no resemblance to the hillbilly decor of the theme park. Just a lot of gold mirrors and sleek mauve furniture spread across the broadloom. Dollywood makes sure that our relation to what might or might not be left of mountain culture is full of irony.

Theme-park tourism calls into question the piousness of authentic reconstructions. The commodities it hawks lie at several removes from the rusty ploughs of the more "realistic" parks. That distance is unavoidable, for the past is never available to us *as the past*. Yet people yearn for some kind of connectedness, of continuity, and it seems they're often willing to purchase it in a gift shop.

Cades Cove: Connections Regained

At Dollywood I saw tourists cramming bags of hillbilly gewgaws into the trunks of their big cars: carved wood figurines, plastic flowers, Dolly Parton T-shirts, whiskey-still charm bracelets, Christian inspirational plaques, and fake folk medicines. I thought about my own desire for connectedness, wondered what an historic village would look like without the souvenirs, and drove further east into the mountains.

It's not long before I get to Cades Cove, an isolated, fertile valley in Great Smoky Mountains National Park on the border of Tennessee and North Carolina. In the mid-nineteenth century Cades Cove was a settlement of six hundred or seven hundred people. When the park was established in 1934, the government bought and expropriated land from the inhabitants of the cove, granting lifetime leases to the people who wanted to stay. The feeling at the time was that once the old homesteads were abandoned, they would be razed and the park returned to its original state.

But original states are never uncomplicated. By the 1960s, park administrators realized that the cultural heritage of the park was as interesting as its natural heritage. They left what buildings were still standing in the valley and brought in others that were scattered around the park, all with the aim of representing a nineteenth-century mountain community.

Today a dirt road travels the circumference of the cove, winding in and out of the rich edge of old-growth forest. The centre of the basin is still used as pasture and cropland by farmers who live outside the park. As I take the driving tour through the valley I realize how perfect a model it is of what is often thought of as an English pastoral aesthetic: steep mountains enclosing an inviting, peaceful valley of haystacks and grazing horses and cows.

Tucked into the edges of the valley are homesteads — single cabins, barns and outbuildings, a school, a mill, and a blacksmith shop — the same collection of buildings seen in all heritage villages. Yet here the differences are instructive. Most of the buildings are original; in fact Cades Cove probably has the most comprehensive collection of old log buildings in North America. It is also the simplest. There are no attendants playing historical roles, no paving, no marigolds, curtains, or furniture. Just the buildings themselves, empty, with weeds growing up to their open doors. It is an enchanting place, popular with tourists. The buildings have been *placed* on the land, either by their long-dead builders or subsequent park staff. They have an organic relationship to their sites, gathering together the ample valley and wooded slopes. By leaving only the buildings on their rough patches of land, Cades Cove takes our attention away from *things* — which easily transform themselves into commodities — and focuses it on the physical traces of human culture on the land. An intelligent brochure produced by the Great Smoky Mountains Natural History Association develops this theme. It tells about the physical changes of the valley, from early Native settlement and displacement, to the ruptures of the Civil War, to the destruction left by the lumber and aluminum industries early in the twentieth century. It also tells of the conditions that remain the same: honeybees in the apple trees, grains growing along Adams Creek, snow brightening long winter days. Through these twenty-odd buildings, with their adze marks and racoon shit, it all somehow connects.

Cades Cove enthrals not because it is more "authentic" than other theme parks. While authenticity is often a goal for the designers of historical museums, it is a notion irrelevant to a discussion of cultural history. Contemporary culture and ideologies always intervene between people and historical objects. It is difficult for our experience of an old farmstead, for example, to be uncontaminated by a gauzy commercial with Grandma sitting at her spinning wheel and serving up Kraft slices. Our experience of historical landscapes is all too easily appropriated by the marketers of nostalgia and the status quo.

Yet if we can't directly experience the past in outdoor museums, aren't there places somewhere where the history of the land can at least be read? Despite its understated contrivances, Cades Cove comes close to that for me. The very surface of the valley is scratched, its views composed, and these scratchings and compositions reveal a material history of human settlement. That history is something we need access to *spatially,* perhaps today more than ever. We need to be reminded in our cities of the lost warehouses where there are now parking lots, and in the country of roads that were once farm lanes or portages. In such places rests the possibility of imagining a future on this land.

Heritage USA

Heritage USA is not a village, and it lies some distance from the eastern foothills of the Appalachians. I include it here because it wants to be a village, a community; and it wants desperately to be part of the traditions of the Southern

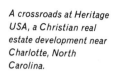

A crossroads at Heritage USA, a Christian real estate development near Charlotte, North Carolina.

Appalachians. I also include it to illustrate the regressive appropriation of the idea of "heritage."

Heritage USA is a twelve-hundred-hectare real estate development located outside Charlotte, North Carolina. Once past the entrance kiosk, where a smiling attendant greets you with "Praise the Lord," Angel Boulevard opens up to reveal what could be yours with membership: a constructed lake, several housing developments, a few hotels, a time-sharing resort, some amusement areas, a campground, a TV studio, a couple of shrines, and several satellite dishes. The intention is, or was, to make this place into a small city. In the event, Heritage USA is not a city, and certainly not a village or community. In fact, it is merely a confusing and inoffensive place, not very different from almost any exurban development you'd find within a couple of miles of an interstate highway anywhere in the United States.

Heritage USA was built by the PTL Club (variously glossed as Praise The Lord and People That Love), an evangelical Christian corporation best known for its television network, which at one time reached fifty-two countries. PTL began construction of its "21st-century Christian retreat center" in 1978, and before Jim and Tammy Bakker fell from grace ten years later it was getting about six million visitors a year. At one time plans called for a 125,000-square-metre Crystal Palace Ministry Center (modelled after the Victorian Crystal Palace in London). It would have been able to hold a projected thirty thousand residents for Sunday services. Other plans called for shopping centres, housing projects with names like Villages of the World and Old Jerusalem, and a Bible Land theme park.

On paper it sounds like Walt Disney's original plans for EPCOT Center, which was to be both an amusement park and a city with residents. But as seen from the car window, Heritage USA is a mess. Hydro transmission corridors barge through campgrounds, parking lots overlap with footpaths, boulevards lead to cul-de-sacs, and vistas are cluttered with service buildings. The park's incongruous and perverse design forms a superb example of unregulated development. It is an entrepreneurial utopia, PTL's vision of how a Christian society organizes itself in space. For obvious political reasons, Heritage USA is fascinated with tradition, which in this case means whatever can be expediently retrieved from a past understood only as a justification for the present. In pre-modern or non-modern societies, tradition is big enough to welcome change, but at Heritage USA history is as rigorously controlled as the time of day — from the first prayer meeting at dawn to those often necessary late-night counselling sessions. The development is planned, so to speak, around leisure, conspicuous consumption, and prayer meetings, a cultural practice widespread in the Southern mountain states. There is little evidence of work or its culture.

It's hard to describe Heritage USA without using quotation marks every few words. There is a "steam" train, an "old" farm with "log" houses, a "Main Street" mall with "Georgian" architecture. Inside most of the buildings we are enveloped by air conditioning, perfume, and discreet music "from yesterday and today." There are also the usual boutiques, and like Dollywood's these too are full of things. But the things are not of this place; some of them seem scarcely of this planet. There are Bibles and inspirational books, Tammy Faye's special line of makeup, and Jim and Tammy's autobiography, now marked down to $5 (from $100). In a nearby auditorium, an auctioneer for Christ sells off mammon: Winnebagos and furs, jewellery and microwaves — all this that the work of God may be done.

I do finally venture out of the car at one of the shrines. The Upper Room is a place of prayer. Two gracious ladies in church bonnets offer to pray with me or, as they put it, to "agree with my belief in prayer." You can pray in the main chapel or in a Private Prayer Closet. The closet looks like a confessional, although presumably nobody but Jesus listens. There's a bench, a Bible, and a box of Kleenex. At the exit is a plexiglass bin full of prayer requests and bulletin boards covered with photos and photocopies of people being prayed for. If you drop by in the afternoon, you can hear testimonials and witness miracles. For people unable to visit in person, you can also pray by phone. A brochure notes, "Concerned individuals answer the line 24 hours a day, able to help with your financial needs, a battle with drugs, sex or alcohol, or happy to share a praise report."

Heritage USA has a number of social programs for residents and visitors. Retreat programming, for example, is extensive: everything from marriage counselling, women's workshops, family workshops, and a Pastors and Spouses Workshop to Inner Healing and a Spring Break Get-Away and Afterglow for college students.

There is also Kevin's House, a home for disabled kids, and Fort Hope for homeless men brought from cities around the United States. Fort Hope offers vocational training and "the chance to enter a new lifestyle of Christian discipleship." You can even get to sing in the New Hope Choir. "Other organizations get people off the streets," the promotion for Fort Hope reads. "We work to get the streets out of the people."

Then there's the Heritage USA version of rural life, called Farmland USA. Promotional material calls it a "a glimpse into the country life of the 19th century surrounded by a tranquil setting of trees and gentle sloping hills." It's hard to locate this reproduction of a settlement in time or place. The farm is a single very large reproduction of a Victorian house with a barn and a few outbuildings. "Old" here evidently means frilly curtains on the windows, winding paths, and a gazebo amid relentless lawns. Down the slope, muddy and unfinished, is another artificial lake. The barn — called a Livery Stable — is fitted out as a petting zoo, and kids can go on accompanied horse and carriage rides. Scattered around those gently sloping hills and at various stages of construction are a Country Chapel for weddings, a windmill, an aviary, a Rustic Workshop displaying antique farm implements, and the Grist Mill Restaurant. Future plans call for Heritage Village, with "400 unique shops" and a Country Expo with ferris wheel and carousel. Accommodation includes the Bunkhouse Hotel, the 1100 Club Mansion, and the Country Inn Farmhouse.

1-800-HISTORY

Assuming good intentions and some kind of common need to re-create a "lost" time and culture, the four re-created Appalachian villages differ considerably. But to some extent they all use history as a retreat from the present crisis of the land. With the arguable exception of Cades Cove, they pointedly avoid making links between their reconstructed farmsteads and contemporary rural economies or settlement patterns. The past is history, as they say; theme parks mobilize its material artifacts to convince us that an organic rural life is no longer possible.

Heritage parks and "living history museums" are another element in this puzzle. They are most often established on sites considered to be of national cultural interest. Some are merely fields, like the Plains of Abraham or a natural landmark on the Santa Fe Trail. Others are plaques that remind us, like a quotation, of a cultural artifact now gone. More typically, heritage parks are forts or lighthouses, battlegrounds, canals, forges, or shipyards; they can be single

A family in stocks at Colonial Williamsburg, Virginia. John D. Rockefeller, Jr. called the park "a beacon light of freedom to the world."

buildings or entire villages. In recent years, nineteenth-century industrial areas, like parts of Lowell, Massachusetts, have been turned into heritage parks. Every level of government has been involved in establishing and maintaining heritage parks. Some, like Colonial Williamsburg or Henry Ford's Greenfield Village in Dearborn, Michigan, have been built by wealthy individuals; others are the work of community organizations.

Unlike theme parks, heritage parks cloak themselves in historicity, downplaying their commercial aspects (even though many do a good business in historical reproductions). Like nature reserves, they have come to rely on interpretive programs to help convey what life might once have been like there. In recent years, display cases and audio-visual presentations have given way to animators in period costumes who demonstrate trades, cooking, commerce, and other aspects of daily life in and among the old buildings. Heritage sites have nurtured architectural restoration movements throughout North America.

Like nature reserves too, heritage parks often promote patriotism and nostalgia. Sanctioned sites like the Liberty Bell aim to construct an idealized national past that legitimates the objectives of the modern state. Far too often, the tidy historical programming of the parks avoids social conflict. Indeed, few heritage parks even broach the kinds of questions that would give us a sense of how a given society organized itself socially and ecologically. Who actually lived in the town? Who were the immigrants, and what was their status? Were there slaves? What kind of work did women do? Who went to war? Where did water, food, and fuel come from, and where did wastes go? What kind of forestry was practised?

These are questions about our own times and places as well. In a way, it is easier to ask them at a heritage site than it is in a nature reserve, where our human traces have been concealed, sometimes physically and sometimes by the very notion that human and natural history are distinct. We never approach the natural world without carrying with us the accretions of decades and centuries of ideas about what nature means. Nor can we enter a re-created eighteenth-century village without recognizing — or being forced not to recognize — the placement of its streets and houses or the ways of its gardens.

If heritage parks used to discuss — or, as they say, present — history without causing discomfort to visitors, that has changed. Certainly, by the 1970s people had begun to complain about the parks' sanitized narratives and suburban landscaping. Younger curators who had been trained in social history were anxious to leave the charm of "bygone eras" to Disney and themselves rigorously examine the tenets of historical reconstructions. Since that time, there has been much debate about when to restore, reconstruct, reproduce, or preserve structures or landscapes, and when to leave them to rot and erode back into the earth. These debates have spilled over into such professions as museum conservation and ecological restoration. They have broad cultural implications as well, for strict criteria about restoration only begin to address the thorny issues at the intersection of nation, land, and history. English historian Patrick Wright has written about the contradictions of preserving material culture in a capitalist society that depends on widespread social change and demolition. But given the close relationship between the modern state and private industry, Wright concludes, conflict with the preservation lobby typically ends in "the restoration of harmony among private property, public interest and national imagination."

Many of these issues have come to a head at Colonial Williamsburg, a reconstructed eighteenth-century town situated along the Atlantic seaboard of the United States. Williamsburg was the second capital of Virginia, an English agricultural colony of tidewater towns and plantations based on slave labour. In the mid-1920s, John D. Rockefeller Jr. bought most of the town and began to rebuild it as a monument to his idea of Colonial America and its values. "May this restored city stand as a beacon light of freedom to the world," he proclaimed. Opened in 1932, Williamsburg (whose toll-free telephone number for information is 1-800-HISTORY) was an immediate success, and it now attracts about a million visitors a year. Its architectural reconstructions have been reproduced everywhere in the United States — from chic suburban manses to A&P shopping centres; and by the 1960s many buildings of its vintage had been tarted up and decked out with eagles and U.S. flags.

Colonial Williamsburg has built its reputation on the kind of flag-waving patriotism that still gets U.S. presidents elected. Under the direction of Winthrop Rockefeller II, Williamsburg became a "shrine of the American faith" during the Cold War. Its mission was to proclaim five concepts "of lasting importance to all men everywhere: opportunity, individual liberties, self-government, the integrity of the individual, and responsible leadership." Educational programs in the reconstructed houses of the planter elite talk about these concepts as the lessons of the American Revolution, yet they seem strangely congruent with contemporary ideas about private property and the free market.

Colonial Williamsburg's version of the past also promotes the U.S. empire. In the 1960s, Winthrop Rockefeller and Dean Rusk both gave speeches from its hallowed streets in support of the U.S. war in Southeast Asia. Many of the park's directors have worked at the State Department, and since the 1950s Williamsburg has functioned as a reception centre for foreign diplomats on their way to Washington, D.C. Its distinguished visitors have included Winston Churchill, the Shah of Iran, Queen Elizabeth II, and most of the 1960s administrators of South Vietnam. The park has been host to U.S. soldiers on their way overseas, and in 1983 Ronald Reagan led a parade of the leaders of the seven wealthiest countries down Duke of Gloucester Street.

Links to U.S. foreign policy are figured in the local geography. The park lies near the confluence of the James and York rivers with Chesapeake Bay and the Atlantic Ocean. The region's broad estuaries are occupied by over a dozen military installations, including the largest nuclear-submarine base in the world (and its attendant ocean waste-dumps). Much of this strategic landscape is visible along the Colonial Parkway, the formal entrance to the park.

By the late 1970s, Williamsburg was in crisis. New curators wanted to provoke the visitors. Amid much controversy they replaced some of the tidy gardens with grimy blacksmith shops and began to leave the horse shit on the streets. They expanded the slave quarters. To comment on the history of American attitudes to mental illness they refitted the public hospital with graffiti, soiled beds, handcuffs, and tranquillizers.

Curators were also interested in commenting on the idea of reconstruction itself. Rockefeller had purged Williamsburg of everything built after 1800. Yet there is much to be learned from the subsequent glosses and reinterpretations of the town's physical history. Perhaps the most interesting changes have taken place at Carter's Grove, an old plantation on the James River southeast of Williamsburg. There the big house has undergone several reconstructions. Throughout the mid-century period it was owned by Molly McCrea, a Virginia socialite who in the 1930s had begun to decorate it in the then-popular Colonial Revival style. Like Dollywood, it was crammed with souvenirs from here and there and showed little concern with arid debates about authenticity. When the Williamsburg park bought the property in the 1960s, they removed McCrea's historical knick-knacks and restored it to a properly austere eighteenth-century agricultural manor. But later there was a change of heart. Park historians decided that the most useful building would be a restoration of McCrea's 1930s interpretation of the colonial era. They brought back her collections of iron cauldrons and spinning wheels, rehung the modern screen doors, and set out McCrea's toaster, telephones, and gaudy soaps. Today visitors hear big-band music on the radio in the upstairs sitting room.

A Canadian equivalent of Williamsburg doesn't really exist, since the nature of Canadian confederation doesn't allow for a single galvanizing cultural site. The most extensive historical reconstruction in the country is at Louisbourg, an early eighteenth-century French settlement on the Atlantic coast of Cape Breton Island. The British demolished the town after the conquest of New France in 1760, and about 20 per cent of the thirty-hectare site has been reconstructed from the foundations. Visitors leave their cars in a parking lot well back from the Atlantic shore and are bused to a beach outside the town gates. There fishing boats come and go, nets are hauled up on the shore for repair, and cod is salted and hung to dry. In the town, costumed townspeople — watched by tourists — wander round doing what we recognize as everyday things: trading and baking, weeding and sewing, repairing tools. Their work is also work for us as tourists — serving us meals and cleaning the washrooms — although the site's directors have chosen not to highlight this relationship.

National and Natural History

The abundance of heritage parks in the contemporary landscape underscores their function as sentimental keepsakes, static utopias that remind us as much of the uncertain future as they do of the past. But they are also places that allow us to explore the full spatial and temporal dimensions of the present land crisis. Whatever the problems with museum villages, and they are many, I think they do achieve this: by stripping away at least some of the detritus of commodity culture, they allow us to see the structure of the relations between human settlement and the natural world. They are tactile places, full of the history of material life: of the birch bark, pine sap, and cedar root that linked Native cultures of the northeast to the rivers and rocks they travelled, and of the crucifixes and contaminated blankets that accompanied the conquest.

The struggle over public memory and its relation to everyday landscapes is exceedingly complex, and here I can only signal the general outlines of its politics. As conservative as the movement to preserve landscape and built form often seems, the attempt has at least some of its roots in the anti-modern movements of the nineteenth century. Following the opening of Skansen outside Stockholm in 1891, "outdoor folk museums" were constructed across Northern Europe. These celebrated the rural lifeways that were quickly being driven into retreat by industrial capitalism. Some of this impulse is visible in Henry Ford's quirky and nostalgic fascination with "the common man" at Greenfield Village.

While today the idea of heritage is frequently appropriated by right-wing politics — Heritage USA and the Heritage Foundation are the most obvious examples — it also enjoys some currency among oppositional cultures. Heritage language programs have undermined the dominance of English in many Canadian and U.S. schools. Gardeners collect and distribute (often for free) "heritage seed," the fertile seed of old fruit and vegetable varieties that are being displaced by the patented and sterile varieties of modern agriculture. The Seed Savers Exchange, based in Iowa, promotes the "timeless kinship of gardeners" who grow, eat, propagate, and exchange plants that live a precarious existence in the interstices of the transnational economy — endangered and heirloom varieties passed from one generation to another or among Native, Amish, or Cajun communities.

What the contradictions of contemporary landscape show is that the binary opposition between city and country, past and present, no longer serves us well. Restoring continuity to human settlements means moving beyond these oppositions — in fact it means moving beyond abstraction altogether. The practical terms of this work will be defined differently from one place to another, as we develop and propagate the natural skills and knowledge necessary to living on this Earth in a new way.

A Ducks Unlimited pond
at Oak Hammock Marsh,
north of Winnipeg,
Manitoba. Ducks
Unlimited is a
conservation organization
that rearranges wetlands
and builds "duck parks"
for hunters.

7. From Reserve to Microenvironment
Nature Parks and Zoos

Even though our intervention [in nature] is obvious, we prefer to maintain an illusion that nature — or God — is in charge, and we don't like to be reminded otherwise because that might get in the way of our feelings about the land and our role in it.

— Tom Bonnicksen

The history of nature parks and zoos differs little from that of fairs and theme parks. Today there are many kinds of parks — not just natural areas but historical and cultural sites, conservation areas, biosphere reserves, land trusts, zoos, safari parks, aquariums, and biological parks. But like suburban lawns and gardens or scenic roads, parks of all kinds are cultural landscapes. The history of their creation and policy is rife with contradictions and compromise, for parks are the site of struggles over conservation, preservation, profit, and development, the site of shifts in the value and meaning of natural areas and animal collections.

The parks that form green patches on our North American roadmaps have many origins. Some derive from the ages-old communal spaces of large and small human settlements the world over: cemeteries, market squares, temple precincts, and commons. In Europe the first established public parks — originally called promenades, pleasure-gardens, or *Volksgarten* — were private reserves that by the late eighteenth century gradually allowed public access. In the nineteenth century, an owner of extensive private property in or near a city sometimes bequeathed land to the city to be used as a public park.

Urban parks have always had an explicit relationship with the less-settled lands outside the city. But the idea of locating a park outside the city — in nature, so to speak — was quite foreign, certainly in North America, until the mid-nineteenth century. The earliest rural parks in Europe were established to protect game from being hunted by the peasantry. When Europeans began to settle North America, the hinterlands were variously described as a wilderness or desert — often as an ugly place — inhabited by savages. While in contemporary culture the word "desert" retains its connotation as a wasteland, "wilderness" has undergone a number of shifts in meaning over the course of this century. Chief Standing Bear, an Ogalala Sioux, pointed out the conflict his people felt with the Europeans who colonized their land in the Great Plains in the late nineteenth century:

We did not think of the great open plains, the beautiful rolling hills and the winding streams with tangled growth as "wild." Only to the white man was nature a "wilderness" and only to him was the land "infested" with "wild" animals and "savage" people. To us it was tame. Earth was bountiful, and we were surrounded with the blessings of the Great Mystery. Not until the hairy man from the east came and with brutal frenzy heaped injustices upon us and the families we loved was it "wild" for us. When the very animals of the forest began fleeing from his approach, then it was that for us the "Wild West" began.

A movement to establish national parks in North America began to form in the 1860s and 1870s, at about the time community organizations were lobbying for public parks and playgrounds in the increasingly dense, industrialized cities. The arguments for the establishment of national parks were in part conservationist: naturalists, bureaucrats, and industrialists were concerned about the loss and mismanagement of natural and scenic resources. Yet there were other factors. The first parks in both Canada and the United States were in the West, far from most white settlement. As that settlement moved across the continent, however, the cultural value of wilderness began to change and a trade in nature became possible. For many years after its establishment in 1872, for example, Yellowstone National Park was used as a sport hunting ground for tourists from the Atlantic cities and Europe. The creation of parks in the West was also spurred by the monumentality of the landscape itself.

Between 1870 and the Depression of the 1930s, Canadian and U.S. governments created scores of national, state, and provincial parks across North America. They established some of them as auxiliaries to road and railway building, as a way of opening up new lands to development. Many of the parks were the fruit of the early conservation movement, which was in part an attempt to regulate private speculation and control supply and value in the marketplace. The leadership of the movement, many of them men of the professional classes, promoted the application of scientific techniques — what Samuel P. Hays calls "the gospel of efficiency" — to resource management, thus centralizing power and expertise in a disorganized industry. These are the same changes that came to agriculture as large companies wrested control over production methods and distribution from farmers. The rationalization of the resource

Yellowstone National Park, Wyoming. For European colonizers, the early national parks were unpeopled and "wild." But to its original inhabitants, North America was tame and bountiful.

Green Gables golf course, Prince Edward Island National Park, Canada. For at least a hundred years, park creation and development have been closely tied to the political economy of tourism.

industry coincided with the introduction of national policies to "protect" wild-lands from haphazard development by local entrepreneurs. This was especially true in Canada, where a wilderness ethic was slow to develop given the sparse white settlement of the West and the vastness of the wild lands in the North. In both countries, however, the interpretation of park mandates has varied widely depending on the government in power.

Sometimes governments created parks for the most expedient political reasons. Prime Minister William Lyon Mackenzie King established Prince Albert National Park in Saskatchewan as a way of thanking his constituents, who had elected him to Parliament. During wartime, national parks have been used to detain conscientious objectors, prisoners, and — most infamously — non-white people the state regards as a security threat. In 1985, when a U.S. icebreaker traversed the Northwest Passage without Canadian permission, the Progressive Conservative government looked for a quick way to assert sovereignty in the Arctic. Cabinet gave immediate approval to a Parks Canada report calling for a park on Ellesmere Island, the most northerly lands in Canada.

In other cases, governments have created parks to preserve forests from local settlers or natural "predators" like fire, so the lands can then be properly harvested by timber companies, as was the case with Algonquin Park, established in 1893 in Ontario. The Adirondack Reserve in New York State was established to enhance the aquifers of the cities of the Hudson River watershed. Such is the legacy of the early conservation movement.

For at least a hundred years, park creation and development have been closely tied to the political economy of tourism. In the capitalist democracies of North America, the conflict between preservation and profit lies at the heart of nature parks. In many cases, parks have been created to stimulate the local tourist industry. Conservation policies have been developed only secondarily, as a response to the pressures of social movements. This is most transparently the case in Canada, where the government established the first national park, Banff, in 1885 as a luxury resort for the Canadian Pacific Railway. (It was not until 1968 that Parks Canada policy was open to public scrutiny and hearings became required for development plans.)

Park development is also related to resource management and extraction. In state and provincial parks, governments have all along permitted forestry, hydro development, mining, and grazing, in addition to recreational uses such as hunting and fishing, boating, and camping. This is usually called "mixed" or "multiple use," a policy much in dispute today. Multiple use is based on an industrial model: it proposes a land-management regime that optimizes human use of the forest for profit while still providing a wholesome habitat for native species of plants and animals. A U.S. Forest Service brochure from the 1960s describes a ranger's job as a "manager of renewable resources." The ranger "must intensify management and development so that each resource — water, timber, wildlife, forage, recreation — will produce forest products and services at as high a level of supply as can be sustained without harming the land's ability to produce, now and in the future."

Multiple use became the founding principle of the national forests in the United States after Gifford Pinchot, a silviculturist, led a vociferous revolt from the ranks of the preservationists at the turn of the century. Throughout the postwar period, the U.S. Forest Service simultaneously increased the number of its timber leases and ran a campaign entitled "The National Forests — America's Playgrounds."

The principal proponents of multiple use continue to be the resource industries, and men's sporting organizations like fishing and gun clubs; until recently the policy has also had strong government support. In recent years, however, multiple-use policy has been seriously undermined by the habitat and ecosystem models that have emerged from the ecological sciences. While the policy is still favoured by most state forest-management bodies, park bureaucrats have by and large renounced it. But timber berths are still held by resource companies in the Rocky Mountain parks of Canada, and it is not inconceivable that the government will someday allow exploitation of the large coal veins there, as well as of the probable natural gas deposits.

Parks Canada now occasionally uses the term "traditional use," a kind of subset of multiple use. It refers to the approval of such land uses as ranching in Grasslands National Park in Saskatchewan and commercial fishing in Gros Morne on the west coast of Newfoundland. These exceptions have usually been necessary conditions for park establishment. In the Northern parks, Native people are permitted to continue their lifeways, including gathering food, hunting, and lumbering.

Park Boundaries: Buffers and Barriers

Boundaries are important, because they limit the meanings parks are allowed in the culture. They establish the privileged status of nature reserves by restricting access to them and physically separating them from other land uses. Although policies change, boundaries go on prohibiting certain kinds of development and providing a buffer against the demands of a market economy. Perhaps most importantly, park boundaries usually prohibit human habitation as well.

Park boundaries have been regularly manipulated by governments right from the beginning. Banff National Park has been reduced in size twice, once so the provincial government could dam the Spray Lakes to get hydro and irrigation for Southern Alberta. In Yosemite National Park in California, the state government allowed the city of San Francisco to flood the renowned Hetch Hetchy Valley, just years after the park was created.

Establishing park boundaries has become a formidable task since the enactment of the first environmental protection legislation in the 1960s. These laws have by and large been the state's response to the conflicting demands of the resource industry, the environmental movement, and indigenous peoples. One of the results of the legislation has been the classification of lands that lie outside of the traditional productive economy. This takes place through a legislative process that resembles the investment decisions of a corporation. Any land considered for a park is first reviewed for its resource potential. Government agencies regularly take inventories from air and land, research the future conditions of the resource market, and determine how much they're able to offer as incentives to private resource industries. ("Like the grocer who has to know the amount and variety of stock on his shelves," a Saskatchewan government forestry pamphlet begins.) It is difficult today to preserve land that contains timber or ore deposits that might be valuable in the future. When the Canadian federal government established Pacific Rim National Park on the west coast of Vancouver Island in 1970, for example, the British Columbia government delayed the enabling legislation long enough for much of the area to be logged.

Today, the less profit-oriented the land is, the more eligible it is for protection. This includes lands "of no economic value" that have never seen development of any kind, as well as disturbed tracts that were once logged, burned, or mined. An anomalous example of this last would be the formerly inhabited but now abandoned lands covered under the Eastern Wilderness Act passed in the United States in 1975. Once protected, land is able to re-enter the realm of the natural or "unspoiled."

Land considered superfluous to resource exploitation is usually available for park status, especially if it will stimulate a local tourist economy. Balancing preservation with profit and accessibility has been the task of park administrators for most of this century. Scenery is of value to tourism, after all, only if it is still there to be enjoyed. The bureaucratic solution to this dilemma has been to define the natural in legal terms and to allow for mixed use.

Thus a "wild" river, where no development is permitted, is considered more natural than a "scenic" river, which is more natural than a "recreational" river, and so on. The state accords each of these types of environment specific protection in law. Boats in a particular park, for example, might be restricted to low-horsepower or non-motorized types or be banned altogether. Roads and power-transmission corridors may or may not be permitted. Certain kinds of tourist development, such as golf courses, might be acceptable, while ski resorts or hunting might not. Aboriginal land rights are sometimes honoured in parks; at other times parks have been created to keep Native people away from an area, as a way of invalidating their rights to land.

The Making of New Parks

In the postwar years, governments and resource industries promoted outdoor recreation as part of more intensive land development underway outside urban areas. Many new resource-extraction facilities, such as lakes impounded for power generation or forests cleared for timber, were developed with recreational components such as campgrounds, picnic areas, and trail systems. These are true multiple-use parks. In the United States, the government began massive land acquisition for national parks in the 1950s. In Canada, in the years following the centennial celebration of 1967, federal and provincial governments began aggressively creating new parks as well. In 1967 the Canadian Outdoor Recreation Demand Study identified the characteristics of park visitors and recommended expansion at every level. Since that time, the amount of land in Canada's national parks has doubled. In both countries, the past thirty years have seen a tremendous expansion of park infrastructures such as roads, interpretive centres, and other visitor services. This has corresponded with a tremendous increase in park use, which went up by 400 per cent between 1950 and 1965.

Since the 1960s there has been a rash of new parks, and especially new kinds of parks and reserves. Some of these were established to commemorate cultural sites or national monuments such as canals or villages. Internationally, for example, UNESCO began a program of World Heritage Sites and Biosphere Reserves. Various levels of government in North America have established conservation areas, national recreation areas, national seashores, national monuments, landmarks, and wildlife refuges, environmental education centres, wilderness areas and marine parks, as well as wild, scenic, heritage, and recreational river systems. In the United States, the Bureau of Land Management and the Fish and Wildlife Service both maintain reserves. There are also private parks run by organizations such as the Audubon Society, Ducks Unlimited, or the Nature Conservancy, or by private corporations. Lastly, there are local land trusts, usually run by rural communities, and the sacred spaces of Native people such as the Black Hills in South Dakota or the Queen Charlotte Islands in British Columbia.

Some of these parks — especially areas with complex nomenclatures, such as the river systems — are the result of environmental legislation. Others are the result of constant pressure from the environmental movement. (In the United States, many of the protected river systems were established after local protest against impoundment.) When governments have been slow to act to protect the earth, people have often simply squatted land. And certainly the claims of the First People of this continent, which have been heard everywhere in the past thirty years, are now beginning to influence the way the dominant culture thinks of parks and nature reserves.

For their part, governments have been busy trying to manage the many social forces at work in the area of environment. The demands of our capitalist economies on the natural resources of North America are perhaps greater than ever today. Yet new ideas about what parks do, as well as new knowledge about the environment, have influenced policy as well.

Parks are now expected to preserve culturally significant landscapes and important ecosystems. This is in part an exercise in conservation, very much like the work of contemporary zoos. Out of the twenty-five thousand estimated species of plants native to North America, two hundred are already extinct, and the Centre for Plant Conservation in Boston estimates that another seven hundred may become extinct by the end of the millennium. The causes are the familiar ones leading to the destruction of habitat, and the areas of particular threat are in the subtropical portions of the continent: California, Texas, Florida, and Hawaii, as well as the U.S. dependency of Puerto Rico. Animals are also part of this equation, and wildlife management is an important part of most park operations. Some species, such as the black bear or salmon, are recognized as "indicator species," meaning that their health is an indicator of the well-being of the entire forest or river they inhabit.

The Changing Culture of Parkland

Two new policies in Canadian national parks are evidence of larger social changes over the past thirty years. In the 1970s Parks Canada implemented a national development plan to identify locations for future parks. The document, drawing heavily on research carried out in the ecological sciences in the 1960s, divided the country into sixty-eight physiographic regions — thirty-nine terrestrial and twenty-nine marine. The guidelines are a virtual catalogue of Earth forms, which have been given names such as Strait of Georgia Lowlands, Mackenzie Delta, Central Boreal Uplands, and Ungava Tundra Plateau. Within these regions, the document identifies specific areas that include the broadest range of local natural "themes" (biologic, geologic, physiographic, geographic, and oceanographic). Planners select potential parks from this inventory, the idea being that each region of Canada should be represented by a national park; and, conversely, each national park should be a microcosm of a Canadian biogeography. At present about half the regions have representative parks.

In the 1970s this policy inspired northern affairs minister Jean Chrétien's campaign to acquire several parklands in the North. But the creation of the Northern parks has anticipated a number of conflicts that cannot be resolved for some time to come — or perhaps will never be resolved until parks have a different relation to human settlement, until they are something more than uninhabited land. It has always been easy to expropriate lands from territorial governments that have virtually no power in Canadian confederation, be it for national parks, oil extraction, or military facilities. What is clearly not so easy is ongoing negotiation about the rights of aboriginal peoples in the North (and elsewhere), and their very contradictory relation to the history of nature reserves in this country. At present, Native people are allowed to carry on a subsistence economy in the Northern parks, since the government considers this a "traditional" use. What Native people themselves consider traditional has yet to be fully pondered by parks enthusiasts — or for that matter by many in the environmental movement. The official Parks Canada policy calls for maintaining an "appropriate balance between the rights of the public to understand and enjoy Canada's natural heritage, the rights of local people to continue certain traditional uses and the requirement to protect the wilderness of the area."

The events surrounding the creation of South Moresby National Park in the southern portion of the Queen Charlotte Islands, or Haida Gwai, in 1987, provide a good example of the conflict inherent in such a policy. The Haida nation disputes Canadian authority over the islands, which are off the northwest coast of British Columbia. Despite this conflict, transnational timber companies have extensively logged the old-growth forests of the islands over much of this century. In recent years the methods of logging have become even more destructive and wasteful than ever. When the Haida prepared a court case to remove the logging companies from their ancestral lands, they formed an uneasy alliance with local environmental groups, who helped set up roadblocks.

The Haida proposed establishing an autonomous and living "tribal park." The environmental position, however — insofar as it can be spoken of in a unitary way — favoured the creation of a national park. The conflict gained international attention, not least because of the high status of Haida culture among Western anthropologists and art historians. When the Haida lost their legal bid to halt logging, the federal government — whose policy since the early Trudeau years has been to extinguish aboriginal rights wherever possible — stepped in with its solution of a national park on the most scenic of the disputed lands.

Such a solution does more than ignore aboriginal rights. It narrows the terms of the relationship between human livelihood and the physical world. The integrity of Haida society depends, in the words of its constitution, on "cultivating a respect for and intimacy with the land and sea." That intimacy has been gained from living in one place for a very long time, developing local and traditional knowledge about the land. Reconciliation with the First Nations of this continent will not take place until settler societies open themselves to that possibility. None of this is to say that aboriginal land stewardship will necessarily meet the approval of the environmental movement.

The other new Canadian parks policy has been a response to conflicts over roads, townsites, ski areas, motels, and other tourist development in the parks. Park administrations have always been interested in promoting tourism, but in the past few decades intensive park use has endangered many local ecosystems, particularly where there are towns in the parks. Consequently, in 1978 Parks Canada set up zones within each park to try to manage the tension between development and preservation. The objective is to concentrate tourist facilities

National Park Natural Regions

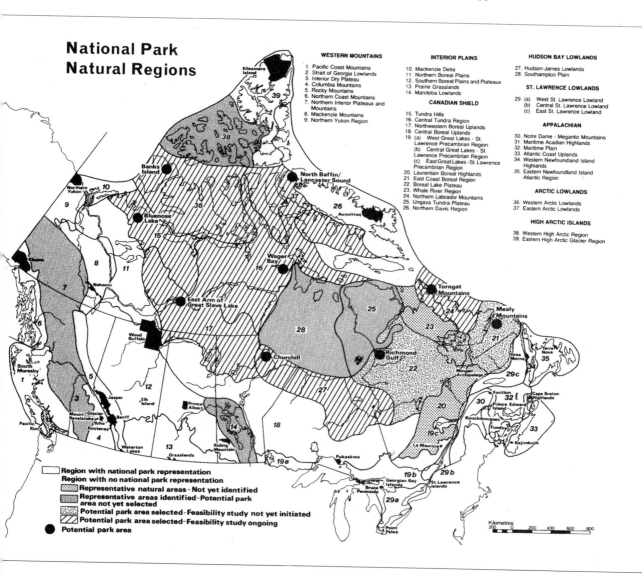

WESTERN MOUNTAINS
1. Pacific Coast Mountains
2. Strait of Georgia Lowlands
3. Interior Dry Plateau
4. Columbia Mountains
5. Rocky Mountains
6. Northern Coast Mountains
7. Northern Interior Plateaux and Mountains
8. Mackenzie Mountains
9. Northern Yukon Region

INTERIOR PLAINS
10. Mackenzie Delta
11. Northern Boreal Plains
12. Southern Boreal Plains and Plateaux
13. Prairie Grasslands
14. Manitoba Lowlands

CANADIAN SHIELD
15. Tundra Hills
16. Central Tundra Region
17. Northwestern Boreal Uplands
18. Central Boreal Uplands
19. (a) West Great Lakes - St. Lawrence Precambrian Region
    (b) Central Great Lakes - St. Lawrence Precambrian Region
    (c) East Great Lakes - St. Lawrence Precambrian Region
20. Laurentian Boreal Highlands
21. East Coast Boreal Region
22. Boreal Lake Plateau
23. Whale River Region
24. Northern Labrador Mountains
25. Ungava Tundra Plateau
26. Northern Davis Region

HUDSON BAY LOWLANDS
27. Hudson-James Lowlands
28. Southampton Plain

ST. LAWRENCE LOWLANDS
29. (a) West St. Lawrence Lowland
    (b) Central St. Lawrence Lowland
    (c) East St. Lawrence Lowland

APPALACHIAN
30. Notre Dame - Megantic Mountains
31. Maritime Acadian Highlands
32. Maritime Plain
33. Atlantic Coast Uplands
34. Western Newfoundland Island Highlands
35. Eastern Newfoundland Island Atlantic Region

ARCTIC LOWLANDS
36. Western Arctic Lowlands
37. Eastern Arctic Lowlands

HIGH ARCTIC ISLANDS
38. Western High Arctic Region
39. Eastern High Arctic Glacier Region

Region with national park representation
Region with no national park representation
Representative natural areas - Not yet identified
Representative areas identified - Potential park area not yet selected
Potential park area selected - Feasibility study not yet initiated
Potential park area selected - Feasibility study ongoing
● Potential park area

The Canadian Parks Service aims to have a park in each biogeographical zone of the country.

so that the majority of parklands can be preserved as wilderness. The zones are, in decreasing order of "primitiveness": Special Preservation, Wilderness, Natural Environment, Outdoor Recreation, and Park Services. Special Preservation areas are endangered ecosystems to which human access is strictly controlled or prohibited. The policy permits private cars only in the last two zones. In the marine parks the zones reach into other dimensions: temporal zoning allows for restrictions on a daily or seasonal basis, to protect spawning grounds, for example; vertical zoning might extend protection to a seafloor, while activities at or near the surface of the water column can continue.

Zoning has succeeded in relieving some of the pressure in more sensitive areas of parks. It has also allowed for the development of a more diversified tourist industry. Self-sufficient backcountry types can try to imagine a nature unmediated by human culture in preserved areas, while the majority of people can languish among their RVs in the semi-urbanized park centres. Outdoor-equipment manufacturers now outfit a multiplicity of experiences in nature parks: canoe and rafting trips, trailer camping, dune and crosscountry skiing, hiking, winter camping, climbing, and mountain biking. Camping gear has become very sophisticated. The big developments have been in synthetic fabrics for clothing and such equipment as tents and packs, but consider the other developments: waxless skis, breathable-waterproof raingear, advances in optics, footwear, sleeping gear, cooking equipment, and bicycle fashions. There are also many kinds of on-road and off-road vehicles.

Ideally, the people who establish park zones rely on land classification criteria such as soil characteristics, watershed quality, slope conditions, and the state of forest regeneration. These are the same criteria used by the resource managers who set up multiple-use schemes in less protected areas. While it doesn't allow for nearly the variety of land uses, zoning is similar to multiple-use management. Its fragmentation of the landscape has its counterpart in the diversification of tourist markets and the specialization of outdoor equipment.

In recent years parks policies have become complicated. Since nature reserves are cultural artifacts as much as they are natural systems, there are always difficult questions about how far to go in manipulating them. Should fires be permitted? Should alien species be eliminated? Should native species be reintroduced? From time to time park administrators have attempted to draw up management principles. In 1963 the Leopold Committee in the United States enunciated one of these principles:

The goal of managing the National Parks ...should be to preserve, or where necessary to recreate, the ecologic scene as viewed by the first European visitors. As part of this scene, native species of wild animals should be present in maximum variety and reasonable abun-

dance. Protection alone . . . is not adequate to achieve this goal. Habitat manipulation is helpful and often essential to restore or maintain animal numbers. . . . Active management aimed at restoration of natural communities of plants and animals demands skills and knowledge not now in existence.

The Leopold Committee report was prescient. It recognized that by 1960 wild lands were no longer wild — they were thoroughly penetrated by the human mind and the physical presence of our societies. Modern parks, the report argued, needed substantial, sensitive, and continuing human intervention. The skills the committee called for are those of ecological restoration, an activity that would not be widely practised until the late 1970s. Ecological restoration, in part an arbitrary exercise in cultural memory, is always a question of what to save, what to put back, what to take apart. What moment in the history of human-natural relations becomes the model? For the Leopold Committee, just as at the University of Wisconsin arboretum, it was the moment of first contact of European peoples with this continent, although it is curiously posed as a visit to an "ecologic scene" rather than an encounter with its inhabitants, the many and diverse aboriginal peoples.

The difficulty the report's writers had in recognizing Native people points to the thorniest question facing parks policy-makers: to what extent is human presence in the parks welcome? The myth of the national park in North America is that of an unpeopled sanctuary amid the extensive terrestrial exploitation and settlement that surrounds it. This notion has often encouraged intensive commercial development along park boundaries — witness the flood of activity at the two main entrances to Great Smoky Mountains National Park in the southern Appalachians. Spiritually, too, nature reserves are widely thought of almost as sacred places, places to retreat to when we are overwhelmed with the unfortunate "side-effects" of civilization. (The U.S. Wilderness Act of 1964 defined wild land as "an area where the earth and its community of life lie untrammelled by man, where man himself is a visitor who does not remain.") In practice, this is an inadequate way of thinking about either parks or settled lands. Our relations with the natural world are rarely that simple. Recent policies on park acquisition and management, however, are beginning to suggest a way out of this bind: that human settlement need not be disruptive of natural systems.

The reasons for establishing parks have multiplied. In addition to traditional concerns about stimulating the tourist economy, there are now more scientific and philosophical reasons to create a park. These have to do with national identity, scientific exploration, and preservation of valuable habitat. What is valuable is determined by the culture of the time; certainly in the past

**Ecoclimatic Provinces
of Canada, 1990**

*A map of the effects of
global climate change on
Canadian biogeography,
developed by the
Sustainable Development
Corporate Policy Group at
Environment Canada.*

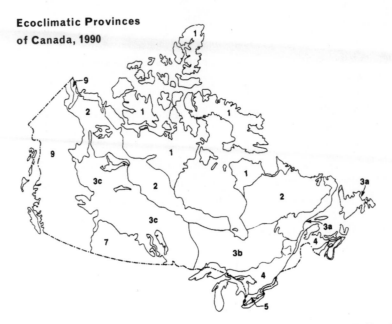

Ecoclimatic Provinces

1. Arctic
2. Subarctic
3. Boreal
   - 3a. Maritime Boreal
   - 3b. Moist Continental Boreal
   - 3c. Dry Continental Boreal
4. Cool Temperate
5. Moderate Temperate
6. Transitional Grassland
7. Grassland
8. Semi-desert
9. unclassed,
   cordilleras not shown

**Ecoclimatic Provinces:
A 2050 Scenario**

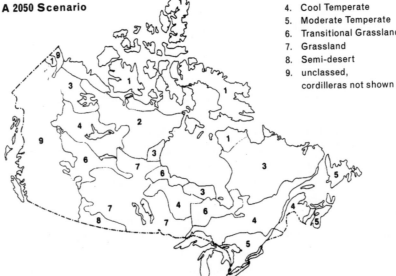

ten years it has become legitimate to set aside tracts of land *for its own sake*. The Canadian government established Northern Yukon National Park, for example, to preserve the feeding grounds and migration routes of the Porcupine caribou herd, the largest in North America. The current ecological crisis has lent park creation a new urgency. Global climate change, for example, will hasten what already appears to be a general floral and faunal collapse. Many scientists recognize that the biotic diversity necessary to support most life on the planet will depend in part on the preservation (and restoration, if possible) of entire biological communities *in situ*. These insights are based on subdisciplines that have only emerged from the science of ecology in the last twenty years: community ecology, island biogeography, animal demographics, and ecological genetics.

In sum, non-economic arguments for park creation are now more popular than ever — even in official policy, as demonstrated by this 1987 document from the Canadian environment minister's Task Force on Park Establishment:

National parks and other protected places are our lifeline to an ecologically stable future. They are places where the forces that animate our planet and make it unique are allowed to operate with minimal interference by man; places where we can wonder and pay respect to other living things and the intricacies of ecosystems; places that produce oxygen, stabilize the hydrological cycle, grow abundant fish and wildlife, stay erosion, pour out no man-made toxicants into air or water. They are places where people can study the vital functions of nature, to understand better the potentially threatening human impacts elsewhere. They do not impede our future. They anchor it. They are not a repudiation of economic development. They balance it.

World Heritage and Biosphere Reserves

In the late 1950s, park managers began to talk about "natural heritage" interchangeably with "natural resource." Since the mid-1970s, the term has been used to denote places that are representative of both natural and cultural history. Historic parks were first established early in this century and tended to focus on military history, perhaps because the relic structures of warfare were sturdy and the lands easily available for expropriation. Recently, however, attention has shifted towards commemoration of cultural or industrial history and its relationship to geography. This is an important step, for it begins to blur the rigid distinctions between cultural and natural history.

Canada and the United States are among about one hundred countries that adhere to UNESCO's World Heritage Convention, adopted in 1972. The convention promotes the protection of cultural and natural sites throughout the world by designating heritage properties and providing financial assistance for their preservation. Approved sites — of which there are about three hundred — include Old Havana, Dinosaur Provincial Park and Head-Smashed-In Bison Jump in Alberta, the city of Quebec, the Galapagos Islands, the city of Quito, Islamic Cairo, Mont St. Michel and Chartres Cathedral in France, Tikal, the Kathmandu valley, Mesa Verde National Park and Independence Hall in the United States, and the Wieliczka salt mine and Auschwitz, both in Poland. While including familiar conditions such as uniqueness and authenticity, the criteria for approval also emphasize that heritage is not only something of the past: the convention is eager to protect sites that are examples of human interaction with environment, as well as the settlements of "cultures which have become vulnerable under the impact of irreversible change."

UNESCO recognizes development as a global problem and maintains that preservation of wild, historical, or sacred sites must be undertaken outside of the interests of states and corporations. It explicitly outlines the threats: pollution, age, urbanization, tourism, vandalism, and property speculation. The agency has often played an advocacy role in its citations. Its designation of the Queen Charlotte Islands, for example, was helpful in preventing at least part of those Native lands from being logged; likewise it intended its designation of Old Jerusalem as a World Heritage Site to help end Israeli occupation.

The World Heritage Convention charter goes beyond the new parks policies. A UNESCO brochure explains:

The Convention presents a profoundly original characteristic which encompasses new and important ideas. It joins together the concepts of nature and culture which up to now were considered different and even in opposition to each other. Indeed, for a long time these concepts were locked in conflict: man was supposed to conquer his hostile natural surroundings while culture symbolized spiritual values. However, nature and culture are complementary: the cultural identity of different peoples has been forged in the environment in which they live and frequently, the most beautiful man-made works owe part of their beauty to the place where they are erected. And in our modern world both our cultural wealth and natural sites appear to be equally threatened by all kinds of degradation.

Under a program called — in a UN language still infected with sexism — "Man and the Biosphere," UNESCO has also established yet another international network of protected areas, called Biosphere Reserves. These areas too are chosen as representative of particular biogeographical "provinces," or land types, on each continent — only here the system is different. Most of North America is part of the Nearctic Realm, which contains twenty-two provinces, local variants of a global system of fourteen biomes, such as grasslands, evergreen scrub forests, coniferous forests, cold-winter deserts, broadleaf woodlands, and temperate rainforests. Geographer Miklos Udvardy formulated the classificatory system in 1975, using both vegetational and faunal analysis.

About two hundred and fifty biosphere reserves have been set aside in over sixty countries; about fifty of them are in North America. They are used for conservation, manipulative research, monitoring of ecosystem changes over time, and as training grounds for resource managers. The reserves are an adaptable concept and often include lands that would never meet the conceptual or practical criteria of traditional parks.

Given that the biosphere is the thin layer of the Earth — the air, soil, and water — where all life is concentrated, it's important to note that these reserves are not the standard nature reserves. They are a new kind of park, born of another time, a time of ecological science and a scarcity of wild lands. Formally, the reserves are built on the idea of the ecosystem: an aggregation of relationships, a self-regulating community of innumerable species, including *homo sapiens,* and their physical environment.

Natural areas in a biosphere reserve are assigned to a "core" area, often an existing traditional park, which serves as both a conservation area and as a kind of control group for research. This core area is surrounded by a "buffer" zone of disturbed or manipulated land used for problem-oriented research, environmental monitoring, and education. The buffer zone demonstrates the same ecosystem organized to meet human needs, particularly by traditional means. It is meant to be a place of reconciliation, a model of a human community in harmony with the natural world.

If necessary, there are also areas set aside for ecological rehabilitation or restoration. Beyond all of these zones is the more customary multiple-use area, where human communities are encouraged to co-operate and be open to some of the lessons learned in the inner zones. Boundaries are often indefinite and fluctuate over time, depending on the scope and character of human activity. There are no fees or hours of entry, for the park is meant to overlay land and landscape.

Administration of the biosphere reserves differs from one to another. Management committees are typically formed of government and private landowners as well as local organizations interested in the program. At the United Nations end, biosphere reserves are sponsored by the Man and the Biosphere (MAB) program. MAB, launched in 1971, was an outgrowth of the International Biological Program (IBP) of the 1960s, which promoted the emerging science of ecology by studying tundra, rainforest, and grassland ecosystems. Participants criticized the IPB because it often ignored the relationships between ecosystems as well as the interconnections between biology and human culture. Much of the initial funding for MAB came from the Soviet Union and the

United States, especially after Nixon and Brezhnev agreed in 1974 to establish reserves in their two countries. Today the United States, the Soviet Union, and the Central European countries contain nearly half of the world's biosphere reserves. There are four reserves in Canada: Mont-Saint-Hilaire (Quebec), Long Point and Point Pelee (Ontario), and Waterton Lakes (Alberta).

MAB's mandate is to study ecosystems and propose means of sustainable resource development, train people to carry it out, and educate the public. A given project might involve specialists in local history, climate, hydrography, medicine, tourism, geology, soils, vegetation, wild and domestic animal life, and pastoral practices. Each biosphere reserve gives a geographic focus to these projects; it is meant to be the very ground of scientific research, and the place where science can be held accountable to society.

Like most UN projects, MAB is about international co-operation. It is a global effort to co-ordinate the local research and development decisions of scientific, corporate, and government managers. MAB maintains a computerized data base at its offices at the UNESCO Secretariat in Paris and regularly issues several series of reports in English, Spanish, and French. Its researchers co-operate through a tangle of other UN professional organizations, including the Food and Agriculture Organization (FAO), the United Nations Environment Program (UNEP), the International Union for Conservation of Nature and Natural Resources (IUCN), the World Health Organization (WHO), the International Hydrological Program (IHP), the International Council of Scientific Unions (ICSU), and the International Geological Correlation Program (IGCP). The logos of these agencies tend to play on organic shapes or symbols of the globe — which in turn remind us of the global presence of logos themselves. The MAB logo is an ankh, an Egyptian hieroglyph of a human figure in the cosmos. In traditional interpretations the ankh is a sign of eternal life.

The logo of UNESCO's Man and the Biosphere program.

There are usually about a thousand interdisciplinary MAB projects underway at a given time, in scores of countries and including perhaps ten thousand scientists. The most challenging projects involve local residents in nurturing lifeways that are ecologically and socially stable. The Kuna Yala Biosphere Reserve off the coast of Panama, for example, is managed by the Kuna indigenous people, who are trying to integrate scientific management practices into the traditional knowledge base of their culture. (The Kuna, by the way, are paid royalties for everything that is made on or collected from their lands, including pharmaceuticals.) Unfortunately, such areas are not common in the biosphere reserve system.

Recent MAB projects include studies of the effects of human modification of ecosystems, through settlement and migration, grazing, engineering works, and irrigation. There are also studies of estuarine and island ecosystems, pest

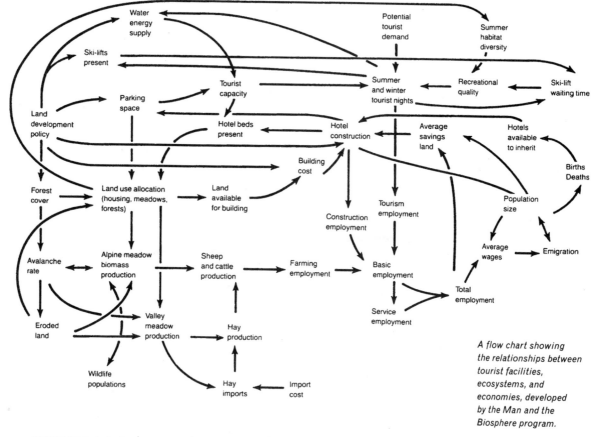

A flow chart showing the relationships between tourist facilities, ecosystems, and economies, developed by the Man and the Biosphere program.

management strategies, germplasm conservation, and energy utilization. MAB has also studied environmental perception and the interrelations between environmental modifications and the adaptive, demographic and genetic characteristics of humans.

Because biosphere reserves don't always look like parks and are about relationships rather than scenery, there is often nothing to "see" there unless you spend weeks and months tramping around, working the land, talking to people who live there — in short, doing all the things traditional rural people do. The reserves are often talked about as being a step towards getting rid of parks altogether. In the words of Girard Collin, curator of the Ecomusée at Mont Lozère in the Cévennes biosphere reserve in southern France:

This insane human adventure, called the technological society, needs to take pause, become wiser, and reconsider its direction. We must be able to leave the consumer society behind and go to places where the natural and human heritage looms large — offering us models of equilibrium and lessons on how to live. And then perhaps it may be possible for us to imagine another kind of time, a slower time ...when, having learned how to live with our cultural and natural environment, taking it into account in our everyday life, and in our projects of technological development, it will not be necessary to legislate the setting aside of parks and protected areas. These measures exist only because the heritage of the past — our heritage — is neglected or poorly loved.

Land Trusts

Whether parks can continue to perform their traditional role of preserving wild lands from development has become more and more uncertain. In recent years governments and industry have put tremendous pressure on lands in every corner of North America, (to say nothing of the rest of the world). While environmental and indigenous movements continue to resist further development and destruction of habitat, park creation is not always a viable part of the solution. In Amazonia, for example, parks put power in the hands of the central government and break the profound connections between traditional rainforest cultures and the land. The land will only be saved if people live on it in a way that restores it — and helps the rest of us to survive.

Parks are usually created in areas that the culture deems *special* in some way. In the past this has meant landscapes with "unique" features, such as geysers or mountains — although, ironically, early European tourists regarded the Rockies as hideous, likening them to boils and other skin disorders. It was not until the late eighteenth century that the settler cultures began to see the Rockies as a paragon of scenic excellence. Since the 1960s, parks have been created to preserve "representative" features of the landscape. But nowhere are nature parks concerned with vernacular landscapes, with the natural history of the worked lands that most of us live on.

But today there are alternatives to traditional parks, alternatives that recognize that it is humans who will ultimately determine the course of evolution on this planet. Strictly speaking, these new places are not all parks. In some areas, people have established land trusts. In others, people have worked at co-ordinating restoration and management programs on privately owned lands — and in the case of forest management, small private landowners have usually done a far better job than corporations and public agencies. In cities neighbours have established parks and community gardens on abandoned or speculative land. These grassroots efforts are born of a desire for local control over the use and meaning of land in the culture. In an era of increasingly centralized social and economic power, land trusts and locally directed restoration projects offer an alternative to the bureaucratic regimes of park administrations and UN agencies. They tend to be organized around bioregions — a loose term that defines an area by its watershed and history of human settlement.

Local geographies lend cohesion and identity to their human communities. In its early years the environmental movement grew most quickly in regions with prominent (and valorized) geographical features: the San Francisco Bay Area, the Gulf Islands, the Sierra Nevada, the Great Lakes, Cape Breton, and the Everglades. Bioregional movements have since discovered that organizing people on the basis of a watershed can lead to political empowerment.

In the late 1970s, people living in the environmentally distressed Mattole Valley in northern California began to notice that the salmon were gone from their streams. A few of them started to gather together the bioregional history of the valley and its eroded tributaries and cut-over slopes — the valley had lost 91 per cent of its forests, almost all of them old-growth, since 1947. The information they found was not collected or stored as a watershed. It existed only as twenty-year-old fish counts, alphabetical lists of the county's voters, timber leases, liquor licences, state maps made from photographs taken from a plane at fifteen-minute intervals, and so on. The Mattole residents collected this official information, analysed it, added the recollections of local people, and distributed it to the local population. This social and natural history of the area became local knowledge and the basis of social power.

Residents established the Mattole Restoration Council to restore natural lands and rebuild a sustainable economic base for their community. They first decided what needed immediate attention: a fish ladder through a culvert, a landslide, revegetation of a gully, a road repair. They sought government, private, and community money according to their own priorities and hired people from the community to carry out the projects. The Council now provides information for people on how to restore land on their properties. It has also integrated work into the curricula of local elementary and secondary schools: an entire generation of kids has now planted trees and released salmon into the wild every year of their lives. Above all, the work built a common language and a common experience of reinhabitation of the land.

Land trusts, another way of going at this problem, have a troubled history — as you'd expect from an effort that tries to take power away from central government. The Islands Trust is an association of people living on about five hundred islands in the southern part of the Strait of Georgia in British Columbia. During the 1970s there were growing concerns on the islands that development decisions were not only being made elsewhere but also depended on the requirements of the market rather than the knowledge of local residents. In 1974 the provincial government set up the Trust, a locally elected body that on paper was given all planning power in the islands. The Trust advocated parks where suitable, but since the islands are widely, if sparsely, settled, its work tended to focus on promoting sustainable development. Watershed protection, logging practices, and coastal zone management were the important issues. In the early 1980s, however, the provincial government had a change of heart, and it has slowly been eroding the power of the Trust ever since.

A more recent and hopeful example is the Madawaska Highlands Regional Trust in southern Ontario. The highlands, northwest of the confluence of the Ottawa and St. Lawrence rivers, are not a heavily settled area of the province, but because they're within two or three hours drive of about eight million people, there is pressure on the land. The local economy is typical for eastern Canada. People farm the few areas where the soil is deep enough to permit it, there is a scattering of towns with one or two industries, and the slack is taken up by tourism — services for cottages and the sorts of low-impact recreation common in the Canadian Shield: canoeing, hunting and fishing, hiking, and camping.

The trust was formed as a grassroots response to a provincial timber-management plan that proposed to eliminate the few scattered old-growth forests in the region. Old-growth forest, sometimes called virgin or climax forest, describes a complex ecosystem of several strata: canopy trees of varied age, a rich understorey, and a forest floor that varies with the amount of light provided by occasional openings. Old-growth forests are stable, diverse, and self-managed: their plant and animal species constantly reproduce themselves without major disruptions to the ecosystem. Old-growth forests in North America are few and far between, and they are concentrated on public lands. While they once covered the entire eastern part of the continent, it is estimated that by the Second World War fewer than 20 per cent of forests in the United States were old-growth — most of them in the West.

Until the early twentieth century, old-growth forests were selectively cut: some large trees, anywhere from 100 to 250 years old, were removed along with damaged or diseased species to be used for fencing. This left young and middle-aged trees to mature amid a diverse understorey, with wildlife and watersheds undamaged. Modern forestry practice favours clearcutting, however, and regards a hundred-year-old tree as over-mature. The belief is that young, second-growth forests of few (or even a single) species encourage wildlife and revitalize the ecosystem, while providing jobs for local residents, profits for their employers, and trickle-down benefits for the local economy. The Madawaska Trust has challenged all of those assumptions. Residents have researched alternative thinking in silviculture, wildlife management, and local economies.

But to stop the logging the Trust did not propose a park. It proposed an economic development plan based on the ecological integrity of the region. A locally controlled body would regulate land use — permitting some hunting, logging, and trapping — over a 4,000-square-kilometre area. It would seek voluntary agreements with landowners, offering tax breaks to participants in the

Community initiated parks risk coming into conflict with resource industries. Volunteers with the Western Canada Wilderness Committee built this boardwalk through temperate rainforest in the Carmanah valley on Vancouver Island; it was vandalized in late 1990, as logging operations resumed.

A Haida woman gathering cedar bark in the tribal park on Haida Gwaii, British Columbia. New alternatives to nature parks blur the old boundaries between human settlement and wild lands.

plan. The Trust's objectives are superficially similar to those of multiple-use advocates. Yet its charter begins with the health of the land, rather than profit: it calls for a "new land ethic" based on regional economic development that protects local ecosystems.

It will not be easy to wrest control over local ecosystems from government resource agencies; and not everyone in a region is likely to support ecological integrity. In the case of Madawaska, the Ontario Federation of Anglers and Hunters has opposed the land trust and its proposals. Given current pressure on most lands in North America, however, a land trust is likely to gain far more local support than a new park, which conceptually and practically removes wild lands from most people's everyday lives and work. The Trust for Public Land and Turtle Island Earth Stewards both offer council to the growing number of communities who want to establish land trusts and local preservation programs.

The other alternative to parks is the traditional land use proposed by indigenous people in the many land-claims struggles of the past thirty years. Tribal parks have been proposed as a resolution to land disputes in the Temagami area in northern Ontario, the Queen Charlotte Islands in British Columbia, and Humboldt County, California.

Parks and natural areas have changed much in this century. Their geographical emphasis has shifted away from large reserves and towards the microenvironments of a multiplicity of wild land types. This fragmentation has been a function of the character of ecological science, the pressures of a profit-oriented economy, and the strategies of modern marketing. It is also related to contemporary demands for the decentralization and diffusion of power. But if the land itself has in a way shrunk, our experience of it has expanded. New parks, and their alternatives, promise a new proximity to nature. They hold out the possibility of blurring old boundaries between human settlement and wild lands, and perhaps of reorienting our technologized society towards the models of integrated and stable communities we find in the natural world and among the traditional cultures that live close to it.

Zoos as Microenvironments

Like parks, the story of zoos is very much bound up with the recent history of environmental degradation. When there is no more wild, the meaning of the zoo changes.

Zoos, safari parks, and aquariums are explicit, even intentional, models of relations between human cultures and the natural world. Like parks, they are constructed environments that often tell us more about ourselves than they do about what we're ostensibly looking at. Traditional zoos remove animals from their physical (and often social) matrix and place them in virtual prisons where they're on display for humans. If the only place we saw humans was in jail, we might be reluctant to make many generalizations about their societies. Similarly, the history of zoos and safari or game parks has at least as much to tell us about human culture and history as it does about animals in captivity.

The history of zoos is a long one: people have kept animals in captivity for thousands of years. The earliest organized zoos were the royal aviaries and menageries of ancient Persia, Egypt, and China. Later, European royalty established parks and hunting grounds, where they were able to expand their dominions to include the natural world.

The zoo as park or microenvironment is a much more recent phenomenon. In the late nineteenth century, private zoos expanded to become large botanical and zoological reserves with public access. Like the circus or bullring, these zoos were organized as spectacle and were very much a part of the history of conquest and empire. The new zoological gardens displayed exotic plants and animals gathered from the European colonies, which once occupied more than half the land mass of the world. Zoos in garden settings were also partly the result of the public parks movement in Europe and North America.

Today the physical plant of a zoo typically includes electrical transformers and generators, water softeners and dechlorinators, pumping stations, kitchens and commissaries, nurseries, ponding systems, sewers, and boilers. Like the infrastructures of theme parks or shopping malls, these internal workings have themselves become part of the experience of the zoo. On the monorail ride that takes visitors around the Metro Toronto zoo, for example, narration on the P.A. offers a long list of statistics: how large the zoo is, how many tonnes of horse meat, fish, and mosquitoes are fed to the animals every year, the capacity of the polar bear swimming tank, the size (in football fields) of the giraffe compound.

If early zoos were largely about display and domination, recent zoos show more of a concern with habitat and environmental education. Confinement strategies have moved from cages to moated pens to invisible barriers. The very terms suggest a reversal of concerns — from a focus on the method of containment of the animals to an examination of viewing, and of the relationships between and among species. The audience is different too. Contemporary zoo visitors have already seen most of the animals on TV, or at the movies. The animals seen on film were probably in their natural habitat and exhibited more "typical" behaviour.

Zoos in the latter half of the twentieth century no longer represent the vastness of empire or the abundance of the natural world. Today the inhabitants of zoos are often the last remnants of a species or community. Their exoticism is an exoticism of imminent loss. Zoo directors now predict that within the next few decades the vast majority of terrestrial wildlife will be either the "living dead" species institutionalized in zoos and reserves, or extinct.

This is a momentous shift, due largely to the destruction of habitat all over the globe. The very subject of the zoo has changed as wetlands have been drained for extensive agriculture, forests cut for firewood or cattle grazing, marine ecosystems destroyed by resource exploration, and the atmosphere asphyxiated by a tangle of industrial pollutants. A rare or endangered animal has a different currency in the culture — sometimes literally so. In recent years a number of zoo scandals have involved the illegal sale of rare and endangered animals to private collections and laboratories.

These changes have worked their way well past the economy. In a culture in which hunting has become a sport, jet fighters are named after birds of prey, and an animal-rights movement has interjected previously unspoken questions, all relations with our animal companions on this Earth have been thrown into crisis. That crisis is present at the zoo in the very glances traded between animal captives and their human keepers.

In technical terms, changes have been underway for some time. The inoculation episodes of *Wild Kingdom* foreshadowed strategies in wide use today by zoologists and animal welfare agencies. Breeding programs, for example, use the kinds of technologies familiar to animal husbandry in Europe and North America. Lab workers implant sperm, fertilize eggs *in vitro,* and split embryos to make twins. Some of this work is done to reproduce captive species that will not reproduce themselves, and thus to replenish a zoo's own stock. Many zoos also breed their captive animals so the offspring can be placed back in wild habitats. This has been the case with the California condor. The last wild member of the species, with a nine-and-a-half-foot wingspan, was captured in April 1987. Now known as AC-9, it is part of a captive-breeding program that aims to release young birds to the wild over the next decade. A collective project called the International Species Inventory System (ISIS) stores census data collected on endangered species in captivity. Przewalski's horse, the North American bison, and the wood buffalo are all species whose survival is due in large part to captive propagation.

Conservation biology has become an important part of contemporary wildlife preservation, although its usefulness in the longer term is under considerable debate. Preserving a few rare or curious species of animals in a zoo does nothing to prevent the destruction of the complex natural systems they used to inhabit — in fact, it may have the opposite effect. This problem presents a dilemma for the environmental movement. By rescuing some endangered plants and animals from an impending development, or restoring an abandoned open-pit mine, are we discouraging responsible ways of living on this Earth?

Some North American zoos sponsor land conservation and reclamation projects. The New York Zoological Society and the World Wildlife Fund both have projects underway around the world. There are other changes in contemporary zoos, mostly to do with design, education, and marketing, which have shifted the discussion away from the animals themselves and onto their viewers: the humans whose cultures so often seem to determine the very survival of wildlife. For all these reasons, contemporary zoos can no longer be simply about biology. They have had to begin to teach people about animal ecology, and why that's important. These changes parallel those made on TV nature programs.

The other crisis facing many zoo planners and directors is one peculiar to consumer capitalist economies: how to continue to attract a market while exhibiting the same old merchandise? There is stiff competition for what in the business is called the "family recreation dollar." Hardly visible thirty years ago, theme parks, waterslides, aquariums, campgrounds, heritage parks, and museums now clutter the North American continent.

Zoo administrations have had to consider how to attract more and more visitors in a climate of rising capital costs and declining state support. Surely new exhibits, which owe much to the display techniques of theme parks and merchandisers, have helped. But the costs of hiring more consultants and technicians, not to mention raising money for wildlife preservation, are enormous. Some zoos have gone in for blockbuster programming similar to the King Tut or Picasso exhibitions that have brought millions of dollars to museum treasuries in the past fifteen years. Current zoo promotion and display techniques have drawn a few lessons from department-store sales managers too. When the Metro Toronto Zoo director received two pandas from China, he told the press: "The drop in the panda population has made Qing Qing and Quan Quan priceless. There are more Rembrandts in the world than there are pandas."

Quin Quin and Quan Quan were two of many giant pandas who toured North American zoos in the mid-1980s with the co-operation of the China Wildlife Conservation Association. The animals were to help publicize the delicate situation in China, where urban and industrial development threatens the habitat of the fewer than one thousand pandas surviving on the northeastern slopes of the Himalayas. Many of the animals now live in reserves in Sichuan.

Judging from the experience in Toronto, these tours were a massive operation by any standards. The pandas, who travelled in couples, were given Chinese names and flown to North America on donated flights filled with journalists and sponsors. Exhibitors had special displays built for the animals and had food, mostly fresh-cut bamboo, flown in every day from California.

With costs for the exhibit running around $5 million or $6 million, corporate sponsorship was essential. The logos of CP Air, McDonald's, Kodak,

Coca-Cola, and Emery Worldwide were on every sign and pamphlet. A local radio station raffled off private showings of the animals, and car dealerships provided "pandamobiles" for disabled visitors and the animals themselves. Four-colour zoo press releases shrieked "pandamania" as they announced panda record deals, stuffed panda toys, T-shirts, a Pennies for Pandas charity, and plenty of photo opportunities. A panda logo was designed, and it too was everywhere. Some zoos sold breakfast and dinner dates with the panda couple, pleading, "The beautiful and rare pandas can only be saved from extinction with your help."

The Chinese Association of Zoological Gardens continues to lease pandas to about four zoos a year, with a waiting list of close to fifty zoos. The typical stay is three months, for a fee of between $500,000 and $1,000,000. The celebrity animals often go to cities as part of publicity for other celebrations, such as the Olympics or a bicentenary.

The operation has not been without its critics. In 1988 the international arm of the World Wildlife Fund decided to oppose further panda loans, arguing that the publicity generated for an admittedly grave ecological situation in China did not warrant removing pandas of breeding age from their habitats. The WWF, which has used the panda as its logo since 1961, has been long involved in studying the diet and habitat of the animals at the Wolong Reserve in south-central China. The U.S. chapter took legal action against the panda tours, successfully lobbying the U.S. Fish and Wildlife Service to revoke the permits for the animals. The Chinese government has since refused to send pandas to the United States.

Biological Parks: Habitat and Community

Older zoo design emphasized taxonomy. Its models, like those of botanical gardens, science museums, and aquariums, were medicine and the old natural sciences. To each species a separate cage, the better to observe and know. (The Chinese emperor Wen Wang's zoo, built about 1000 B.C., was called the Garden of Intelligence.) Cages were arranged along both sides of paths, and people strolled past them talking and eating and joking and acting very social, occasionally stopping to stare or smile or poke at the animals. The animals, on the other hand, were usually solitary, having been yanked from their social communities, sometimes in the belief that they'd be happier that way.

By contrast, our newest zoos emphasize habitat and community — an organicism that has been a long time in the works. In the early twentieth century, a new movement swept zoological parks and gardens in Europe and North America. Variously called romanticism and naturalism by contemporary zoo historians, the movement owed much to the work of Carl Hagenbeck, a German national who designed zoos in Hamburg, Paris, St. Louis, and Detroit. Hagenbeck introduced the cageless zoo, in which the animals were confined to large open-air compounds separated from the viewing areas by moats, ha-has, and concealed fences so visitors could see the animals under the open sky. They could also look across consecutive exhibits to see compositions of predator and prey and other relations in the background. Hagenbeck's sensitivity to sightlines and cross-viewing were key contributions: the moats, groves of trees, artificial lakes, mountains — and later the berms contributed by landscape architects — not only framed these vistas but also prevented zoo-goers from concentrating their gaze on other viewers.

These moated zoos were necessarily large and often built outside cities. Thus their gardens as well as the surrounding landscape figured in the design. In many ways, Hagenbeck's ideas owed much to the English landscape parks of the eighteenth century. In contemporary interpretations of the moated, cageless zoo, however, modernism has played a large role. Path, water, and lawn configurations, as well as sculptural elements like fake mountains and glaciers, have drawn heavily from modernist work in painting, sculpture, and landscape design.

Cageless exhibits first caught on in North America in the 1930s, in San Diego, the Bronx, the National Zoo, and Chicago Brookfield, for example. The Metro Toronto Zoo, built in the early 1970s and divided into six zoo-geographical regions, is one of the most recent examples. All of this design work, in which architects played a far more important role than in the past, imposed a distance — often quite considerable — between zoo-goer and captive animal. While zoo design has since taken other directions, the moated cageless version is still widespread. This design is also common in "safari parks," ambitious environments where visitors drive through animal habitats that usually have an African theme. (At the Tokyo Zoo, animal lovers ride in armoured buses.) The African referent has to do with the stature of African animal species, both physically in the savannah and culturally in imperial myths about Africa and "big-game hunting." Safari parks are an example of how colonialism continues to be part of the whole idea of the zoo, and perhaps of parks of all kinds. African themes also have a specific historical basis. It was to Africa that big-game hunters turned after the buffalo and antelope had virtually disappeared in North America. Those animals were hunted to near extinction in the American West in the late 1880s, in a campaign to starve the Lakota who had resisted incarceration on reserves. Theodore Roosevelt, who had participated in the last commercial buffalo hunt on the Great Plains in 1883, went on a well-publicized safari in East Africa in 1909. The case of Roosevelt is telling, for aside from being a big-game hunter and military adventurer overseas, he was also an ardent conservationist who helped win government support for the establishment of national parks in

African Lion Safari park, Ontario. Colonialism continues to be part of the whole idea of the zoo – and perhaps of parks as well.

the U.S. West. In the same period European nations began to build animal reserves in their African colonies, largely for the pleasure of international tourists.

In recent years new directions in zoo design have emerged. One new objective is to immerse viewers in the habitat of the animals. Landscape immersion, as this design has been known professionally since the early 1980s, conceals the barriers between people and the animals so well that we're never sure whether the animals can approach us or not. The work is based on ongoing research into our understanding of plant and animal communities, as well as of human psychology — the results of which have only begun to emerge in the past ten or fifteen years. If older exhibits aimed for naturalism, contemporary exhibition technology aims for realism.

The replication of habitat is a central part of this new design. Wild animals don't live in manicured parks; any naturally functioning ecosystem is full of weeds and mud, bugs, and dead trees. Habitat is also specific. Animals live in relation to very particular plant and animal communities, after all: bogs, tundra, sub-humid forests, savannahs, and so on. A sign at the National Zoo in Washington, D.C., describes the plants in an animal compound as "inseparable partners, not decor." While the replication of specific landscapes is increasingly common in the work of contemporary landscape designers, at zoos this replication extends to the architecture of service buildings, which might use materials like adobe, thatch, or corrugated metal, depending on the cultural reference points the designers want to call attention to.

Zoo designers now work with anthropologists, animal ecologists, and comparative psychologists to determine how to replicate wild habitat on a small scale and still come up with something both wholesome for the animals and edifying for visitors. At the gorilla exhibit in Woodland Park, Seattle — now the model for contemporary zoo design — the primates live in a tropical forest clearing that demonstrates the process of plant succession. A glass-fronted lean-to at one side is the only vantage point for the visitor. A series of boulders, heated by electric cables in the cool Seattle winter, attract the gorillas to an area directly in front of the lean-to. But the gorillas don't have to linger in the viewing area. They can escape to more distant boulders or cross a stream to a group of caves. This ability to escape is related to "flight distance" — a technical term for the amount of non-social space an animal needs to feel safe. (This concept has also been used in the design of visiting areas in nursing homes.) Yet by constricting the field of vision from the lean-to and judiciously arranging plantings, the distance of the gorillas' flight seems greater than it really is, and visitors end up feeling immersed in the landscape.

Zoo-geographical fidelity, proximity to the animals, and lack of visual distraction are the keys to landscape immersion. Sometimes the exhibits use tricks like slightly elevating the animal areas or installing non-glare glass to heighten the visitor's sense of being part of the world on display. More often they rely on the work of restoration ecologists who drag in rocks and tree stumps or construct marshes. The new exhibits have proved useful for animal ecologists, since the social behaviour of captive animals in these new exhibits seems similar to that of animals in the wild. At the San Diego Zoo, visitors walk and climb through a twelve-metre-high rock outcropping that is home to innumerable small African mammals and reptiles. The barriers are glass kick-panels obscured by foliage. Visitors can wander around on their own, on or off the paths, and come close to encountering the animals in the nooks and crannies they ordinarily inhabit. At the Audubon Zoo in New Orleans, a boardwalk crosses a Louisiana swamp inhabited by black bears, cougars, otters, alligators, migratory birds, and mosquitoes.

Aquariums are also part of these new trends. The Monterey Bay Aquarium in California is a recently built example. Once inside its warehouse exterior along Cannery Row, the building opens out at once to the bay that is its subject. The architecture repeatedly juxtaposes massive glazing and outdoor terraces — with views out over the littoral and its marine culture — to the giant tanks themselves, some of which are connected to the ocean. Visitors can view the tanks from above or below the water line, and the magnificent size of the aquarium exaggerates the sense of the ocean. "Touch pools" allow visitors to handle some of the animals. Like in the zoos, the life displayed in the tanks is classified according to marine community rather than species, only here the emphasis is almost exclusively on communities local to Monterey Bay. There are kelp tanks, sandy shore aviaries, and tide pools. All of these exhibits are constructed — that is to say simulated — environments, but they extend outdoors along the rocks and under the sky, abutting the real space of the bay itself.

With these new exhibits zoos hope to make a more useful contribution to nature education. While television wildlife programming cultivated more sophisticated audiences in the 1970s and 1980s, many zoos continued to reproduce well-worn stereotypes about animals and our relation to them. Zoological societies now take some blame for educating people to hold their noses and shuffle quickly past antiseptic cages or for encouraging them to make jokes about giraffes standing around as bored as plastic flamingoes on a suburban lawn. As wildlife preservation has become a priority, it's not only cages that are disappearing. Many zoos no longer post feeding times or give animals names like Dumbo or Pixie. Some zoos have ripped up their sidewalks and replaced them with dirt paths. They've left lawns to go to seed and had moats converted to wetlands. Some zoos now call themselves biological parks, and have begun to include flowers, trees, and art in their exhibits. Unglamorous animals like invertebrates (which account for 98 per cent of all animal life) are the subjects of new buildings at parks in Washington, D.C., and Montreal.

All of these developments are encouraging. Some questions remain, however. Do the new designs somehow disguise the confinement that is the primary fact of the zoo? Do wild-animal displays conceal and mystify the ways some human cultures continue to dominate the natural world? Can we really see ourselves looking? These are questions that apply to parks as well.

Zoos and parks have changed a great deal over the past forty years, as have all popular representations of natural areas and ecosystems. Their organizational strategies have shifted away from the encyclopaedic, the taxonomic collection, the idea of multiple use. Their design now emphasizes models of ecosystem, ideas of habitat — changes we've seen in garden design and wildlife movies as well. If the discourse of conservation is now often posed as a matter of survival, clearly that survival is cultural as well as biogeographical. It's as if these new places on the Earth acknowledge the wall or hedge between civilization and the natural world; but at the same time refuse to push that wall further into the bush.

The new parks and zoos are obviously not enough. At most they are an interim measure, a way of instructing us about the possibilities that lie ahead at the place where human and natural economies meet. Their contradictions, however, will not be resolved until we have real functioning (and inhabited) models of humans living mutually with the other native species of each region.

Parks and zoos will be part of that project, but we will also need to look elsewhere for ideas. Perhaps then there will be no need for either.

Gary Nabhan's story of two oases in the Sonoran desert of Arizona and Mexico illustrates the point. Fed by perennial springs, A'al Waipia and Ki:towak have been inhabited by the Papago for centuries, and their fields and orchards traditionally attracted wildlife from the entire region. A'al Waipia was taken over by Organ Pipe Cactus National Monument in 1937. By the early 1960s, the National Park Service had removed all the Papago and declared the oasis a wildlife refuge. But a strange thing happened. Once people stopped working the land at A'al Waipia, trees died and wildlife declined. At Ki:towak, where Papago continued to work the land, seventy-two plant species, native and cultivated, medicinal and culinary, thrived — among them pomegranate, fig, mesquite, elderberry, date, wolfberry, and palo verde. Some plants considered endangered at Organ Pipe still grow in houseyards and fields in Ki:towak. Moreover, there are twice as many bird species at Ki:towak as at the wildlife refuge. When asked to account for the difference in bird populations, a Papago elder remarked:

I've been thinking over what you say about not so many birds living over there any more. That's because those birds, they come where the people are. When the people live and work in a place, and plant their seeds and water their trees, the birds go live with them. They like those places, there's plenty to eat and that's when we are friends to them.

A hunter at Long Point Provincial Park and Biosphere Reserve on the north shore of Lake Erie. The contradictions of parks won't be resolved until we have functioning models of humans living mutually with the other native species of each region.

LIVE BETTER
ELECTRICALLY

DAD IS PROUD THAT HE HELPED BUILD THE FIRST NUCLEAR PLANT.

BUT FROM WHAT I REMEMBER, ALL HE EVER TALKED ABOUT WAS HIS CREW HAVING TO TAKE SHOWERS.

8. On the Frontiers of Capital
Nuclear Plants and Other Environmental Architectures

We have spent more than two billion dollars on the greatest scientific gamble in history, and we have won....It is an awful responsibility which has come to us. We thank God that it has come to us instead of to our enemies. And we pray that He may guide us to use it in His ways and for His purposes.
> — Harry S. Truman, announcing the atomic bombing of Japan, 1945

So far we have looked at a number of characteristics of the contemporary North American landscape in order to understand in them our social relations and our ideas about the Earth — and how these two are connected. We've come to see that geographies of agriculture, leisure, and even wilderness are all cultural spaces, inscriptions on the land that are derived from and in turn shape our changing ideas about this Earth.

There remains one kind of inscription on the land to consider, and that is the explicit landscape of technology. Of course technology suffuses nearly all the geographies of the modern industrial state, as well as our bodies and perceptions. Yet there are certain built environments that are meant to be models of a world dedicated to the progressive expansion of human mastery. These are the structures and machines that clearly demonstrate a will to dominate the Earth: dams, oil rigs, nuclear-power plants, and military installations.

Dams and power plants are the appurtenances of modern industry, geographical evidence of human work and the transformation of nature. These and other technologies fully occupy the industrial and post-industrial landscape of North America, from the petroleum-based farms of Saskatchewan to the militarized deserts of the American West to the relentless electric grid of the Tennessee River watershed. These environments are not coincidentally linked; their conception, history, operations, and public image form a unity that even Dwight Eisenhower was able to recognize as the military-industrial complex. But technology is not autonomous. Its development, introduction, and use are part of social history. Thus the environmental architectures of energy extraction and

Opposite:
No Immediate Threat.
Photograph by Carole
Condé and Karl Beveridge.

A 1950s ad for electric power. Energy extraction technologies organize both landscape and social relations.

transformation are nodes that alternately reveal and disguise the interconnected webs of social and physical power.

But in the late twentieth century, technology is not merely a collection of tools and machines or a representation of power. It is also a sensorium, a field of perception. If the land is wired, so are we. Technology has become an organizational principle of our everyday lives. It provides the framework for scientific thought and public discussion — in short, the whole range of social relations.

For example, in scientific terms energy is the capacity to do work. Transforming that capacity into useful tasks depends on a number of factors: the quality and quantity of fuels, the availability of human labour and appropriate technics, and the type of work the energy will be used to do. Once transformed into work, energy is called power. Its production, organization, distribution, and end use are all deeply social matters. Yet the language of the power industry is saturated with mystification. Sometimes the language is a joke, other times it is an outright lie. We hear about "harnessing nature to meet the needs of man." The Army Corps of Engineers calls floods "high-water events." The atomic industry calls radioactive discharges at nuclear plants "unusual events." The military refers to malfunctioning weapons deliveries (of which nearly fifty have been reported since the Second World War) as "incidents." Serious nuclear-weapons accidents — of which thirty-seven have been reported, all of them "too politically sensitive for public discussion" — are called "broken arrows." Scientific jargon has monopolized truth, contaminating not only the internal utterances of professionals but public discourse as well. In thinking about energy, and power, we must move beyond the self-justifying narratives of science.

Understanding figures of power in the landscape — the large industrial and military installations that have been placed in every region of this continent — means thinking about scientific discourse and its relationship to technology and management — what U.S historian Stanley Aronowitz calls "the two most important forms of intellectual labour." My goal in this chapter is to put history back into these places, to show in these dystopian landscapes the physical and social continuum of energy, capital, and war.

The Tennessee Valley Authority

Late one September day in 1987 I stop at a picnic area in Panther Creek State Park, established by the Tennessee Valley Authority (TVA) in 1971. As I tuck into some food I've brought along, a van pulls up. A loaded van: venetian blinds, big smoked-glass windows, ice machine, gun rack. Six talkative Americans get out. They've come to look at the view. They leave the engine running, walk across the road, and stare out.

A hundred metres down a steep embankment is Cherokee Lake. It's a big lake, winding off in many directions, surrounding islands and moving up old river and creek beds into farmlands and patches of bush. The lake is low, with broad shores of red mud. Getting into the water would be a lot of work. Joggers come by and pause. Cars and pickups slow or stop. This is the only view of the lake in the park, except for what you can see at the boat ramp.

An electric stove and washing machine being delivered in Hamilton County, Tennessee, 1947. For the Tennessee Valley Authority, rural electrification programs meant encouraging and subsidizing the purchase of electrical appliances.

It's a ten-minute drive from the campground, itself a large and open place with few trees and lots of electrical hookups. At the overlook, you can't get down to the lake. There is just the view. It's a small view. It closes off the world, rather than gathering us into it.

Nearby is an earlier park, Big Ridge. It was built during the 1930s by the TVA, the Civilian Conservation Corps, and the National Parks Service. The park is centred on a small dammed stream, deep in a hollow. Its buildings are clustered as a village might be, down close to the water. The components of the landscape — swimming area, recreation hall, bridge, remnant hardwood forest, docks, boathouse, and cabins — gather the land together as you walk from one to the other.

From the time it was established by an act of Congress in 1933, the Tennessee Valley Authority was an immense project. Only four months after taking office, Franklin D. Roosevelt called for a corporation "clothed with the power of government but possessed of the flexibility and initiative of a private enterprise." According to Roosevelt, the TVA would have the responsibility of "planning for the proper use, conservation, and development of the natural resources of the Tennessee River drainage basin and its adjoining territory for the general social and economic welfare of the nation." The TVA, he declared, "transcends mere power development: it enters the wide fields of flood control, soil erosion, afforestation, elimination from agricultural use of marginal lands, and distribution and diversification of industry."

As a large government-owned development agency, the TVA's jurisdiction extends over parts of seven states in the southeast quadrant of the United States. For almost sixty years the agency has extensively reworked mountain, highland, and bottomland topographies, transforming them into models of modern industrial, agricultural, and recreational development. Its thirty-nine dams — most of them built in the early years, especially during the Second World War — provide flood control, navigation, drinking water, and electrical power. In the 1990s the agency employs about twenty-seven thousand people and is the largest producer of electricity in the United States.

Needless to say, such a project entails social transformations on a grand scale. The goal of the TVA was to bring the impoverished southern Appalachians "into the twentieth century." After industrialization, rural electrification was the next priority for the agency, including programs to encourage and subsidize the purchase of all kinds of electrical machines and appliances. Demonstration "Electro-development farms" promoted water pumps, refrigeration equipment, milling machines, toasters, electric ranges, freezers, radios, and vacuum cleaners.

For its bureaucrats, the TVA built the town of Norris, Tennessee, in 1934, a prototype of the mass-produced suburb. The agency also developed an infrastructure for the tourist industry that would come into full use after the Second World War. The development of that infrastructure reveals the geographical links between resource extraction and tourism. The TVA converted construction camps to tourist camps, borrow pits to marinas, crane sites to observation platforms. Its recreational installations include scores of parks, boat ramps, beaches, nature trails, campgrounds, cabins, resorts, wildlife refuges, and demonstration forests. On a neck of land between the dammed Tennessee and Cumberland rivers in Kentucky, the TVA operates Land Between the Lakes, a tourist development and education centre opened in 1963. Over the years the recreational developments have changed. The old parks were built down in the hollows. More recently, with many of the hollows flooded, parks — like Panther Creek — have been cut out of the forests adjacent to the new reservoirs.

Electricity generation was the key to the TVA project. With electrification, it was believed, the region's social and economic malaise would vanish. Industry would be lured with cheap electricity, industrial jobs would contribute to a rising standard of living, and waged labourers could be organized into new markets for consumer products. This is the Fordist logic of a consumer society that we've seen from the New York World's Fair onwards. In her 1929 book *Selling Mrs. Consumer,* home economist Christine Frederick laid out its logic:

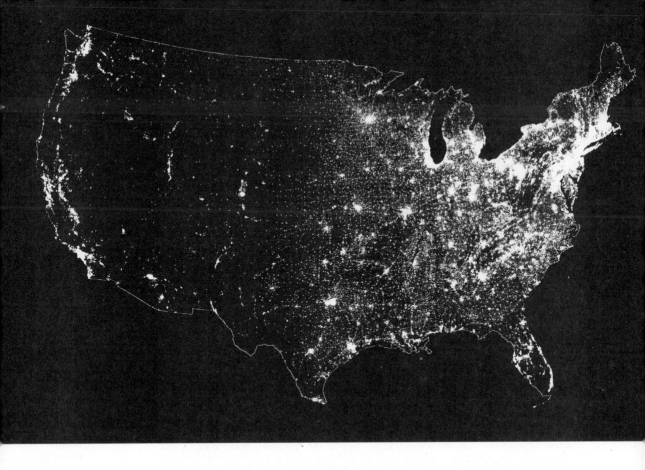

The United States of America at night, mid-1980s.

Consumptionism is the name given to the new doctrine; and it is admitted today to be the greatest idea that America has to give to the world — the idea that workermen and masses be looked upon not simply as workers and producers, but as consumers....Pay them more, sell them more, prosper more is the equation.

Initially, most of the power came from hydroelectric plants the TVA built along the Tennessee and Cumberland rivers and their tributaries. After the Second World War, the agency built twelve coal-fired plants to meet the demand it had created by encouraging energy-intensive industries, nuclear-weapons production, and household electricity use twice the national average.

By the mid-1950s, most electricity in the Valley was being generated from coal rather than hydro, and the TVA had become the largest consumer of coal in North America. Just one of its generating plants consumed a railroad car of coal every six minutes. The long-term contracts the TVA signed with regional mines recapitalized an industry crippled by competition from cheap Middle Eastern oil. This in turn led to a concentration of ownership, the introduction of new extraction technologies, and the proliferation of strip mines all through the Appalachian Basin.

The shift to strip mining (which the industry calls surface mining) signals several changes. With the rise of energy monopolies — by the 1970s, most coal, natural gas, and uranium reserves in the United States were owned by oil companies — prices were increased and mining activity was further mechanized. Profits were invested in a westward expansion, first to the Illinois Basin, and in the late 1970s and 1980s to the eastern slope of the Rockies, the Green River watershed of Colorado, Utah, and Wyoming, and the Athabasca watershed of Alberta and Saskatchewan. In the years when oil prices were high and public panic could be organized, governments invested in the extraction and production of synthetic fuels from oil shales and sands, much of these on Native lands.

Mining is an activity that is destructive of the surface of the Earth. Traditional shaft mines consume whole forests for reinforcing timbers and smelting. Modern mineral excavation and processing require large quantities of electricity and water and produce equally large quantities of toxic waste. With strip mining, all of this activity became visible as never before, particularly in the fragile ecosystems of the West and North. Strip mining replaces the old dark and damp galleries deep in the Earth with gargantuan craters, machines the size of buildings, and small mountains of sterile slag. The mining process is perhaps still our most potent symbol of

A tar sands excavating machine in northern Alberta. The mining industry is a potent symbol of industrial society and its will to dominate.

industrial society and its will to dominate. Social critic Lewis Mumford reminds us of its syntax: "mine: blast: dump: crush: extract: exhaust."

In *Technics and Civilization* Mumford discusses the relationship between the industrial process and modern warfare, and his description of fifteenth-century Europe is helpful in understanding the destructive calculus of the TVA's industrial strategy during the Cold War:

> *War, mechanization, mining and finance played into each other's hands. Mining was the key industry that furnished the sinews of war and increased the metallic contents of the original capital hoard, the war-chest: on the other hand, it furthered the industrialization of arms, and enriched the financier by both processes. The uncertainty of both warfare and mining increased the possibilities for speculative gains: this provided a rich broth for the bacteria of finance to thrive in.*

TVA policies promoted far more than the coal industry. Industrial expansion in the southern Appalachians encouraged the extraction of iron, sand, gravel, stone, and timber. Sand and gravel were used to construct dams, which produced electricity and aided the transportation of primary materials. Electricity in turn helped produce aluminum for aircraft (ALCOA used four dams to power its factories in the Valley), as well as enrich uranium for weaponry. By 1950 the hundreds of millions of pine trees planted for erosion control had attracted large pulp and paper companies to the valley.

The TVA also promoted the industrialization of agriculture, through its fertilizer and food-processing plants. The National Fertilizer Development Center in Muscle Shoals, Alabama, is a key locale in the Tennessee Valley. During the First World War the Army Corps of Engineers built a dam on the Tennessee River at Muscle Shoals to supply electricity for a munitions plant. After the war, the property was put up for sale, and Henry Ford entered a low bid with the idea of building a privately owned manufacturing city of one million people. The petroleum-based synthetic nitrates of the munitions plant would be used for fertilizers, and additional dams, mines, mills, and smelters would provide the infrastructure for the mass production of automobiles.

Ford's proposal was never approved by Congress. Perhaps it was his bargain-basement bid. Or perhaps Ford's capitalist utopia — which linked agriculture, industry, and consumerism into a single system on the land — was too tidy, too unitary a vision of the future for the U.S. government of the day. By the time of the New Deal, however, those worries were being ignored by state and industrial planners, who very likely envisioned the U.S.-dominated global economy that would emerge after the Second World War. With the co-operation of universities and the petrochemical industry, the Muscle Shoals facility

TVA electricity also powered the production of synthetic nitrogen fertilizers. Corn is more energy intensive than any other North American crop.

has since developed three-quarters of the synthetic fertilizers in use in the United States. Its products have also played an important role in the export of industrial agricultural technology to the rest of the world, through food aid programs and corporate initiatives like the Green Revolution, another product of the Cold War years.

The other important TVA town is Oak Ridge, Tennessee. In 1942 the U.S. government bought the towns of Wheat, Scarboro, Robertsville, and Elza and over corn and tobacco fields built a high-security settlement for the seventy-five thousand people working on the Manhattan Project. After the war, Rear Admiral Hyman Rickover, an electrical engineer, headed a team of Oak Ridge technicians charged with building a nuclear-powered submarine. They completed the submarine, the *Nautilus,* in 1953, and while arranging its manufacture, Rickover built the infrastructure for the nuclear-power industry. It was Rickover who funnelled research contracts to Westinghouse and General Electric (which would become the two largest suppliers of nuclear technology), convinced MIT to begin training nuclear engineers, and persuaded the U.S. government to make commercial nuclear-power generation official state policy. For the Pentagon, commercial nuclear fission was a godsend: it ensured a steady and legitimate supply of plutonium for weapons. For the State Department, nuclear reactors could be used like synthetic fertilizers to bring Third World nations within the U.S. technological domain.

The TVA was an integral part of this process. The Oak Ridge National Laboratory was established in the Tennessee Valley because the TVA was the only utility capable of supplying the enormous amounts of electricity necessary to manufacture uranium fuel for reactors — and the TVA secured this capacity during the Cold War by building immense coal-fired generators. The coal-generated electricity was used to enrich uranium; the enriched uranium fuelled nuclear reactors; and the reactors in turn produced plutonium for bombs. They also produced heat, which could be converted to electricity, which was then dumped back into the grid to enrich more uranium. The nuclear-fuel cycle is a maddeningly circular (and enormously wasteful) process. Nuclear power makes good sense as physics — but not much else. The energy that reactors turn out — once touted as "too cheap to meter" — requires mammoth amounts of electricity to produce. And each time energy is converted from one form to another, there is a net loss. Only a third of the heat generated by fission, for example, can be used to produce steam. It's a complicated way to boil water.

The Atomic Age

The town of Oak Ridge sprawls across the foothills of the Cumberland Mountains, just north of the Clinch River and a short drive downstream from the town

of Norris, where the TVA built its first dam, and the home of the Museum of Appalachia. It is a thoroughly suburban place, dispersed and unfocused. The town centre is a shopping mall, and the access road to its parking lot is called Main Street.

The action in Oak Ridge takes place in a number of long, fenced-off valleys surrounding the town. In these valleys the Martin Marietta corporation runs a number of "nuclear facilities" for the Atomic Energy Commission (AEC) and the U.S. Department of Energy. As you take the official Oak Ridge motor tour, over a distant knoll you can see one of these installations, called a gaseous diffusion plant, code-named K-25. The plant enriches uranium by turning it into a gas and pumping it through pipes in a building that stretches over hundreds of hectares. Over another couple of ridges there is a cluster of research reactors and laboratories, and down along the Clinch River there is a TVA coal-powered generator and an experimental breeder reactor run by the AEC. Along the highway, roads with locked gates lead away to weapon-components factories and waste dumps.

The only facility that can be visited is X-10, a graphite reactor that was used for plutonium production during the war and is now a National Historic Landmark. The reactor is no longer in operation, but it is the type still used by the U.S. military at their Savannah River and Hanford plants, as well as by the Soviet government at Chernobyl.

To get more of a sense of the invisible work done at Oak Ridge, authorities encourage tourists to visit the American Museum of Science and Energy. It used to be called the Atomic Museum, and it too is run by the U.S. Department of Energy. Its lavish, hands-on displays are testimony to the sophistication of the nuclear industry and reveal much about how science is talked about in popular culture. There is a brief history of the town, some discussion of nuclear physics, and lots of talk about the abundant, fun, and above all safe future that awaits all U.S. citizens regardless of their station. The historical exhibits don't reveal the links between nuclear power and the military. Nor do they mention how documents such as the Non-Proliferation Treaty reinforce that link by requiring signatories to export "peaceful" nuclear expertise to the developing world.

In the section on nuclear physics, the displays move seamlessly from drawings of atoms to diagrams about how reactors work. It is as if nuclear power were a "natural" outcome of physical theory. Caricatures of Einstein instruct us that reactors are part of the illustrious history of scientific progress: light bulbs, automobiles, vaccines, fountain pens, rockets. The displays obscure any sense of the human decision-making processes that underlie the introduction of these technologies.

Thus, "energy" is an abstraction, something that lies outside of the social or political. The syntax of a typical display at the Oak Ridge museum joins lightning bolt to nuclear reactor to electric toothbrush. Electricity is a "natural" component of nature, unmediated by science, engineering, state funding, industrial priorities, marketing strategies, or indeed human intervention of any kind. Similarly, radiation becomes a natural property of matter, as if it were a requirement of human health as well. A film called *Radiation ...Naturally* declares, "Until recently, man could only worship nature, or fear it [image of aboriginal people dancing around a fire, audience laughter]....Now we understand it" [image of scientist in lab]. The film introduces an Environmental Protection Agency scientist by the name of Goldie Watkins who takes us hiking in the Rockies. While setting up camp, Watkins measures the "cosmic radiation" present in the Rockies. As it turns out, St. Mark's Square in Venice is radioactive, and so is Grand Central Station. "There is even radioactivity in our own bodies." Properly controlled, the argument goes, radiation can be harnessed for use in industry, art museums, medicine, scientific research, and our own homes. Our scientist then measures the radiation outside a nuclear plant, and she finds it "equivalent to what you'd get in a crosscountry flight or by standing in front of Grand Central Station for thirty-six hours. Of course, a lot could happen to you if you stood in front of Grand Central Station for thirty-six hours." All in all, the film concludes, "We live in a restless landscape of change. We must learn to adapt to our environment, and channel it to our use."

Science museums like the one in Oak Ridge function in a critical vacuum. For the most part, scientists are unable to address the social aspects of science by their very constitution as professionals whose methods are putatively uncontaminated by society. The media, on the other hand, do not treat science museums seriously except as tourist destinations. Science journalism is today little more than public relations, a testament to the impoverished public debate about science and technology in this thoroughly technologized society. Thus science remains the ultimate source of truth and useful knowledge in this society, scientists the only people competent to make decisions — leaving no social control over the direction or application of scientific research.

Never has the marriage of science and industry been more destructive than it has been with respect to nuclear fission. Fission is through and through a technology that inhibits human freedom. It was conceived and developed in secret. Its production requires massive (hidden) investment and infrastructure, centralized control, and sweeping police powers. The whole process is supervised by a virtual priesthood of experts who speak a jargon that does little other than promote deference to authority.

Public relations has been a central part of the nuclear industry since 1946, when the U.S. Congress passed the Atomic Energy Act. Its preamble reads:

It is reasonable to anticipate . . . that tapping this new source of energy will cause profound changes in our present way of life. Accordingly, it is hereby declared to be the policy of the people of the United States that the development and utilization of atomic energy shall be directed toward improving the standard of living, strengthening free competition among private enterprises so far as practicable, and cementing world peace.

ATOMIC ENERGY *of* CANADA LIMITED

The Act also established the Atomic Energy Commission (now innocuously called the Energy Research Development Administration, a part of the Department of Energy), which was charged with overseeing nuclear production. President Truman appointed five industrialists to the commission, including David Lielenthal, chair of the TVA. Their job, wrote *Life* magazine at the time, was "to hold atomic energy in trust until the world can agree on how it should be used without danger to enrich the life of men."

Plans for that enrichment were not long in coming, for the government was anxious to dissociate nuclear reactors from the bomb as quickly as possible. In the words of Alvin Weinberg, a Manhattan Project alumnus and later director of the Oak Ridge labs, the objective was to transform fission from the greatest evil into "the noblest of all technological dreams."

Canada passed its own Atomic Energy Control Act in 1946. With a mandate identical to that of the U.S. agency, the act called for the establishment of the Atomic Energy Control Board (AECB) to regulate the industry and the materials it uses, as well as control all information related to it in the interests of national security. The federal government later established Atomic Energy of

Old and new logos of Atomic Energy of Canada Limited, the government agency that promotes and markets nuclear technology.

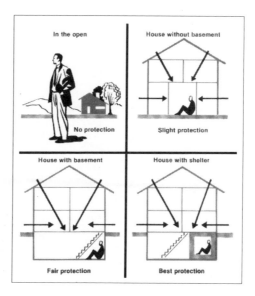

How to protect yourself from a nuclear explosion, from a 1980 brochure produced by Emergency Preparedness Canada and Public Works Canada.

Canada Limited (AECL) to promote and market its nuclear technology. Both agencies are under the aegis of the Ministry of Energy, Mines and Resources, and receive large subsidies from Parliament.

Science writers quickly took up the challenge of promoting nuclear technology, and the hype they wrote is now as infamous as the bomb itself. Nuclear power was unabashedly presented as an inexhaustible source of energy, the greatest invention since the discovery of fire. In no time at all atomic flying cars would be operated by remote control from the back seat, where families could play Monopoly in air-conditioned comfort. The few highways still needed would be paved by an atomic device that would, according to a *Popular Mechanics* article, "fuse all the dirt in its path into lava." Mini-reactors the size of a typewriter would power homes and factories. Nuclear energy would run desalinization plants that would transform deserts into plantations. Atomic medicine would cure cancer and slow the aging process. In a chilling anticipation of the Green Revolution and later biotechnological research, radioactive fertilizers would serve as agents of genetic changes in plants, enabling them to "kill" weeds. Atomic enthusiasm was by no means confined to popular science writers. Harold E. Stassen, Eisenhower's Special Assistant on Disarmament, proclaimed in the pages of *Ladies' Home Journal* in 1955 that nuclear energy would create a world

in which there is no disease ...where hunger is unknown ...where food never rots and crops never spoil ...where "dirt" is an old-fashioned word, and routine household tasks are just a matter of pushing a few buttons ...a world where no one stokes a furnace or

*Opposite:
A 1990 ad from the Canadian Nuclear Association, a corporate advocacy group. Public relations has been a central part of the nuclear industry since 1946.*

curses the smog, where the air is everywhere as fresh as on a mountain top and the breeze from a factory as sweet as from a rose.

"Imagine the world of the future," Stassen gushed. "The world that nuclear energy can create for us." This is the technocratic lingo familiar from world's fairs and advertising throughout the twentieth century. It proposes technological solutions to social problems.

"Atoms for Peace," a slogan first uttered by Eisenhower in a 1953 speech to the United Nations, became the U.S. government's stock response to what it called "nuclearosis." The propaganda was backed with billions in research grants. Project Plowshares, for example, investigated the possibilities of using nuclear explosions to drill for oil, dredge harbours, move mountains, alter weather patterns, and put out forest fires. A related project studying a nuclear blast-constructed "Panatomic Canal" across Central America received government funding from 1957 to 1970. The U.S. Air Force and the AEC set up a joint Aircraft Nuclear Propulsion program, which worked on a long-range nuclear plane from 1946 until 1961.

Atoms for Peace provided the military with the research and budgetary infrastructure to expand nuclear industries and make weapons production a central part of the U.S. economy. During the 1950s the U.S. government spent an estimated $35 billion a year (in 1974 dollars) on "strategic capabilities." Atoms for Peace gave respectability to a technology that could never win acceptance from a fully informed populace.

The Nuclear Landscape

Aside from Oak Ridge, there were early centres of nuclear research at Savannah River, South Carolina; the Argonne Laboratories in Chicago (where nuclear physicist Enrico Fermi supervised the first "pile"); Los Alamos, New Mexico; Arco, Idaho; Hanford, Washington; and Chalk River, Ontario. This dispersal across North America happened first of all because military security called for decentralization. Secondly, the long and complicated fuel production process begins with uranium deposits located in places well away from the urban and military settlements where fission usually takes place. Lastly, the U.S. government moved quickly to distribute research and production right across the country — and into Canada — so it could build a broad constituency for nuclear development. President Ronald Reagan's Strategic Defense Initiative, which apparently involved contracts in every congressional district, followed the same pattern. Similarly, reactors and related technologies have been sold round the world, mostly by U.S. and Canadian companies. Today there are about five hundred reactors operating (or more often not operating) in almost forty countries.

Most uranium is mined in Canada, Australia, Namibia, France, the United States, and the Soviet Union. The transport of nuclear materials — by road, sea, and air — is extensive. It is not unusual for each stage of production to be carried on in a different country: mining, milling, enrichment, fuel fabrication, fission, reprocessing, weapons manufacture, decommissioning, and waste storage. Each stage produces materials hazardous to life over the course of many generations — hazards that include increased incidence of leukemia and other cancers, miscarriages and infant mortality, immunological and genetic diseases, and mental and physical disabilities of all kinds. People most vulnerable to these disorders are those who work with or live near fission materials and microwave radiation. These hazards, in fact, are on an order of magnitude greater than those of any other industrial process. Yet commercial uranium mining operations in the United States had no health regulations until 1967 — almost twenty years after the mines opened. For reasons of "national security," neither the Canadian nor the U.S. government has revealed the full extent of the health hazards associated with the nuclear fuel cycle. They would be unable to gain popular acceptance if they did so.

The hazards of nuclear technology — and these hazards are, we must remember, the reason fission was developed in the first place — also raise enormous security problems for the nuclear state. The U.S. Department of Energy, for example, admits there is "statistical uncertainty" about the location of four to five tons of nuclear-weapons materials. The globally dispersed production of life-threatening materials, carried out in an unstable economic and geopolitical atmosphere, requires nothing short of authoritarian rule. That will to power is figured in the nuclear plant itself. Unlike a dam or a steel mill, a nuclear-power operation does not reveal the larger economy that surrounds it. There is no smoke, for example — just what is euphemistically called "steam." The plant's work — the transformation of mineral energy into heat to boil water — is invisible.

At the Pickering Nuclear Generating Station outside Toronto, eight reactors are lined up along the shore of Lake Ontario. Once they get past the security gate, visitors enter an information centre where their visit is framed by several rooms of displays, a slide show, and a movie. Then we're given a hard hat and shiny yellow boots, ushered onto a bus, and taken to the main building. Inside, it looks like a hospital. Everything is clean, and it's very quiet save for the white noise of distant machinery. The hallways stretch further than your eyes can focus, though you can see a series of doors with numbers on them — how many football fields long did they tell us?

Every so often, like in a game, we have to stand on a machine to see if our boots have picked up any radioactive dust. (In the movie it had been explained that there is "confusion" about radiation.) There are signs everywhere advising workers to be careful, to wear the right protective clothing, to uphold the high safety standards of the Canadian nuclear industry.

Finally, we get to the control room: masses of dials and meters and valves. But it's the reactor everyone wants to see — the control room is only an approximation of what takes place in this plant. We see the entrance to the reactor, sealed off by countless doors ("air locks," they call them), surrounded by warning signs and radiation detectors. But of course we can't go in, or we'd die.

At the centre of this unimaginably immense enterprise there is an absence. The very *place* where the human economy meets nature is invisible — and

deadly. We have always been able to experience this place — the fire — but we cannot experience it here.

The other large nuclear installation in Ontario is the Bruce Energy Centre on Lake Huron. It is larger than Pickering, and newer, and was built with a strikingly different relation to the surrounding landscape. First of all, the site has been severed from neighbouring farms by five-metre-high Israeli anti-tank fencing: an unequivocal break. The reactor inside is surrounded by a "nature preserve." The utility company trucked in trees, meadows, ponds, deer, and fish. The inhabitants of the preserve have no contact with the ecosystems outside the anti-tank fencing; they can relate only to the reactor. This sealed preserve functions as a place for workers to relax, and its animals provide both a laboratory for researchers to study the effects of low-level emissions on living tissue and a warning of radiation releases (like canaries in mines). The animals have another purpose, however, and that is to illustrate the safety and naturalness of nuclear power.

The Ontario nuclear industry is run by Ontario Hydro, which, like the TVA, is an enormous government monopoly with virtually no public accountability. It operates outside of the market, and its huge debt — nearly $27 billion in 1991 — is serviced by tax revenues. Just as in the United States, the Canadian government got into commercial reactors early on. Canadian scientists participated in the

Tailings wall, Elliot Lake, Ontario. The sand dune is made up of radioactive mill wastes from uranium mining. The stream in the foreground drains into the Great Lakes. Each stage of nuclear production produces materials hazardous to all life over many generations.

Map of the Canadian nuclear landscape. A similar map of the U.S. would include weapons production facilities and bomb test sites. The nuclear fuel cycle – mining, milling, enrichment, fuel fabrication, fission, reprocessing, weapons manufacturing, decommissioning, and waste storage – is dispersed across the globe.

Nuclear Canada

Northwest Territories
1) Kiggavik (proposed uranium mine/mill – Urangesellschaft Canada Ltd.)

Saskatchewan
2) Beaverlodge and other mines (closed)
3) Cluff Lake Uranium Mine/Mill (Amok)
4) Key Lake Uranium Mine/Mill (Key Lake Mining Corp.)
5) Cigar Lake (proposed uranium mine/mill – Cidar Lake Mining Corp.)
6) Rabbit Lake Uranium Mine (closed)
7) Collins Bay "B" Uranium Mine/Mill (CAMECO)

Manitoba
8) - Underground Nuclear Research Laboratory (AECL's test site for high level radioactive waste disposal)
   - Whiteshell Nuclear Reseach Establishment (AECL)
   - WR-1 Reactor (shutdown 1985)
   - SLOWPOKE Demonstration Reactor (2 MWt/200kWe) (1987)

Ontario
9) - Elliot Lake Uranium Mines and tailings sites
   - Blind River Uranium Refinery (CAMECO)
10) Espanola area uranium tailings
11) Bruce Nuclear Power Development (Ontario Hydro)
   - Bruce A Nuclear Generating Station (4 x 750 MWe reactors) (1976)
   - Bruce B Nuclear Generating Station (4 x 750 MWe reactors) (1984)
   - Douglas Point Reactor (200 MWe – 1966 – shutdown 1984)
   - Radioactive Waste Operations Sites 1 & 2 (incineration, compaction and storage of radioactive waste from Ontario Hydro's nuclear generating stations)
   - Douglas Point Radioactive Waste Storage Facility (storage of waste from the old Douglas Point reactor – no new waste)
   - Bruce Heavy Water Plants A, B & D (B & D mothballed)
12) - Pickering Nuclear Generating Station A (Ontario Hydro – 4 x 500 MW) (1971)
   - Pickering Nuclear Generating Station B (Ontario Hydro – 4 x 500 MWe (1982)
13) - Darlington Nuclear Generating Station (Ontario Hydro – 4 x 850 MW) (1989-1992)
   - Darlington Tritium Removal Facility
14) - Port Granby Waste Management Facility (CAMECO)
   - Welcome Waste Management Facility (CAMECO)
   - Port Hope Uranium Refinery (CAMECO)
15) Bancroft area uranium tailings
16) Nuclear Power Demonstation (NDP) Reactor (Ontario Hydro/AECL – 22 MW) (1962–shutdown 1987)
17) Chalk River Nuclear Laboratories
   - NRU Reactor
   - NRX Reactor
   - Maple-X10 Reactor (20 MW) (under construction)
   - radioactive waste sites
   - Tritium Extraction Plant
   - Industrial Materials Processing Linear Accelerator (IMPELA)

Québec
18) - Gentilly-1 Nuclear Power Station (CANDU-BLW) (AECL/Hydro Québec – 250 MWe – 1971 – Shutdown 1979)
   - Gentilly-2 Nuclear Power Station (Hydro-Québec – 600Mwe – 1982)
   - Gentilly Radioactive Waste Facilities
   - LaPrade Heavy Water Plant (AECL – 1974 – mothballed 1978)

New Brunswick
19) Point Lepreau Nuclear Generating Station (New Bruswick Electric Power Commission – 600 MW – 1982)

Additional Nuclear Facilities (not on map)

Research Reactors
University of Toronto, Toronto, Ontario
  - Subcritical Assembly
  - SLOWPOKE-2 – 20kW(t)
McMaster University, Hamilton, Ontario
  - Swimming Pool Reactor – 5Mw(t)
École Polytechnique, Montréal , Québec
  - Subcritical Assembly
  - SLOWPOKE-2 – 20kW(t)
Dalhousie University, Halifax, Nova Scotia
  - SLOWPOKE-2–20kW(t)
University of Alberta, Edmonton, Alberta
  - SLOWPOKE-2 – 20kW(t)
Saskatchewan Research Council, Saskatoon, Saskatchewan
  - SLOWPOKW-2 – 20kW(t)
Nordion International Inc., Kanata, Ontario
  - SLOWPOKE-2 – 20kW(t)
Royal Military College of Canada, Kingston, Ontario
  - SLOWPOKE-2 – 20kW(t)

Fuel Fabrication
- General Electric Canada Inc., Peterborough, Ontario
- General Electric Canada Inc., Toronto, Ontario
- Zircatec Precisions Industries Inc,. Port Hope, Ontario

Irradiation Facilities
- Agriculture Canada, Sts. Hyacinthe, Quèbec
- AECL/Nordion, Kanata, Ontario
- Ethicon Ltd., Peterborough, Ontario
- Institut Armand-Frappier, Laval, Quèbec
- Sterirad, Markham, Ontario

Manhattan Project, which used uranium mined near Great Bear Lake in the Northwest Territories. The Canadian government started up a reactor in the eastern Ontario town of Chalk River in 1945. It was there, in 1950, that the first recorded "accident" at a nuclear plant occurred (in this case, a hydrogen explosion that demolished the core).

Ontario is one of two key nuclear provinces in Canada (the other is Saskatchewan) and the showroom of Canadian nuclear reactor technology. Well over half its electricity is generated at one of almost twenty Canadian Deuterium Uranium (Candu) reactors around the province, mostly in large "nuclear parks" where much of the operation is concentrated. The Candu uses deuterium oxide (heavy water) as a coolant, and is widely regarded as the safest reactor type. It is also the most efficient producer of plutonium (named after the Greek god of the dead) and tritium, most of which is exported to the United States for weapons production. Because Candu reactors can be refuelled while in operation, it is possible to steal or divert additional weapons materials without detection.

As in the United States, Canadian nuclear policy is built on global expansion. Despite Candu's relatively good record, however, only eight reactors have been sold overseas: to Pakistan, India, Taiwan, Argentina, South Korea, and the last one to Romania in 1981. The federal government's response to the slump has been to develop food irradiation technology and a small Slowpoke reactor designed for hospitals and universities. The government has also promoted southeastern Manitoba as an international nuclear-waste dump.

Canada's other major nuclear site is Saskatchewan, where about one-third of the world's supply of uranium lies under the Canadian Shield. Saskatchewan is now the largest producer and exporter of uranium in the world, selling to the United States, France, West Germany, the United Kingdom, Sweden, Finland, Japan, and Korea. The mines — owned by two crown corporations, the Saskatchewan Mining and Development Corporation and Eldorado, in partnership with private French, German, Japanese, and Korean syndicates, some of which are involved in weapons production — underwent huge expansion in the 1970s. The largest project, the Cigar Lake mine, contains high-grade uranium at 430 metres below the surface, uranium so radioactive that workers have to rotate on one-hour shifts. All of the sites are operated under the strictest state security, and most information about them is generated by the government and its crown corporations.

Military Landscapes

The least populated regions of the continent, the U.S. western interior and the Canadian north — those areas that Walt Disney referred to as "incredibly ugly, yet fantastically beautiful" — are not coincidentally the site of large military

installations. Throughout the Great Basin of the western United States — in Nevada, Utah, Texas, New Mexico, Arizona, California, Oregon, Washington, and Idaho — the armed forces have established "Military Operations Areas." These off-limit zones of millions of square kilometres are used for bombing practice, waste dumps, gunnery ranges, weapons production, and missile deployment. In addition to these fixed installations, jet training corridors link the Strategic Air Command headquarters in Nebraska to Nevada, a state almost entirely controlled by the military. Similar low-level flight paths stretch across British Columbia, the Northwest Territories, Alberta, Saskatchewan, Ontario, Quebec, and Labrador.

These extraordinary landscapes put to rest the myth of the West as the final uncontaminated frontier. The largest installation, the Nevada Test Site, was built on Shoshone land in 1950, during the Korean War when the United States was afraid of losing its test sites in the South Pacific. Since then the U.S. military has conducted at least six hundred nuclear blasts in Nevada, close to two hundred of them above ground — although the exact number of U.S. tests, which include blasts all over the Pacific, is not public knowledge. The full extent of these nuclear landscapes cannot be seen, even through the miles of

Sedan Crater, Nevada Test Site. The U.S. government detonated a thermonuclear device here in 1962 to test the use of bombs for widening the Panama Canal.

A Canadian Nuclear Association diagram of an underground repository of high-level radioactive waste.

chain-link fences that surround them. Some of them are places that people or animals will not be able to reinhabit for centuries.

The U.S. military is by far the largest producer of hazardous wastes in the world. From the Second World War until the Carter administration in the late 1970s, the Atomic Energy Act exempted the military from all state and federal environmental legislation. During those thirty-five years, weapons plants all across the country indiscriminately released radioactive materials into air, water, and soil. In the late 1980s the U.S. Environmental Protection Agency estimated that there were fifteen thousand contaminated sites on military reserves, ninety-six of them so dangerous that they were on the National Priorities List of the agency's Superfund. The most notorious of these installations is Hanford Reservation, a one-thousand-square-kilometre development straddling the Columbia River in south-central Washington state. Its nine reactors and three reprocessing plants have produced half of all the plutonium in the U.S. arsenal. At least 800 billion litres of liquid wastes have been dumped at Hanford over the years, most of them directly into the soil — with few records kept. Some accounts have escaped the paper shredder, however. In 1986, the Department of Energy was forced to release documents showing that more than once Hanford scientists deliberately released radioactive iodine into the air to see how far the winds would spread it. Technicians subsequently tested members of communities downwind (without telling them what the tests were for). Plant officials claim they have kept no records of the tests, just as the army has denied the existence of medical records of soldiers who have worked in weapons-testing areas.

The Rocky Mountain Arsenal near Boulder, Colorado, was originally a plutonium processing plant. Since then the U.S. army has used the site to produce mustard and nerve gases, incendiary balms, Napalm, explosives, and military viruses. Despite its long history of fires and accidents, the army leased the plant to Shell Oil for the production of aldrin and dieldrin, broad-spectrum insecticides that have since been banned. Shell abandoned the site in the mid-1980s, and since then the two institutions have been in court arguing about responsibility for severe soil and water contamination. The army believes the pollution can be "cleaned up," and has announced plans to open the Arsenal to the public as a wildlife refuge. Other public agencies have different ideas. The FBI is investigating criminal violations of toxic waste laws. The Army Corps of Engineers, for its part, calls the Arsenal "the most contaminated square mile on Earth" and has suggested that cleanup costs will be so high that the area might become the first place in the United States to be permanently fenced off to prevent future human use.

At the Idaho National Engineering Laboratory, in a sagebrush desert near the Teton Mountains in southeastern Idaho, the Exxon Nuclear Idaho Company operates a nuclear reprocessing plant for the Department of Energy. The plant recovers weapons materials from "high-level wastes" generated by terrestrial and marine reactors all over the world. Since the 1950s, the Idaho installation has also been a "temporary" storage depot for low-level waste such as contaminated tools, equipment, and clothing. Many of these wastes are buried or dissipated in wells that reach into the vast Snake River aquifer, used to irrigate local croplands. In late 1988 the governor of Idaho ordered police to stop further shipments of nuclear wastes at the border.

Storage of nuclear wastes has become an acute problem for the nuclear industry. The U.S. Nuclear Waste Policy Act of 1982 mandated the development and operation of underground storage facilities by the early 1990s. A Department of Energy (DOE) brochure I picked up in Oak Ridge said that waste would be shipped first to Tennessee, where it would be packaged into "little capsules" and prepared for shipment by rail to sites in Texas, Nevada, or Washington. Those plans have since changed. Texas and Washington refused to accept the wastes; and the DOE, which took over the management of seventeen nuclear-weapons facilities from the Atomic Energy Commission in 1977, became embroiled in scandal for covering up a long history of radioactive contamination.

In late 1989, under pressure from some of its former scientists, the DOE admitted that its research for a planned storage facility at Yucca Mountain, Nevada, was invalid. Undaunted, the department started construction of the Waste Isolation Pilot Plant in an old salt mine near Carlsbad, New Mexico. Admiral James Watkins, the secretary of energy, called the storage facility, where high-level wastes would boil for a thousand years, "part of the peace through strength concept."

The North

Canadians live uneasily in the narrow space between the technological dynamo to the south and one of its objects: the great expanse of the North. I mean North as it's used casually by most people: the High Arctic of frozen seas and tundra barrens, and the sub-Arctic of vast boreal forests, shallow lakes, bogs, and muskeg. The North is a crucial site for the conflict between industrial society and everything pitted against it. It is an ancient landscape inhabited by many distinct aboriginal nations. Now it too is highly technologized, its natural features overlaid with oil-drilling platforms, pipelines, military communications facilities, jet airfields, NATO and NORAD practice-flight ranges, lead, uranium, and asbestos mines, hydroelectric projects, as well as radioactive garbage dumped from space. The Canadian North has also been a test range for Cruise missiles and B-1 bombers rehearsing for the day they would collide with enemy weaponry.

While resource extraction in the Canadian North has not been as secretive as the U.S. military development, its installations bear a remarkable similarity to the off-limits zones of the U.S. West. In this new and perhaps last colony of industrialism, modern resource extraction has restructured entire environments. One of the prime examples is "the project of the century," as its promoters call it, a scheme to generate twenty-seven thousand megawatts of electricity to sell to the United States. The James Bay hydroelectric project is a series of hundreds of dams and dikes that if finished will collect and divert all the moving water in a 350,000-square-kilometre area of Northern Quebec — an area more or less the size of France.

The $60 billion project started in 1971, and its first phase, involving the generation of 15,000 megawatts of electricity, was near completion by 1990. In a book promoting the project in the early 1970s, Quebec premier Robert Bourassa described Quebec as "a vast hydroelectric plant in the bud, and every day, millions of potential kilowatt hours flow downhill and out to sea. What a waste." He went on to announce that "Quebec must occupy its territory; it must occupy James Bay." That occupation is immense. Hydro-Quebec, the crown corporation overseeing the project, has dammed, diverted, eliminated, or reversed entire rivers. Filling the reservoirs has already caused small earthquakes, moving the Cree, among the traditional inhabitants of the region, to call electricity *nimischiiuskutaau,* the fire that shakes the land. In the completed sections of the project, the hydro company now manages river flows according to power demands, effectively reversing the natural water cycle.

In other words, to run electric heaters and air conditioners in the south, rivers rage during the coldest months of winter and the hottest months of summer, ordinarily the times of lowest water. In spring and fall, ordinarily times of high water, rivers are reduced to a trickle. The water diversions, which are now opposed by many North American environmental organizations, threaten the habitat of whales, fish, caribou, and migratory birds, as well as a rare species of freshwater seal.

Ancillary development includes the deforestation of an area the size of Maine, Vermont, and New York states; the flooding of ancient camps and communities, as well as hunting and fishing areas; and the imposition of new towns, airports, transmission corridors, bars, swimming pools, and arenas — all in a region that previously had no roads. For its part, the flooding has released methane, which contributes to the greenhouse effect. It has also released mercury from the bedrock and introduced it into the food chain. Mercury poisoning is now common among the Cree, whose diet is based on fish. Jean Bernier, general secretary of Hydro-Quebec, calls the mercury "a natural phenomenon [that] will stabilize over time, probably 10, 15 or 20 years."

The Quebec government began construction before notifying the Cree or Inuit living in the region (at the time the Natives were denied the right to vote) and conducted no environmental review. In 1975, four years into construction of the project, Quebec awarded aboriginal residents $225 million over a twenty-year period, although the agreement required most of the money to be invested in Quebec bonds and blue-chip stocks. The compensation thus functioned as a loan to the financial interests promoting the development. In its fury to complete the project, the government has broken many parts of the agreement, and in 1990 the Cree filed suit against Quebec in the World Court, arguing that the development is incompatible with their way of life and the local environment.

The James Bay Project has indeed devastated a society based on worship of the land. The progression of changes is familiar from similar projects all over the world, for large-scale environmental manipulation destroys the social fabric of human communities: flooded ancestral lands, relocated villages, changes in diet, the introduction of a cash economy, substance abuse, suicide, and violence.

The ruthlessness of the James Bay project was graphically demonstrated

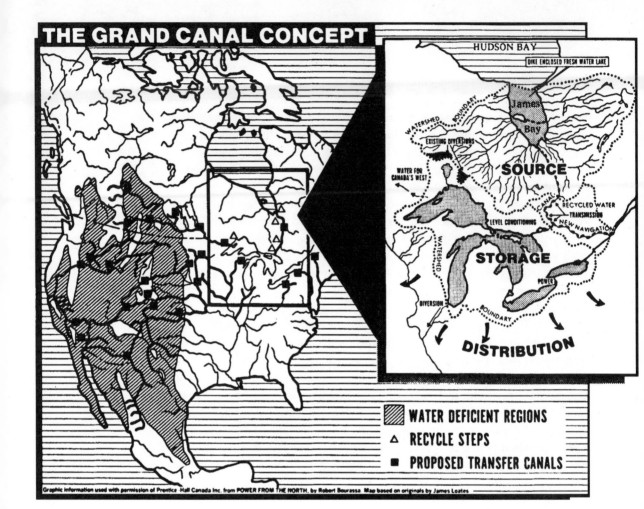

THE GRAND CANAL CONCEPT

HUDSON BAY

DIKE ENCLOSED FRESH WATER LAKE

WATERSHED BOUNDARY

James Bay

EXISTING DIVERSIONS

WATER FOR CANADA'S WEST

SOURCE

CANAL

RECYCLED WATER

TRANSMISSION

NEW NAVIGATION

LEVEL CONDITIONING

WATERSHED

STORAGE

POWER

DIVERSION

BOUNDARY

DISTRIBUTION

⬚ WATER DEFICIENT REGIONS
△ RECYCLE STEPS
■ PROPOSED TRANSFER CANALS

Graphic information used with permission of Prentice-Hall Canada Inc. from POWER FROM THE NORTH, by Robert Bourassa. Map based on originals by James Loates

The Grand Canal project proposes to ship water from southern Hudson Bay to the arid regions of western North America.

to the world in the fall of 1984. During the height of caribou migration, Hydro-Quebec released a large quantity of water to test the gates on one of its dams, and ten thousand caribou trying to cross the Caniapiscau River at their traditional ford near Limestone Falls died in the floodwaters. In a televised operation, the carcasses were removed by helicopter to a fish-processing plant at Kuujjuaq on the Atlantic coast, where they were later processed into dog food.

If it is completed, the Quebec project has even more sinister implications, for behind every new dam in Canada rests the possibility of water sales to the south, especially to the expanding desert areas of the western states. For nearly twenty years a consortium of Canadian businessmen has quietly promoted something called the Grand Canal. The scheme involves separating James Bay from Hudson Bay by a dike and turning it into a freshwater sea, a highly marketable commodity on a warming planet. In this engineering logic, the Great Lakes would become a giant pumping station for water on its way south

to irrigate agricultural plantations and lawns. It's not an entirely new or bizarre idea: Great Lakes water has for some time been drawn off through the Chicago River and into the Mississippi watershed to flush pollution and raise water levels for shipping. The promoters of the canal speak of water as an "export product" for the branch-plant Canadian economy. Indeed, the city of Santa Barbara, California, is already considering bringing water by ship from British Columbia.

The fear of "water basin transfers," as their promoters call them, has been heightened by the Free Trade Agreement, a treaty signed by the Canadian and U.S. governments in 1987 and approved by the House of Commons (after an intervening federal election) in December 1988. The agreement, whose chief Canadian negotiator, Simon Reisman, is linked to the Grand Canal scheme, gives the United States permanent and unrestricted access to many Canadian resources. Whether those resources include water remained open to interpretation.

In recent years the rush to extract the last resources from this planet has produced other Northern environments as well: oil and natural gas infrastructures have come to dominate the landscape. Oil provides by far the most energy to the industrialized world, although its uses are very specific. Some 90 per cent of world petroleum production is dedicated to the manufacture and fuelling of North American automobiles. Since the late 1960s, a large percentage of this oil and gas has been retrieved from the Arctic coast, stretching from the National Petroleum Reserve in northwest Alaska to the Mackenzie Delta and Beaufort Sea in Canada. The centrepiece of this development was to be Prudhoe Bay, opened along the Arctic coast of Alaska in 1968: the largest industrial complex in the world, a 1,500-square-kilometre area that has obliterated the North Slope ecosystem. Even when the production at Prudhoe Bay started to wind down in the late 1980s, there were six hundred reported oil spills a year, and the EPA's Superfund was listing several sites of severe contamination. By 1990 new exploration was under way in Bristol Bay on the south coast of Alaska, the Chukchi Sea on the west coast, and the Beaufort Sea to the north. The shallow waters of the Beaufort lie along the coast of the Arctic National Wildlife Refuge, the principal calving ground of the 180,000-head Porcupine caribou herd. The U.S. government wants to open drilling in the refuge itself to tap into a potential supply of 3.5-billion barrels of oil — or seven months' worth — for the U.S. market.

While onshore extraction poisons soils and thaws the permafrost, offshore drilling from drill ships or artificial islands disrupts fragile marine life. U.S. writer Michael Brown estimates that one exploratory drill ship alone produces as much smog as twenty-five thousand cars each travelling twenty-nine thousand kilometres. The "drilling muds" used to lubricate the drills are contaminated with oil, polychlorinated biphenyls, polycyclic aromatic hydrocarbons, and heavy metals. When they're exhausted the muds are dumped on the sea floor. Most oil from the Arctic is removed by pipelines, which the U.S. Congress has exempted from environmental laws.

Concentrating on the North, however, obscures the global reach of the petroleum economy. In spring 1989, for example, the Exxon Valdez spilled eighteen million litres of oil into Prince William Sound off the southern Alaskan coast. Calling this spill an accident obscures the fact that accidents are a normal part of any large-scale industrial system. The Exxon spill was the four hundredth in Prince William Sound since Valdez became a transhipment port for oil from Alaska's North Slope. In the twelve months before the Exxon spill, at least eight million litres of oil were spilled in Alaska, British Columbia, Antarctica, Hawaii, Delaware, Rhode Island, Texas, the Mediterranean, and the Persian Gulf. Then again, the American Petroleum Institute estimates that *every two-and-a-half weeks* home car mechanics discharge as much oil down drains and into vacant lots as the Exxon Valdez dumped into the sea. The cleanup of Prince William Sound, such as it was, has itself produced enormous wastes: journalist Jill Kunka has written, "One ton of spilled crude produces ten tons of toxic garbage — bags of oily gravel, mountains of synthetic absorbent booms and pads, discarded coveralls and the assorted refuse of 10,000 cleanup workers." Much of this waste was burned in temporary incinerators in Valdez; the rest was to be sent to toxic waste disposal sites. In short, the Exxon Valdez's cargo would have been spilled anyway — it's just taken a different route round the world.

Outer Space

Today, military and technological environments extend well beyond the surface of the Earth. Domination has a new frontier, as Senator Lyndon Johnson pointed out with characteristic aplomb in the late 1950s. "Control of [outer] space means control of the world, far more certainly, far more totally than any control that has been achieved by weapons or by troops of occupation. Space is the ultimate position, the position of total control over Earth." Total control of the universe is thankfully something that remains beyond U.S. technological capabilities, despite Ronald Reagan's Strategic Defense Initiative. But as historian Michael L. Smith has pointed out, the greatest achievement of the space program — and especially its most spectacular moment, the moon landing — has been not so much the colonization of outer space as the "simulation of territorial and scientific conquest." In other words, the most important function the space program has had in contemporary culture is its *display value,* its ability to win prestige for the military and build consensus about the proper role for science and technology in the world.

No discussion of technology and landscape can overlook what is sometimes called the electronic environment, whose invisible reach extends around the entire globe and into our very organs. One of the key instruments of this sensorium, the satellite, has changed the way we perceive the Earth. Like nuclear reactors, satellites too are a technology developed by the military, and their "commercial applications" have been numerous. The objectives of modern military satellites are to gather information on potential targets and attack routes, to provide early warning of attack, and (more recently) to confirm compliance with arms-control treaties. After World War II, rocket engineering made it possible to gather intelligence from space, rather than using balloons or planes closer to Earth, and satellites played a crucial role during the U.S.-Soviet arms race of the 1950s and 1960s. The Carter administration invested heavily in satellite technology in the late 1970s as part of its reform of the CIA, replacing many clandestine agents with mechanical information-gatherers.

This investment spurred the development of sophisticated imaging technologies through the National Reconnaissance Office at the Pentagon and led to three major developments: resolution, real-time imaging, and photo enhancement. Current military satellites such as the KH-12 (whose existence is denied) have a resolution of a few inches and can gather data in the dark. This means something as small as a golf ball can be seen from space, at night. Real-time imaging means that the photograph is converted to digits and transmitted to Earth within a second — time enough for an operator (or a computer on Earth) to zoom in on an object (or person) of interest. Photo-enhancement machines can manipulate the digits to sharpen, realign, or alter a photograph. They can also, undetected, add or subtract elements of a terrestrial image.

At present, non-military satellite photography, which cannot focus on objects much smaller than a house, can be manipulated to create a three-dimensional filmic representation of the Earth. Using reinterpreted still-photography images from Landsat, for example, *L.A.: The Movie* creates a representation of Los Angeles from a moving plane. This hypothetical plane can fly anywhere in the photograph, and perspectives and building shadows alter with its changing position. This mapping technology was developed to guide Cruise missiles.

Satellites also monitor and transmit audio signals. Military versions collect microwaves and relay them to Earth stations for analysis and possible scrambling. Analysis, most of which is done by computers, is the most complicated aspect of all. Military satellites record and interpret tens of thousands of audio and visual messages each day.

Most satellites are launched by rocket and powered by a combination of electro-chemical and solar power. The Pentagon, the Department of Energy, and the National Aeronautics and Space Administration (NASA) are currently developing SP-100, a space-based nuclear reactor that they hope will power satellites, weapons, space telescopes, explorations vehicles, and space stations. After use, the reactor would be discarded in space, where there's already a remarkable amount of human garbage. As the U.S. Space Command puts it, there are "20,000 manufactured objects larger than a softball" in the Earth's orbit.

Although remote-sensing equipment came out of military research labs, like many technologies it has potentially redemptive uses if introduced at a rate that allows for broad social discussion. As satellite images of Earth have circulated in North American culture, the aggregate effects of land development have become newly visible. Earth-observation satellites like Landsat TM and SPOT were first put into orbit in the early 1980s. They are able to interpret a wide range of light and radiation reflecting off the Earth's surface and thus track things like biotic islands and corridors, plant succession, erosion, and water

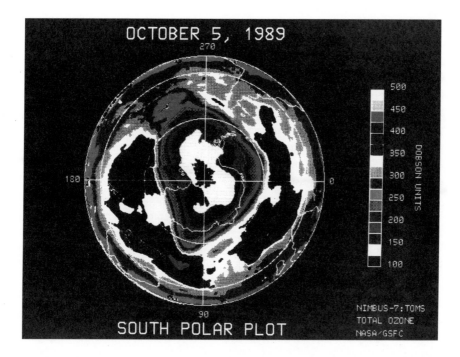

OCTOBER 5, 1989

SOUTH POLAR PLOT

A photograph of ozone distribution in the southern hemisphere. Data were gathered from a Total Ozone Mapping Spectrometer on NASA's NIMBUS-7 satellite.

quality. When — and if — these images become publicly accessible, the information forms invaluable educational and political tools.

It might seem odd that we need to see some of these things from space just to grasp the regional impact of changes in landscape. Yet often the earliest or "first" development of a region has the strongest effect on how we perceive our surroundings. Each development can obscure the possibility of repairing and linking together once again both human and natural communities. Satellite images might help us see how to do this. They also change the way we experience the world; I've seen some sophisticated 3-D bicycle maps of the hills south of San Francisco, maps made from satellite images. Writing in a very different context, Lucy Lippard reminds us that maps help us locate ourselves in the world, giving meaning to the discontinuities of time and place. We come back to the ambiguous image of the Earth seen from space, the whole Earth.

Technology as Environment: The Ultimate Fix

In many ways, the Tennessee Valley Authority is the perfect model of modern technology on the land. Its narratives — "electrification" and "Atoms for Peace" — are the bedtime stories we know well from world's fairs and corporate annual reports. They are the tales of progress, of Gross National Product and Rising Standard of Living. North American institutions have exported the TVA model of industrial development all over the world, as John F. Kennedy pointed out on a visit to the valley in 1963: "The work of TVA will never be over. There will always be new frontiers for it to conquer. For in the minds of men the world over, the initials of TVA stand for progress, and the people of this area are not afraid of progress."

The TVA is also a model of another kind. Its grandiose project of harnessing the Tennessee River and its tributaries is a material model of social and ecological organization — a virtual outdoor factory based on the division of labour. Like all science, its project is to manage the unpredictable or hostile forces of nature — in this case floods and disease.

The historical conjuncture that the TVA represents is now behind us. Today the Tennessee Valley, like the North, is a geography in crisis, a place that everywhere reveals the ruptures of an expansionist industrial society. The intervening years have seen the rise of a broad resistance to that society. Our presidents and prime ministers can no longer count on consensus about the doctrine of progress. Indeed, refusal has become so total that it obstructs not only the building of dams and airport expansion but also the whole promotional apparatus of world's fairs and olympic games.

The sinister unity of the TVA towns of Muscle Shoals and Oak Ridge has also been shattered by two decades of ecological disasters. Yet disasters seem, ironically, to fuel the very system that creates them, a system that feeds off its own failures, always ready to substitute a new technology to ostensibly heal the wounds inflicted by its now outmoded predecessor. Thus the technological fixes touted everywhere: that last bit of oil under a caribou herd, the magic of nuclear power, ever larger dams, biodegradable garbage bags, a safe way to dispose of toxins. The ultimate fix, as social critic George Bradford points out, is biotechnology, which offers us the illusion of total biological control.

Massive technological environments (and they are still being madly built) do something more than accelerate the destruction of the Earth or signal "the end of nature." They also reduce economics to production, further mystifying the relationship between human livelihood and natural systems. It may well be that the productive economy is beginning to collapse under its own weight, opening up the possibility of creating alternatives in our regions and communities. Yet the terms of survival into the next century will not be found within the technological arena but from within the culture that surrounds and produces it. We urgently need to imagine environments that are not about domination and war. We need to tell new stories about settlement and work on this Earth.

Perhaps this speculative task is best left to art, to gardens, to books and movies. *That* work — everything that goes on under the name of culture — has a history too. It will be enough to recall *Beaver Valley* or Jacques Cousteau's sea adventures to realize that for all the possibilities those investigations of nature might have opened up in their day, they are no longer adequate to the task of imagining a future in which technology, culture, and nature are fully integrated. We now need a larger perspective. We need to gain a sense of how our constructed environment connects to the natural one surrounding it, and to its history. Only then can we be mobilized to restore nature and to assure it, and ourselves, a future.

*Don Valley Parkway and
Riverdale Park in Toronto.
Photograph by Robert
Burley.*

Notes on Sources

Introduction

Two books have been alongside my desk throughout the years I've spent on this manuscript. My first encounter with Frederick W. Turner, *Beyond Geography: The Western Spirit Against the Wilderness* (New York: Viking Press, 1980) was a revelation, for the book was able to engage cultural history, geography, and comparative religion all at once. Although Turner's subject — a spiritual history of European civilization in the Americas — seems to lie at some distance from my own, his book has inspired and I hope influenced this one. Hans Peter Duerr, *Dreamtime: Concerning the Boundary Between Wilderness and Civilization,* first published in 1978 and translated into English in 1985 (Oxford: Basil Blackwell), attempts to recover the voices of pre-modern cultures that have been all but silenced by everything we call modernity. It continues to give me hope for the future.

Other theoretical and historical works I've found useful are Theodore Roszak, *Person/Planet: The Creative Disintegration of Industrial Society* (New York: Anchor, 1978) and *Where the Wasteland Ends: Politics and Transcendence in Postindustrial Society* (Garden City: Doubleday, 1972). Denis E. Cosgrove, *Social Formation and Symbolic Landscape* (London: Croom Helm, 1984), is a thorough and provocative examination of the idea of landscape in Western history. And Neil Evernden, *The Natural Alien: Humankind and Environment* (Toronto: University of Toronto Press, 1985), offers a good introduction to current thinking in natural philosophy. *A Primer for Daily Life* by Susan Willis (London: Routledge, 1991), is a book that shared its beginnings with *The Culture of Nature* in a series of ambulatory discussions about contemporary culture and everyday life.

The work of two U.S. geographers has been indispensable to me. Carl O. Sauer's luminous writing is perhaps best first encountered in his *Selected Essays 1963–1975*

(Berkeley: Turtle Island, 1981). The other groundbreaking geographer in the American tradition is J. B. Jackson, whose many collected essays I list immediately below. D. W. Meinig,
ed., *The Interpretation of Ordinary Landscapes* (Oxford: Oxford University Press, 1979), is a useful collection of current English thinking about landscape.

Good social histories of the 1950s and 1960s are Marty Jezer, *The Dark Ages: Life in
the United States, 1945–1960* (Boston: South End Press, 1982), Douglas T. Miller and Marion
Nowak, *The Fifties: The Way We Really Were* (Garden City: Doubleday, 1977), and the collection *The 60s Without Apology* (Minneapolis: University of Minnesota Press, 1984). Samuel P.
Hays, *Beauty, Health and Permanence: Environmental Politics in the United States 1955–1985*
(Cambridge: Cambridge University Press, 1985), gives a good sense of the historical context
of the environmentalist movement as it rose to prominence in the postwar years.

Lastly, Hans Magnus Enzensberger's prescient "A Critique of Political Ecology," in his
Critical Essays, ed. Reinhold Grimm and Bruce Armstrong (New York: Continuum, 1982)
alerts us to the pitfalls of ecological politics. I hope I've learned some of its lessons.

❂

Anil Agarwal. "Beyond Pretty Trees and Tigers: The Role of Ecological Destruction in
　　　the Emerging Patterns of Poverty and People's Protests." *South Asian Anthropologist,*
　　　Vol. 6, No. 1 (1985).

Jay Appleton. *The Experience of Landscape.* London: Wiley, 1975.

Rudolf Bahro. "The Logic of Deliverance: On the Foundations of An Ecological Politics."
　　　London: Schumacher Society Lecture, 1986.

Rudolf Bahro. "Socialism, Ecology and Utopia." *History Workshop,* Vol. 16 (1983).

Julian Burger, ed. *The Gaia Atlas of First Peoples.* New York: Anchor Doubleday, 1990.

J. Baird Callicott, ed. *Nature in Asian Traditions of Thought: Essays in Environmental
　　　Philosophy.* Albany: State University of New York Press, 1989.

Ward Churchill, ed. *Marxism and Native Americans.* Boston: South End Press, 1983.

Barry Commoner. *Making Peace with the Planet.* New York: Pantheon, 1990.

Consumer Reports, ed. *I'll Buy That: 50 Small Wonders and Big Deals that Revolutionized the
　　　Lives of Consumers.* Mount Vernon, N.Y.: Consumers' Union, 1986.

William Cronin. *Changes in the Land: Indians, Colonialists and the Ecology of New England.*
　　　New York: Hill and Wang, 1983.

Ben Crow, "Lost in Forests of Aboriginal Goodness?" [review of *The State of India's
　　　Environment 1982: A Citizens' Report*], *Radical Science,* No. 14 (1984).

Richard Drinnon. *Facing West: The Metaphysics of Indian Hating and Empire Building.* New
　　　York: Schocken, 1980, 1990.

Richard T.T. Forman and Michel Godron. *Landscape Ecology.* New York: Wiley, 1986.

Eric F. Goldman. *The Crucial Decade and After: America, 1945–1960.* New York, 1960.

Robert Hay. "Toward a Theory of Sense of Place." *Trumpeter,* Vol. 5, No. 4 (Fall 1988).

Thomas Hine. *Populuxe.* New York: Knopf, 1986.

Ivan Illich. *H₂O and the Waters of Forgetfullness*. London: Marion Boyers, 1986.

J.B. Jackson. *Landscapes: Selected Writings of J. B. Jackson*. Amherst: University of Massachusetts Press, 1970.

J.B. Jackson. *The Necessity for Ruins and Other Essays*. Amherst: University of Massachusetts Press, 1980.

J.B. Jackson. *Discovering the Vernacular Landscape*. New Haven, Conn.: Yale University Press, 1984.

David Nicholson-Lord, *The Greening of the Cities*. London: Routledge and Kegan Paul, 1987.

Edmund C. Penning-Rowsell and David Lowenthal. *Landscape Meanings and Values*. London: Allen and Unwin, 1986.

John V. Punter. "Landscape Aesthetics: A Synthesis and Critique," in J.R. Gold and J. Burgess, eds., *Valued Environments*. London: George Allen and Unwin, 1982.

Edward Relph. *Place and Placelessness*. London: Pion, 1976.

Joni Seager, ed. *The State of the Earth Atlas*. Toronto: General, 1990.

Paul Shepard. *Man in the Landscape: A Historic View of the Esthetics of Nature*. New York: Knopf, 1967.

John R. Stilgoe. *Common Landscape America 1580–1845*. New Haven, Conn.: Yale University Press, 1982.

Edward Soja. *Post-Modern Geographies: The Resurrection of Space in Critical Social Theory*. London and New York: Verso, 1989.

David Suzuki and Anita Gordon. *It's a Matter of Survival*. Toronto: Stoddart, 1990.

William J. Thomas, ed. *Man's Role in Changing the Face of the Earth*. Chicago: University of Chicago, 1956.

Keith Thomas. *Man and the Natural World: A History of the Modern Sensibility*. New York: Pantheon, 1983.

May Theilgaard Watts. *Reading the Landscape of America* (1957). New York: Collier, 1975.

Raymond Williams. *Keywords: A Vocabulary of Culture and Society*. London: Fontana, 1976.

Judith Williamson. *Decoding Advertisements: Ideology and Meaning in Advertising*. London: Marion Boyers, 1978.

Alexander Wilson. "Art, Geography and Resistance." *Massachusetts Review,* Vol. 31, Nos. 1 & 2 (Summer 1990).

Wilbur Zelinsky. *The Cultural Geography of the United States*. Englewood Cliffs, N.J.: Prentice-Hall, 1973.

1. The View from the Road: Recreation and Tourism

The standard texts on tourist culture in North America are Dean McCannell, *The Tourist: A New Theory of the Leisure Class* (New York: Schocken, 1976) and John Jakle, *The Tourist: Travels in 20th-Century North America* (Lincoln: University of Nebraska Press, 1985).

On the car and its relation to North American geographies and cultures, see John B. Rae, *The Road and the Car in American Life* (Cambridge, Mass.: MIT Press, 1971), David Brodsly, *L.A. Freeway: An Appreciative Essay* (Berkeley: University of California Press, 1981), and Robert Venturi, Denise Scott Brown and Steven Izenour, *Learning From Las Vegas* (Cambridge, Mass.: MIT Press, 1972).

My idea of modernity is drawn from Marshall Berman, *All That is Solid Melts into Air: The Experience of Modernity* (New York: Simon and Schuster, 1982), a tour-de-force that is as sensitive to spatial issues as it is to literary ones. See especially his chapter on Robert Moses, as well as the debate between Berman and Perry Anderson in *New Left Review,* No. 44 (March–April, 1984)

A concise social history of the urban parks and recreation movements in the United States is Galen Cranz, "Changing Roles of Urban Parks: From Pleasure Garden to Open Space," *Landscape,* Vol. 22, No. 3 (Summer 1978).

The Annapurna Conservation Area Project can be contacted at Box 3712, Kathmandu, Nepal.

◉

"Bury my Heart at Peggy's Cove: A Special Summer Issue on Tourism." *New Maritimes,* Vol. 5, No. 11/12 (July/August 1987).

"Guests Nude and Rude." Editorial on tourism, *The Globe and Mail,* October 31, 1986.

Judith Adler. "Tourism and Pastoral: A Decade of Debate," in Verner Smitheram, David Milne, Satadal Dasgupta, eds., *The Garden Transformed: Prince Edward Island 1945–1980.* Charlottetown: Ragweed Press, 1982.

Stanley Aronowitz. "Why Work?" *Social Text.* No. 12 (Fall 1985).

Warren James Belasco. *Americans on the Road: From Autocamp to Motel 1910–1945.* Cambridge, Mass.: MIT Press, 1979.

Elizabeth Boo. *Eco-Tourism: The Potentials and Pitfalls.* Washington, D.C.: World Wildlife Fund, 1990.

Daniel Boorstin. "From Traveler to Tourist: The Lost Art of Travel," in *The Image, or, What Happened to the American Dream?* New York: Atheneum, 1962.

C. Frank Brockman and Lawrence C. Merriam, Jr. *Recreational Use of Wild Lands.* Third edition. New York: McGraw-Hill, 1979.

Barry Buxton, ed. *Parkways: Past, Present, Future.* Boone, N.C.: Appalachian Consortium Press, 1988.

Margaret Cerullo and Phyllis Ewen. "The American Family Goes Camping: Gender, Family and the Politics of Space." *Antipode: A Radical Journal of Geography,* Vol. 16, No. 3 (1984).

Phoebe Cutler. *The Public Landscape of the New Deal.* New Haven, Conn.: Yale University Press, 1985.

Guy Debord, *La société du spectacle.* Paris: Buchet/Chastel, 1967.

Umberto Eco. "Travels in Hyperreality," in *Travels in Hyperreality*. San Diego: Harcourt, Brace Jovanovich, 1986.

Robin Epstein. *Rediscovering Rosalie Edge*. Unpublished manuscript, Department of History, Duke University, April 1985.

James Flink. *Car Culture*. Cambridge, Mass.: MIT Press, 1975.

E.J. Hart. *The Selling of Canada: The CPR and the Beginnings of Canadian Tourism*. Banff, Alta.: Altitude Publishers, 1983.

Alan Hess. *Googie: 50s Coffee Shop Architecture*. San Francisco: Chronicle Books, 1985.

Harley E. Jolley. *Painting with a Comet's Tail: The Touch of the Landscape Architect on the Blue Ridge Parkway*. Boone, N.C.: Appalachian Consortium Press, 1986.

Harley E. Jolley. *Blue Ridge Parkway: The First 50 Years*. Boone, N.C.: Appalachian Consortium Press, 1985.

Journal of Leisure Research. Washington, D.C.: National Recreation & Park Association, 1969 –.

Christian Kallen. "Ecotourism: The Light at the End of the Terminal." *E,* Vol. 1, No. 4 (July/August 1990).

Leisure Studies. London: F.N. Spon, 1982–.

Chester H. Liebs. *Main Street to Miracle Mile: American Roadside Architecture*. Boston: Little, Brown, 1985.

John Marsh. *Scenery Evaluation and Landscape Perception: A Bibliography*. Exchange Bibliography 304. Monticello, Ill.: Council of Planning Librarians, 1972.

T. C. McLuhan. *Dream Tracks: The Railroad and the American Indian 1890–1930*. New York: Abrams, 1985.

Margaret Mead. "Outdoor Recreation in the Context of Emerging American Cultural Values: Background Considerations," in *Trends in American Living and Outdoor Recreation,* a report to the Outdoor Recreation Resources Review Commission. Washington, D.C.: ORRRC, 1962.

Joseph W. Meeker. "Red, White and Black in National Parks," *The North American Review* (1973), reprinted in Gary E. Machlis and Donald R. Field, eds., *On Interpretation: Sociology for Interpreters of Natural and Cultural History*. Corvallis, Oreg.: Oregon State University Press, 1984.

Terry Morden. "The Pastoral and the Pictorial". *Ten.8,* No. 12 (1983).

Peter E. Murphy. *Tourism: A Community Approach*. New York: Methuen, 1985.

Nature in World Development: Patterns in the Preservation of Scenic and Outdoor Recreation Resources. New York: The Rockefeller Foundation, 1978.

Stephanie Ocko. *Environmental Vacations: Volunteer Projects to Save the Planet*. Santa Fe, New Mexico: John Muir Publications, 1990.

Stanley Parker. *The Sociology of Leisure*. London: George Allen and Unwin, 1976.

John Robinson. *Highways and Our Environment*. New York: McGraw-Hill, 1971.

Michael Aaron Rockland. *Homes on Wheels*. New Brunswick, N.J.: Rutgers University Press, 1980.

Chris Rojek. *Capitalism and Leisure Theory.* London: Tavistock, 1985.

Barry Sadler and Allen Carlson. *Environmental Aesthetics: Essays in Interpretation.* Victoria, B.C.: University of Victoria, 1982.

Elizabeth A. T. Smith. "The Drive-in Culture," in Gerald Silk, ed., *Automobile and Culture.* New York: Abrams, 1984.

"The Endless Weekend: A Special Issue on Americans Outdoors." *Life,* September 3, 1971.

E P. Thompson. "Time, Work–Discipline, and Industrial Capitalism." *Past and Present,* No. 38 (1967).

Yi-fu Tuan. *Topophilia: A Study of Environmental Perception, Attitudes and Values.* Englewood Cliffs, N.J.: Prentice-Hall, 1974.

United States. Forest Service, U.S. Department of Agriculture. *A Comprehensive Bibliography on Vacation Homes and Recreational Lands in the United States* (Forest Service Research Paper SE-202). Asheville, N.C.: Southeastern Forest Experimental Station, 1980.

United States. Forest Service, U.S. Department of Agriculture. *Future Recreation Environments* (Forest Service Research Paper NE-301). Upper Darby, Penn., 1977.

John Henry Wadlund. *Ernest Thompson Seton: Man in Nature and the Progressive Era 1880–1915.* New York: Arno Press, 1978.

Geoffrey Wall and John S. Marsh, eds. *Recreational Land Use: Perspectives on Its Evolution in Canada.* Ottawa: Carleton University Press, 1982.

Arthur S. White. *Palaces of the People: A Social History of Commercial Hospitality.* New York: Taplinger, 1970.

Richard Saul Wurman, Alan Levy, and Joel Katz. *The Nature of Recreation.* Cambridge, Mass.: MIT Press, 1972.

2. Nature Education and Promotion

Because education about the natural world takes place within many disciplines and its terms are fiercely debated, there are no comprehensive texts on nature education. Some sense of the diversity of educational materials can be had by looking at the *Environmental Resource Directory* (available from Public Focus, 489 College Street, Toronto, Ont. M6G 1A5), an annually updated survey of environment-related books, pamphlets, kits, and audio-visual material available to teachers.

The standard introduction to nature interpretation is Grant W. Sharpe, ed., *Interpreting the Environment* (New York: Wiley & Sons, 1976, 1982).

Barry Commoner provides a succinct discussion of the current ecological crisis in his report, "The Environment," in *The New Yorker,* June 15, 1987. See also his more recent *Making Peace with the Earth* (New York: Pantheon, 1990), as well as the yearly reports of Lester Brown, et al., *The State of the World: A Worldwatch Institute Report on Progress Toward a Sustainable Society* (New York: W. W. Norton).

Ecological theory is now a vast field of inquiry. A starting point is the work of Rudolf Bahro and Murray Bookchin. See Bahro, *Socialism and Survival* (London: Heretic Books, 1982), *From Red to Green: Interviews with New Left Review* (London: Verso, 1984), and *Building the Green Movement* (Philadelphia: New Society, 1986). Bookchin's important work includes *The Ecology of Freedom* (Palo Alto, Cal.: Cheshire Books, 1982) and *Remaking Society* (Montreal: Black Rose, 1989).

Feminism has considerably broadened and deepened environmentalist thinking. Judith Plant, ed., *Healing the Wounds: The Promise of Ecofeminism* (Toronto: Between the Lines, 1989), and Vandana Shiva, *Staying Alive: Women, Ecology and Development* (London and New Delhi: Zed Books and Kali for Women, 1988), are both good introductions, as is Carolyn Merchant, *The Death of Nature: Women, Ecology and the Scientific Revolution* (San Francisco: Harper and Row, 1980, 1990).

Two long essays by George Bradford, *How Deep is Deep Ecology?* (Ojai, Cal.: Times Change Press, 1989), and "Return of the Son of Deep Ecology: The Ethics of Permanent Crisis and the Permanent Crisis in Ethics," *Fifth Estate,* Spring 1989, help to untangle current debates about the social implications of ecological science. In recent years those debates have centred around the concept of deep ecology. Interested readers should consult Bill Devall, "The Deep, Long-Range Ecology Movement," in *Simple in Means, Rich in Ends: Practicing Deep Ecology* (Salt Lake City: Peregrine Smith, 1988); Murray Bookchin, "Social Ecology Versus Deep Ecology," *Socialist Review,* July–September 1988; Kirkpatrick Sale, "Deep Ecology and Its Critics," *The Nation,* May 14, 1988; Alexander Cockburn, "Socialist Ecology: What it Means, and Why No Other Kind Will Do," *Zeta,* February and April 1989; Michael Albert, "Green Marxism!?" *Zeta,* March 1989; Frances Moore Lappé and J. Baird Callicott, "Marx Meets Muir: Toward a Synthesis of the Progressive Political and Ecological Visions," *Tikkun,* Vol. 2, No. 4 (September 1987); and Murray Bookchin and Dave Foreman, "Defending the Earth and Burying the Hatchet," *Whole Earth Review,* Winter 1990.

Animal rights and animal liberation are tangled issues that I've not been able to engage very fully. Helpful texts are three essays of J. Baird Callicott in *In Defense of the Land Ethic: Essays in Environmental Philosophy* (Albany: State University of New York, 1989); John Sanbonmatsu, "Animal Liberation: Should the Left Care?" *Zeta,* October 1989; and the work of Peter Singer and Tom Regan, both mentioned in the section for chapter four.

For my understanding of the history of environmentalism, I've relied on Samuel P. Hays, *Beauty, Health and Permanence: Environmental Politics in the United States, 1955–1985* (Cambridge: Cambridge University Press, 1985). Stephanie Mills, *Whatever Happened to Ecology?* (San Francisco: Sierra Club Books, 1989) is a good autobiographical account of the post-1960s movement in the United States. Covering the same period, but focusing more on the political history of environmentalism, are Jonathan Lash, Katherine Gillman and David Sheridan, *A Season of Spoils: The Reagan Administration's Attack on the Environment* (New York: Pantheon, 1984) and Robert Paehlke, *Environmentalism and the Future of Progressive Politics* (New Haven, Conn.: Yale University Press, 1989).

The larger context is glimpsed in Anna Bramwell, *Ecology in the 20th Century: A History* (New Haven, Conn.: Yale University Press, 1989) and Donald Worster, *Nature's Economy: A History of Ecological Ideas* (Cambridge: Cambridge University Press, 1977). Pierre Dansereau, "Megalopolis: Resources and Prospect," in Dansereau, ed., *Challenge for Survival: Land, Air and Water in the Megalopolis* (New York: Columbia University Press, 1970) is a brief history of ecology as science. Langdon Winner, *The Whale and the Reactor: A Search for Limits in an Age of High Technology* (Chicago: University of Chicago Press, 1986), includes a good discussion of the ideas of nature at large within environmentalist thought.

❂

"Can Conservation Strategies Lead to Sustainable Development?" Special issue of *Alternatives*, March/April 1990.

"Educating Tomorrow's Environmentalists." Special issue of *New Alchemy Quarterly*, No. 35 (Spring 1989).

"Feminism and Ecology." Special issue of *Heresies*, Vol. 4, No. 1 (1981).

"New Mexico Tells Natural History with Electronic Magic Show." *New York Times*, February 12, 1986.

"Politics of the Environment." Special issue of *Canadian Dimension*, Vol. 23, No. 1 (January/February 1989).

"Protesters and Ideologues: Directions in Environmental Politics," Special issue of *Alternatives*, Vol. 15, No. 4 (November/December 1988).

"The Environment and Environmentalism: Our Progress, Problems and Prospects." Special issue of *Probe Post*, Vol. 11, No. 4 (Winter 1989).

"Investing in the Environment." Special issue of *Moneywise*, June 1989.

"Toxic Environmentalists." Special issue of *Whole Earth Review*, No. 45 (March 1985).

Don Alexander. "Sustaining Development or Developing Sustainability?" *Kick it Over*, August 1989.

Thomas Berry. *The Dream of the Earth*. San Francisco: Sierra Club Books, 1986.

Janet Biehl. "It's Deep, But Is It Broad? An Ecofeminist Looks at Deep Ecology." *Kick it Over*, n.d.

John W. Brainerd. *The Nature Observer's Handbook: Learning to Appreciate Our Natural World*. Chester, Conn.: Globe-Pequot Press, 1986.

Leonie Caldecott and Stephanie Leland. *Reclaim the Earth: Women Speak Out for Life on Earth*. London: Women's Press, 1983.

Canada. *Catalogue of Environmental Education Materials*. Ottawa: Minister of Supply and Services, 1979.

Canada. *State of the Environment Report for Canada*. Ottawa: Environment Canada and Statistics Canada, 1986.

Canada. *Environmental Peacekeepers: Science, Technology and Sustainable Development in Canada*. Ottawa: Science Council of Canada, 1988.

Canada. *The Great Lakes: An Environmental Atlas and Resource Book*. Environment Canada and United States Environmental Protection Agency, 1987.

Canada. *Sustainable Development*. Ottawa: Environment Canada, 1984.

Canada. *The Acid Rain Story*. Ottawa: Environment Canada, 1984.

Canada. *Defence of the Fur Trade*. Ottawa: Department of External Affairs, May 1985.

Jeanne Cannizzo. "Living History Museums." CBC-Radio *Ideas*, January 1987.

Capitalism, Nature, Socialism: A Journal of Socialist Ecology. Santa Cruz, Cal, 1988–.

W. J. Christie, M. Becker, J. W. Cowden and J. R. Vallentyne. "Managing the Great Lakes Basin as a Home." *Journal of Great Lakes Research*, Vol. 12, No. 1 (1986) pp. 2–17.

Alice Cook and Gwyn Kirk. *Greenham Women Everywhere: Dreams, Ideas and Actions from the Women's Peace Movement*. London: Pluto Press, 1983.

Bill Devall and George Sessions. *Deep Ecology: Living as if Nature Mattered*. Salt Lake City: Peregrine Smith, 1985.

Mary Douglas. *Purity and Danger: An Analysis of Concepts of Pollution and Taboo*. London: Ark, 1984.

Yvon Dubé. *The Right to A Healthy Environment*. UNESCO Canada/MAB Report No. 16 (1986).

William Eblem and Ruth Eblem. *Experiencing the Total Environment*. New York: Scholastic Book Services, 1977.

Michael R. Edelstein. *Contaminated Communities: The Social and Psychological Impacts of Residential Toxic Exposure*. Boulder, Col.: Westview Press, 1988.

Yorke Edwards. *The Land Speaks: Organizing and Running Interpretation Systems*. Toronto: The National and Provincial Parks Association of Canada (now the Canadian Parks and Wilderness Society), 1979.

John Ely. "Anti-Modernist Movements in Germany: The Weimar and Bonn Republics." Unpublished manuscript, University of California at Santa Cruz, 1984.

John Ely. "Green Sprouts, Rootlets, Runners and Rhizomes: The Growing Ecology Movement in Europe." *Harbinger*, No. 3 (Fall 1985).

Ethics and Energy. Toronto: Canadian Nuclear Association, 1980–1989.

Thomas W. Foster. "The Taoists and the Amish: Kindred Expressions of Eco-Anarchism." *The Ecologist*, Vol. 17, No. 1 (1987).

Boris Frankel. *The Post-Industrial Utopians*. Madison: University of Wisconsin Press, 1987.

Larry N. George. "Love Canal and the Politics of Corporate Terrorism." *Socialist Review*, No. 66 (November–December 1982).

Frank B. Golley. "Deep Ecology: An Analysis from the Perspective of Ecological Science." *Trumpeter*, Vol. 6, No. 1 (Winter 1989).

Great Lakes Science Advisory Board. *The Ecosystem Approach: Scope and Implications of an Ecosystem Approach to Transborder Problems in the Great Lakes Basin*. Windsor, Ont.: International Joint Commission, 1978.

Susan Griffin. *Woman and Nature: The Roaring Inside Her.* San Francisco: Harper and Row, 1978.

Daniel Halpern, ed. *On Nature: Nature, Landscape and Natural History.* Berkeley: North Point Press, 1986.

Thom Henley. *Rediscovery: Ancient Pathways, New Directions: A Guidebook to Outdoor Education.* Vancouver: Western Canada Wilderness Committee, 1979.

S.G. Hilts and A.M. Fuller. *The Guelph Seminars on Sustainable Development.* Guelph, Ont.: University School of Rural Planning and Development, University of Guelph, 1990.

Humane Society of the United States. "The Dangers of Project Wild." Washington, D.C.: Humane Society of the United States.

International Union for the Conservation of Nature and Natural Resources (IUCN), with United Nations Environment Programme (UNEP) and World Wildlife Fund (WWF). *World Conservation Strategy: Living Resource Conservation for Sustainable Development.* Gland, Switzerland, 1980.

Journal of Business Ethics, Dordrecht, Netherlands.

William Leiss. *The Domination of Nature.* Boston: Beacon Press, 1972.

William Leiss, ed. *Ecology versus Politics in Canada.* Toronto: University of Toronto Press, 1979.

Aldo Leopold. *A Sand County Almanac.* Oxford: Oxford University Press, 1949.

Raymond Lindemann. "The Trophic-Dynamic Aspect of Ecology," in Hazen, W.E., ed., *Readings in Population and Community Ecology.* Philadelphia: W.B. Saunders, 1964.

John A. Livingston. "Moral Concern and the Ecosphere." *Alternatives,* Vol. 12, No. 2 (Winter 1985).

Thomas J. Lyon. *This Incomperable Lande: A Book of American Nature Writing.* Boston: Houghton Mifflin, 1989.

Gary E. Machlis and Donald R. Field, eds. *On Interpretation: Sociology for Interpreters of Natural and Cultural History.* Corvallis, Oreg.: Oregon State University Press, 1984.

Jim MacNeill, "Agenda for Change," interim report of the World Commission on Environment and Development, 1985.

Christopher Majka. "Anti-Environmentalism: Ideology on the Front Lines." *New Maritimes,* Vol. 4, No. 10 (June 1986).

Mary Mellor. "Turning Green: Whose Ecology?" *Science as Culture,* No. 6 (1989).

Carolyn Merchant, ed. "Women and the Environment," special issue of *Environmental Review,* Vol. 8, No. 1 (Spring 1984).

Arne Naess. "The Shallow and the Deep, Long Range Ecology Movement: A Summary." *Inquiry,* Spring 1973.

Dennis Frank Owen. *What is Ecology?* New York: Oxford, 1974.

Ray Raphael. *Tree Talk: The People and Politics of Timber.* Covelo, Cal.: Island Press, 1981.

Alejandro Rojas. "Interrogaciones acerca del movimiento ecológico y la naturaleza del poder social." Unpublished manuscript (1987).

Andrew Ross. "The Work of Nature in the Age of Electronic Emission." *Social Text,* No. 18 (Winter 1987–88).

J. Stan Rowe. *Home Place: Essays on Ecology.* Edmonton: NeWest Books, 1990.

George K. Russell. "Biology, the Study of Life." *Orion,* Vol. 6, No. 1 (Winter 1987).

Kirkpatrick Sale. "The Forest for the Trees: Can Today's Environmentalists Tell the Difference?" *Mother Jones,* November 1986.

Judith Salisbury. *A Teacher's Manual to the Green Classroom.* East Falmouth, Mass.: New Alchemy Institute, 1989.

John Seed and Joanna Macy. *Thinking Like a Mountain: Toward a Council of All Beings.* Philadelphia: New Society, 1988.

Vandana Shiva. "I am Nature." *The Illustrated Weekly of India,* September 17, 1989.

Ginny Shrivastava, Nandini Narula and Rajesh Tandon. *Women and Wasteland.* New Delhi: Society for Participatory Research in Asia, n.d.

Henryk Skolimowski. *Eco-Philosophy: Designing New Tactics for Living.* Boston: Marion Boyars, 1981.

Gary Snyder. *The Real Work: Interviews and Talks, 1964–1979.* New Haven, Conn.: New Directions, 1980.

Gary Snyder. *The Practice of the Wild.* San Francisco: North Point Press, 1990.

Starhawk. *Dreaming the Dark: Magic, Sex and Politics.* Boston: Beacon Press, 1982.

Kathleen Stecher Mayer and R. Kent Schrieber. *Acid Rain: Effects on Fish and Wildlife.* Washington, D.C.: U.S. Department of the Interior, Fish and Wildlife Service, 1985.

Dan Stoffman. "The Greening of Ontario." *Challenges,* Fall 1989.

Christopher D. Stone. "Should Trees Have Standing? Toward Legal Rights for Natural Objects." *Southern California Law Review,* Vol. 45 (1972).

Freeman Tilden. *Interpreting Our Heritage.* Chapel Hill, N.C.: University of North Carolina Press, 1957, 1977.

Michael Tobias, ed. *Deep Ecology.* San Diego: Avant Books, 1985.

Brian Tokar. "Politics Under the Greenhouse." *Zeta,* March 1989.

Toronto. *Healthy Toronto 2000.* Toronto: Toronto Board of Health, 1988.

William A. Tracy and Patricia Myers. "The Genesis of an Ecomusée: The Frank Slide Interpretive Centre." *NeWest Review,* Summer 1986.

William Tucker. *Progress and Privilege: America in the Age of Environmentalism.* Garden City, N.J.: Doubleday/Anchor, 1982.

UNESCO. Man and the Biosphere/Canada. *Methods and Interpretation of Environmental Perception Research.* Canada/MAB Report No. 9, 1977.

UNESCO. *Perception of Environmental Quality.* MAB Report Series No. 9, 1973.

UNESCO, "Vancouver Declaration on Survival in the 21st Century," press release, 1989.

Lindsy Van Gelder. "It's Not Nice to Mess with Mother Nature." *Ms.,* January/February 1989.

Steve Van Matre. *Acclimatization: A Sensory and Conceptual Approach to Ecological Involvement*. Martinsville, Ind.: American Camping Association, 1972, 1989.

Steve Van Matre. *Acclimatizing: A Personal and Reflective Approach to a Natural Relationship*. Martinsville, Ind.: American Camping Association, 1974.

Joe Weston, ed. *Red and Green: The New Politics of the Environment*. London: Pluto Press, 1986.

Lynn White Jr. "The Historical Roots of Our Ecologic Crisis." *Science,* Vol. 155, No. 3767 (March 10, 1967). Also in Paul Shepard and Daniel McKinley, eds. *The Subversive Science*. New York: Houghton-Mifflin, 1969.

World Commission on Environment and Development. *Our Common Future*. Oxford: Oxford University Press, 1987.

3. Nature at Home: A Social Ecology of Postwar Landscape Design

This discussion of the recent social history of landscape aesthetics in North America is drawn from my own experiences working in horticulture, landscape design, and construction over the past fifteen years, as well as travels throughout most of the continent.

The theoretical and historical work on this subject is dispersed across many disciplines. Among the useful contributions is the work of J.B. Jackson, mentioned in the section for the Introduction. Two books that provide an inspiring aesthetics of the garden are Charles W. Moore et al., *The Poetics of Gardens* (Cambridge, Mass.: MIT Press, 1988) and Mark Francis and Randolph T. Hester, Jr, eds., *The Meaning of Gardens* (Cambridge, Mass.: MIT Press, 1990).

My brief comments about landscape and gender rely on Carolyn Merchant, *The Death of Nature: Women, Ecology and the Scientific Revolution* (New York: Harper and Row, 1980) and Lucy Lippard, *Overlay: Contemporary Art and the Art of Prehistory* (New York: Pantheon, 1983). See also Marilyn French, *Beyond Power: On Women, Men and Morals* (New York: Ballantine, 1985); Mary Daly, *Gyn/Ecology: The Metaethics of Radical Feminism* (Boston: Beacon Press, 1982); and Mariana Valverde's response, "The Religion of the 'Race' of Women: A Critique of Mary Daly," *Rites,* October 1985. On "captivity narratives," as white desertions to aboriginal societies are known, see the bibliography in Frederick W. Turner, *Beyond Geography: The Western Spirit Against the Wilderness* (New Brunswick, N.J.: Rutgers University Press, 1983); and Richard Drinnon, *Facing West: The Metaphysics of Indian Hating and Empire Building* (New York: Schocken, 1980, 1990).

On housing, gender, and family, the work of Dolores Hayden is indispensible, especially *The Grand Domestic Revolution: A History of Feminist Designs for American Homes, Neighbourhoods and Cities* (Cambridge, Mass.: MIT Press, 1981) and *Redesigning the American Dream: The Future of Housing, Work and Family Life* (New York: Norton, 1984). See also Gwendolyn Wright, *Building the Dream: A Social History of Housing in America* (New York: Pantheon, 1981).

On modernism and its influence on garden design, Elizabeth B. Kassler, *Modern Gardens and the Landscape* (New York: Museum of Modern Art, 1964, 1984) and Peter Shepheard, *Modern Gardens* (London: The Architectural Press, 1953) are both good and well-illustrated introductions.

Until very recently there has been little writing on the relation of landscape design to natural systems. The essential early work is Ian McHarg, *Design With Nature* (Garden City, N.J.: Doubleday/Natural History Press, 1969) and Garrett Eckbo, *Landscape for Living* (New York: F.W. Dodge Corporation, 1950). More recent and sophisticated discussions are Anne Whiston Spirn, *The Granite Garden: Urban Nature and Human Design* (New York: Basic Books, 1984); Michael Hough, *City Form and Natural Process* (New York: Van Nostrand Reinhold, 1984); "Nature in the City," *Landscape Architecture,* September 1989; and *Out of Place: Restoring Identity to the Regional Landscape* (New Haven, Conn.: Yale University Press, 1990).

W.R. Jordan, et al., *Restoration Ecology: A Synthetic Approach* (Cambridge: Cambridge University Press, 1987), John J. Berger, ed., *Environmental Restoration: Science and Strategies for Restoring the Earth* (Washington, D.C. and Covelo, Cal.: Island Press, 1990), and *Ecological Restoration in the San Francisco Bay Area: A Descriptive Directory and Sourcebook* (Berkeley: Restoring the Earth, 1990), are all good introductions to ecological restoration. Further information can be had from the Society for Ecological Restoration, based at the University of Wisconsin Arboretum in Madison. The Society publishes the lively *Restoration and Management Notes.*

Sam Bass Warner, Jr. and Hansi Durlach, *To Dwell is To Garden: A History of Boston's Community Gardens* (Boston: Northeastern University Press, 1987) contains a brilliant short history of community gardens.

Over the past ten years there has been an increasing interest in gardens and landscape, and I include below some of the popular books that have helped to broaden the subject.

❂

"Helping Nature Heal: A Special Issue on Environmental Restoration." *Whole Earth Review,* No. 66 (Spring 1990).

"Plants as Teachers." Special section of *Whole Earth Review,* No. 64 (Fall 1989).

Chris Baines and Jane Smart. *Guide to Habitat Creation.* London: Greater London Council, 1984.

Sharon Begley with Seth Zuckerman and Lisa Drew. "Making Nature Whole Again." *Newsweek,* January 18, 1988.

Richard Britz, et al. *The Edible City Resource Manual.* Los Altos, Cal.: William Kaufmann, 1981.

John Brookes. *The Small Garden.* London: Cavendish House, 1977.

John Brookes. *The Country Garden.* New York: Crown, 1987.

A.E. Bye. *Art Into Landscape, Landscape Into Art.* Mesa, Ariz.: PDA Publishers, 1983.

Murray Campbell. "Canada's Grassroots Obsession." *The Globe and Mail,* July 8, 1989.

M. Chinery. *The Natural History of the Garden*. New York: Collins, 1977.

Thomas Church, et al. *Gardens are for People*. New York: McGraw-Hill, 1955, 1983.

Thomas Church. *Your Private World: A Study of Intimate Gardens*. San Francisco: Chronicle Books, 1969.

Grady Clay. *Close-Up: How to Read the American City*. New York: Praeger, 1973.

Malcolm Collier. "Jens Jensen and Columbus Park." *Chicago History*, Vol. 4, No. 4 (Winter 1975–1976).

Malcolm Collier. "Prairie Profile: Jens Jensen." *Nineteenth Century*, Vol. 3, No. 1 (Spring 1977).

John F. Collins and Marvin I. Adleman. *Livible Landscape Design*. Ithaca, N.Y.: Cornell Cooperative Extension Information Bulletin 211, 1988.

Alfred W. Crosby. *Ecological Imperialism: The Biological Expansion of Europe, 900–1900*. Cambridge: Cambridge University Press, 1986.

John Diekelmann and Robert Schuster. *Natural Landscaping: Designing with Native Plant Communities*. New York: McGraw-Hill, 1982.

Robert S. Dorney. *The Professional Practice of Environmental Management*. New York: Springer-Verlag, 1989.

Leonard K. Eaton. *Landscape Artist in America: The Life and Work of Jens Jensen*. Chicago: University of Chicago, 1974.

Garrett Eckbo. *The Art of Home Landscaping*. New York: McGraw-Hill, 1956.

J. Ronald Engel. *Sacred Sands: The Struggle for Community in the Indiana Dunes*. Middletown, Conn.: Wesleyan University Press, 1983.

Nan Fairbrother. *Men and Gardens*. New York: Knopf, 1956.

Nan Fairbrother. *New Lives, New Landscapes: Planning for the 21st Century*. New York: Knopf, 1970.

Albert Fein. *Frederick Law Olmsted and the American Environmental Tradition*. New York: Braziller, 1972.

Robert Fishman. *Bourgeois Utopias: The Rise and Fall of Suburbia*. New York: Basic Books, 1987.

Tom Fox, Ian Koeppel and Susan Kellam. *Struggle for Space: The Greening of New York*. New York: Neighborhood Open Space Coalition, 1985.

Mark Francis, Lisa Cashdan and Lynn Paxson. *Community Open Spaces: Greening Neighborhoods Through Community Action and Land Conservation*. Covelo, Cal.: Island Press, 1984.

Edgar W. Garbisch. *Highways and Wetlands: Compensating Wetland Losses*. Washington, D.C.: U.S. Department of Transportation, Federal Highway Administration, Report No. FHWA-IP-86-22, 1986.

David Goode. *Wild in London*. London: Michael Joseph, 1986.

David Gordon, ed. *Green Cities: Ecologically Sound Approaches to Urban Space*. Montreal: Black Rose, 1989.

Richard Gorer. *The Growth of Gardens*. London: Faber and Faber, 1978.

Barrie B. Greenbie. *Spaces: Dimensions of the Human Landscape*. New Haven, Conn.: Yale University Press, 1981.

Barrie B. Greenbie. *Space and Spirit in Modern Japan*. New Haven, Conn.: Yale University Press, 1988.

Gene W. Grey and Frederick J. Deneke. *Urban Forestry*. New York: Wiley, 1978.

Lawrence Halprin. *Cities*. Cambridge, Mass.: MIT Press, 1963.

Carrol L. Henderson. *Landscaping for Wildlife*. St. Paul, Minn.: Minnesota Department of Natural Resources, 1987.

Alan Hess. "Eichler Homes." *arts and architecture*, Vol. 3, No. 3 (1984).

Gary L. Hightshoe. *Native Trees, Shrubs, and Vines for Urban and Rural America*. New York: Van Nostrand Reinhold, 1988.

Hort Ideas. Gravel Switch, Kentucky.

Jane Jacobs. *The Death and Life of Great American Cities*. New York: Vintage, 1961.

Geoffrey and Susan Jellicoe, Patrick Goode and Michael Lancaster, eds. *The Oxford Companion to Gardens*. Oxford: Oxford University Press, 1986.

Geoffrey and Susan Jellicoe. *The Landscape of Man*. London: Thames and Hudson, 1987.

Jens Jensen. *Siftings* (1956). Baltimore: Johns Hopkins University Press, 1990.

Jens Jensen. "Natural Parks and Gardens." *Saturday Evening Post*, March 8, 1930.

Jens Jensen. "The Camp Fire or Council Fire," in Emma Doeserich and Mary Sherburne, eds., *Outdoors with the Prairie Club*. Chicago: Paquin Publishers, 1941.

Hugh Johnson. *The Principles of Gardening*. New York: Simon and Schuster, 1979.

William R. Jordan III, "Restoration: Shaping the Land, Transforming the Human Spirit," *Whole Earth Review*, No. 66 (Spring 1990).

Robert Kourik. *Designing and Maintaining Your Edible Landscape Naturally*. Santa Rosa, Cal.: Metamorphic Press, 1986.

Jon A. Kusler and Mary E. Entula. *Wetlands Creation and Restoration: The Status of the Science*. Washington, D.C.: Island Press, 1990.

Ian C. Laurie, ed. *Nature in Cities: The Natural Environment in the Design and Development of Urban Green Space*. Chichester and Toronto: Wiley, 1979.

Barry Lopez. "The American Geographies." *Orion Nature Quarterly*, Fall 1989.

Kevin Lynch. *Managing the Sense of the Region*. Cambridge, Mass.: MIT Press, 1980.

Kevin Lynch. *A Theory of Good City Form*. Cambridge, Mass.: MIT Press, 1981.

Richard Manning. *Nature in the City: The Creation of Nature-Like Landscapes in European Parks and Residential Open Spaces*. Thesis, Landscape Architecture Program, Cornell University, 1988.

Clare Cooper Marcus. "Alternative Landscapes: Ley-Lines, Feng-Shui and the Gaia Hypothesis." *Landscape*, Vol. 29, No. 3 (1987).

Malcolm Margolin. *The Earth Manual: How to Work on Wild Land Without Taming It* (1975). Berkeley: Heyday Books, 1985.

Linda Martin and Kerry Segrave. *City Parks of Canada*. Oakville, Ont.: Mosaic Press, 1983.

Esther McCoy. "Garrett Eckbo: The Early Years." *arts and architecture*, Vol. 1, No. 4, n.d.

Craig McGregor. "Return to Awfulville," in *Pop Goes the Culture*. London: Pluto, 1984.

Carolyn Merchant. "Restoration and Reunion with Nature." *Restoration and Management Notes*, Winter 1986.

Robert W. Miller. *Urban Forestry: Planning and Managing Urban Greenspaces*. Englewood Cliffs, N.J.: Prentice-Hall, 1988.

Bill Mollison. *Permaculture: A Designers' Manual*. Tyalgum, New South Wales: Tagari, 1988.

Flávio L. Motta. *Roberto Burle Marx e a nova visão paisagem*. São Paulo: Livraria Nobel, 1984.

National Gardening Association. *The Prison Garden Book*. Burlington, Vt., n.d.

National Gardening Association. *Successful Senior Citizen Gardens*. Burlington, Vt., 1987.

National Gardening Association. *Starting a Community Garden*. Burlington, Vt., 1987.

National Gardening Association. *A Leader's Guide to Youth Gardening*. Burlington, Vt., 1987.

David Nicholson-Lord. *The Greening of the Cities*. London: Routledge and Kegan Paul, 1987.

Helga and William Olkowski. "Entomophobia in the Urban Ecosystem, Some Observations and Suggestions." *Bulletin of the Entomological Society of America*, Vol. 22, No. 3 (September 1976).

Ruth Parnall. "Advocate for the Land." *Women in Natural Resources*, Vol. 12, No. 1.

Organic Gardening. Emmaus, Pennsylvania.

Michael Pollan, Daniel B. Botkin, Dave Foreman, James Lovelock, Frederick Turner, and Robert D. Yaro. "Only Man's Presence Can Save Nature." *Harper's*, April 1990.

Michael Pollan, "Why Mow?: The Case Against Lawns." *New York Times Magazine*, May 28, 1989.

Sarah Pollack. "A Time to Mend." *Sierra*, September/October 1988.

Gary O. Robinette. *Plants/People/and Environmental Quality: A Study of Plants and Their Environmental Functions*. Washington, D.C.: U.S. Department of the Interior, National Parks Service; and American Society of Landscape Architects Foundation, 1972.

Elizabeth Barlow Rogers, et al. *Rebuilding Central Park: A Management and Restoration Plan*. Cambridge, Mass.: MIT Press, 1987.

Allan R. Ruff. *Holland and the Ecological Landscapes*. Deanwater Press, 1979.

Allan R. Ruff and Robert Tregay. *An Ecological Approach to Urban Landscape Design*. Department of Town and Country Planning, University of Manchester, 1982.

P. Russell. *The Awakening Earth*. London: Routledge, 1982.

Bob Scarfo. "Socialization of the Emerging Professional Landscape Architect." Paper delivered at Environmental Design Research Association conference, Ottawa, May 1987.

Bob Scarfo. "Stewardship of the Land as a Professional Practice." Paper delivered at
    Ontario Association of Landscape Architects Fall Seminar, 1982.

Keith Schneider. "Restoring Natural Landscape Emerges as a Major Goal." *The New York
    Times,* March 5, 1988.

Dale Shank. *Hortus Northwest: A Pacific Northwest Native Plant Directory and Journal.* 1990
    (Available from Box 955, Canby, Oregon. 97013)

Larry Sommers. *The Community Gardening Book: New Directions for Creating and Managing
    Neighborhood Food Gardens in Your Town.* Burlington, Vt.: National Gardening
    Association, 1984.

Robert A.M. Stern. *The Anglo-American Suburb.* London: Architectural Design, 1981.

John R. Stilgoe. "Gardens in Context." *Orion,* Vol. 4, No. 2 (Spring 1985).

John R. Stilgoe. *Borderland: Origins of the American Suburb 1890–1939.* New Haven, Conn.:
    Yale University Press, 1988.

S.B. Sutton, ed. *Civilizing American Cities: A Selection of Frederick Law Olmsted's Writings on
    City Landscape.* Cambridge, Mass.: MIT Press, 1971.

Judith B. Tankard and Michael R. Van Valkenburgh. *Gertrude Jekyll: A Vision of Garden and
    Wood.* New York: Abrams/Saga Press, 1988.

Tamara Plakins Thornton. "Cultivating the American Character: Horticulture as Moral
    Reform in the Antebellum Era." *Orion,* Vol. 4, No. 2 (Spring 1985).

J. William Thompson. "Standard-Bearer of Modernism" [on Garrett Eckbo]. *Landscape
    Architecture,* February 1990.

Patricia M. Tice. *Gardening In America 1830–1910.* Rochester, N.Y.: The Strong Museum,
    1984.

Robert Tregay. "Urban Woodlands," in Laurie, *Nature in Cities.*

Nancy Jack Todd and John Todd. *Bioshelters, Ocean Arks, City Farming: Ecology as the Basis
    of Design.* San Francisco: Sierra Club Books, 1984.

Frederick Turner. "Cultivating the American Garden: Toward a Secular View of Nature."
    Harper's, August 1985.

Frederick Turner. "A Field Guide to the Synthetic Landscape." *Harper's,* April 1988.

Michael Van Valkenburgh. "Two Views of Landscape Design: Dan Kiley and A. E. Bye."
    Orion, Vol. 4, No. 2 (Spring 1985).

Edwinna Von Baeyer. *Rhetoric and Roses: A History of Canadian Gardening.* Toronto:
    Fitzhenry and Whiteside, 1984.

Simon Watney. "Gardens of Speculation: Landscape in *The Draughtsman's Contract.*"
    Undercut, Nos. 7/8 (Summer 1983).

William H. Whyte. *The Social Life of Small Urban Spaces.* Washington, D.C.: The
    Conservation Foundation, 1980.

William H. Whyte. *The Last Landscape* (1968). Garden City, N.J.: Anchor, 1970.

Alexander Wilson. "Toward a Culture of Diversity: Politics in the Urban Ecosystem."
    Borderlines, Winter 1985/86.

William H.W. Wilson. *Landscaping With Native Plants and Wildflowers*. San Francisco: Ortho Books, 1984.

4. Looking at the Non-Human: Nature Movies and TV

The history of relations between humans and other animals is long and complicated. David Guss's sensitive anthology, *Language of the Birds: Tales, Texts and Poems of Interspecies Communication* (San Francisco: North Point Press, 1985) provides good access to this history among traditional, tribal, and peasant cultures the world over. Hans Peter Duerr's *Dreamtime,* mentioned in the Introduction section, and John Berger's *Once in Europa* (New York: Pantheon, 1987) and *Pig Earth* (New York: Pantheon, 1979) examine how non-modern cultures in Europe have looked at and lived with animals. Berger's seminal essay "Why Look at Animals?" in *About Looking* (New York: Pantheon, 1980), which has been republished in the Guss anthology and elsewhere, has helped shape my arguments about our experience of animals in contemporary culture.

Many books discuss the place of animals (and other non-human beings) in aboriginal North American cultures. See especially: Hugh Brody, *Maps and Dreams: Indians and the British Columbia Frontier* (Vancouver: Douglas and McIntyre, 1981, 1988); Adrian Tanner, *Bringing Home Animals: Religious Ideology and Mode of Production of the Misstassini Cree Hunters* (New York: St Martin's Press, 1979); Richard Nelson, *Make Prayers to the Raven: A Koyukon View of the Northern Forest* (Chicago: University of Chicago Press, 1983); Jerome Rothenburg, *Shaking the Pumpkin: Traditional Poetry of the Indian North Americas* (New York: Alfred van der Marck, 1986); Howard Norman, ed., *Where the Chill Came From: Cree Windigo Tales and Journeys* (San Francisco: North Point Press, 1982); Gisday Wa and Delgam Uukw, *The Spirit in the Land: The Opening Statement of the Gitksan and Wet'suwet'en Hereditary Chiefs in the Supreme Court of British Columbia,* May 11, 1987; Calvin Martin, *Keepers of the Game: Indian-Animal Relationships and the Fur Trade* (Berkeley: University of California, 1978).

Contemporary discussion of animals seems to be focused on two issues: conservation and animal rights. Peter Matthiessen, *Wildlife in America* (1959) (Harmondsworth: Penguin, 1977), is a good natural history of animals in North America; and John A. Livingston, *The Fallacy of Wildlife Conservation* (Toronto: McClelland and Stewart, 1981), is a succinct critique of commonsensical thinking about their conservation. The useful animal rights literature includes: John A. Livingston, "Rightness or Rights? Dominance, Domestication and the Paradox of Animal Rights," *Borderlines,* No. 5 (Summer 1986); Peter Singer, *Animal Liberation: A New Ethics for Our Treatment of Animals* (New York: Avon, 1977); Tom Regan, *All That Dwell Therein: Animal Rights and Environmental Ethics* (Berkeley: University of California, 1982); the first three essays in J. Baird Callicott, *In Defense of The Land Ethic;* and John Sanbonmatsu, "Animal Liberation: Should the Left Care?" *Zeta,* October 1989. Donna Haraway, *Primate Visions: Gender, Race and Nature in the World of Modern Science* (New York: Routledge, 1989), and *Simians, Cyborgs and Women* (New York: Routledge, 1991) helps place many of these debates in their full historical and cultural context.

Current literature on the history of science will be discussed in the sections for chapters five and eight. Sources on the history of environmentalism are given in the section for chapter two. Science journalist David Suzuki's best work is perhaps on TV and radio, but see also his *Inventing the Future: Reflections on Science, Technology and Nature* (Toronto: Stoddart, 1989) and, with Anita Gordon, *It's a Matter of Survival* (Toronto: Stoddart, 1990). For a sense of the resistance to this kind of work from within the scientific community, see Stephen Strauss, "No Takers for *A Planet for the Taking;* Western Man is not Enemy of Nature," *The Globe and Mail,* March 25, 1985; and "David Suzuki Reveals Himself as a Politician in a Lab Coat," *The Globe and Mail,* November 24, 1990.

Lastly, there is now a substantial literature on television and its culture. Interested readers should consult Patricia Mellencamp, ed., *Logics of Television: Essays in Cultural Criticism* (Bloomington: Indiana University Press, 1990); Cynthia Schneider and Brian Wallis, eds., *Global Television* (Cambridge, Mass.: MIT Press, 1988), Todd Gitlin, *Watching Television* (New York: Pantheon, 1986); Raymond Williams, *Television: Technology and Cultural Form* (London: Fontana, 1974); Robert C. Allen, ed., *Channels of Discourse: Television and Contemporary Criticism* (Chapel Hill: University of North Carolina, 1987); Janet Bergstrom and Mary Ann Doane, eds., "The Spectatrix," *Camera Obscura,* Nos. 20/21 (1990); and Joyce Nelson, *The Perfect Machine: TV and the Nuclear Age* (Toronto: Between the Lines, 1987).

❂

"Animals Are Us." Special section of *Utne Reader,* No. 19 (January/February 1987).

"The Fate of Animals in the 21st Century." Special issue of *Orion,* Vol. 8, No. 2 (Spring 1989).

Robert Ardrey. *African Genesis.* New York: Dell, 1961.

Robert Ardrey. *The Territorial Imperative.* New York: Atheneum, 1966.

Jean M. Auel. *The Clan of the Cave Bear.* New York: Bantam, 1980.

Derek Bousé. "Wildlife on Film: A Neglected Tradition." Unpublished manuscript, Annenberg School of Communications, University of Pennsylvania, 1989.

Jacques-Yves Cousteau, with James Dugan. *The Living Sea.* New York: Harper and Row, 1963.

"Cruel Camera," broadcast on CBC-Television, *The 5th Estate,* 1982.

Walt Disney. "The Lurking Camera." *The Atlantic Monthly,* August 1954.

Neil Evernden, *The Natural Alien: Humankind and Environment.* Toronto: University of Toronto Press, 1985.

Matthew Fisher. "Capturing Facts: Video Cameras Set to Record Truth of Trapped Animals' Fate." *The Globe and Mail,* January 13, 1986.

Gary Genosko. "Animals in the Army." *Borderlines,* No. 9/10 (Fall/Winter 1987/88).

Samuel P. Hays. *Conservation and the Gospel of Efficiency: The Progressive Conservation Movement, 1890–1920.* New York: Atheneum, 1969.

Barbara Berch Jamison. "Amazing Scripts by Animals." *The New York Times Magazine,* July 18, 1954.

Stephen R. Kellert. "Americans' Attitudes and Knowledge of Animals." Proceedings of Forty-Fifth North American Wildlife Conference.

Nora Lee. "20 Years with National Geographic, Part II." *American Cinematographer,* November 1985.

John A. Livingston. *Canada: A Natural History.* Toronto: Viking, 1988.

Konrad Lorenz. *On Aggression.* New York: Harcourt, Brace and World, 1966.

T.C. McLuhan. *Touch the Earth: Native American Testimony* (1971). New York: Harper and Row, 1978.

Mary Midgley. *Animals and Why They Matter.* Athens: University of Georgia, 1983.

Desmond Morris. *The Naked Ape: A Zoologist's Study of the Human Animal.* New York: McGraw-Hill, 1967.

Farley Mowat. *Sea of Slaughter.* Toronto: McClelland and Stewart, 1984.

Rob Nixon. "Plastic Stone Age. *Borderlines,* No. 5 (Summer 1986).

Thomas W. Overholt and J. Baird Callicott. *Clothed-in-Fur and Other Tales: An Introduction to an Ojibwa World View.* Washington, D.C.: University Press of America, 1982.

D. Pepper. *The Roots of Modern Environmentalism.* London: Croom Helm, 1984.

Marlin Perkins. *My Wild Kingdom: An Autobiography.* New York: Dutton, 1982.

Tom Regan. *The Case for Animal Rights.* Berkeley: University of California, 1983.

Boyce Richardson, ed. *Drum Beat: Anger and Renewal in Indian Country.* Toronto: Assembly of First Nations and Summerhill Press, 1989.

Rural Advancement Fund International. *Biotechnology's Bitter Harvest: Herbicide-Tolerant Crops.* Pittsboro, N.C., 1990.

Richard Schickel. *The Disney Version: The Life, Times, Art and Commerce of Walt Disney.* New York: Simon and Schuster, 1968, 1985.

Peter Steinhart. "Wildlife Films: End of an Era?" *National Wildlife,* Vol. 18, No. 1 (December 1979).

Marty Stouffer. *Wild America.* New York: Times Books, 1988.

Marianna Torgovnick. *Gone Primitive: Savage Intellects, Modern Lives.* Chicago: University of Chicago Press, 1990.

Susan Willis. "Fantasia: Walt Disney's Los Angeles Suite." *Diacritics,* Vol. 17, No. 2 (1987).

5. Technological Utopias: World's Fairs and Theme Parks

My sense of the role American world's fairs have played in the history of urban design is drawn from Giorgio Ciucci, et al., *The American City: From the Civil War to the New Deal* (Cambridge, Mass.: MIT Press, 1979). On the two New York fairs, see Edward Ball, "Degraded Utopias," *The Village Voice,* Fall Art Special, 1989, and *Dawn of a New Day* (Queens, New York: Queens Museum, 1980).

Much has been written about Disney's films, especially the animation, but there is little on the parks or other environmental installations. Among the worthwhile essays are Louis Marin, "Disneyland: A Degenerate Utopia," *Glyph* 1 (1977); and Michael Wallace, "Mickey Mouse History: Portraying the Past at Disney World," *Radical History Review,* No. 32 (March 1985). I've also cited (in the section for chapter four) Schickel, *The Disney Version.*

Disney's environments are closely connected to the history and geography of Los Angeles. Reyner Banham, Los Angeles: *The Architecture of Four Ecologies* (Harmondsworth: Penguin, 1971), is a classic study of the city; David Brodsly, *L.A. Freeway: An Appreciative Essay* (Berkeley: University of California Press, 1981), engages both the history and aesthetics of transportation in the Los Angeles Basin.

The other critical axis of this chapter is technology and society. Here my arguments have been shaped by two books: John Zerzan and Alice Carnes, eds., *Questioning Technology: A Critical Anthology* (London: Freedom Press, 1988); and Arthur Kroker, *Technology and the Canadian Mind: Innis/McLuhan/Grant* (Montreal: New World Perspectives, 1984). The periodicals *Radical Science* (now *Science as Culture*), and *Science for the People* are indispensable for an understanding of contemporary science in a social context.

I end this chapter with a discussion of agriculture. There is now a vast critical literature on agriculture, and I'll cite some of these sources in the section for chapter six.

❧

"Science and Technology; Survival and Well-Being." Special Issue of *Alternatives,* Vol. 13, No. 2 (April 1986).

Robert Anderson and Eleanor Wachtel. *The Expo Story.* Madeira Park, B.C: Harbour Publishing, 1986.

Aronowitz, Stanley. *Food, Shelter and the American Dream.* New York: Seabury, 1974.

Bahro, Rudolf. "Who Can Stop the Apocalypse? Or the Task, Substance and Strategy of the Social Movements," in Bahro, *Socialism and Survival.* London: Heretic Books, 1982

Warren J. Belasco. *Appetite for Change: How the Counterculture Took on the Food Industry, 1966–1988.* New York: Pantheon, 1989.

James P. Blair. "World's Fair in New York Reopens." *National Geographic,* Vol. 127, No. 4 (April 1965).

Trevor Boddy. "Bread and Surfaces: Architecture at Expo 86." *Canadian Art,* Spring 1986.

Robert Caro. *The Power Broker: Robert Moses and the Fall of New York.* New York: Random House, 1974.

Linda Cekal, et al. *On Site! 86: The Best of Expo.* North Vancouver, 1986.

Joseph J. Corn and Brian Horrigan. *Yesterday's Tomorrows: Past Visions of the American Future.* New York: Summit Books/The Smithsonian Institution, 1984.

Joseph J. Corn, ed. *Imagining Tomorrow: History, Technology and the American Future.* Cambridge, Mass.: MIT Press, 1986.

Chris Creighton-Kelly. "Artists, Technology and Cultural Production: How is Social Meaning Made?" *Parallelogramme*, 1985.

Sara Diamond. "Expo 86: A Political Guide for Cultural Producers." *Fuse*, Vol. 9, No. 6 (February/March 1986).

Robert Fishman. *Urban Utopias in the 20th Century*. Cambridge, Mass.: MIT Press, 1982.

Robert Fulford. *This Was Expo*. Toronto: McClelland and Stewart, 1968.

Buckminster Fuller. *Utopia or Oblivion?: The Prospects for Humanity*. New York: Overlook Press, 1969.

William H. Galchutt and William John Wallis. "Disney's Other World: Mickey-Mousing Florida's Water Supplies?" *Landscape Architecture*, Vol. 63, No. 1 (October 1972).

Yaakov Jerome Garb. "The Use and Misuse of the Whole Earth Image." *Whole Earth Review*, March 1985.

Jim Hightower. "Hard Tomatoes, Hard Times: The Failure of the Land Grant College Complex," in Richard Merrill, ed., *Radical Agriculture*. New York: New York University Press, 1976.

Pam Hobbs. "Disney's Secret World." *The Globe and Mail*, September 5, 1987.

Andrew Holleran. "The Mouse and the Virgin." *WigWag*, August 1990.

Ebenezer Howard. *Garden Cities of Tomorrow*. London, 1902.

John F. Kasson. *Amusing the Million: Coney Island at the Turn of the Century*. New York: Hill and Wang, 1978.

Harvey Levenstein. *Revolution at the Table: The Transformation of the American Diet*. Oxford: Oxford University Press, 1988.

John A. Livingston. "Man and His World: A Dissent." *Wilderness Canada*. Toronto: Clarke, Irwin, 1970.

James Lovelock. *Gaia: A New Look at Life on Earth*. Oxford: Oxford University Press, 1979.

Jon Nordheimer. "In Orlando, Disney is Making Itself a World Apart." *The New York Times*, January 18, 1986.

Kevin Robins and Frank Webster. "Athens Without Slaves or Slaves Without Athens? The Neurosis of Technology." *Science as Culture*, No. 3 (1988).

Robert Schwartzwald. "an/other Canada, another Canada? other Canadas." *The Massachusetts Review*, Vol. 21, Nos. 1 & 2 (Spring-Summer 1990).

Barbara Smalley. "EPCOT: Disney's Dream Come True." *Express*, April 1983.

Warren Strugatch and Thom McMenemy. "Abusement Park: The Disney Empire Extends to Central Florida's Mickey Mouse Government." *In These Times*, July 4–7, 1990.

David Suzuki. *Inventing the Future: Reflections on Science, Technology and Nature*. Toronto: Stoddart, 1989.

Alvin Toffler. *Previews and Premises*. Montreal: Black Rose Books, 1983.

Walt Disney Productions. *Walt Disney World: The First Decade*. 1982.

Gloria Webster. *Spirit Lodge: The Story Behind the Haunting Show Presented by General Motors at the 1986 World's Fair*. Bob Rogers and Co., 1986.

Alexander Wilson. "The Managed Landscape: The Organization of Disney World." *Impulse,* Summer 1985.

Alexander Wilson. "The Betrayal of the Future: Walt Disney's EPCOT Center." *Socialist Review,* No. 84 (November-December 1985), and *Utne Reader,* No. 17 (August-September 1986).

Frank Lloyd Wright. *The Living City* (originally published as *When Democracy Builds*). New York: New American Library, 1958.

6. City and Country

Critiques of modern agriculture include Brewster Kneen, *From Land to Mouth: Understanding the Food System* (Toronto: NC Press, 1989); Lois Ross, *Prairie Lives: The Changing Face of Farming* (Toronto: Betweeen the Lines, 1985); Frances Moore Lappé and Joseph Collins, *Food First: Beyond the Myth of Scarcity* (Boston: Houghton Mifflin, 1977); and Jack Doyle, *Altered Harvest: Agriculture, Genetics and the Fate of the World's Food Supply* (New York: Penguin, 1985).

The indispensable work on sustainable agriculture and its relation to culture includes Wendell Berry, *The Unsettling of America: Culture and Agriculture* (San Francisco: Sierra Club Books, 1977); Wes Jackson, Wendell Berry and Bruce Colman, eds., *Meeting the Expectations of the Land: Essays in Sustainable Agriculture and Stewardship* (San Francisco: North Point Press, 1984); and Gary Paul Nabhan, *Enduring Seeds: Native American Agriculture and Wild Plant Conservation* (San Francisco: North Point Press, 1989).

A wonderfully speculative essay is Gianfranco Baruchello and Henry Martin, *How to Imagine: A Narrative on Art and Agriculture* (New Paltz, N.Y.: MacPherson & Co., 1983).

The overall frame for this chapter is the historical relationship between city and country. This is a subject Raymond Williams explored in *The Country and the City* (London: Chatto and Windus, 1973) and returned to late in his life in an essay from which I've drawn the epigraph for this chapter, "Between Country and City," in Richard Mabey, ed., *Second Nature* (London: Jonathan Cape, 1984). The same essay has been reprinted in Simon Pugh's useful collection, *Reading Landscape: Country-City-Capital* (Manchester: Manchester University Press, 1990).

The literature on the history of land use in North America is quite dispersed, including work by Lewis Mumford, Ian McHarg, and Kevin Lynch as well as J. B. Jackson, Carl Sauer, and Jane Jacobs. This work has influenced most everything this book is about and is included in the sources for the Introduction and chapter three. Two recent books synthesize older material and lend a new political urgency to the reconciliation of city and country. While it focuses on recent developments in England and on the European continent, David Nicholson-Lord, *The Greening of the Cities* (London: Routledge and Kegan Paul, 1987), has broad lessons for North Americans. Tony Hiss, *The Experience of Place* (New York: Knopf, 1990), drawn from two series of articles in *The New Yorker,* is a pithy and inspiring survey of new thinking about land use and the emerging "science of place" in the United States.

Patrick Wright, *On Living in an Old Country: The National Past in Contemporary Britain* (London: Verso, 1985), opened up for me the larger issues of popular historiography. Michael Wallace, "Visiting the Past: History Museums in the United States," *Radical History Review*, No. 25 (1981), is a thoughful and well researched discussion of the important U.S. heritage parks.

◉

Anil Agarwal and Sunita Narain. *Toward Green Villages: A Strategy for Environmentally-Sound and Participatory Rural Development*. New Delhi: Centre for Science and Environment, 1989.

Wendell Berry. *The Gift of Good Land: Further Essays Cultural and Agricultural*. San Francisco: North Point Press, 1981.

Fergus M. Bordewich. "Williamsburg: Revising Colonial America." *The Atlantic,* December 1988.

David Brown, Michael MacLean and Dieter Sijpkes. "The Indoor City: Can it be Successfully Integrated into the Urban Fabric?" *City Magazine*, Vol. 7, No. 4 (Fall 1985).

Roger Burbach and Patricia Flynn. *Agribusiness in the Americas*. New York: Monthly Review Press and North American Congress on Latin America, 1980.

Joseph Collins. *What Difference Could a Revolution Make? Food and Farming in the New Nicaragua*. San Francisco: Institute for Food and Development Policy, 1982.

Colonial Williamsburg Foundation. *Teaching History at Colonial Williamsburg*. Williamsburg, Va., 1985.

Richard Conviser. "Postmodern Agricultures." *Trumpeter*, Vol. 6, No. 3 (Summer 1989).

Evan Eisenberg. "Back to Eden" [on Wes and Dana Jackson]. *The Atlantic,* November 1989.

Masanobu Fukuoka. *The Natural Way of Farming: The Theory and Practice of Green Philosophy*. Tokyo: Japan Publications, 1985.

Masanobu Fukuoka. *The One-Straw Revolution: An Introduction to Natural Farming*. Emmaus, Penn.: Rodale Press, 1978.

Susan George and Nigel Paige. *Food for Beginners*. London: Writers and Readers, 1982.

Charlie Hosmer. *Preservation Comes of Age*. Charlottesville, Va.: University of Virginia Press.

Wes Jackson. *New Roots for Agriculture*. San Francisco: Friends of the Earth, 1980.

Wes Jackson. *Altars of Unhewn Stone: Science and the Earth*. San Francisco: North Point Press, 1987.

J.B. Jackson. "New Fields." *art and architecture*, Vol. 1, No. 4 (n.d.).

Jack Kloppenburg. *First the Seed: The Political Economy of Plant Biotechnology*. New York: Cambridge University Press, 1988.

Philip Kopper. *Colonial Williamsburg: The Modern Era*. New York: Abrams, 1986.

Bruce Krushelniki. "Shopping Centres: Public Agora or Privileged Place?" *City Magazine*, Vol. 7, No. 4 (Fall 1985).

Christopher B. Leinberger and Charles Lockwood. "How Business is Reshaping America." *The Atlantic*, October 1986.

Nicholas Lemann. "Naperville: Stressed Out in Suburbia." *The Atlantic*, November 1989.

Barry Lopez. "Unbounded Wilderness." *Aperture*, No. 120 (Summer 1990).

James Lorimer and Carolyn MacGregor, eds. *After the Developers*. Toronto: James Lorimer & Co., 1981.

Scott Malcolmson. "Work Ethics". *The Village Voice*, March 4, 1986.

George Melnyk. *Radical Regionalism*. Edmonton: NeWest Books, 1981.

Richard Merrill, ed. *Radical Agriculture*. New York: New York University Press, 1976.

Tom Naylor. "Modern Agriculture Soaked Up by Oil Companies." *Now*, August 2–8, 1990.

Joyce Nelson. "Culture and Agriculture: The Ultimate Simulacrum." *Borderlines*, No. 18 (Spring 1990).

Michael Olmert. *Official Guide to Colonial Williamsburg*. Williamsburg, Va.: The Colonial Williamsburg Foundation, 1985.

Todd Oppenheimer. "Triangle 2000: A Sprawl Odyssey." *The Independent* (Durham, N.C.), March 14–27, 1986.

David Plowden. *Industrial Landscape*. New York: Chicago Historical Society/W.W. Norton, 1986.

Darrell Yates Rist (with Marcia Pally). "I was the Queer at a Christian Theme Park: Back to the Closet of my Faith." *The Village Voice*, July 1, 1986.

Carl O. Sauer. *Agricultural Origins and Dispersals: The Domestication of Animals and Foodstuffs* (1959). Cambridge, Mass.: MIT Press, 1969.

The "Official" West Edmonton Mall Souvenir Book: Everything From A to Z. Edmonton: ChrisCam Publications, 1987.

Sim Van der Ryn and Peter Calthorpe. *Sustainable Communities: A New Design Synthesis for Cities, Suburbs and Towns*. San Francisco: Sierra Club Books, 1986.

John Zerzan. "Agriculture: Essence of Civilization." *Fifth Estate*, Vol. 23, No. 2 (Summer 1988).

7. From Reserve to Microenvironment: Nature Parks and Zoos

Leslie Bella, *Parks for Profit* (Montreal: Harvest House, 1987), is a good critical history of Canadian national parks. The debate that has emerged over the management of Yellowstone National Park is a good example of the contradictions of park policy. See Alston Chase, *Playing God in Yellowstone* (Boston and New York: Atlantic Monthly Press, 1986), as well as two reviews of this book in *Restoration and Management Notes*, Vol. 5, No. 1 (Summer 1987). The 1989 fires brought this debate into the public eye and taught us many new lessons. See

Thomas Hackett, "Fire," *The New Yorker,* October 2, 1989; and William H. Romme and Don G. Despain, "The Yellowstone Fires," *Scientific American,* Vol. 261, No. 5 (November 1989).

From a biological standpoint, parks as islands of wilderness in an unbroken sea of cleared and developed land are almost useless. In recent years, especially in the West, the best discussion of wild lands has been displaced to issues related to forestry. Here the essential texts are Larry D. Harris, *The Fragmented Forest* (Chicago: University of Chicago Press, 1984); Chris Maser, *The Redesigned Forest* (San Pedro, Cal.: R. & E. Miles, 1988 and Toronto: Stoddart, 1990); Catherine Caufield, "The Ancient Forest," *The New Yorker,* May 14, 1990; and Gordon Robinson, *The Forest and the Trees* (Covelo, Cal.: Island Press, 1988). See also the periodical *Inner Voice,* published out of Eugene, Oreg., by the Association of Forest Service Employees for Environmental Ethics.

Much forestry work is now community initiated. Freeman House, "To Learn the Things We Need to Know: Engaging the Particulars of the Planet's Recovery," *Whole Earth Review,* Spring 1990, draws profound lessons from the experience in the Mattole Valley of California. See also the Mattole Restoration Council, *Elements of Recovery: An Inventory of Upslope Sources of Sedimentation in the Mattole River Watershed, with Rehabilitation Prescriptions and Additional Information for Erosion Control Prioritization,* Box 160, Petrolia, California 95558, 1989. Alex and Katie Lipkis, *The Simple Act of Planting a Tree: A Citizen Forester's Guide* (Los Angeles: Jeremy Tarcher, 1990) gives a good sense of the voluntary forestry work going on in many cities today.

On the idea of bioregions, see Kirkpatrick Sale, *Dwellers in the Land: The Bioregional Vision* (San Francisco: Sierra Club Books, 1985), and the excellent anthology edited by Van Andrus, et al., *Home: A Bioregional Reader* (Philadelphia, Pa., Santa Cruz, Cal., and Gabriola, B.C.: New Catalyst/New Society, 1990). Ernest Callenbach's novel *Ecotopia* is a wonderful narrative treatment of the subject. The Planet Drum Foundation (Box 31251, San Francisco, Cal. 94131) publishes the bioregional journal *Raise the Stakes.* For more information contact the Turtle Island Bioregional Congress (formerly the North American Bioregional Congress), c/o Realistic Living, Box 140826, Dallas, Tex. 75214.

The relations between aboriginal and environmental groups are complex. Native land stewardship has been attacked by anthropologists and science journalists. To get a sense of the tenor of these critiques, it is enough to look at Stephen Strauss, "Native Peoples Adept at Upsetting Nature if Given a Chance," *The Globe and Mail,* September 22, 1990, and the many angry letters in response, and Daniel A. Guthrie, "Primitive Man's Relationship to Nature," *Bioscience,* No. 21 (July 1971). A fuller treatment of these issues can be found in J. Baird Callicott, "American Indian Environmental Ethics," in *In Defense of the Land Ethic;* "The Chippewa and the Other," *Cultural Studies,* Vol. 2, No. 3 (October 1988); and several years of interviews from the *New Catalyst,* now collected in Christoper Plant and Judith Plant, eds., *Turtle Talk: Voices for a Sustainable Future* (Philadelphia, Pa., Santa Cruz, Cal. and Lillooet, B.C.: New Catalyst/New Society, 1990).

☉

"Emerging States: A Bioregional Directory." *Raise the Stakes,* No. 12 (Spring 1987).

"Man and the Biosphere." Special issue of *UNESCO Courier,* April 1981.

"Small is Vital: The Fourth World." Special issue of *The New Catalyst,* No. 15 (Fall 1989).

A Green City Program for San Francisco Bay Area Cities and Towns. San Francisco: Planet Drum, 1989.

Ronald Arnold. "Loggerheads Over Land Use: Organizing Against Environmentalists." *New Catalyst,* Winter 1988/89.

Asia-Pacific People's Environmental Network. "International Wildlife Trade: Japan as Number One." *New Catalyst,* Winter 1988/89.

Jeffery Tyhson Banighen. "Intentional Communities and Land Stewardship Trusts." *Trumpeter,* Vol. 7, No. 1 (Winter 1990).

Peter Berg, ed. *Reinhabiting a Separate Country: A Bioregional Anthology of Northern California.* San Francisco: Planet Drum, 1978.

Gary Braasch. *Secrets of the Old Forest.* Salt Lake City: Peregrine Smith, 1988.

Orville Camp. *The Forest Farmer's Handbook: A Guide to Natural Selection Forest Management.* Berkeley: Sky River Press, 1984.

Canada. *Parks Canada Policy.* Ottawa: Environment Canada, 1982.

Canada. *National Marine Parks Policy.* Ottawa: Environment Canada, 1986.

Canada. "Our Forests — Riches That Grow." *Annual Report 1957–1958.* Ottawa: Department of Northern Affairs and National Resources, 1958.

Canada. "Wisdom's Heritage: The National Parks of Canada." *Annual Report 1956–1957.* Ottawa: Department of Northern Affairs and Natural Resources, 1957.

Canada. *Our Parks — Vision for the 21st Century.* Report of the Minister of the Environment's Task Force on Park Establishment. Ottawa: Environment Canada, 1987.

Neil H. Cheek, Jr. "Sociological Perspectives on the Zoological Park," in Neil H. Cheek, et al., eds., *Leisure and Recreational Places.* Ann Arbor, Mich.: Ann Arbor Science Publications, 1976.

Chief Standing Bear, *Land of the Spotted Eagle* (Boston, 1933), in T.C. McLuhan, *Touch the Earth: Native American Testimony.* New York: Harper and Row, 1971, 1978.

David G. Dodge. "Madawaska: A Land Ethic in the Making." *Borealis,* Vol. 1, No. 1 (Fall 1988).

J. Ronald Engel. "Renewing the Bond of Mankind and Nature: Biosphere Reserves as Sacred Space." *Orion,* Summer 1985.

Rowe Findley and James P. Blair. "Endangered Old-Growth Forests." *National Geographic,* Vol. 178, No. 3 (September 1990).

Janet Foster. *Working for Wildlife: The Beginning of Preservation in Canada.* Toronto: University of Toronto Press, 1978.

George Francis. *Nomination of Canadian Biosphere Reserves:* Canada/MAB Committee Report No. 15. Ottawa: UNESCO, 1982.

Melissa Greene. "No Rms, Jungle Vu." *The Atlantic Monthly,* December 1987.

William P. Gregg, Jr. and Betsy Ann McGean. "Biosphere Reserves: Their History and Their Promise." *Orion,* Summer 1985.

Gonzalo Halffter. "Biosphere Reserves: Conservation of Nature for Man." *Parks,* Vol. 10, No. 3 (1985).

Karl Hansen. "Ethical Struggles Over Forest Elixirs." *Now,* June 28–July 4, 1990.

Rose Harvey and Evelyn Lee. "Forming a Land Trust." *Trumpeter,* Vol. 7, No. 1 (Winter 1990).

Freeman House. "Restoring Your Local Watershed." *New Catalyst,* Winter 1988/89.

Institute of the American West. *Parks in the West and American Culture.* Sun Valley, Idaho: Sun Valley Center for the Arts and Humanities, 1984.

Stephen R. Kellert and J.K. Berry. "Knowledge, Affection and Basic Attitudes Toward Animals in American Society." Washington, D.C.: U.S. Government Printing Office (No. 024-010-00-625-1), 1980.

Robert Lamb. *World Without Trees: Dutch Elm Disease and Other Human Errors.* London: Wildwood House, 1979.

Land Trust Alliance. *Starting a Land Trust.* Washington, D.C., 1990

W.F. Lothian. *A History of Canada's National Parks.* Ottawa: Parks Canada, 1976.

Chris Maser. *Forest Primeval.* San Francisco: Sierra Club Books, 1989.

Peter Morrison. *Old Growth in the Pacific Northwest: A Status Report.* Washington, D.C.: The Wilderness Society.

Bob Mullan and Garry Marvin. *Zoo Culture: A Book about Watching Man Watching Animals.* London: Weidenfeld and Nicholson, 1987.

Gary Paul Nabhan. *The Desert Smells Like Rain: A Naturalist in Papago Indian Country.* San Francisco: North Point Press, 1987.

Roderick Nash. *Wilderness and the American Mind.* Third edition. New Haven, Conn.: Yale University Press, 1982.

Natural Areas. [periodical].

Nature Conservancy of Canada. *Parks 2000: Vision for the 20th Century/Parcs 2000: Perspectives pour le 21 siècle.* Toronto: n.d.

J.G. Nelson, ed. *Canadian Parks in Perspective.* Proceedings of the conference, "The Canadian National Parks Today and Tomorrow," Calgary, October 1968. (Montreal: Harvest House, 1969).

Richard Nelson. *The Island Within.* San Francisco: North Point Press, 1989.

Richard Nilsen. "Reforming the Forest Service from Within: The Crusade of Jeff DeBonis." *Whole Earth Review,* No. 64 (Fall 1989).

Randal O'Toole. *Reforming the Forest Service.* Washington, D.C., and Covelo, Cal.: Island Press, 1988.

Christopher Plant. "Indian Self-Government: Triumph or Treason?" *Borderlines,* No. 13 (Winter 1988–89).

Kenneth J. Polakowski. *Zoo Design: The Reality of Wild Illusions*. Ann Arbor, Mich.: School of Natural Resources, University of Michigan, 1987.

Ray Raphael. *Tree Talk: The People and the Politics of Timber*. Washington, D.C., and Covelo, Cal.: Island Press, 1981.

Ray Repetto and Malcolm Gillis. Public Policies and the Misuse of Forest Resources. New York: Cambridge University Press, 1988.

Boyce Richardson, ed. *Drum Beat: Anger and Renewal in Indian Country*. Toronto: Assembly of First Nations and Summerhill Press, 1989.

Norbert Ruebsaat. "Speaking with Diane Brown: A Work in Progress." *Borderlines*, No. 16 (Fall 1989).

Second North American Bioregional Congress Proceedings. Dallas: Turtle Island Bioregional Congress, 1986.

D. Scott Slocombe. "CITES, The Wildlife Trade and Sustainable Development." *Alternatives*, Vol. 16, No. 1 (March/April 1989).

Robert Sommer. "What Do We Learn at the Zoo?" *Natural History*, Vol. 81, No. 2 (August 1972).

Susan Foster Swensen. "A Comparison of Visitors at Different Types of Zoo Facilities." Unpublished paper, School of Forestry and Environmental Studies, Yale University, Spring 1984.

Jamie Swift. *Cut and Run: The Assault on Canada's Forests*. Toronto: Between the Lines, 1983.

Third North American Bioregional Congress Proceedings. Dallas: Turtle Island Bioregional Congress, 1988.

Frederick W. Turner. *Rediscovering America: John Muir in His Time and Ours*. New York: Viking, 1985.

Robert D. Turner and William E. Rees. "A Comparative Study of Parks Policy in Canada and the United States." *Nature Canada*, Vol. 2, No. 1 (January/March 1973).

Amei Wallach. "How Visitors View Exhibitions." *Newsday*, February 20, 1983.

David S. Wilcove. *National Forests: Policies for the Future*. The Wilderness Society.

Steve Yates. *Adopting a Stream: A Northwest Handbook*. Seattle: Adopt-a-Stream Foundation and University of Washington Press, 1988.

8. On the Frontiers of Capital: Nuclear Plants and Other Environmental Architectures

The critique of progress and technology that runs through this book is informed, as it has been for many people, by the work of Lewis Mumford, especially *The Myth of the Machine,* Vol. 1, *Technics and Human Development* (New York: Harcourt, Brace and World, 1966) and *The Myth of the Machine,* Vol. 2, *The Pentagon of Power* (New York: Harcourt Brace Jovanovich, 1970).

James Ridgeway's anthology *Powering Civilization: The Complete Energy Reader* (New York: Pantheon, 1982), is a succinct social history of energy. George Bradford's analysis of the

Exxon Valdez spill has also been very helpful: "Stopping the Industrial Hydra: Revolution Against the Megamachine," *Fifth Estate,* Vol. 24, No. 3 (Winter 1990).

The case against large dams has been exhaustively made by Edward Goldsmith and Nicholas Hildyard, *The Social and Environmental Effects of Large Dams* (San Francisco: Sierra Club Books, 1986).

Michael L. Smith's "Selling the Moon: The U.S. Manned Space Program and the Triumph of Commodity Scientism," in Richard Wightman Fox and T.J. Jackson Lears, eds., *The Culture of Consumption: Critical Essays in American History, 1880–1980* (New York: Pantheon, 1983), is a lively discussion of science, popular culture, and media.

Good critical histories of science are Stanley Aronowitz, *Science as Power: Discourse and Ideology in Modern Society* (Minneapolis: University of Minnesota, 1988); Richard Lewontin, Steven Rose and Leon Kamin, *Not in Our Genes: Biology, Ideology and Human Nature* (New York: Pantheon, 1984); and Richard Lewontin, "Biology as Ideology: The Doctrine of DNA," CBC-Radio, Massey Lecture, November 1990.

More speculative work on science I've found useful includes Morris Berman, *The Reenchantment of the World* (New York: Bantam, 1984); Daniel B. Botkin, *Discordant Harmonies: A New Ecology for the 21st Century* (Oxford: Oxford University Press, 1990); and Rupert Sheldrake, *The Presence of the Past: Morphic Resonance and the Habits of Nature* (New York: Vintage, 1988).

On nuclear fission and its culture, Rosalie Bertell, *No Immediate Danger: Prognosis for a Radioactive Earth* (London and Toronto: The Women's Press, 1985) is at once thorough and inviting. Stephen Croall and Kaianders Sempler, *Nuclear Power for Beginners* (London: Writers and Readers, 1980) is characteristically forthright. The film *The Atomic Cafe* is a fascinating compendium of nuclear propaganda by both the military and the media. Crispin Audrey, ed., *Nukespeak: The Media and the Bomb* (London: Comedia, 1982), is a collection of essays on cold war propaganda. Joyce Nelson pursues many of those connections in *The Perfect Machine: TV in the Nuclear Age* (Toronto: Between the Lines, 1987).

❂

"No Clear Reason: Nuclear Power Politics." *Radical Science,* No. 14 (1984).

Special issue on nuclearism. *Fifth Estate,* Vol. 14, No. 2 (April 18, 1979).

"Nuclear Power and Nuclear Bombs." *Not Man Apart,* Vol. 10, No. 8 (August 1980).

Paul Adler. "Technology and Us." *Socialist Review,* No. 85, (January-February 1986).

Australopithecus. "Militarization of the West Continues." *Earth First!,* Mabon, September 1985.

Hilary Bacon and John Valentine. *Power Corrupts: The Arguments Against Nuclear Power.* London: Pluto Press, 1981.

John Berger. "The Sixth of August 1945," in *The Sense of Sight.* New York: Pantheon, 1985.

Thomas R. Berger, ed. *The Arctic: Choices for Peace and Security: Proceedings of a Public Inquiry.* West Vancouver: G. Soules Book Publishers, 1989.

Thomas R. Berger. *Northern Frontier, Northern Homeland: The Report of the Mackenzie Valley Pipeline Inquiry* (1977). Vancouver: Douglas and McIntyre, 1988.

Thomas R. Berger. *Village Journey: Report of the Alaska Native Review Commission.* New York: Hill and Wang, 1985.

Bradford, George. "Incinerator Logic: The Hidden Cost of Progress." *Detroit Trash Incinerator: We Say No!* Detroit: The Evergreen Alliance, 1988.

Paul Brodeur. *The Zapping of America: Microwaves, Their Deadly Risk and the Cover-up.* New York: Norton, 1977. [See also Brodeur's many follow-up articles in *The New Yorker.*]

Hugh Brody. *The People's Land: Whites and the Eastern Arctic.* Harmondsworth: Penguin, 1975.

Michael Brown. *The Toxic Cloud.* New York: Harper and Row, 1987.

W.F. Bynum et al. eds. *Dictionary of the History of Science.* Princeton: Princeton University Press, 1981.

Campaign Against the Model West Germany. "The Atomic State and The People Who Have to Live in It." 1979. (Available from Box 282, Station E, Montreal, Quebec, H2T 3A7)

Canada. *Canada's North Today.* Ottawa: Ministry of Indian and Northern Affairs, 1981.

Canada. *Under the Beaufort: Canada Drills in the Arctic.* Ottawa: Ministry of Indian and Northern Affairs, 1980.

Canadian Arctic Resources Committee. *Northern Perspectives* [periodical]. Ottawa.

Catherine Caufield. *Multiple Exposures: Chronicles of the Radiation Age.* Toronto: Stoddart, 1988.

Ward Churchill. "Last Stand at Lubicon Lake." *Zeta,* September 1989.

Kenneth Coates and Judith Powell. *The Modern North: People, Politics and the Rejection of Colonialism.* Toronto: James Lorimer & Co., 1989.

Barry Commoner. *The Poverty of Power.* New York: Bantam, 1977.

Robert del Tredici. *The People of Three Mile Island.* San Francisco: Sierra Club Books, 1981.

Earthscan. "Natural Disasters: Acts of God or Acts of Man?" (available from: 1717 Massachusetts Ave. NW, Suite 302, Washington, D.C. 20036).

Neil Evernden. "Science in Industrial Society," in Ian Angus and Sut Jhally, eds., *Cultural Politics in Contemporary America.* New York: Routledge, 1989.

H. Bruce Franklin. "The Superweapon and Its Cultural Images." *Zeta,* January 1989.

Ursula Franklin. *The Real World of Technology.* Toronto: CBC Enterprises and University of Toronto Press, 1990.

Christine Frederick, *Selling Mrs Consumer* (1929), in Stuart Ewen, *Captains of Consciousness.* New York: McGraw-Hill, 1976.

Ian Gill. "Earth: The Sequel." *Vista,* November 1989.

Peter Goin. "Ground Zero: Nevada Test Site." *Landscape,* Vol. 30, No. 1 (1988).

Thane Grauel. "Dishonorable Discharges: The Military's Peacetime War on Earth." *E,* Vol. 1, No. 4 (July/August 1990).

Heinz Haber. *The Walt Disney Story of Our Friend the Atom*. New York: Golden Press, 1961.

Bill Harding. *Uranium Mining in Northern Saskatchewan: Correspondence with the Premier*. Regina: Regina Group for a Non-Nuclear Society, 1979.

Gaetan Hayeur, Gilles Schooner and Jean A. Robitaille. *The Salmon of the Koksoak*. Montreal: Hydro-Québec, 1984.

Robert Horvitz, ed. "Radio Earth." Special section of *Whole Earth Review*, No. 68 (Fall 1990).

Marcia J. Jones. "Ambivalence Toward Wilderness: The Idaho National Engineering Laboratory as a Case Study." *Parks in the West and American Culture*. Sun Valley, Idaho: Institute of the American West, 1984.

Tara Jones. *Corporate Killing: Bhopals Will Happen*. London: Free Association Books, 1988.

Joel Kovel. *Against the State of Nuclear Terror*. Boston: South End Press, 1984.

Patricia Kullberg. "Nuclear Emergency: An 'Unusual Event.'" *Science as Culture*, No. 6 (1989).

Jill C. Kunka. "Report from Alaska," *Metro Times* (Detroit) September 27–October 3, 1989.

Winona Laduke. "James Bay: A Northern Sacrifice Area." *Zeta*, Vol. 3, No. 6 (June 1990).

Richard S. Lewis. *The Nuclear Power Rebellion: Citizens vs. The Atomic Industrial Establishment*. New York: Viking, 1972.

Barry Lopez. *Arctic Dreams: Imagination and Desire in a Northern Landscape*. New York: Scribners, 1988.

Amory Lovins and Hunter Lovins. *Energy/War: Breaking the Nuclear Link*. San Francisco: Friends of the Earth, and New York: Harper and Row, 1981.

Hunter Lovins and Leonard Ross. "Nuclear Power and Nuclear Bombs." *Not Man Apart*, August 1980.

E. Magnuson. "They Lied to Us: Unsafe, Aging U.S. Weapons Plants are Stirring Fear and Disillusion." *Time*, October 31, 1988.

Jack Manno, *Arming the Heavens: The Hidden Military Agenda for Space, 1945–1995*. New York: Dodd, Mead, 1984.

John May, ed. *The Greenpeace Book of the Nuclear Age: The Hidden History, The Human Cost*. Toronto: McClelland and Stewart, 1989.

Kevin A. McNamee. "Wilderness or Oil Fields?" *Probe Post*, Vol. 12, No. 1 (Spring 1989).

Debbie S. Miller. *Midnight Wilderness: Journeys in Alaska's Arctic National Wildlife Refuge*. San Francisco: Sierra Club Books, 1990.

Richard Misrach. *Bravo 20: The Bombing of the American West*. Baltimore: Johns Hopkins University Press, 1990.

Scott L. Montgomery. "The Cult of Jargon: Reflections on Language in Science." *Science as Culture*, No. 6 (1989).

Lewis Mumford, *Technics and Civilization*. New York: Harcourt, Brace and Co., 1934.

National Audubon Society. *Arctic Refuge: Vanishing Wilderness?* [Video]. WETA and Turner Broadcasting Company, 1990.

Dorothy Nelkin. *Nuclear Power and Its Critics.* Ithaca, N.Y.: Cornell University Press, 1971.

Sheldon Novick. *The Careless Atom.* Boston: Houghton Mifflin, 1969.

Michael Peake. "Grand Dams." *Toronto Sun,* July 1–3, 1990.

André Picard. "James Bay: A Power Play." *The Globe and Mail,* April 13–15, 1990.

Steven Rose. "The Limits to Science." *Science for the People,* November/December 1984.

Rebecca Solnit. "Reclaiming History: Richard Misrach and the Politics of Landscape Photography." *Aperture,* No. 120 (Summer 1990).

David Suzuki. *James Bay: The Wind That Keeps on Blowing* [Video]. CBC, 1991.

Diana Swift. "The Anti-Nukes: Shadows on the Wall." *AECL Ascent,* Summer 1984.

Tennessee Valley Authority. *A History of the Tennessee Valley Authority.* Knoxville, Tenn., 1986.

Randy Thomas. "Georgia Strait: Crisis and Opportunity." *The New Catalyst,* No. 18 (Summer 1990).

Lloyd Timberlake and Jon Tinker. "The Environmental Origins of Political Conflict." *Socialist Review,* No. 84 (November-December 1985).

Frederick Turner. "Life on Mars: Cultivating a Planet — and Ourselves." *Harper's,* August 1989.

United States. *You Can Survive.* Washington, D.C.: U.S. National Security Resources Board, 1950.

United States. *The Family Fallout Shelter.* Washington D.C.: Office of Civil and Defense Mobilization, 1959.

United States. *Individual and Family Survival Requirements.* Washington, D.C.: Office of Civil and Defense Mobilization, 1959.

Warman and District Concerned Citizens Group. *Why People Say No to a Uranium Refinery at Warman, Saskatchewan.* Regina: Regina Group for a Non-Nuclear Society, 1980.

Spencer R. Weart. *Nuclear Fear: A History of Images.* Cambridge, Mass.: Harvard University Press, 1988.

Langdon Winner. *Autonomous Technology: Technics-Out-of-Control as a Theme in Political Thought.* Cambridge, Mass.: MIT Press, 1977.

Christa Wolf. *Accident: A Day's News* [about Chernobyl]. New York: Farrar, Straus Giroux, 1989.

Picture Credits

Many thanks to the following people for help obtaining pictures:
Bob Burley, Cees van Gemerden, Bill Shilvock, Doug Curran, John Lougheed, R.G. Outram, Eileen O'Meara, Dave Foreman, Paul Baglole, Graeme Ellis, Sue Lagasi, Lynne Cohen, Nancy Checko, Dan Strickland, Julia Langer, Stephanie Thorson, Julie Gelfand, James Parsons, Kalle Lasn, Anne Doremus, Pat Bardon, Peter Menzel, Pegi Dover, Richard Beharriel, Kelly Brine, Karen Sotiropoulos, Debbie Adams, Christopher Grampp, Garrett Eckbo, Terry Murphy, Michael Levenston, Alejandro Tomás, Jeanetta Ho, Suzanne H. Hryb, Lucie Charbonneau, Andre Davis, Hubert Gariépy, Victor Barac, Rose Kallal, Vid Ingelevics, Larry Leonard, Line Séguin, Brewster Kneen, Cathleen Kneen, Wendy Simpson Lewis, Ted Manning, Patrick Lang, Bob Taylor, Cathy Callaghan, Beth Russell, Art McLeod, Tom Huff, Toby Styles, André Guindon, Carole Condé, Karl Beveridge, Robert Del Tredici, Ed Aduss, Irene Kock, William Lee, Susan North, Marguerite Hudson, Deirdre Shimwell, Christine Leask, Karen Ewing-Wilson, and Cheryl Oakes.
— Lorraine Johnson

Cover
Jeff Wall, *Steves Farm, Steveston* 1980. Collection of Ydessa Hendeles. Courtesy of the Ydessa Hendeles Foundation.

Frontispiece
2   Forest History Society, Inc.

Acknowledgements
6   Cees van Gemerden, from series *No Trespassing*

Introduction

10 Ontario Ministry of Natural Resources
12 Ministry of Tourism, Province of British Columbia
13 Royal Ontario Museum

1. The View from the Road: Recreation and Tourism

18 Douglas Curran
21 Archives of Ontario
23 Camp Associates
26 Evinrude Motors
29 Asphalt Institute
35 Alexander Wilson
38 Bankers Trust Company
39 National Archives of Canada C-137392; Adrian Raeside
40 Dave Foreman, The Big Outside, P.O. Box 5141, Tucson, Arizona 85703
48 Prince Edward Island Department of Tourism and Parks
50 Graeme Ellis, Pacific Biological Station

2. Nature Education and Promotion

52 Lynne Cohen, Canadian Museum of Contemporary Photography/ Musée canadien de la photographie contemporaine
54 Alexander Wilson
58 Alexander Wilson
59 Ontario Ministry of Natural Resources, Algonquin Provincial Park
65 Ontario Ministry of Natural Resources
66 Canadian Wildlife Federation
67 Ontario Ministry of Natural Resources
72 U.S. Forest Service
74 World Wildlife Fund
76 Ontario Ministry of the Environment
78 MacMillan Bloedel
79 Media Foundation/David Bowes

80 Loblaw International Merchants
80 Bank of Montreal
81 Environment Canada
83 Mattole Restoration Council, Box 109, Petrolia, California 95558 USA

3. Nature at Home: A Social Ecology of Postwar Landscape Design

88 Peter Menzel
93 *Probe Post* magazine, Kelly Brine
95 New York City Parks Photo Archive
98 B. F. Goodrich
101 Christopher Grampp
102 Garrett Eckbo
102 Alexander Wilson
109 Michael Levenston
111 Alejandro Tomás
111 Alexander Wilson
112-13 Ian McHarg
114 Jeanetta Ho. Photographed at Cleveland Metroparks, Brecksville Reservation, Ohio

4. Looking at the Non-Human: Nature Movies and TV

116 Preservation Society of Newport County
122 National Film Board of Canada
126 National Film Board of Canada
133 World Wildlife Fund
138 AGF and World Wildlife Fund
138 Greenpeace U.S.A.
142 *Money*; copyright 1983, The Time Inc. Magazine Company
151 *Millennium: Tribal Wisdom and the Modern World*
153 Ontario Ministry of Natural Resources

5. Technological Utopias: World's Fairs and Theme Parks

156 Rose Kallal
160 Vid Ingelevics
161 CALTRANS

163   National Archives of Canada/
       PA 168605

168   NASA

171   The Province of British Columbia

172   NASA

177   Vid Ingelevics

178   Vid Ingelevics

188   NASA

6. City and Country

192   Vid Ingelevics

195   Cathleen Kneen, *Ram's Horn*

196   Ontario Ministry of Natural
       Resources

198   West Edmonton Mall

202-03 E. W. Manning, Environment
       Canada

209   Alexander Wilson

213   Alexander Wilson

216   Alexander Wilson

7. From Reserve to Microenvironment: Nature Parks and Zoos

222   Robert R. Taylor

225   Ansel Adams, National Archives
       Trust Fund Board

226   Canadian Parks Service

233   Environment Canada, Parks
       Service

236   Canadian Parks Service

240   MAB

245   Art McLeod/Exceptional
       Photography

245   Thom Henley; Rediscovery

252   African Lion Safari

255   Ontario Ministry of Natural
       Resources

8. On the Frontiers of Capital: Nuclear Plants and Other Environmental Architectures

256   Carole Condé/Karl Beveridge

258   Babcock & Wilcox

260   Tennessee Valley Authority

262   Argonaut Press

263   Peter Christopher

265   Tennessee Valley Authority

267   Robert Del Tredici

269   AECL

270   Canadian Nuclear Association

271   Emergency Preparedness Canada
       and Public Works Canada

272   U.S. Council for Energy
       Awareness, Washington, D.C.

275   Robert Del Tredici

276-77 Nuclear Awareness Project,
       Box 2331, Oshawa, Ontario
       L1H 7V4 Tel. (416) 725-1565

279   Robert Del Tredici

289   NASA

Notes on Sources

292   Bob Burley

Index

(Numbers in **bold** refer to photographs, drawings, or maps)

Abbott, Stan, 35, 114
aboriginal land rights, 66, 231
acclimatization, 66–69
Adirondack Reserve, New York, 227
Adopt-a-Stream Foundation, 70
Africa,
    as film location, 121
    as theme in zoos and game preserves,
      30, 121
    as tourist destination, 48
African-Americans,
    and outdoor recreation, 27
African Lion Safari, Ontario, **252**
African mammals,
    in zoos, 251, **252**
Agarwal, Anil, 12
agriculture,
    and energy, 186
    industrial, 184–90, **187**, 193–95, **200**,
      264
    and land use, 193
    and the nursery industry, 105
    and school curricula, 61
    and transportation, 32–33
    urban, 91, **109**

air conditioning, 37, **38**
Akeley, Carl, 124
Alaska, 120, 142
Algonquin Park, Ontario, **59**
America the Beautiful program, 65
American Forestry Association, 109
American Museum of Natural History, 124
American Museum of Science and Energy,
    267
American West,
    as film location, 120
animal abuse, 123, 177
animals,
    as companions, 126–28, 248
    domestication of, 128–29
Annapurna Conservation Area Project,
    Nepal, 51
Antarctica, 83
anthropology,
    and nature movies, 130, 148–51
anthropomorphism, 128–31, 144, 154
aquariums, 253–54
Arctic National Wildlife Refuge, 148, 286
Ardrey, Robert, 130
Aronowitz, Stanley, 77, 259

Atomic Energy Act, (U.S.), 269
Atomic Energy Commission (U.S.), 267,
    269
Atomic Energy Control Act (Canada), 269
Atomic Energy Control Board (Canada),
    269
Atomic Energy of Canada Ltd., 269
Atomic Museum, *see* American Museum
    of Science and Energy
Atoms for Peace, 137, 272
Audubon Society, 71, 148, 230
Audubon Zoo, New Orleans, 253
automobiles,
    and settlement patterns, 91
    and tourism, 25, 28–39
    and urban design, 158

Back to Chernobyl, 146
Bakker, Jim and Tammy, 213
Banff National Park, 58, 227–28
Barragán, Luis, 103
Bear, The, 152
Bear Country, 129
beaux-arts design, 100
Beaver Dam, 131
Beaver Valley, 120, 129, 290
Berger, John, 126
biological parks, 254
bioregionalism, 113, 242
biosphere reserves, 238–42, **240, 241, 255**
biotechnology,
    in the nursery industry, 106, 290
bison, 134, 248
Blacksmith, Sam, 149
Blade Runner, 179
Blue Ridge Parkway, 33–37, **35**
Bourrasa, Robert, 282
Bradford, George, 86, 290
British Columbia,
    government of, **12,** 169, 229
Brookes, John, 101
Brown, Lancelot ("Capability"), 94
Brown, Michael, 286
Bruce Energy Centre, Ontario, 275
Brundtland Report, *see* World
    Commission on Environment and
    Development

Bye, A.E., 103

Cades Cove, 211–12
California,
    and landscape design, 104–05
Camp Fire Girls, 24
Canadian Broadcasting Corporation (CBC),
    134, 147
Canadian Nuclear Association, **270, 280**
Canadian Outdoor Recreation Demand
    Study, 57, 230
Canadian Pacific Railway (CPR), 169, 227
Canadian Parks Service, 231–32
CANDU nuclear reactor, 278
Cape Hatteras National Seashore, 60
Cape Lookout National Seashore, 60
caribou, 148, 283, 286
Carson, Rachel, 57
Carter's Grove, 219
Center for the Defense of Free Enterprise,
    78
Center for Plant Conservation, 231
Central Park, New York, 65, **95**
Centre for Conflict Studies, 78
Chernobyl, 267
Chinese Association of Zoological
    Gardens, 250
Chrétien, Jean, 231
Church, Thomas, 100, **102**
Claw and the Tooth, The, 152
Cody, Buffalo Bill, 133
Collin, Girard, 241–42
community gardens, 108–10, **109**
condor, California, 135, 248
conservation biology, 248
conservation movement, 131–37
    relation to tourism and resource
        development, 39–41
Le Corbusier, 158
corporate environmentalism, 77–81
Cousteau, Jacques, 137–40, 290
Cree, 149, 150, 283
Cree Hunters of Mistassini, 149
Cries from the Deep, 137–40
Crow, Ben, 13
cruise missiles, 282
Cry of the Wild, **126**

Daly, Mary, 96
dams, 256
Dances with Wolves, 95
Debord, Guy, 51
Defense Highway Act, 29
Disney Studios, 117–21, 123, 125, 128–31,
    151, 154
Disney University, 178
Disney, Walt, 129, 161, 176, 183
Disney World, 11, **160,** 176–90, **177, 178**
Disneyland, 160–62, **160**
Dollywood, 208, **209**
Downing, Andrew Jackson, 94
Drapeau, Jean, 166
Ducks Unlimited, 71, **222,** 230

East Bay Regional Park District,
    California, 70
Eastern Wilderness Act, 229
Eastman, George, 124
East of Eden, 32
Eckbo, Garrett, 100, **102,** 104
ecological restoration, 17, 18, 113, **114,**
    253
ecology,
    and education, 61
    and landscape design, 110–15
    origins of, 144–46
    as politics, 86
    social implications of, 85–87
ecotourism, 49
Eisenhower, Dwight, 257
electrification, rural, **260,** 261
Ellesmere Island, 227
Elliot Lake, Ontario, **275**
Emergency Preparedness Canada, **270**
endangered species, **74**
environment, electronic, 287–88
environmental advocacy,
    by corporations, 77–81
    in movies, 147,
environmental movement,
    rise of, 136
Environmental Protection Agency (EPA),
    177, 268, 280
environmental studies, 62
EPCOT Center, 176, **178,** 183–90, **185**

evergreens,
    in landscape design, 92
Evernden, Neil, 121
Expo 67, Montreal, 162–68, **163**
Expo 86, Vancouver, 168–75, **171**
Exxon Valdez, 78, 286–87

Filming Nature's Mysteries, 123, 125
fire ecology, 72, 114
fishery, North Atlantic, 137–40, **138**
Florida,
    as film location, 134
Floridan aquifer, 177
food irradiation, 278
Ford, Henry, 183, 220, 264
Fowler, Jim, 133
Frank Slide Interpretive Centre, Alberta, 60
Frederick, Christine, 261
Free Trade Agreement, Canada-U.S., 285
French, Marilyn, 96
Fuller, Buckminster, 180, 190

garden centres, 106
gardening, organic, 100, 107
gender, and gardening, 44, 97–100
General Motors,
    pavilions at world's fairs, 158, 174–75
    and public transportation, 28
George, Chief Dan, 164
Gitksan Wet'suwet'en, 173
global climate change, **236,** 237
Goodall, Jane, 140
Grand Canal Project, **284**
Grassland National Park, Saskatchewan,
    228
Great Smokey Mountains National Park,
    Tennessee, **54,** 209, 211, 235
green commodities, 79–81, **80**
Greene, Lorne, 135
Greenfield Village, 220
Greenpeace, **138,** 139
Green Revolution, 189, 266, 271
Grizzlies, The, 142
Grizzly!, 141
Gros Morne National Park,
    Newfoundland, 228

Habitat, 67, 165
habitat models,
     in zoo and park design, 252, 254
Hagenbeck, Carl, 250–51
Haida, 173, 232
Haida Gwaii, 69, 232, 238, **245**
Hanford Reservation, Washington, 267,
     273, 280–81
Hang Your Hat on the Wind, 132
Hays, Samuel P., 53, 224
Heritage USA, 212–15, **213**
highways,
     and gasoline taxes, 30
     interstate, 29
highway architecture, 33
Hiss, Tony, 204
Hough, Michael, 92
horticultural industry,
     standardization of, 105–07
hunting, 121
Hydro-Quebec, 283–84

Idaho National Engineering Laboratory,
     281
Institute for Earth Education (IEE), 66–69
International Species Inventory System,
     (ISIS), 248
Islands Trust, British Columbia, 243

Jackson, Wes, 183
James Bay hydroelectric project, 282–85
Japanese landscape design,
     influence of, 103–04
Jensen, Jens, 104, 114
Jetsons, The, 162
Johnson, Lyndon Baines, 287
Johnson, Martin and Osa, 124, 141
Jordan, William R., 114

Kennedy, John F., 290
Kiley, Daniel Urban, 60, 100
King, William Lyon Mackenzie, 159
Knott's Berry Farm, California, 205
Kraft, 182, 184–93
Kuna Yala Biosphere Reserve, Panama,
     240
Kunka, Jill, 287

Kwakwaka'wakw, 174

Lakota, 251
land grant universities, 105, 186
Land Institute, Kansas, 71
Landsat, 15, 288
landscape architecture, 33, 113, 251
landscape immersion, 252
landscape park,
     English, 94–96, 211
land trusts, 242–46
lawns, **93,** 93–96, 110, **111**
Leopold, Aldo, 114
Leopold Committee, 234–35
Lielenthal, David, 269
Lippard, Lucy, 96
Living Desert, The, 118
Livingston, John A., 148, 154
Lopez, Barry, 203
Lorenz, Konrad, 145
Los Angeles,
     and urban design, 88, 161
Louisbourg, Cape Breton Island, 219
Lovelock, James, 167

MacKenzie Delta, 286
MacMillan Bloedel, **78**
Madawaska Highlands Regional Trust,
     Ontario, 244
Makuna, **151**
Man and the Biosphere Program (MAB),
     238–42, **240, 241**
Marey, Etienne-Jules, 124
Marx, Roberto Burle, 103
Mason, Bill, **122**
Mattole Restoration Council, California,
     83, 243
McHarg, Ian, 111, **112**
McLuhan, Marshall, 166–167
McKibben, Bill, 155
McPhee, John, 15
Mead, Margaret, 44
media image anticipation, 172
Merchant, Carolyn, 61
Metro Toronto Zoo, 247, 249
military-industrial complex, 257
Millennium, 150, **151**

mining, 263
    uranium, 273–74, **275**
modernism,
    in landscape design, 90, 100–104, **101,
        102,** 251
Monterey Bay Aquarium, 253–54
Morris, Desmond, 130
Moses, Robert, 160
Mowat, Farley, 151
multiple use policy, **39,** 227–28
Mumford, Lewis, 111, 263
Muscle Shoals, Alabama, 183, 264
Museum of Appalachia, Tennessee, 206
Muybridge, Eadweard, 124
Muzak, 182

Nabhan, Gary, 255
National Aeronautics and Space
    Administration (NASA), **188,** 288, **289**
National Film Board of Canada (NFB), 131,
    148
National Geographic Society, 127, 136–37,
    140–44
national parks, 224–34
National Zoo, Washington, D.C., 252, 254
Native North Americans,
    and outdoor recreation, 27
native plants,
    in landscape design, 104, 110
natural landscaping, 91, 103, 111–15
Nature, 136
nature interpretation, 54–57
nature tourism, 22–25, 28, 43
Nature of Things, The, 127, 144, 147
Nature's Half Acre, 117
Navaho, 132, 150, 181
Nevada Test Site, **279**
Never Cry Wolf, 151
New Alchemy Institute, 64
New Deal, 34, 41
New York World's Fair, 1939, **156,** 157
New Wilderness, 127, 135
New York Zoological Society, 249
Nicholson-Lord, David, 14
Non-Proliferation Treaty, 268
Norris, Tennessee, 207, 261
North American Air Defense (NORAD), 165

Northwest Territories, 174
Nova, 144, 146
Nuu-Chah-Nulth, 173
nuclear fission, 269
nuclear fuel cycle, 266, **276-77**
nuclear power industry, 79, 256, **276-77**
nuclear waste, 278–82
nursery industry, 105

Oakland Museum, 60
Oak Ridge, Tennessee, 208, 266
Oberlander, Cornelia Hahn, 103
Oka, Quebec, 11
old-growth forest, **12,** 244
Olmsted, Frederick Law, 65, 94, **95,** 114
Olympics, Los Angeles, 1984, 172
One Day in Teton Marsh, 119, 130
Ontario Hydro, 275
Organ Pipe Cactus National Monument,
    255
outdoor recreation,
    and Native and African-Americans, 27
Outdoor Recreation Resources Review
    Commission (ORRRC), 43-44
outer space, 287

Pacific Rim National Park, British
    Columbia. 229
panda, giant, 249
Papago, 235
parks movement, 24, 247
parkways, 33-35
Parks Canada, *see* Canadian Parks Service
pastoralism,
    in landscape design, 94-96, **95**
Perkins, Marlin, 132-34
Pee-wee's Playhouse, 189
permaculture, 108
pesticides, 92-93, **99,** 196
petrochemicals, **194**
photography,
    colour, 43
    and the eye, 121
    and hunting, 45, 121, **142**
    and tourism, 43, 45
photo opportunities, 172
Piaget, Jean, 68

Pickering Nuclear Generating Station, Ontario, 274-75
Pinchot, Gifford, 136, 227
Planet for the Taking, A, 148
playgrounds movement, 24
prairie ecosystems,
    in landscape design, 103, **111, 114**
prairie school of design, 103-04
Prince Albert National Park, Saskatchewan, 226
Prince Edward Island, tourism in, 48
Prince Edward Island National Park, **226**
Project Plowshares, 273
Project Wild, 63
Prudhoe Bay, Alaska, 286
PTL Club, 49, 213-14

Queen Charlotte Islands, *see* Haida Gwaii

radiation, 268
Raven, 175
recreation movement, 25-27
recreational vehicles (RV), 28, 32, 49
Rediscovery Camps, 69
regionalism,
    and landscape design, 92, 103-04, 110
Reisman, Simon, 285
remote sensing, *see* satellite photography
Research Triangle Park, North Carolina, 201
restoration,
    ecological, 17-18, 113-14, 253
risk and risk assessment, 75
risk-benefit analysis, 76
rivers,
    wild and scenic, 229
roadless areas, **40**
roadside architecture, 33
Rockefeller, John D., Jr., 217
Rockefeller, Winthrop, 218
Rocky Mountain Arsenal, Colorado, 281
Roosevelt, Franklin, D., 260
Roosevelt, Theodore, 251
Rose, James, 100

safari parks, 251

Safdie, Moshe, 165
St. Lawrence River, 166
San Diego Zoo, 253
Saskatchewan Mining and Development Corporation, 278
satellite photography, 15, 34, 167, 288
satellites, **172**
Savannah River plant, 267, 273
scenery evaluation, 31, 47
science,
    rise of in West, 14
science journalism, 144-47, 269
science museums, 267-69
seal hunting, 120, 139
second homes, 30
shopping centres and malls, 107, 180, 196-99
Shoshone, 279
SITE design group, 170
Smokey the Bear, **72**
Standing Bear, Chief, 224
Star Wars, *see* Strategic Defense Initiative
Stassen, Harold E., 271
Strategic Defense Initiative (SDI), 273, 287
Streep Meryl, 148
South Moresby National Park, British Columbia, 232
suburbs,
    construction of, 89-94, 202
Suzuki, David, 77, 147

Tasmanian devil, 135
technology,
    and communications, 170
    promotion of, 168-69
Tenneco, 162
Tennessee Valley Authority (TVA), 41, 207, 259
Thunderbird, 175
Tilden, Freeman, 55
tourism,
    adventure, 49
    and modernity, 21-22
    social, 49
tourist industry, 41-47, 261
trailers, 31

tribal parks, 232
trucking industry, 32
Tuktu and His Animal Friends, 148-49

Udvardy, Miklos, 239
UNESCO, 82, 85, 230
U.S. Council for Energy Awareness, 272
U.S. Fish and Wildlife Service, 77, 250
U.S. Forest Service, 227
University of Wisconsin Arboretum, 114, 235

Vancouver,
    real estate development in, 169, **171**

water diversions, 284
water shortages,
    and landscape design, 110, **111**
Watkins, Admiral James, 282
Weinberg, Alvin, 269
Wen Wang, 250
West Edmonton Mall, 197-99, **198**
Whitehead, William, 148
whale watching, **50**
Whole Earth image, 167, **168**
Wild Wild World of Animals, 134

Wilderness Act, U.S., 45, 235
wilderness ethic, 25
Wild Kingdom, 127, 132-34, 248
Williams, Raymond, 12
Williamsburg, Virginia, **216,** 217-19
Williamson, John, 124
wolves,
    as primates, **126,** 127-28
Woodland Park, Seattle, 253
World Commission on Environment and
    Development, 82-85
World Conservation Strategy, 82
World Heritage Convention, 237
World Wildlife Fund, 50, 71, 249, 250
Wright, Frank Lloyd, 103, 158, 179, 184
Wright, Patrick, 217
Wye Marsh, Ontario, 57, **58**

xeriscaping, 110

Yellowstone National Park, Wyoming,
    224, **225**
YMCA, 224
Yosemite National Park, California, 228

zoos, 246-55